MW00477707

Mormonism Unveiled

Mormonism Unveiled

The Life and Confession
of John D. Lee
and the Complete Life
of Brigham Young

John D. Lee

UNIVERSITY OF NEW MEXICO PRESS   ALBUQUERQUE

University of New Mexico Press edition published 2008.

Reprinted from the 1891 edition published by D. M. Vandawalker & Co. as *Mormonism Unveiled: Autobiography of John D. Lee, a Bishop and "Enforcer" of Secret Terrorist Organizations of the Mormon Church during the Years of 1838 to 1875.*

14 13 12 11 10 09 08   1 2 3 4 5 6 7

Library of Congress Cataloging-in-Publication Data

Lee, John Doyle, 1812–1877.
Mormonism unveiled : the life and confession of John D. Lee and the complete life of Brigham Young / John D. Lee.
p. cm.
Originally published: St. Louis : D.M. Vandawalker, 1891.
ISBN 978-0-8263-4567-7 (pbk. : alk. paper)
1. Lee, John Doyle, 1812–1877. 2. Mountain Meadows Massacre, Utah, 1857.
3. Mormon Church—History—19th century. 4. Young, Brigham, 1801–1877. I. Title.
F826.L475 2008
979.2′02092—dc22
[B]
2008005179

PUBLISHERS' PREFACE

JOHN D. LEE'S prominent connection with the Mormon Church, and the almost universal desire on the part of the public to know the secrets that he could tell, give a peculiar interest to the life and doings of this man, and led to a general inquiry for his Autobiography and Confessions. This has caused the publication of several pretended "Lives and Confessions of John D. Lee," the materials for which were collected from fragmentary newspaper reports, and advertised by certain unscrupulous publishers so genuine. We therefore deem it but simple justice to those who may read this book, to state how we obtained the *true* and *only* LIFE AND CONFESSIONS OF JOHN D. LEE.

It was stated at the time of Lee's execution that he had left the manuscripts of his Life and Confessions with his confidential attorney for publication. We at once wrote to Col. Wm. Nelson, U. S. Marshal of Utah Territory, requesting him to give us the address of Lee's attorney. He replied promptly, stating that Mr. W. W. Bishop, of Pioche, Nevada, was the man. We immediately entered into correspondence with Mr. Bishop, and made a contract with him for the publication of the work.

In proof of the fact that this is the genuine *and only genuine* Life and Confessions of John D. Lee, we refer to Col. Wm. Nelson, U. S. Marshal Utah Territory; Hon. Wm. Stokes, Deputy U. S. Marshal, U. T.; Hon. Sumner Howard, U. S. Attorney, U. T.; the editor of the *Salt Lake Tribune*; Col. Geo. M. Sabin, Pioche, Nevada; Mr. Wm. W. Bishop, of the same place, and to John D. Lee's letter to Mr. Bishop, on page 34 of this book. Lee wrote his Life and Confessions, in prison, after his sentence to death, and subsequent to his execution, his manuscripts were copied and prepared for publication by Mr. Bishop. They were at no time out of his possession or from under his immediate control, until they were delivered to the express company on the 17th day of May

1877, to be forwarded to us.

The Mormon leaders were so greatly alarmed at the prospect of the publication of Lee's writings, and the consequent revelation of their secrets and crimes, that they sent their "Blood Atoners" to threaten the life of Mr. Bishop, and, if possible, compel him to give up the manuscripts. The danger was so great that he was compelled to have his office guarded while engaged in copying the papers; and when they were ready to be forwarded to the publishers, the Wells, Fargo Co. Express refused to receive them until they were furnished with an armed guard to protect them until they were beyond the reach of the Mormons.

The fears of the Mormon dignitaries were well founded, for Lee's revelations of crimes committed by them were of the most startling character.

THE PUBLISHERS

PREFACE

I WAS requested by John Doyle Lee, after he had been sentenced to be shot for the part he took in the commission of the Mountain Meadows Massacre, to publish an account of his life and confessions, in order to inform the world how it was that he had acted as he had, and why he was made a scapegoat by the Mormon Church. I accepted the trust, and, in giving publicity to the facts now, for the first time fully brought to light, I am only performing what I believe to be a duty - to him, and to the public.

The Mountain Meadows Massacre stands without a parallel amongst the crimes that stain the pages of American history. It was a crime committed without cause or justification of any kind to relieve it of its fearful character. Over one hundred and twenty men, women and children were surrounded by Indians, and more cruel whites, and kept under constant fire, from hundreds of unerring rifles, for five days and nights, during all of which time, the emigrants were famishing for water. When nearly exhausted from fatigue and thirst, they were approached by white men, with a flag of truce, and induced to surrender their arms, under the most solemn promises of protection. They were then murdered in cold blood, and left nude and mangled upon the plain. All this was done by a band of fanatics, who had no cause of complaint against the emigrants, except that the authorities of the Mormon Church had decided that all the emigrants who were old enough to talk, should die; revenge for alleged insults to Brigham Young, and the booty of the plundered train being the inciting causes of the massacre. John D. Lee was *one, and only one of fifty-eight* Mormons, who there carried out the *orders* of the Mormon Priesthood. He has died for his crimes - shall the others escape?

The entire history of this atrocious crime is given in the confession.

How it was done, and why it was the wish of the Mormons that it should be done, all is fully stated. As one of the attorneys for John D. Lee, I did all that I could to save his life. My associates were, and are able men and fine lawyers, but *fact* and *fate* united to turn the verdict against us. The history of the first and second trials is familiar to most of the American people; therefore, I will not describe them here, any more than to say, Mormonism prevented conviction at the first trial, and at the second trial Mormonism insured conviction.

After Brigham Young and his worshippers had deserted Lee, and marked him as the victim that should suffer to save the Church from destruction, on account of the crimes it had ordered; after all chances of escape had vanished, and death was certain as the result of the life long service he had rendered the Church, the better nature of Lee overcame his superstition and fanaticism, and he gave to me the history of his life, and his confession of the facts connected with the massacre, and wished me to have the same published. Why he refused to confess at an earlier day, and save his own life by placing the guilt where it of right belonged, is a question which is answered by the statement, that he was still a slave to his Endowment and Danite oaths, and trusted until too late to the promises of protection made to him by Brigham Young. John D. Lee was a fanatic, and as such, believed in the Mormon Church, and aided in carrying out the orders of that Church. I believe it to my duty to publish this work, to show mankind the fruits resulting from obedience to Mormon leaders, and to show that Mormonism was as certainly the cause of the Mountain Meadows Massacre, and it is that fanaticism has been the mother of crime in all ages of the world. I also wish the American people to read the facts, as they are told by a mistaken and fanatical follower of the Mormon doctrines, yet, one who was a brave man, and, according to his ideas and teaching, a good man; who did not believe he was doing wrong when obeying the commands of the Mormon priesthood. I wish the American people to read this work, and then say, if they can, what should be the fate of those who caused the crime to be committed. The following pages contain simply true copies of material, furnished me by John D. Lee, for the purpose of being published; all of which was written by him while in prison, and after the jury had returned its verdict of guilty.

I have no excuses to offer for publishing the work just as it is. It is what it purports to be, a full history of the Mountain Meadows Massacre, and also a sketch of the life of John D. Lee, embracing a revelation of the secret history of Mormonism, from its inception down to the death of Lee; with a correct copy of his confession as given to me for publication. If any feel injured by the facts, I cannot help it. If this publication shall, in any degree, aid in securing the much needed legislation, demanded by the American citizens of Utah, from the National Government, so that Church criminals, as well as Gentiles, can be convicted in Utah, I shall feel that I have been paid well for all the vexations I have endured in the land of the *Saints*, where they murder men, women and children for the glory of God, and the upbuilding of His kingdom.

I also believe this publication will be an advantage to the large number of naturally good and honest people who inhabit Utah, who joined the Church, and moved to Utah, believing it their Christian duty to do so. To that class of people I am indebted for many favors, and wish them future prosperity.

WM. W. BISHOP,
Confidential Att'y of John D. Lee
PIOCHE, NEVADA, May 17, 1877

CONTENTS

CONTENTS

CONTENTS

LIST OF ENGRAVINGS

INTRODUCTORY

ONE hundred and twenty men, women, and children were murdered by Mormons and Indians, at the Mountain Meadows, on Friday, September 16, 1857, or thereabouts. The victims were members of a train under command of Captain Fancher, and are generally known as the Arkansas Emigrant Company. At that time Brigham Young was Governor of Utah Territory, and also the head of the Church of Jesus Christ of Latter-Day Saints. Acting as Governor of the Territory, he and his followers had, for a series of years, violated the laws of the United States, with insulting impunity, and then were standing in hostile attitude towards the government. Brigham Young had the audacity to declare Utah under martial law, and call out his legions of fanatics to oppose the forces of the United States, which had been ordered to Utah to enforce obedience to the Government. As leader and head of the Mormon Church, he had taught his followers to believe that he was an inspired man, and as such, receiving orders and revelations direct from the God of Heaven; that the time had arrived when Christ was to come to earth and reign a thousand years, and that *all* who did not accept the Book of Mormon, and the teachings of Brigham Young, as God's holy religion, were to suffer death, and the wealth of the unbelievers to become the property of the so-called Saints. He had also taught the doctrine that all who opposed his orders or refused obedience to his commands should die, and if they had been members of the Mormon Church their blood was to be shed in order to save their souls. At that time Brigham Young had the *sole* control of everything in Utah; his word was law; his orders were given under the pretense that they emanated from God, and to disobey his orders was treason to the Church and punishable by death. The Mormon people were willing followers of their designing leader. They believed in polygamy, blood atonement, and the inspiration of the priesthood. Their intelligence made their fanaticism the more dangerous. No crime was so great that it would not be ordered by Brigham Young, if he believed it would benefit Mormonism, and no order could be given by him but what his deluded followers considered it their bounden duty to unquestioningly obey.

The oaths taken by the Mormons in their various ceremonies bound them under fearful penalties to lay aside all individuality, and become the willing tools of a cruel and treasonable priesthood. Blind obedience to Brigham Young was the test of Christian excellence. Salvation and celestial glory were offered by the Church leaders, and confidently expected by the brethren, as the reward to be received for the most fearful crimes. Brigham Young held the keys of Heaven, so it was said, and so his followers believed, and certain it was he held the life of every man in the Territory of Utah in his hand. Law and justice were unheard of, or at least unknown. The so-called reformation was then at its height. The members of the Church were confessing their sins to each other in public and being rebaptized under promise of certain salvation. Superstition, fanaticism, and satanic influences of every character had changed the dwellers in Utah from American citizens, with reasoning faculties, into blind zealots, anxious to do any act that their so-called prophet commanded. It was while this condition of affairs existed in Utah that Captain Fancher attempted to cross the Territory, on the way to the pleasant valleys of the Golden State, where the company intended to settle and build homes for themselves and their children.

In support of the charge that Brigham Young favored the shedding of blood as atonement for sin, I quote the following compilation of extracts, which were kindly furnished me by the *Salt Lake Tribune*, and as they speak for themselves, comment is useless:

EXTRACTS FROM BRIGHAM YOUNG'S SERMONS

"I could refer you to plenty of instances where men have been righteously slain in order to atone for their sins."

"But now I say, in the name of the Lord, that if this people will sin no more, but faithfully live their religion, their sins will be forgiven them without taking life."

"Now, when you hear my brethren telling about cutting people off from the earth, that you consider in strong doctrine; but it is to save them, not to destroy them."

"All mankind love themselves; and let these principles be known by an individual, and he would be glad to have his blood shed. That would be loving themselves even unto eternal exaltation."

"This is loving our neighbor as ourselves; if he needs help, help him; if he wishes salvation, and it is necessary to spill his blood upon the ground in order that he be saved, spill it."

"Any of you who understand the principles of eternity, if you have sinned a sin requiring the shedding of blood, except the sin unto death, would not be satisfied or rest until your blood should be spilled, that you might gain the salvation you desire. This is the way to love mankind."

"It is true the blood of the Son of God was shed for sins through the fall and those committed by men, yet ye men can commit sins which it can never remit. As it was in the ancient days, so it is in our day; and though the principles are taught publicly from this stand, still the people do not understand them; yet the law is precisely the same."

"I have known a great many men who have left this Church, for whom there is no chance whatever of exaltation; but if their blood had been spilled, it would have been better for them. The wickedness and ignorance of the nations forbid this principle being in full force, but the time will come when the law of God will be in full force."

"Will you love your brothers and sisters likewise, when they have committed a sin that cannot be atoned for without the shedding of their blood? Will you love that man or woman well enough to shed their blood? That is what Jesus Christ meant. He never told a man or woman to love their enemies in their wickedness. He never intended any such thing."

"I have known scores and hundreds of people for whom there would have been a chance in the last resurrection if their lives had been taken and their blood spilled upon the ground as a smoking incense to the Almighty, but who are now angels to the devil, until our elder brother, Jesus Christ, raises them up, conquers death, hell, and the grave."

"There are sins that can be atoned for by an offering upon an altar, as in ancient days; and there are sins that the blood of a lamb, of a calf, or of turtle doves cannot remit, but they must be atoned for by the blood of the man. That is the reason why men talk to you as they do from this stand; they understand the doctrine, and throw out a few words about it. You have been taught that doctrine, but you do not understand it."

"Now, take a person in this congregation, who has a knowledge of being saved in the kingdom of our God and our Father, and being an exalted one, who knows and understands the principles of eternal life, and sees the beauty and excellency of the eternities before him, compared with the vain and foolish things of the world; and suppose he is overtaken with a gross fault, that he has committed a fault which he knows will deprive him of that exaltation which he desires, and that he cannot attain to it without the shedding of blood; and also knows that by having his blood shed, he will atone for that sin and be saved, and be exalted with the gods, is there a man or woman in this house but what would say, 'I shed my blood, that I may be saved and exalted with the gods?'"

Brigham Young had also written letters to his chief men throughout the territory, inciting them against the people of the United States. That it may be understood what kind of language he used to his bishops in these circulars, I copy the one sent to Wm. H. Dame, the man who was colonel and commander of the militia in southern Utah, and who afterwards, and while standing upon Mountain Meadows examining the bodies of those that he had directed Haight to slaughter, said: "I would not have given the orders if I had thought there were so many of them." The circular bears date two days before the massacre is charged to have been committed, and the supposition is that it had been delivered to Dame at the time he issued his orders for the massacre. It explains itself, and reads as follows:

"GREAT SALT LAKE CITY, Sept. 14, 1857.

"Colonel William H. Dame, Parowan, Iron Co.:

"Herewith you will receive the Governor's Proclamation, declaring martial law. You will probably not be called out this fall, but are requested to continue to make ready for a big fight another year. The plan of operations is supposed to be about this: In case the U.S. Government should send out an overpowering force, we intend to desolate the territory and conceal our families, stock, and all of our effects in the fastnesses of the mountains, where they will be safe, while the men waylay our enemies, attack them from ambush, stampede their animals, take the supply trains, cut off detachments and parties sent to canons for wood or on other service. To lay waste everything that will burn - houses, fences, trees, fields, grass - that they cannot find a particle of anything that will be of use to them, not even sticks to make a fire for to cook their suppers. To waste away our enemies, and lose none. That will be our mode of warfare. Thus you see the necessity of preparing. First secure places in the mountains where they cannot find us, or if they do, where they cannot approach in any force, and then prepare for our families, building some cabins, *caching* flour and grain. Flour should be ground in the latter part of winter, or early in the spring, in order to keep.

Sow grain in your fields early as possible this fall, so that the harvest of another year may come off before they have time to get here. Conciliate the *Indians*, and make them our fast friends. In regard to letting people pass or repass, or travel through the territory, this applies to all strangers and suspected persons. Yourself and Bro. Isaac C. Haight, in your district, is authorized to give such permits. Examine all such persons strictly before giving them permits to pass, keep things perfectly quiet and let all things be done peacefully, but with firmness, and let there be no excitement. Let the people be united in their feelings and faith, as well as works, and keep alive the spirit of the reformation; and what we said in regard to sowing the grain and provisions, we say again, let there be no waste; save life always when it is possible - we do not wish to shed a drop of blood if it can be avoided. This course will give us great influence abroad.

[Signed]   "BRIGHAM YOUNG"

[Signed]   "DANIEL H. WELLS"

Next, take the proclamation declaring martial law in the Territory, and put these facts together, and no fair minded person can deny that the massacre was the result of the teachings of Brigham Young, and that the Mormons in Church Council decided that the emigrants should be killed as they were afterwards killed.

I claim that Brigham Young is the *real criminal*, and that John D. Lee was an instrument in his hands. That Brigham Young used John D. Lee, as the assassin uses the dagger, to strike down his unsuspecting victim; and as the assassin throws away the dagger, to avoid its bloody blade leading to his detection, so Brigham Young used John D. Lee to do his horrid work; and when discovery becomes unavoidable, he hurls Lee from him, cuts him away from the Church and casts him far out into the whirlpool of destruction. The assassin has no further use for his weapon. I also claim that if religious fanaticism can clear a man from his crime, that John D. Lee was guiltless, for he was one of the most intensely fanatical Mormons that infested Utah In 1857. But I do not claim that the fact of his being a fanatic and blinded believer of Brigham Young's so-called revelations excused him - far from it. In place of excusing him, it added to his crime. Such insanity as that which religious fanaticism breeds, can only, and should only, be treated by the executioner, and there are many thousands in Utah who are afflicted with the disease, that calls for that radical treatment which was administered to Lee. The

Mormons around Cedar City, especially, were insane dreamers, and to them the Danites, Destroying Angels and Blood Atoners became objects of ecstatic admiration. The Mormons had come into existence to combat the doctrines of Protestants and Catholics alike. They were infatuated followers of designing leaders, anxious to earn the martyr's crown by giving up life if necessary to advance the interest of the Mormon Church, or please one of the priesthood.

The Templars and Knights of St. John were no more willing servants of the Cross, in its war with the Crescent, than were the deluded followers of Brigham Young to overthrow all established government, and shed the blood of all who were marked as victims by the false prophet who directed their assassin-like actions. They had no law but the will of Brigham Young. No purpose but what they called the will of God. Their discipline was perfect, and their devotion absolute.

Such was the condition of affairs when the fair plains of Utah were wetted with the blood of over one hundred and twenty human beings, that had been doomed to death by the unanimous voice of the Satanic crew that claimed to be servants of the ever-living God. Since that time every force has been brought forward which Mormonism could wield to prevent the facts from becoming known. Brigham Young has shielded and rewarded those that he well knew were engaged in the unholy work.

I cannot explain the facts connected with the Mormons and the massacre, in any other way, so fully and clearly, and yet so truly, as I can by giving extracts from the speech of Judge Cradlebaugh, which he delivered in Congress, in the year 1863. Judge Cradlebaugh was an educated, honorable gentleman, whose word no man that ever knew him can honestly dispute. He was speaking about the Mountain Meadows Massacre, and calling upon Congress for needed legislation for the Territory of Utah. The entire speech is one that every lover of our institutions should be familiar with, as it most clearly portrays the evils of the Mormon system. I would like to publish the entire speech, but will content myself by giving only a part. In regard to what Mormonism is, he says:

MR. CRADLEBAUGH - "Mr. Speaker, having resided for some time among the Mormons, become acquainted with their ecclesiastical policy, their habits, and their crimes, I feel that I would at be discharging my duty if I failed to impart such information as I have acquired in regard to this people in our midst, who are building up, consolidating, and daringly carrying out a system subversive of the Constitution and laws, and fatal to morals and true religion.

"The remoteness of Utah from the settled regions of our country, and the absence of any general, intercourse between the Mormons and the masses of our people, have served to keep the latter in almost complete ignorance of the character and designs of the former. That ignorance, pardonable at first, becomes criminal when the avenues to a full knowledge are open to us.

"Mormonism is one of the monstrosities of the age in which we live. It seems to have been left for the model Republic of the world, for the nineteenth century, when the light of knowledge is more generally diffused than ever before, when in art, science and philosophy we have surpassed all that ages of the past can show, to produce an idle, worthless vagabond of an impostor, who heralds forth a creed repulsive to every refined mind, opposed to every generous impulse of the human heart, and a faith which commands a violation of the rights of hospitality, sanctifies falsehood, enforces the systematic degradation of women, not only permits, but orders, the commission of the vilest lusts, in the name of Almighty God himself, and teaches that it is a sacred duty to commit the crimes of theft and murder. It is surprising that such faith, taught too, in the coarsest and most vulgar way, should meet with any success. Yet in less than a century it girdles the globe. Its missionaries are planted in every place. You find them all over Europe, thick through England and Wales, traversing Asia and Africa, and braving the billows of the southern oceans to seek proselytes. And, as if to crown its achievements, it establishes itself in the heart of one of the greatest and most powerful governments of the world, establishes therein a theocratic government overriding all other government, putting the laws at defiance, and now seeks to consummate and perpetuate itself by acquiring a State sovereignty, and by being placed on an equality with the other states of the Union.

"Mormonism is in part a conglomeration of illy cemented creeds from other religions, and in part founded upon the eccentric production of one Spaulding, who, having failed as a preacher and shopkeeper, undertook to write a historic novel. He had a smattering of biblical knowledge, and chose for his subject 'the history of the lost tribes of Israel'. The whole was supposed to be communicated by the Indians, and the last of the series was named Mormon, representing that he had buried the book. It was a dull, tedious, interminable volume, marked by ignorance and folly. The work was so flat, stupid and insipid, that no publisher could be induced to bring it before the world. Poor Spaulding at length went to his grave, and the manuscript remained a neglected roll in the possession of his widow.

"Then arose Joe Smith, more ready to live by his wits than by the labor of his hands. Smith had, early in life, manifested a turn for pious frauds. He had figured in several wrestling matches with the devil, and had been conspicuous in giving in eventful experiences in religion at certain revivals. He announced that he had dug up the book of Mormon, which taught the true religion; this was none other than poor Spaulding's manuscript, which he had purloined from the widow. In his hands the manuscript became the basis of Mormonism. Joe became a prophet; the founder of a religious sect; the president of a swindling bank; the builder of the City of Nauvoo; mayor of the city; general of the armies of Israel; candidate for President of the United States, and finally a martyr, as the Saints choose to call him. But the truth is that his villainies, together with the villainies of his followers, brought down upon him the just vengeance of the people of Illinois and Missouri, and his career was brought to an end by his being shot while confined in jail in Carthage. It was unfortunate that such was his end, for his followers raised the old cry of martyrdom and persecution, and, as always proved, 'the blood of the martyr was the seed of the Church.'

"Mormonism repudiates the celibacy imposed by the Catholic religion upon its priesthood, and takes in its stead the voluptuous impositions of the Mohammedan Church. It preaches openly that the more wives and children its men have in this world, the purer, more influential and conspicuous will they be in the next; that wives, children, and property will not only be restored, but doubled in the resurrection. It adopts the use of prayers and baptism for the dead, as a part of its creed. Mormons claim to be favored with marvelous gifts - the power of speaking in tongues, of casting out devils, of curing the sick, and of healing the lame and the halt. They claim that they have a living prophet, seer and revelator who holds the keys of the Kingdom of Heaven, and through whose intercession alone access can be had. They recognize the Bible, but they interpret it for themselves, and hold that it is subject to be changed by new revelation, which, they say, supercedes old revelation. One of their doctrines is that of continued progression to ultimate perfection. They say God was but a man, who went out developing and increasing until he reached his present high capacity; and they teach that Mormons will be equal to him; in a word, that good Mormons will become gods. They teach the shedding of blood for remission of sins, or, in other words, that if a Mormon apostatizes, his throat shall be cut, and his blood poured out upon the ground for the remission of his sins. They also practice other revolting doctrines, such as are only carried out in polygamous countries, which is evidenced by a number of mutilated persons in their midst. They hold that the prophet's revelations are binding upon their consciences, and that they are bound to obey him in all things. They say that the earth and the fullness thereof is the Lord's; that they are God's chosen people on earth; that their mission on earth is to take charge of God's property, and, as faithful stewards, that it is their duty to obtain it, and are taught that, in obtaining it, they must not get in debt to the Lord's enemies for it; in other words, they teach that it is a duty to rob and steal from Gentiles. They have christened themselves 'The Church of Jesus Christ of Latter-Day Saints.' They claim that Mormonism is to go on spreading until it overthrows all the nations of the earth, and if necessary for its accomplishment, its success shall be consummated by the sword; that Jackson County, Missouri, is to be the seat of empire of the Mormon Church; that here the Mormons are to be finally gathered, and that from that Zion shall proceed a power that will dethrone kings, subvert dynasties, and subjugate all the nations of the earth.

"I have said that their doctrines were repulsive to every refined mind. Every other false faith which has reigned its evil time upon this goodly world of ours, has had some kindly and redeeming features. Even the semi-theocracy of the Aztecs, as Prescott tells you, disfigured as it was by horrid and bloody rites, was not without them. Buddhism and Brahmanism, with all their misshapen fables, still inculcated, in no small degree, a pure code of morals. Nor, is the like assertion untrue of Mohammedanism. It was reserved for Mormonism, far off in the bosom of our beloved land, to rear its head, naked in all its hideous deformity, and unblushingly, yes, defiantly, proclaim a creed without the least redeeming feature, and of such character that the Thugism of India cannot match it.

"So at variance is the practice of polygamy with all the instincts of humanity, that it has to be pressed upon the people with the greatest assiduity as a part of their religious duty. It is astonishing with what pertinacity through all their 'sermons and discourses' it is justified and insisted on. Threats, entreaties, persuasions, and commands, are continually brought in play to enforce its cheerful observance. So revolting is it to the women, that to aid in its enforcement they are brutalized, their modesty destroyed by low, vile, vulgar expressions, such as I could not repeat, and would not ask the clerk to read in your hearing. If, however, my conjugal friend, the Delegate from Utah, will undertake such task, I will most cheerfully furnish them for him; certainly he ought not to hesitate. If they are proper to be repeated before large congregations of women and children in Salt Lake City, the representative of the Church ought not to be ashamed at reading them to this House. Will the Delegate from Utah read them?

CONDITION OF THE WOMEN

"But their teachings, officially reported by themselves, give you a better idea of their estimation of woman than anything I could say. I shall read to you from a few of their sermons on this subject, only observing that you may pick other passages inculcating similar doctrines, containing like threats, rebukes, and complaints, in nearly every sermon published in the Church organ.

"President J.M. Grant, in a sermon delivered September 21, 1856, reported in the *Deseret News*, (volume 6, page 235) said:

'And we have women here who like anything but the celestial law of God; and, if they could, would break asounder the cable of the Church of Christ; there is scarcely a mother in Israel but would do it this day. And they talk it to their husbands, to their daughters, and to their neighbors, and say that they have not seen a week's happiness since they became acquainted with that law, or since their husbands took a second wife. They want to break up the Church of God, and to break it from their husbands and from their family connections.'

"President Brigham Young, in a sermon delivered the same day, reported in the same paper, said:

"'Now, for my proposition; it is more particularly for my sisters, as it is frequently happening that women say that they are unhappy. Men will say, "my wife, though a most excellent woman, has not seen a happy day since I took my second wife; no, not a happy day for a year." It is said that women are tied down and abused; that they are misused, and have not the liberty they ought to have; that many of them are wading through a perfect flood of tears, because of the conduct of some men, together with their own folly.

"'I wish my women to understand that what I am going to say is for them, as well as all others, and I want those who are here to tell their sisters, yes, all the women of this community, and then write it back to the States, and do as you please with it. I am going to give you from this time to the 6th day of October next for reflection, that you may determine whether you wish to stay with your husbands or not, and then I am going to set every woman at liberty, and say to them, "now go your way, my women with the rest; go your way." And my wives have got to do one of two things; either round up their shoulders to endure the afflictions of this world, and live their religion, or they may leave, for I will not have them about me. I will go into Heaven alone, rather than have scratching and fighting around me. I will set all at liberty. "What, first wife too?" Yes, I will liberate you all.

"'I know what my women will say; they will say, 'you can have as many women as you please, Brigham.' But I want to go somewhere and do something to get rid of the whiners; I do not want them to receive a part of the truth and spurn the rest out of doors. • • • •

"'Let every man thus treat his wives, keeping raiment enough to clothe his body; and say to your wives, "take all that I have and be set at liberty; but if you stay with me you shall comply with the law of God, and that, too, without any murmuring and whining. You must fulfill the law of God in every respect, and round up your shoulders to walk up to the mark without any grunting.

"'Now, recollect, that two weeks from tomorrow I am going to set you all at liberty. But the first wife will say, "it is hard, for I have lived with my husband twenty years, or thirty, and have raised a family of children for him, and it is a great trial for me for him to have more women than will bear children." If my wife had borne me all the children that she ever would bear, the celestial law would teach me to take young women that would have children. • • • •

"'Sisters, I am not joking; I do not throw out my proposition to banter your feelings, to see whether you will leave your husbands, all or any of you. But I do know that there is no cessation to the everlasting whinings of many of the women of this territory. And if the women will turn from the commandments of God and continue to despise the order of Heaven, I will pray that the curse of the Almighty may be close to their heels, and that it may be following them all the day long. And those that enter into it and are faithful, I will promise them that they shall be queens in heaven and rulers for all eternity.'

"President Heber C. Kimball, in a discourse delivered in the

Tabernacle, November 9, 1856 (*Deseret News*, volume 6, page 291), said:

"'I have no wife or child that has any right to rebel against me. If they violate my laws and rebel against me, they will get into trouble just as quickly as though they transgressed the counsels and teachings of Brother Brigham. Does it give a woman a right to sin against me because she is my wife? No; but it is her duty to do my will as I do the will of my Father and my God. It is the duty of a woman to be obedient to her husband, and unless she is, I would not give a damn for all her queenly right and authority, nor for her either, if she will quarrel and lie about the work of God and the principles of plurality. A disregard of plain and correct teachings is the reason why so many are dead and damned, and twice plucked up by the roots, and I would as soon baptize the devil as some of you.'

"October 6, 1855 (volume 5, page 274), Kimball said:

"'If you oppose any of the works of God you will cultivate a spirit of apostasy. If you oppose what is called the spiritual wife doctrines, the patriarchal order, which is of God, that course will corrode you with apostasy, and you will go overboard. Still a great many do so, and strive to justify themselves in it; but they are not justified in God. • • •

"'The principle of plurality of wives never will be done away, although some sisters have had revelations that when this time passes away, and they go through the vale, every woman will have a husband to herself. I wish more of our young men would take to themselves wives of the daughters of Zion, and not wait for us old men to take them all. Go ahead upon the right principle, young gentlemen, and God bless you for ever and ever, and make you fruitful, that we may fill the mountains and then the earth, with righteous inhabitants.'

"April 2, 1854, President Heber C. Kimball said in the Tabernacle (see *Deseret News*, volume 4, No. 20):

"'There are some ladies who are not happy in their present situation; but that woman who cannot be happy with one man cannot be happy with two. You know all women are good, or ought to be. They are made for angelic beings, and I would like to see them act more angelic in their behavior. You were made more angelic, and a little weaker than man. Man is made of rougher material - to open the way, cut down bushes and kill the snakes - that women may walk along through life, and not soil and tear their skirts. When you see a woman with ragged skirts you may know she wears the unmentionables, for she is doing the man's business, and has not time to cut off the rags hanging about her. From this time henceforth you may know what woman wears her husband's pants. May the Lord bless you. Amen.'

"President Heber C. Kimball, in a lengthened discourse, delivered in the Tabernacle on the 4th day of April, 1857, took occasion to say:

"'I would not be afraid to promise a man who is sixty years of age, if he will take the counsel of Brother Brigham and his brethren, he will renew his age. I have noticed that a man who has but one wife, and is inclined to that doctrine, soon begins to wither and dry up, while a man who goes into plurality looks fresh, young and sprightly. Why is this? Because God loves that man, and because he honors his work and word. Some of you may not believe this; but I not only believe it, but I also know it. For a man of God to be confined to one woman is a small business, for it is as much as we can do to keep under the burdens we have to carry, and do not know what we should do if we only had one woman apiece.'

"President Heber C. Kimball used the following language in a discourse, instructing a band of missionaries about to start on their mission:

"'I say to those who are elected to go on missions, go, if you never return, and commit what you have into the bands of God - your wives, your children, your brethren and your property. Let truth and righteousness be your motto, and don't go into the world for anything else but to preach the Gospel, build up the kingdom of God, and gather the sheep into the fold. You we sent out as shepherds to gather the sheep together; and remember that they are not your sheep; they belong to him that sends you; then don't make a choice of any of those sheep, don't make selections before they are brought home and put into the fold. You understand that! Amen.'

"Such, then, to Mormonism in regard to all that beautifies life in the conjugal relation; such are their sentiments and commands pronounced under the assumed authority of God upon the female sex. When President Kimball calls his numerous wives his 'cows,' he but reflects the Mormon idea of woman in the social scale.

"The view is sickening. I turn with loathing and disgust from their legalized status of systematic debauchery and lust. Before it the entire nature recoils. No wonder that it requires the whole enginery of the Mormon Church, threats and intimidations to compel the women to submit to it. I pity that man or women who can for, one moment look upon this organized, systematic, enforced degradation and prostitution with any other feeling then that of abhorrence and disgust. In matters of affection woman is a monopolist - she wants the whole heart, or she wants none. But in Utah she is compelled to take part only of the smallest of hearts - a Mormon's heart - little attention and no devotion.

"The church government established by the Mormons to carry into operation the teachings from which I have so copiously extracted, is one of the most complete despotisms on the face of the earth. The mind of one man permeates through the whole mass of the people, and subjects to its unrelenting tyranny the souls and bodies of all. It reigns supreme in Church and State, in morals, and even in the minutest domestic and social arrangements. Brigham's house is at once tabernacle, capital and harem; and Brigham himself is king, priest, lawgiver, and chief polygamist. Is treason hatched in Utah? - Brigham is the head traitor. Is a law enacted? - Brigham's advice determines it. Is an offending 'Gentile' or an Apostate Mormon to be assassinated? - The order emanates from Brigham.

"In addition to all this, he heals the afflicted by the laying on of hands, and comforts the widow by becoming her husband. It may be asked, does he do this without compensation? No, his pay is both high and certain. He taxes his deluded followers to the extent of all surplus property upon their arrival in the Territory. He subsequently taxes them to the extent of one tenth of their annual productions and labor, and if reluctant to pay, he mercilessly snatches all they have. He has through the Legislature unrestricted license to tax merchants. By legislation, all estrays in the Territory are impounded and sold, and the proceeds paid over to him. By like authority he seizes upon the great highway between our Atlantic and Pacific possessions, grants exclusive rights to erect bridges and ferries across all the streams in the Territory, and fixes the toll at enormous rates, ranging from five to ten dollars for a team, expressly providing in the law that a portion of the receipts shall be paid over to himself, by which means, whether willing or unwilling, the emigrant to the Pacific Coast is forced to build up the Church, and furnish money to emigrate pious sisters to Zion to replenish the harems of the hoary-headed leaders of the Church; and as if to consummate the matter of pay, all escheats in the Territory are to him; the property of the emigrant, and even the habiliments of the deceased may be sold, and the proceeds paid over to him. He selects for himself the choicest spots of land in the Territory, and they yield him their productions, none daring to interfere.

"The timber in the mountains for a great distance from Salt Lake City belongs to him, and it is only by delivering each third load, as he shall order, that the gates are opened and the citizen allowed to pass up City Creek canyon to obtain it. Having appropriated all that he desires for his own use, he has quite extensive tracts of country furnished him by the Federal Government as capital for his Church. He sends his agents, denominating them missionaries, to Europe, who represent Utah as a paradise, and go into the market offering each proselyte who will come to Zion, a homestead of a quarter of a section of land, being in return compensated by the addition of females to fill the harems, and the tithing which will in the future accrue to him. The cattle on a thousand hills exhibit his brand. He fixes his pay - pays himself. His pampered but plebeian body reposes in a palace, and scores of bright eyed women call him husband. His deluded followers yield him implicit obedience and a Church organization known as 'Danites' or 'Destroying Angels,' stands ready to protect his person, or avenge his wrongs, and to execute his pleasure.

"The legislators of the Territory are Mormons. The endowment oaths bind them to yield an implicit obedience to Brigham, as the head of the Church, and political head of the Territory. His mandates are superior to all law. The Mormons are fanatics; they will keep their oath to obey him. Did not their religion induce, their fears would compel obedience, for the vengeance of Brigham, though silent, is swift, and fearful as the horrors of death can make it. Mormon punishment for Mormon Apostasy is like the old curse of former Popes, it extends from the soles of the feet to the hairs of the head. It separates the husband from the wife; it reaches from the confiscation of property to the severance of the windpipe. Armed with such power over the hearts and lives of the people, Brigham defiantly drives the barbaric chariot of Mormon robbery, murder, polygamy and incest over all law, in defiance of all Federal officials in the Territory. Brigham not only controls the legislation, but he controls the courts. He uses the one to aid in accomplishing the other.

"As one of the Associate Justices of the Territory of Utah, in the month of April, 1859, I commenced and held a term of the District Court for the Second Judicial District, in the city of Provo, about sixty miles south of Salt Lake City. General A. S. Johnston, in command of the Military Department, furnished a small military force for the purpose of protecting the court. A Grand Jury was empaneled, and their attention was pointedly and specifically called to the great number of crimes that had been committed in the immediate vicinity, cases of public notoriety both as to the offense and the persons who had perpetrated the same; for none of these things had 'been done in a corner.' Their perpetrators had scorned alike concealment or apology before the arrival of the American forces. The Jury, thus instructed; though kept in session two weeks, utterly refused to do anything, and were finally discharged as an evidently useless appendage to a court of justice. But the Court was determined to try a last resource to bring to light and to punish those guilty of the atrocious crimes, which had been committed in the Territory, and the session continued. Bench warrants, based upon sworn information, were issued against the alleged criminals, and United States Marshal Dotson, a most excellent and reliable officer, aided by a military posse, procured on his own request, had succeeded in making a few arrests. A general stampede immediately took place among the Mormons; and what I wish to call your attention to as particularly noticeable, is the fact that this occurred more especially among the Church officials and civil officers. Why were these classes so peculiarly urgent and hasty in flight? The law of evidence, based on the experience of ages, has but one answer. It was the consciousness of guilt which drove them to seek a refuge from the avenging arm of the law, armed at last, as they supposed, with power to vindicate its injured majesty. It is a well known fact that many of the bishops and presidents of 'Stakes' remained secreted in the mountains until the news was confirmed beyond doubt, which announced the retrograde course of the administration at Washington.   •   •   •   •   •   •

Sitting as a committing magistrate, complaint after complaint was made before me of murders and robberies. Among these I may mention as peculiarly and shockingly prominent, the murder of Forbes, the assassination of the Parishes and Potter, of Jones and his mother, of the Aiken party, of which there were six in all; and worst and darkest in this appalling catalogue of blood, the cowardly, cold blooded butchery and robbery at the Mountain Meadows. At that time there still lay, all ghastly under the sun of Utah, the unburied skeletons of one hundred and nineteen men, women and children, the hapless, hopeless victims of the Mormon creed."

Judge Cradlebaugh then gives a full history of his visit to the scene of the massacre and of his utter failure to procure the arrest of one of the guilty parties; and also gives the reasons why the courts were powerless to bring offenders to justice. After giving the history of many of the crimes committed by the priestly crew, the speech closes with the following eloquent sentences:

"There can be no doubt that the mass of the Mormon community are misled in their errors by a set of heartless, fanatical leaders. Their success may be much attributed to their isolation. That isolation the fast filling up of the Great Basin, because of its vast mineral deposits, will soon do away with. Nevada now has a population equal to Utah. Thriving towns and cities are springing up on the Humboldt River - and in near proximity to the Mormons. Brigham sees this, and he knows and feels that he must place himself in a position to prevent the consequences to his system which will grow out of this contiguity of settlement. He feels that he cannot keep his women where they have a chance to get away, unless he can protect himself by legislation further than he is able to do while his community remains under the general jurisdiction of the Government. It is on that account that he manifests so great a desire to become an independent State. I say he desires to become a State, for under his tyrannical sway, and with the system that is now prevalent, Brigham would be the State and the State would be Brigham.

"The people of Utah have nothing but ill will towards our government. The great mass knows nothing of our institutions; they came to Zion, not to America. They are hurried through the settled portions of our country without being allowed to become acquainted with our people or institutions. Upon arriving in Utah they hear nothing but abuse of our people; the whole fountain of patriotism is polluted, and they are taught they owe neither allegiance nor love to our government. Treason and insubordination are openly taught. God forbid that this people should be admitted into the Union as an independent State; I protest against it in the name of humanity, which it would violate by the admission; I protest against it on behalf of my constituents, who have a deep interest in the institutions that are to prevail in the great American Basin; I protest against it in the name and on behalf of the murdered victims of the cruel Mormon faith, whose mouldering bones are bleaching in almost every valley in the Territory; I protest against it on behalf of the downtrodden and undone women of Utah, who, with their female - posterity, in all time to come, will bless those that would not aid in keeping them in bondage."

The foregoing is, in my judgment, sufficient to show what Mormonism was, and the influences that were brought to bear upon the citizens of Utah at the time of the commission of the massacre.

The Territory was practically without courts of justice from 1857 until after the passage of the "Poland Bill", since which time the Federal officers in Utah have made great and praiseworthy exertions to enforce the laws in the Territory.

ORGANIZATION OF THE COURT AT BEAVER CITY

The Second District Court convened in Beaver City, Utah Territory, on the seventh day of September, A.D. 1874. A grand jury was summoned for the 7th of September, but the panel was not completed until the 9th of September. This was the first grand jury under the *Poland Bill.* This was the *first* term of this court at which a Federal or Gentile officer had charge of the grand jury.

This grand jury consisted of fifteen men, ten Gentiles, four Mormons, and one Apostate.

Wm. Stokes and B. L. Duncan rendered efficient service in procuring witnesses to go before this grand jury.

This grand jury was in session from the 9th to the 25th day of September 1874. The indictment against John D. Lee and others, charging them with the crime of murder at the Mountain Meadows, was returned into court on the 24th day of September 1874. Twenty-eight indictments for various crimes were found and returned by this jury. D. P. Whedon, Esq., acted as deputy United States Attorney, and drew all the indictments presented at that term of court. Great credit is due to Judge Whedon for the able manner in which he discharged his duty while acting as deputy United States Attorney in Utah.

Hon. Jacob S. Boreman was the presiding judge during all of the time since 1874, in that district.

General George R. Maxwell, the United States Marshal for Utah, was an efficient officer. He resigned his position after the first trial of Lee, and was succeeded by Colonel William Nelson, the present United States Marshal for Utah.

James R. Wilkins, the clerk of the court, is an affable, educated gentleman, in every way qualified for his position.

Hon. William Carey, United States Attorney, who prosecuted at the first trial, was succeeded by Hon. Sumner Howard, who secured a conviction of Lee, by beating the Mormons at their own game of trickery.

At the first trial, a jury was sworn to try the case on the 24th day of

July 1875.

The prosecution was conducted by William Carey, United States Attorney for Utah, D. P. Whedon, deputy United States Attorney, R. N. Boskin, Presley Denney, Charles H. Swift and C. M. Hawley.

The defendant was represented by J. G. Sutherland, E. D. Hoge, Wells Spicer, John McFarland and Wm. W. Bishop.

After several days of legal strife, the case was given to the jury, and failing to agree (nine being for Not Guilty, and three being for Guilty), the jury were discharged and the case continued.

At the succeeding May term of the court, the prosecution being without money to carry on the base, or procure witnesses, and the defendant insisting upon a trial, the court admitted him to bail in the sum of ten thousand dollars, which bail was at once given, and Lee was then discharged from custody, and remained at liberty until a few days before the commencement of the second trial, at which time he was surrendered to the court by his Mormon bondsmen, they having been ordered by the Church authorities to withdraw all assistance and sympathy from John D. Lee, as he had been selected as a victim to shoulder the sins of the people of the Mormon Church. Daniel H. Wells was present in person at Beaver, to see that the treachery of the Mormon leaders was completely carried out.

September 14, 1876, a jury was empaneled to try the case the second time. Twelve jurymen were found who were considered safe by the Church authorities, and all other parties concerned, and the trial commenced. The attorneys for the defendant had been furnished a list of the Jurymen, and the list was examined by a committee of Mormons, who marked those who would convict with a dash (--), those who would rather not convict with a star (*), and those who were certain to acquit John D. Lee, under all circumstances, with two stars (**). It is sufficient on that subject to simply say, all the jurymen accepted were marked with *the two stars* in the list, and they acted as the Church directed - they convicted! As a matter of explanation, I may be pardoned for saying that the Mormons, who gave us the list so marked, had shown it to Howard before they gave it to us, and informed him that he had nothing to fear! The law and evidence, and also Brigham Young and the Mormon Church, were then all against Lee, hence his conviction was a foregone conclusion. The evidence is given in full in the body of this work, and speaks for itself.

The jury brought in a verdict of guilty of murder in the first degree, and the court passed sentence of death upon Lee. The case was appealed to the Supreme Court of Utah Territory, and the judgment of the District Court affirmed. Lee was again taken to Beaver and sentenced to be shot. The sentence was carried into effect on the 23rd day of March, A.D. 1877.

At the last trial the prosecution was conducted by Sumner Howard, U.S. Attorney for Utah, and Presley Denney, Deputy U.S. Attorney. The defendant was represented by Wells Spicer, J. Q. Foster and W.W. Bishop.

After John D. Lee had been convicted, he consented to make, a full confession of all that he knew concerning the Mountain Meadows Massacre, and at his request I assisted him in writing up the confession. He then made an assignment of all his writings to me, and requested me to publish the same. I have over one thousand pages of his manuscripts and writings, in his own handwriting. I have corrected the same as I have seen fit, by correcting the spelling and punctuation; otherwise I give the writings and confessions in the exact language of John D. Lee.

Several persons having made claim to the possession of the true confession of Lee, I can only say that what I have published was given to me by him for the purpose of publication, and that he insisted up to the moment of his execution his statements were true.

As my authority for publishing his life and confessions, I give the following letter, which he wrote to me, and which, with others that I have since received from him, and still retain, give me the sole right to publish his writings. The letter reads as follows:

BEAVER CITY, UTAH TERRITORY, SEPT. 30, 1876.

"W.W. BISHOP:

"*Dear Sir* - Having acted for me as one of my Attorneys, and having in all respects done your utmost for my acquittal and interest generally; now that I am awaiting sentence of death on the charge of having aided in the Mountain Meadows Massacre, in case of my death, or final imprisonment, I wish you to still continue my counsel and friend, and as such to publish to the world the history of my life and of my connection with the affair for which I have been tried. You are familiar with the facts, and have my *statements*, which are true. My journals and private papers will be furnished you by my family, the same to be returned when examined. In justice to myself, and to my family, I wish you to publish the *true history* of my life, after the expenses are paid for the publication, I expect you to divide the profits arising there from with my

PRESENT APPEARANCE OF MOUNTAIN MEADOWS

(From a photograph taken just before Lee's execution)

family. Charging you with this *sacred trust*, and by reason of my own inability to publish my life, by reason of imprisonment, I urge you to carry out this my request.   "Your true friend and no mistake,

Yehu & Lee

The Mountain Meadows are situated in Washington County, Utah Territory, and between the seventh and eight parallels of south latitude, from Salt Lake meridian. If the government survey was extended over that portion of Utah Territory, then the particular portion of the Meadows where the massacre was committed would be within the limits of township thirty seven, south of range twelve west. The monument, erected at the place of the massacre, is three hundred and twenty miles southwest from Salt Lake City, by road measure, as the road ran in 1857. A line extended two hundred miles due south, from Salt Lake City, and then ran, at right angles, seventy-five miles due west would terminate at the monument. The Meadows are thirty-six miles southwest of Cedar City, where the massacre was finally planned by Haight, Higby, Klingensmith and the Mormon authorities then in council.

At the time of the massacre, if the evidence of the vampires who acted as Church slaves to secure the conviction of Lee are to be believed, the Meadows were covered with an abundance of rank, nutritious grasses, and was a beautiful, smiling spot of earth, inviting the beholder to rest and repose.

Now it is an arid waste, with but little vegetation upon its plains. The springs, once furnishing a bounteous supply of water, now comparatively dry and wasted away. The Meadows are such only in name; all that gave them beauty has long since faded and gone. They lie there as one of the cursed spots of earth; surrounded by desolation so intense that a fanatic, seeking death in order to escape from the troubles of this sin cursed earth; seeking death in order to obtain the CELESTIAL reward offered by some self-styled apostle, anxious to give up life at once, and try the realities of the *hereafter*, would forego his promised joys and dwell in this land of sorrow, for a season, rather than lay down the body that he was so anxious to separate from and leave it to moulder upon the unsightly spot where so much of wrong has been done in the name of religion. Mormon tradition informs us that the ghosts of the slaughtered emigrants meet nightly at the springs, and with phantom-like stillness, but with perfectness of detail, act over in pantomime the cruelties and horrors connected with the massacre.

I acknowledge myself greatly indebted to D. P. Whedon, Esq., Hon. Wm. Nelson, Wm. Stokes, Esq., John Ward Christian, Esq., General George R. Maxwell, Hon. Sumner Howard, A. S. Patterson, Esq., and the Salt Lake *Tribune* Publishing Company for many favors extended to me by them, in furnishing me with valuable documents for use in the work of compiling this manuscript for publication.

I also acknowledge myself under man obligations to Col. Geo. M. Sabin, of Pioche, Nevada, for his valuable services rendered me in the preparation of this work for the press.

I have now kept faith with my unfortunate client, and feel that I have also performed a duty that I owed to myself and the country.

WM. W. BISHOP

PIOCHE, NEVADA, May 17th, 1877.

LIFE OF JOHN D. LEE

CHAPTER I

A STORMY BEGINNING

IN JUSTICE to myself, my numerous family, and the public in general, I consider it my duty to write a history of my life. I shall content myself with giving *facts*, and let the readers draw their own conclusion therefrom. By the world at large, I am called a vile criminal, and have been sentenced to be shot for deeds committed by myself and others nearly twenty years ago. I never willingly committed a crime. I *have acted my religion*, nothing more. I have obeyed the orders of the Church. I have acted as I was commanded to do by my superiors, and if I have committed acts that justify my execution, I ask my readers to say what should be the fate of the leaders in the Church who taught me to believe that I could not and would not commit sin while obeying orders of the priesthood? My sins, if any, are the result of doing what I was *commanded* to do by those who were my superiors in authority in the Church of Jesus Christ of Latter Day Saints. I will now give the facts, which relate to my own history, and leave it to others to say how I should have acted - how they would have acted if situated as I was.

I was born on the 6th day of September, A.D. 1812, in the town of Kaskaskia, Randolph County, Illinois. My father, Ralph Lee was born in the State of Virginia. He was of the family of Lees of Revolutionary fame, and was a relative of General Robert E. Lee, of the late war; he served his time as an apprentice and learned the carpenter's trade in the city of Baltimore. My mother was born in Nashville, Tennessee. She was the daughter of John Doyle, who for many years held the position of Indian Agent over the roving tribes of Indians in south eastern Illinois. He served in the war of the Revolution, and was wounded in one of the many battles in which he took part with the Sons of Liberty

against the English oppressors. About the year 1796, he was appointed Indian Agent, and moved to Kaskaskia, Illinois.

My mother was first married in 1799, to Oliver Reed, and lived with him until he was assassinated by a man named Jones, who entered the house when the family were asleep, and striking Reed with a seat of a loom, knocked his brains out, at the same time severely wounding my half sister, Eliza Virginia, then six months old. The blow and the screams of the child awakened my mother, who sprang from the bed, and recognizing the assassin, said, "For God's sake, Jones, spare my husband's life. Jones said, You know me, G-d--n you! You shall tell no tales. With this, he caught up a sugar trough and struck my mother on the head with it. The blow rendered her senseless. Jones, believing he had completed his work of death, then left the house. My mother soon revived, called upon the neighbors for assistance, and told who had committed the murder. Jones was arrested, convicted and afterwards hung for the crime. The injuries received by my mother, from the blow struck by Jones, affected her all the rest of her life.

After the death of Reed, my mother went back to Kaskaskia and lived in her father's family until she married my father in the year 1808. My mother had two children by my father - that is, William Oliver and myself. My brother, William Oliver, died when about two years old. At the time of my birth my father was considered one of the leading men of that section of country; he was a master workman, sober and attentive to business, prompt and punctual to his engagements. He contracted largely and carried on a heavy business; he erected a magnificent mansion, for that age and country, on his land adjoining the town of Kaskaskia. This tract of land was the property of my mother when she married my father. My grandfather Doyle was a wealthy man. He died in 1809 at Kaskaskia, Illinois, and left his whole fortune to my mother and her sister Charlotte, by will. They being his only children, he divided the property equally between them.

My father and mother were both Catholics, were raised in that faith; I was christened in that Church. William Morrison and Louise Phillips stood as my representative god-father and god-mother. It is from that Church record that I could alone obtain the facts and date that referred to my birth.

When about one year old, my mother being sick, I was sent to a French nurse, a negro woman. At this time my sister Eliza was eleven years old, but young as she was she had to care for my mother and do all the work of the household. To add to the misfortune, my father began to drink heavily and was soon very dissipated; drinking and gambling was his daily occupation. The interest and care of his family was no longer a duty with him; his presence was seldom seen to cheer and comfort his lonely, afflicted wife. The house was one mile from town, and we had no neighbors nearer than that. The neglect and indifference on the part of my father towards my afflicted mother, served to increase her anguish and sorrow, until death came to her relief. My mother's death left us miserable indeed; we were (my sister and I) thrown upon the wide world, helpless, and I might say, without father or mother. My father when free from the effects of intoxicating drink was a kind hearted, generous, noble man, but from that time forward he was a slave to drink - seldom sober.

My aunt Charlotte was a regular spitfire; she was married to a man by the name of James Conner, a Kentuckian by birth. They lived ten miles north of us. My sister went to live with her aunt, but the treatment she received was so brutal that the citizens complained to the county commissioners, and she was taken away from her aunt and *bound* out to Dr. Fisher, with whose family she lived until she became of age. In the meantime the Doctor moved to the city of Vandalia, Illinois. I remained with my nurse until I was eight years of age, when I was taken to my aunt Charlotte's, to be educated, I had been in a family which talked French so long that I had nearly lost all knowledge of my mother tongue. The children at school called me *Gumbo*, and teased me so much that I became disgusted with the French language and tried to forget it - which has been a disadvantage to me since that time.

My aunt was rich in her own right. My uncle Conner was poor; he drank and gambled and wasted her fortune; she in return gave him *thunder and blixen* all the time. The more she scolded, the worse he acted, until they would fight like cats and dogs. Between them I was treated worse than an African slave. I lived in the family eight years, and can safely say I got a whipping every day I was there. My life was one of misery and wretchedness; and if it had not been for my strong religious convictions, I certainly would have committed suicide, to have escaped from the miserable condition I was in. I then believed, as I do still, that for the crime of suicide there was no forgiveness in this world, or that which is to come. My aunt was more like a savage than a civilized woman. In her anger she generally took her revenge upon those around her who were the least to blame. She would strike with anything she could obtain, with which to work an injury. I have been knocked down and beaten by her until I was senseless, scores of times, and I yet carry many scars on my person, the result of my harsh usage by her.

My experience in childhood made a lasting impression upon me; the horrors of a contentious family have haunted me through life. I then resolved in my mind that I would never subject myself to sorrow and misery as my uncle had done. I would marry for love, and not for riches. I also formed the resolution that I would never gamble after I was married, and I have kept that resolution since I was a married man.

Aunt Charlotte had five children, four girls and one boy; i.e., Minerva C., Amanda, Eliza, Maria and John Edger. They, as well myself, were strangers to the affections of a mother, and the pleasures of a home.

When I was sixteen years old, I concluded to leave my aunt's house - I cannot call it home; my friends advised me to do so. I walked one night to Kaskaskia; went to Robert Morrison and told him my story. He was a mail contractor. He clothed me comfortably, and sent me over the Mississippi River into Missouri, to carry the mail from St. Genevieve to Pinckney, on the north side of the Missouri River, *via* Potosi, a distance of one hundred and twenty seven miles. It was a weekly mail. I was to receive seven dollars a month for my services. This was in December 1828. It was a severe winter; snow unusually deep, and roads bad. I was often until two o'clock at night in reaching my stations. In the following Spring I came near losing my life on several occasions when swimming the streams, which were then generally over their banks. The Meramec was the worse stream I had to cross, but I escaped danger, and gave satisfaction to my employer. At my request, I was changed, in the spring of 1829, to the route from Kaskaskia to Vandalia, Illinois, the then capital of the State; the route went by Covington and Carlisle. This was also a weekly route; the distance was about one hundred miles, and I had eighteen hours in which to make the trip. While I was carrying the mail in Missouri, I got a letter from my sister, informing me of her marriage to Josiah Nichols, a nephew of Barker Berry, the sheriff of Fayette County, Illinois, and inviting me to visit them. Nichols was a wealthy man, and lived sixteen miles north of Vandalia. I had not met my sister for many years, so I concluded to visit her. This was one reason why I wished to be put on the Vandalia route. One day, when I arrived at Vandalia, I did not find the postmaster in the post office. I could not find him, so I left the mail at the post office door, and rode up to my brother-in-law's house. I had a pleasant visit there, and returned the next

morning to carry the mail back to Kaskaskia. The postmaster, not knowing where I was, had sent another person with the mail, at my expense.
It cost me $15.00 - a little over my wages for two months. I returned to
Kaskaskia, where my employer received me kindly, and laughed at my
mishap. I agreed to pay all damages if he would change me to another
route, for I could not consent to return again to the scene of my failure.
My employer kindly gave me the place as stage driver from Kaskaskia
to Shawneetown, on the Ohio River. The route ran by Pinkneyville and
Gallatin; and it was one hundred and twenty miles in length, through a
thinly settled country. I drove on that line about one month, when I commenced driving stage from Kaskaskia to Belleville. In traveling this
route, I passed by my aunt Charlotte Conner's place. Uncle Conner had
then gone to the lead mines at Galena. When my aunt and cousins saw
me, they all begged me to return and live with them. They made great
promises of kindness, and I was finally persuaded to agree to return, and
live in the family. I soon quit the stage driving business and returned to
my aunt's.

All I know of my father, after I was eight years of age, is, that he went
to Texas in the year 1820, and I have never heard of him since. What his
fate was I never knew.

When my mother died, my uncle and aunt Conner took all the property - a large tract of land, several slaves, household and kitchen furniture, and all; and, as I had no guardian, I never received any portion of
the property; in fact, I was robbed of all. The slaves were set free by an
act of the Legislature; the land was sold for taxes, and was hardly worth
redeeming when I came of age; so I sold my interest in all the land that
had belonged to my mother, and made a quitclaim deed to it to Sidney
Breeze, a lawyer of Kaskaskia, in consideration of $200. My sister, by
the kindness of Dr. Fisher, her guardian, received a much greater price
for her interest in the land than I did.

I was born on the point of land lying between and above the mouth
of the Okaw or Kaskaskia River and the Mississippi River; in what in
known as the Great American Bottom - the particular point I refer to
was then called Zeal-no-waw, the Island of Nuts. It was nineteen miles
from the point of the bluffs to the mouth of the Okaw River; ten miles
wide up at the bluffs and tapering to a point where the rivers united.
Large bands of wild horses, French ponies called "punt" horses, were to
be found any day feeding on the evergreen and nutritious grasses and
vegetation. Cattle and hogs were also running wild in great numbers;

every kind of game, large and small, could be had with little exertion. The streams were fall of fish; the forests contained many varieties of timber; nuts, berries, and wild fruits of every description, found in the temperate zone, could be had in their season. This point of land is one of the finest on the globe; there I spent my early years; there I had pleasures and sorrows; there I met the maiden that first taught me love's young dream. Near by was the Kaskaskia Reservation of the Kaskaskia Indians; Louis DuQuoin was Chief of the tribe. He had a frame house painted in bright colors, but he never would farm any, game being so plentiful he had no need to labor. Nearly all the settlers were French, and not very anxious for education or improvement of any kind. I was quite a lad before I ever saw a wagon, carriage, set of harness, or a ring, a staple or sit of bows to an ox yoke. The first wagon I ever saw was brought into that county by a Yankee peddler; his outfit created as great an excitement in the settlement as the first locomotive did in Utah; the people flocked in from every quarter to see the Yankee wagon. Every thing in use in that country was of the most simple and primitive construction. There were no saw mills or grist mills in that region; sawed lumber was not in the country. The wagons were two wheeled carts made entirely of wood - not a particle of iron about them - the hubs were of white elm, spokes of white oak or hickory, the felloes of black walnut, as it was soft and would bear rounding. The felloes were made six inches thick, and were strongly doweled together with seasoned hardwood plus; the lynch pin was of hickory or ash; the thills were wood. In fact all of it was wood. The harness consisted of a corn husk collar, hames cut from an ash tree root, or from an oak; tugs were raw hide; the lines also were raw hide; a hackamore or halter was used in place of a bridle; one horse was lashed between the thills by raw hide straps and pins in the thills for a hold back; when two horses were used, the second horse was fastened ahead of the first by straps fastened on to the thills of the cart.

Oxen were yoked as follows: A square stick of timber of sufficient length was taken and hollowed out at the ends to fit on the neck of the ox, close up to the horns, and this was fastened by raw hide straps to the horns. All other implements were made in an equally primitive manner. The people were of necessity self-sustaining, for they were forced to depend upon their own resources for everything they used. Clothing was made of home manufactured cloth or the skins of wild animals. Imported articles were procured at heavy cost, and but few found their way to our settlements. Steamboats and railroads were then unthought of, by us at least, and the navigation of the Mississippi was carried on in small boats, that could be drawn up along the riverbank by means of oars, spikes, poles and hooks. The articles most in demand in the settlements were axes, hoes, cotton cards, hatchels for cleaning flax, hemp and cotton, spinning wheels, knives and ammunition, guns and bar shears for plows. In exchange for such goods the people traded beef, hides, furs, tallow, beeswax, honey, etc. Money was not needed or used by any one - everything was trade and barter.

The people were generous and brave. Their pleasures and pastimes were those usual in frontier settlements. They were hardy, and well versed in woodcraft. They aided each other, and were all in all a noble class of people, possessing many virtues and few faults. The girls were educated by their mothers to work, and had to work. It was then a disgrace for a young woman not to know how to take the raw material - the flax and cotton - and, unaided, manufacture her own clothing. It is a lamentable fact that such is no longer the case.

CHAPTER II

THE INDUSTRIOUS YOUNG MAN

AFTER I settled up with my employer and drew my wages, I had but little money left. But I had learned one good lesson: that men who will lead you into trouble will seldom stand by you to get you out of it. I then knew that a soft answer turned away wrath, and I also found out that a man should never spend money that he had not earned. So I determined to live within my income from that time forward, to be prompt and punctual to all my engagements; making my word my honor and my bond. These rules I incorporated into my creed and tried hard to reduce them to practice.

I formed a liking for Emily Conner, the daughter of Henry Conner, when we were quite young. Her father was Marshal of the State of Illinois, under Ninian Edwards, the Governor of the State. Emily was an orphan, and lived for about four years at my aunt Charlotte's after her mother died, and until her father married again. She had a consoling word for me at all times when I was in trouble. From being friends, we became lovers, and were engaged to be married, when my circumstances would permit. The year after I quit driving stage, I raised a larger crop of grain on my aunt's farm, but she did not think I was entitled to any pay for it. This, after her fine promises, was rather disheartening, but I bore it without complaining. My uncle Conner returned home that Fall, and was much pleased to see me back on the farm again, and by his influence I was well treated the remainder of the Fall and Winter. That Winter I went to a school for three months. Early in the spring the Indian war, known as the Black Hawk war, broke out, and volunteers were called for. I enrolled myself at the first call, in, the company of Captain Jacob Feaman, of Kaskaskia. My uncle Conner was First Lieutenant in the same company. The company was ordered to rendezvous at Fort Armstrong, Rock Island, where the troops were reorganized, and Capt. Feaman was promoted to Colonel, and James Conner became Captain of the company. I served until the end of the war, and

was engaged in many skirmishes, and lastly was at the battle of Bad
Axe, which I think took place on the 4th day of August, A.D. 1831, but
am not certain as to the date.

The soldiers were allowed to go home about the first of September
1831. Our company got to Kaskaskia, and were discharged, I think, on
the first of September 1831. I got back to my uncle's with a broken-
down horse and worn-out clothing, and without money. During that
month I concluded to seek a more genial clime, one where I could more
rapidly better my financial condition. I went to see and talk with Emily,
the friend of my childhood, and the girl that taught me first to love. I
informed her of my intentions. We pledged mutual and lasting fidelity
to each other, and I bid farewell to the old farm, and went to St. Louis
to seek employment. When I landed on the wharf at St. Louis, I met a
negro by the name of Barton, who had formerly been a slave to my
mother. He informed me that he was a fireman on the steamboat
Warrior, running the Upper Mississippi, between St. Louis, Mo., and
Galena, Illinois. I told him I wanted work. He said be could get me a
berth on the Warrior as fireman, at $25.00 a month; but he considered
the work more than I could endure, as it was a hard, hot boat to fire on.
I insisted on making the effort, and was employed as fireman on the
Warrior, at $25.00 per month. I found the work was very hard. The first
two or three times that I was on watch, I feared I would be forced to give
it up; but my proud spirit bore me up, and I managed to do my work
until we reached the lower rapids near Keokuk. At this place the Warrior
transferred its freight, in light boats, over the rapids to the Henry Clay,
a steamer belonging to the same line.

The Henry Clay then lay at Commerce, now known as Nauvoo. I was
detailed with two others to take a skiff with four passengers over the
rapids. The passengers were Mrs. Bogges and her mother, and a lady
whose name I have forgotten, and Mr. Bogges. The distance to the
Henry Clay from where the Warrior lay was twelve miles. A large portion of the cargo of the Warrior belonged to the firm of Bogges Co.
When we had gone nearly halfway over the rapids my two assistants got
drunk and could no longer assist me; they lay down in the skiff and went
to sleep. Night was fast approaching, and there was no chance for sleep
or refreshment, until we could reach Commerce or the Henry Clay. The
whole labor fell on me, to take that skiff and its load of passengers to
the steamer. Mr. Bogges aided me when he could do so, but much of the
distance I had to wade in the water and push the skiff as was most con-

venient. I had on a pair of new calfskin boots when we started, but they were cut out by the rocks in the river long before we reached the end of the journey. After a great deal of hardship I succeeded in getting my passengers to the steamer just as it became dark. I was wet, cold, hungry and nearly exhausted. I had strained every nerve to accomplish my task, and save those ladies from a night of suffering in an open skiff on the river. Yet when we boarded the boat I was forgotten; no one paid any attention to me. I was among strangers. I expected that the passengers that I had so faithfully served would see to my wants, but in this I was mistaken; no one paid any attention to me. I sat down by the engine in my wet clothing and soon fell asleep, without bedding or food. I slept from exhaustion until near midnight, when I was seized with fearful crampings, accompanied by a cold and deathlike numbness. I tried to rise up, but could not. Every time I made an effort to rise, the pains increased. I thought my time had come, and that I would perish without aid or assistance. When all hope had left me, I heard a footstep approaching, and a man came and bent over me and asked if I was ill. I recognized the voice as that of Mr. Bogges. I said I was in the agonies of death, and a stranger without a friend on the boat. He felt my pulse, and hastened away, saying as he left me, "Do not despair, young man, you are not without friends, I will return at once." He soon came to me bringing a lantern and a bottle of cholera medicine; and gave me a large dose of the medicine, then he brought the Captain and others to me. I was soon comfortably placed in bed, and from that time I had every attention paid me, and all the medical care that was necessary. Mr. Bogges sat by me a long time and rubbed my hands and limbs until the cramping gave way. He told me by way of apology for his seeming neglect, that he had supposed I was one of the regular crew of the Henry Clay, and was among friends. That his wife and mother-in-law had noticed that I appeared to be a stranger, and they had seen me when I sat down by the engine alone; that after they retired, his wife was restless and insisted on his getting up and finding me; this was the occasion of his assistance coming as it did. He then asked me why I was there and for a history of my former career. I gave him a brief history of my life, which seemed to interest him very much. He told me he had formed a slight acquaintance with my uncle Conner, at Galena, the year before, and considered him rather a hard case. So the conversation dropped for that night. I recovered rapidly, and by noon next day was up, and reported myself to the

Captain for duty, informing him why I was there, and what I came for. I was set to work loading the steamer. In the meantime, Mr. Bogges had contracted for freighting his goods to Galena, where he resided; and had provided for the passage of himself, wife and mother-in-law. They would go by land from Commerce, as he dreaded the passage of the upper rapids in time of low water, as it then was. After finishing the loading of the steamer, I again began to fire up to get ready for a start. While so engaged, Mr. Bogges came to me, and talked to me for some time. He said steam boating was a hard life at best, that I would be constantly wet, cold, and broken of my rest, and would soon drift into bad habits; that he considered me an honorable young man, and felt an interest in me like a father should feel for a son; that he admired my grit and courage, and said I had manly principles, which was more than the average, that his wife was interested in my welfare, and that, at the suggestion of her and her mother, and of his own wish, he now offered to employ me, and wished me to go to Galena with him, and act as his clerk that winter; that he was doing business as a provision and grocery man, that in the Spring he would furnish me with tools, and every thing I needed, and I could go to mining, if I wished to do so, and he would then give me the half that we could make. He asked me then what wages I was getting. I told him $25. I will give you $50, said he. I said, "You are very kind, indeed, sir. I should not charge you more than I am getting here, except my expenses from Galena to Saint Louis, as I may have that to pay, for I may not suit you; for I have had very little experience in selling goods, though I have traded and trafficked considerably with the people where I have lived. And the services that I rendered you, as we came up the river, was simply my duty. It was what I had been employed to do, and I did it and no more. He said, "I know what you have done, and if you will only go with me, I will pay you double what you are getting here, and perhaps three times as much." "But," said I, "you know I am already employed, and have no right to break my contract, and leave my employer." He said he would arrange that with the Captain, if I would go with him. I consented, and after settling with the Captain of the Henry Clay, who bid me goodbye and good luck, I started for Galena, Illinois, with Mr. Bogges and his family, to take charge of a business then almost new to me.

We reached Galena in safety, and good health. Now a new era in my life commenced. Mr. William Bogges introduced me to John D. Mulligan, his partner. I at once commenced my duties as salesman and bartender at the store, and general outside man for Mr. Wm. Bogges; who placed me in charge of every thing in which he was interested. The business was such that I found it more than play. Many a time I did not get rest or sleep for forty-eight hours at a time. I have frequently taken in $100 in twenty four hours for drinks, at five cents a drink. The receipts, for provisions sold, would average $1000 a day. During the winter, Mr. Mulligan was taken sick, and I had the whole business to attend to for three weeks. I found out that the clerks in stores have as hard work to do, and put in more hours during the day and night than the farm hand has to labor. I paid strict attention to business, making the interest of my employers my interest. On account of my faithful services, I was permitted to prepare hot lunches during the night, to sell to gamblers. What I made was my own. In this way I made from $50 to $100 a mouth extra.

One day while I was absent from the store, looking after the farming interests of Mr. Bogges, a French half-breed, by the name of Shaunce, got on a drunken spree and cleared out the store, and saloon, too; he broke considerable furniture, glassware, and made himself generally troublesome. When I returned at night, Mr. Bogges told me of all the troubles that Shaunce had occasioned, and said if he repeated it, I must give him a good drubbing. I said I would rather have nothing to do with him. Things were quiet for a few days, then the miners got on a spree, and a large number of them came to where I was working. Shaunce was in the crowd. I was then out at dinner. They attacked Mulligan, beat him up badly, and ran him out of the building; then the drunken crowd set things up generally.

Hearing the disturbance, I ran to the store. I entered by the back door, and went behind the counter. As I did so Shaunce ran to the counter and grabbed up a large number of tumblers, and threw them over the house, breaking them all. I said, "Mr. Shaunce, you must either behave, or go out of the house." As I said so, he jumped over the counter, caught me by the throat, and shoved me back against the counter, saying, "You d--d little pup, how dare you insult me!" There was no time to swap knives. I must either receive a severe beating, or do something to prevent it. I remembered the advice that my uncle Conner had given me about fighting. He said, "John, if you ever get in a fight with a man that overmatches you, take one of his hands in both of yours, and let him strike as he may, but get one of his fingers in your mouth and then bite it, and hold on until he gives up." Acting on this advice, I succeeded in getting one of his thumbs in my mouth. I held to it until I dislocated the thumb joint, when he yelled, "Take him off!" This little affair made a quiet man of Shaunce, and my employers were more pleased with me than ever before. They made me a present of $50 for what I had done.

I formed a slight acquaintance with the father of General Grant while in Galena. He was a steady, orderly man. U.S. Grant was then about seventeen years of age. I remember a story that was told at that time about the Grant family by John L. Dickerson, who resided near Galena. Dickerson had a horse that he wanted to sell, and young Grant took a fancy to it and insisted that his father should buy it for him. The father sent young Grant to buy the horse, but directed him to give no more than $60, and said, "You offer him $50, and if he refuses that, offer $55; if he still refuses, you can give $60, but that is as much as I will pay, for he has offered it for that price." Young Grant went to Dickerson and commenced to talk about buying the horse. Dickerson said, "Tell me just what your father said about your trading with me." This made Grant think a few minutes, when he said, "Mr. Dickerson, I expect it is best to tell the truth." Then he informed him what his father had said. Dickerson was so pleased at it that he let Grant have the horse for $55, saying he deducted $5 on account of the lad being so honest.

I made money while with Bogges & Co., and was saving of what I earned. I did not gamble. I took good care of myself, and, having the respect of every person, I admit I was quite vain and proud. I was accused by the gamblers of being stingy with my money. So I thought I would do as others did, and commenced to give money to others as a *stake* to gamble with on shares. Soon I began to play. I won and lost, but did not play to any great extent. Mr. Bogges took me to task for gambling, gave me good advice, and showed me how utterly impossible it was for me to be a successful businessman if I gambled. He also showed me many of the tricks of the gamblers, and I promised him to quit the practice as soon as I got married, and also not to gamble any more while in his employ. I kept these promises.

In the early part of 1832 I received an affectionate letter from my Emily, desiring me to return to her, and settle down before I had acquired a desire for a rambling life. I then had $500 in money and two suits of broadcloth clothing. I was anxious to see Emily, so I settled up with Bogges Co., and started for home. Emily was then living at her sister's house in Prairie de Roache; her brother-in-law, Thos. Blay, kept the tavern there. I boarded with them about two weeks, during which time I played cards with the Frenchmen there, and dealt *vantune*, or twenty-one, for them to bet at. I was lucky, but I lived fast and spent my money freely, and soon found that half of it was gone.

I soon discovered that Emily was dissatisfied with my conduct. I proposed immediate marriage; Emily proposed to wait until the next fall, during which time we were to prepare for housekeeping. Her suggestions were well intended, and she wished to see if I would not reform, for she had serious doubts about the propriety of marrying a gambler. She asked me to quit gambling, and if I had made that promise all would have been well, but I was stubborn and proud and refused to make any promise; I thought it was beneath my dignity. I really intended to never gamble after my wedding, but I would not tell her so; my vanity overruled my judgment. I said to her that if she had not confidence enough in me to take me as I was, without requiring me to give such a promise, I would never see her again until I came to ask her to my wedding. This was cruel, and deeply wounded her; she burst into tears and turned from me. I never saw her again until I went to ask her to attend my wedding. I went up into the country and stopped with my cousins; while there I met the bride of my youth; she was the daughter of Joseph Woolsey and Abigail his wife; they had four daughters, all grown. I attended church, went to parties, picnics, etc., with the girls, and fell in love with Agathe Ann, the oldest girl. The old folks were opposed to my marrying their daughter, but after suffering the tortures and overcoming the obstacles usual in such cases, I obtained the consent of the girl's parents, and was married to Agathe Ann Woolsey on the 24th day of July, A.D. 1833. The expenses of the wedding ended all my money, and I was ready to start the world new and fresh. I had about $50 to procure things to keep house on, but it was soon gone; yet it procured about all we then thought we needed. I commenced housekeeping near my wife's fathers, and had good success in all that I undertook. I made money; or rather I obtained considerable property, and was soon comfortably fixed. I followed trading everything, and for everything that was in the country.

My wife was born January 18, 1814; our first child was born on the 3rd day of July 1834; we named him William Oliver. In October 1834, I moved to Fayette County, Illinois and settled north of Vandalia, near my sister's, and lived there some two years; during that time our oldest child died. I next purchased a farm on Luck Creek, in Fayette County, Illinois, and lived on it until I went to Missouri to join the Mormon Church.

CHAPTER III

LEE BECOMES A MORMON

IN 1836 my second child, Elizabeth Adaline, was born. After I moved to Luck Creek I was a fortunate man and accumulated property very fast. I look back to those days with pleasure. I was blest with everything that an honest heart could wish.

I had a large house and I gave permission to all sorts of people to come there and preach. Methodists, Baptists, Campbellites and Mormons all preached there when they desired to do so. In 1887 a man by the name of King, from Indiana, passed by, or came to my place, on his way to Missouri, to join the Mormons. He had been a New Light, or Campbellite preacher. I invited him to stay at my place until the next Spring. I gave him provisions for his family, and he consented to and did stay with me some time. Soon after that there was a Methodist meeting at my house. After the Methodist services were through I invited King to speak. He talked about half an hour on the first principles of the gospel as taught by Christ and his apostles, denouncing all other doctrines as spurious. This put an end to all other denominations preaching in my house. That was the first sermon I ever heard concerning Mormonism. The Winter before two elders, Durphy and Peter Dustan, stayed a few days with Hanford Stewart, a cousin of Levi Stewart, the bishop of Kanab. They preached in the neighborhood, but I did not attend or hear them preach. My wife and her mother went to hear them, and were much pleased with their doctrine. I was not a member of any church, and considered the religion of the day as merely the opinions of men who preached for hire and worldly gain. I believed in God and in Christ, but I did not see any denomination that taught the apostolic doctrine as set forth in the New Testament.

I read in the New Testament where the apostle Paul recommended his people to prove all things, then hold fast to that which is good; also that he taught that though an angel from heaven should preach any other gospel than this which ye have received, let him be accursed. This forbid me believing any doctrine that differed from that taught by Christ and his apostles. I wanted to belong to the *true* Church or none. When King began to preach at my house I noticed that every other denomination opposed him. I was surprised at this. I could not see how he could injure them if they were right. I had been brought up as a strict Catholic. I was taught to look upon all sects, except the Catholic, with disfavor, and my opinion was that the Mormons and all others were apostates from the true Church; that the Mormon Church was made up of the offscourings of hell, or of apostates from the true Church. I then had not the most distant idea that the Mormons believed in the Old and New Testaments. I was astonished to hear King prove his religion from the Scriptures. I reflected. I determined, as every honest man should do, to fairly investigate his doctrines, and to do so with a prayerful heart. The more I studied the question, the more interested I became. I talked of the doctrine to nearly every man I met. The excitement soon became general, and King was invited to preach in many places. In the meantime, Levi Stewart, one of my near neighbors, became interested in this religion, and went to Far West, Missouri, to investigate the question of Mormonism at headquarters. He joined the Church there, and when he returned he brought with him the "Book of Mormon" and a monthly periodical called the *Elder's Journal*. By this time my anxiety was very great, and I determined to fathom the question to the bottom. My frequent conversations with Elder King served to carry me on to a conviction, at least, that the dispensation of the fullness of time would soon usher in upon the world. If such was the case I wished to know it, for the salvation of my never dying soul was of far more importance to me than all other earthly considerations. I regarded the heavenly boon of eternal life as a treasure of great price. I left off my frivolity and commenced to lead a more moral life. I then began trying to lay up treasure in Heaven, in my Father's rich storehouse, and wished to become an heir of righteousness, to inherit in common with the faithful children the rich legacy of our Father's Kingdom.

A third child had been born to us, a daughter; we called her Sarah Jane. During that year our second child, Elizabeth Adaline, died of scarlet fever. The night she lay a corpse I finished reading the Book of Mormon. I never closed my eyes in sleep from the time I commenced until I finished the book. I read it after asking God to give me knowledge to know if it was genuine and of Divine authority. By careful examination I found that it was in strict accord with the Bible and the gospel therein contained. That it purported to have been given to another people, who then lived on this continent, as the Old and New Testaments had been given to the Israelites in Asia. I also found many passages in the Bible in support of the forthcoming of such a work, preparatory to the gathering of the remnant of the House of Israel, and the opening glory of the Latter-Day Work, and the setting up of the Kingdom of God upon the earth for the reception of the Son of Man, the millennial reign of Christ upon the earth a thousand years, etc.; all of which, to me, was of great moment. My whole soul was absorbed in these things. My neighbor Stewart, who had just returned from Missouri, brought the most cheering and thrilling accounts of the power and manifestations of the Holy Spirit working with that people. That the spiritual gifts of the true believers in Christ were enjoyed by all who lived faithfully and sought them. That there was no deception about it; that every one had a testimony for himself; and was not dependent upon another. That they had the gift of tongues, and the interpretation of those tongues. The power of healing the sick by the laying on of hands; prophesying, casting out devils and evil spirits, etc. All of which he declared, with words of soberness, to be true. Stewart had been my playmate and my companion in former years. His word was considered good by all, and it had great influence on me, and strengthened my conviction that the Book of Mormon was true - that it was a star opening the dispensation of the fullness of time.

I believed the Book of Mormon was true, and if so, everything but my soul's salvation was a matter of secondary consideration to me. I had a small fortune, a nice home, kind neighbors, and numerous friends, but nothing could shake the determination I then formed, to break up, sell out, and leave Illinois and go to the Saints at Far West, Missouri. My friends used every known argument to change my determination, but these words came into my mind, "First seek the righteousness of the kingdom of God, then all things necessary will be added unto you"; and again, "What would it profit a man to gain the whole world and lose his own soul?" or, what could a man give in exchange for his soul? I was here brought to the test, and my action was to decide on which I placed the most value - my earthly possessions and enjoyments, or my reward in future, the salvation of my never-dying soul. I took up my cross and chose the latter. I sold out and moved to Far West. I took leave of my friends and made my way to where the Saints had gathered in Zion. Our journey was one full of events interesting to us, but not of sufficient importance to relate to the public. While on the journey I sold most of my cattle *on time* to an old man, a friend of Stewart's - took his notes, and let him keep them, which, as the sequel shows, was fortunate for me.

We arrived at Far West, the then headquarters of the Mormon Church, about the fourth day of June 1838. The country around there for some fifteen or twenty miles, each way, was settled by Mormons. I do not think any others lived within that distance. The Mormons, who had been driven from Jackson, Ray and Clay counties, in 1833, settled in Caldwell and Daviess counties.

The night after our arrival at Far West, there was a meeting to be held there. Stewart said to me, "Let us go up and hear them speak with new tongues and interpret the same, and enjoy the gifts of the gospel generally, for this is to be a prayer and testimony meeting." My reply was, "I want no signs; I believe the gospel they preach on principle and reason, not upon signs - its consistency is all I ask. All I want are natural, logical and reasonable arguments, to make up my mind from." Feeling in this way, I did no go to the meeting.

The Sunday after, I attended church in Far West Hall. The hall was crowded with people, so much so that I, with others, could not gain admittance to the building. I obtained standing room in one of the windows. I saw a man enter the house without uncovering his head. The prophet ordered the brother of Gideon to put that man out, for his presumption in daring to enter and stand in the house of God without uncovering his head. This looked to me like drawing the lines pretty snug and close; however, I knew but little of the etiquette of high life, and much less about that of the kingdom of heaven. I looked upon Joseph Smith as a prophet of God - as one who held the keys of this last dispensation, and I hardly knew what to think about the rash manner in which the man was treated who had entered the house of God without taking his hat off. But this did not lessen my faith; it served to confirm it. I was fearful that I might in some way unintentionally offend the great and good man who stood as God's prophet on the earth to point out the way of salvation.

We remained at the house of elder Joseph Hunt, in Far West, several days. He was then a strong Mormon, and was afterwards first captain in the Mormon Battalion. He, as an elder in the Church, was a preacher of the gospel; all of his family were firm in the faith. Elder Hunt preached to me the necessity of humility and a strict obedience to the gospel requirements through the servants of God. He informed me that the apostles and elders were our true teachers, and it was our duty to *hear*, *learn* and obey; that the spirit of God was very fine and delicate, and was easily grieved and driven from us; that the more humble we were, the more of the Holy Spirit we would enjoy.

After staying in Far West about a week, we moved about twenty miles, and settled on a stream called Marrowbone, at a place called afterwards Ambrosia. Sunday, June I7, 1888, I attended meeting. Samuel H. Smith, a brother of the prophet, and elder Daniel Cathcart preached. After meeting, I and my wife were baptized by elder Cathcart, in Ambrosia, on Shady Grove creek, in Daviess County, Missouri. I was now a member of the Church, and expected to live in strict obedience to the requirements of the holy priesthood that ruled governed and controlled it. I must do this in order to advance in the scale of intelligence unto thrones, kingdoms, principalities and powers, and through faithfulness and fidelity to the cause, receive eternal increase in the mansions that would be prepared for me, in my Father's kingdom.

My neighbor, Stewart, and myself each selected a place on the same stream, and near where his three brothers, Riley, Jackson and Urban, lived. Urban Stewart is now Treasurer of Beaver County, Utah. On my location there was a splendid spring of pure, cold water; also a small lake fed by springs. This lake was full of fish, such as perch, bass, pickerel mullet and catfish. It was surrounded by a grove of heavy timber, mostly hickory and oak, in nearly all their varieties. We could have fish sufficient for use every day in the year, if we desired. My home on Ambrosia creek reminded me much of the one I had left on Luck creek, Illinois; but it was on more rolling land, and much healthier than the Illinois home had proven to us. I knew I could soon replace, by labor, all the comfort I had abandoned when I started to seek my salvation. I felt that I had greatly benefited my condition by seeking first the kingdom of Heaven and its righteousness; all else, I felt, would be added unto me. But still I knew I must be frugal, industrious, and use much care. I improved my farm as rapidly as I could, and was soon so fixed that we were comfortable. Meetings were held three times a week; also prayer and *testimony* meetings, it the latter sacrament, was administered. In these meetings, as well as in everything I was called upon to do, I tried hard to give satisfaction. I was a devout follower from the first. Whatever duty was assigned me, I tried to discharge with a winning heart and ready hand. This disposition, on my part, coupled with my views of duty, my promptness and punctuality, soon brought me to the notice of the leading men of the Church. The motives of the people who composed my neighborhood, were pure; they were all sincere in their devotions, and tried to square their actions through life by the golden rule - "Do unto others as you would they should do unto you." The word of a Mormon was then good for all it was pledged to or for. I was proud to be an associate with such an honorable people.

Twenty miles northeast of my home was the settlement of Adam-on-Diamond. It was on the east bank of Grand River, near the Three Forks. Lyman White, one of the twelve apostles, was president of that Stake of Zion. In July, 1838, Levi Stewart and myself concluded to visit the settlement of Adam-on-Diamond. We remained over night at the house of Judge Mourning. He was a Democrat. He told us that, at the approaching election, the Whigs were going to cast their votes, at the outside precincts, early in the day, and then rush in force to the town of Gallatin, the county seat of Daviess County, and prevent the Mormons from voting. The judge requested us to inform our people of the facts in the case, and for us to see that the Mormons went to the polls in force, and prepared to resist and overcome all violence that might be offered. He said the Whigs had no right to deprive the Mormons of their right of suffrage, that they had a right to cast their votes as free and independent Americans. I knew that the two political parties were about equally divided in Daviess County, and that the Mormons held the balance of power, and would turn the scale which ever way they desired.

I had heard of Judge Mourning as a sharp political worker, and I then thought he was trying to get up and carry out an electioneering job for his party; therefore I paid but little attention to what he said.

We visited our friends at Adam-on-Diamond, and returned home. While on this trip I formed the acquaintance of Solomon McBrier, and purchased some cattle from him. He wished to sell me quite a number, but as I did not wish to be involved in debt, I refused to take them, for I had a perfect horror of being in debt, for I knew that when a man was in debt he was in nearly every respect a slave, and that if I got in debt it would worry me and keep my mind from that quiet repose so necessary for contemplating the principal beauties of nature, and communing with the Spirit regarding holy subjects.

On Monday, the 6th day of August, 1838, the greater portion of our people in the settlements near me, went to Gallatin to attend the election. In justice to truth I must state, that just before the general election of August, 1838, a general notice was given for all the brethren of Daviess County to meet at Adam-on-Diamond. Every man obeyed the call. At that meeting all the males over eighteen years of age, were organized into a military body, according to the law of the priesthood, and called "The Host of Israel." The first rank was a captain with ten men under him; next was a captain of fifty, that is he had five companies of ten; next, the captain of a hundred, or of ten captains and companies of ten. The entire membership of the Mormon Church was then organized in the same way. This, as I was then informed, was the first organization of the military force of the Church. It was so organized at that time by command of God, as revealed through the Lord's Prophet, Joseph Smith. God commanded Joseph Smith to place the Host of Israel in a situation for defense against the enemies of God and the Church of Jesus Christ of Latter-Day Saints.

At the same Conference another organization was perfected, or then first formed - it was called the "Danites." The members of this order were placed under the most sacred obligations that language could invent. They were sworn to stand by and sustain each other. *Sustain, protect, defend*, and *obey* the leaders of the Church, under any and *all circumstances unto death*; and to disobey the orders the leaders of the Church, or divulge the name of a Danite to an outsider, or to make public any of the secrets of the order of Danites, was to be punished with death. And I can say of a truth, many have paid the penalty for failing to keep their covenants. They had signs and tokens for use and protection. The token of recognition was such that it could be readily understood, and it served as a token of distress by which they could know each other from their enemies, although they were entire strangers to each other. When the sign was given it must be responded to and obeyed, even at the risk or certainty of death. The Danite that would refuse to respect the token, and comply with all its requirements, was stamped with dishonor, infamy, shame, disgrace, and his fate for cowardice and treachery was death.

This sign or token of distress is made by placing the right hand on the right side of the face, with the points of the fingers upwards, shoving the hand upwards until the ear is snug up between the thumb and forefinger.

I here pause, and ask myself the question, "Am I justified in making the above statement? I ask those who think I am not fully justified in telling all I know, to wait until they read the whole story; how I have been ordered, how I have obeyed orders, and how treacherously I have been used and deserted by the Church and its leaders. It is my purpose and intention, for such is my certain duty, to free my mind, and bring to light some of the secret workings, some of the deeds of darkness, that have been the result of the evil teachings of aspiring men, who have tried to couple their vile sets with the Gospel of Truth; and endeavored, alas! too successfully, to palm it off on the credulous and weaker minded brethren, as a religious duty they owed to God, to unquestioningly obey *every* order of the Priesthood.

To return to the election at Gallatin: - the brethren all attended the election. All things seemed to pass off quietly, until some of the Mormons went up to the polls to vote. I was then lying on the grass with McBrier and a number of others. As the Mormons went to the polls, a drunken brute by the name of Richard Weldon, stepped up to a little Mormon preacher, by the name of Brown, and said:

"Are you a Mormon preacher, sir?"

"Yes, sir, I am."

"Do you Mormons believe in healing the sick by laying on of hands, speaking in tongues, and casting out devils?"

"We do," said Brown.

Weldon then said, "You are a d--d liar. Joseph Smith is a d--d impostor."

With this, he attacked Brown, and beat him severely. Brown did not resent it, but tried to reason with him; but without effect. At this time a Mormon, by the name of Hyrum Nelson, attempted to pull Weldon off of Brown, when he was struck by half a dozen men on the head, shoulders and face. He was soon forced to the ground. Just then, Riley Stewart struck Weldon across the back of the head with a billet of oak lumber, and broke his skull. Weldon fell nearly on me, and appeared lifeless. The blood flowed freely from the wound. Immediately the fight became general.

Gallatin was a new town, with about ten houses, three of which were saloons. The town was on the bank of Grand River and heavy timber came near the town, which stood in a little arm of the prairie. Close to the polls, there was a lot of oak timber, which had been brought there to be riven into shakes or shingles, leaving the heart, taken from each shingle block, lying there on the ground. These hearts were three square, four feet long, weighed about seven pounds, and made a very dangerous, yet handy weapon; and when used by an enraged man they were

FIGHT AT GALLATIN, MISSOURI, BETWEEN MORMONS AND "GENTILES"

truly a class of instrument to be dreaded. When Stewart fell, the Mormons sprang to the pile of oak hearts, and each man, taking one for use, rushed into the crowd. The Mormons were yelling, "Save him!" and the settlers yelled, "kill him; d--n him!" The sign of distress was given by the Danites, and all rushed forward, determined to save Stewart, or die with him. One of the mob stabbed Stewart in the shoulder. He rose and ran, trying to escape, but was again surrounded and attacked by a large number of foes. The Danite sign of distress was again given by John L. Butler, one of the captains of the Host of Israel. Butler was a brave, true man, and a leader that it was a pleasure to follow where duty called. Seeing the *sign*, I sprang to my feet and armed myself with one of the oak sticks. I did this because I was a Danite, and my oaths that I had taken required immediate action on my part, in support of the one giving the sign. I ran into the crowd. As I reached it, I saw Nelson down on the ground fighting for life. He was surrounded by a large number, who were seeking to murder him, but he had a loaded whip, the lash wrapped around his hand, and using the handle, which was loaded with several pounds of lead, as a weapon of defense. He was using it with effect, for he had men piled around him in all shapes. As I approached, a man sprang to his feet. He had just been knocked down by Nelson. As the man was rising, Nelson gave him a blow across the loins with the handle of his whip, which had the effect of straitening out the villain on the grass, and rendered him an inoffensive spectator during the remainder of the play. Captain Butler was then a stranger to me, and until I saw him give the Danite sign of distress, I had believed him to be one of the Missouri ruffians, who were our enemies. In this contest I came near committing a serious mistake. I had raised my club to strike a man, when a Missourian rushed at him, and struck him with a loaded whip, and called him a d--d Mormon. The man then gave the *sign*, and I knew how to act.

Capt. Butler was attacked from all sides, but, being a powerful man, he used his oak club with effect and knocked a man down at each blow that he struck, and each man that felt the weight of his weapon was out of the fight for that day at least. Many of those that he came in contact with had to be carried from the field for surgical aid. In the battle, which was spirited, but short in duration, nine men had their skulls broken, and many others were seriously injured in other ways. The severe treatment of the mob by the Danites, soon ended the battle. Three hundred men were present at this difficulty, only thirty of whom were Mormons, and only eight Mormons took part in the fight.

I was an entire stranger to all who were engaged in the affray, except Stewart, but I had seen the *sign*, and, like Sampson, when leaning against the pillar, I felt the power of God nerve my arm for the fray. It helps a man a great deal in a fight to know that God is on his side. After the violence had ceased, Captain Butler called the Mormons to him, and as he stood on a pile of building timber, he made a speech to the brethren. He said that his ancestors had served in the war of the Revolution to establish a free and independent government - one in which all men had equal rights and privileges; that he professed to be half white and free born, and claimed a right to enjoy his constitutional privileges, and would have his rights as a citizen, if he had to fight for them; that as to his religion, it was a matter between his God and himself, and was no man's business; that he would vote, and would die before he would be driven from the polls. Several of the Gentile leaders then requested us to lay down our clubs and go and vote. This Captain Butler refused, saying, "We will not molest any one who lets us alone, but we will not risk ourselves again in that crowd without our clubs." The result was, *the Mormons all voted.* It is surprising what a few resolute men can do when united. After voting, the Mormons returned home, fearing additional violence if they remained.

It may be well for purposes of explanation to refer back to the celebration of the Declaration of Independence on the 4th of July, 1838, at Far West. That day Joseph Smith made known to the people the substance of a revelation he had before received from God. It was to the effect that all the Saints throughout the land were required to sell their possessions, gather all their money together, and send an agent to buy up all the land in the region round about Far West, and get a patent for the land from the Government, then deed it over to the Church; then every man should come up there to the land of their promised inheritance and consecrate what they had to the Lord. In return the Prophet would set apart a tract of land for each Saint - the amount to correspond with the number of the Saint's family and this land should be for each Saint an everlasting inheritance. In this way the people could, in time, redeem Zion (Jackson County) without the shedding of blood. It was also revealed that unless this was done, in accordance with God's demand, as required by Him in the Revelation then given to the people through his Prophet, Joseph Smith, the Saints would be driven from State to State, from city to city, from one abiding place to another, until the members would die and waste away, leaving but a remnant of the Saints to return and receive their inheritance in Zion (Jackson County) in the *Last Days*. Sidney Rigdon was then the mouthpiece of Joseph Smith, as Aaron was of Moses in olden time. Rigdon told the Saints that day that if they did not come up as true Saints and consecrate their property to the Lord, by laying it down at the feet of the apostles, they would in a short time be compelled to consecrate and yield it up to the Gentiles. That if the Saints would be united as one man, in this consecration of their entire wealth to the God of Heaven, by giving it up to the control of the Apostolic Priesthood, then there would be no further danger to the Saints; they would no more be driven from their homes on account of their faith and holy works, for the Lord had revealed to Joseph Smith that he would then fight the battles of His children, and save them from all their enemies. That the Mormon people would never be accepted as the children of God unless they were united as one man, in temporal as well as spiritual affairs, for Jesus had said unless ye are one, ye are not mine; that oneness must exist to make the Saints the accepted children of God. That if the Saints would yield obedience to the commands of the Lord all would be well, for the Lord had confirmed these promises by a revelation which He had given to Joseph Smith, in which it was said: "I, the Lord, will fight the battles of my people, and if your enemies shall come up against you, spare them, and if they shall come up against you again, then shall ye spare them also; even unto the third time shall ye spare them; but if they come up against you the *fourth* time, I, the Lord, will deliver them into your hands, to do with them as seemeth good unto you; but if you will then spare them it shall be accounted unto you for righteousness."

The words of the apostle, and the promises of God, as then revealed to me, made a deep impression on my mind, as it did upon all who heard the same. We that had given up all else for the sake of the gospel, felt willing to do anything on earth that it was possible to do, to obtain the protection of God, and have and receive his smile of approbation. Those who, like me, had tall faith in the teachings of God, as revealed by Joseph Smith, his Prophet, were willing to comply with *every* order, and to obey every wish of the priesthood. The majority of the people felt like Ananias and Sapphira, they dare not trust all to God and His Prophet. They felt that their money was as safe in their own possession as it was when held by the Church authorities. A vote of the people was then had to determine the question whether they would consecrate their wealth to the Church or not. The vote was taken and was unanimous for the consecration. I soon found out that the people had voted as I have often known them to do in Mormon meetings since then, they vote to please the priesthood, then act to suit themselves. I never thought that was right or honest; men should vote their sentiments, but they do not at all times do so. I have been the victim of such hypocrites, as the sequel will show.

The vote, as I said, was taken. It was done by a show of hands, but not a show of hearts. By the readiness with which all hands went up in favor of consecration, it was declared that the people were of a truth God's children, and as such, would be protected by him. The Prophet and all his priesthood were jubilant, and could hardly contain themselves; they were so happy to see the people such dutiful Saints.

Sidney Rigdon, on that day, delivered an oration, in which he said the Mormons were, as a people, loyal to the government, and obedient to the laws, and as such, they were entitled to the protection of the government, in common with all other denominations, and were justified in claiming as full protection, in their religious matters, as the people of any other sect. That the Mormons had long suffered from mob rule and violence, but would no longer submit to the mob or unjust treatment that had so long followed them. Now and forever more would they meet force with force. "We have been driven from Kirkland, Ohio, from Jackson County, the true Zion, and now we will maintain our rights, defend our homes, our wives and children, and our property from mob rule and violence. If the Saints are again attacked, we will carry on a war of extermination against our enemies, even to their homes and firesides; until we despoil those who have despoiled us, and give no quarter until our enemies are wasted away. We will unfurl to the breeze the flag of our nation, and under that banner of freedom we will maintain our rights, or die in the attempt." At the end of each sentence Rigdon was loudly cheered; and when he closed his oration, I believed the Mormons could successfully resist the world. But this feeling of confidence faded away as soon as a second thought entered my mind. I then feared that the ways of liberty for our people had been numbered. First, I feared the people would not give up all their worldly possessions, to be disposed of by and at the will and pleasure of three men. In the second place, I doubted the people being so fully regenerated as to entitle them to the full and unconditional support and favor of God, that had been promised through the Revelation to Joseph Smith, in favor of the Latter-Day Saints. I knew that God was able and willing to do all He had promised, but I feared that the people still loved worldly pleasures so well that God's mercy would be rejected by them, and all would be lost.

About three days after the proclamation of Rigdon had been made, there was a storm of rain, during which the thunder and lightnings were constant and terrible. The liberty pole in the town was struck by lightning, and shivered to atoms. This evidence from the God of nature also convinced me that the Mormon people's liberties, in that section of the country, were not to be of long duration.

CHAPTER IV

THE SAINTS ARE BESET WITH TROUBLES

THE Saints did not consecrate their possessions as they had so recently voted they would do; they began to reflect, and the final determination was that they could manage their worldly effects better than any one of the apostles; in fact better then the Prophet and the priesthood combined. Individual Saints entered large tracts of land in their own names, and thereby secured all of the most desirable land round about Far West. These landed proprietors became the worst kind of extortionists, and forced the poor Saints to pay them large advances for every acre of land that was settled, and nothing could be called free from the control of the money power of the rich and headstrong Mormons who had defied the revelations and wishes of God.

So things went from bad to worse, until the August election at Gallatin. The difficulty on that day had brought the Church and Saints to a stand-still; business was paralyzed; alarm seized the stoutest hearts, and dismay was visible in every countenance. The Prophet soon issued an order to gather all the people at Far West and Adam-on-Diamond, under the leadership of Col. Lyman White, for the purpose of protecting the people from mob violence, and to save the property from lawless thieves who were roaming the country in armed bands.

The Gentiles and Mormons hastened to the executive of the State. The Gentiles asked for a military force to protect the settlers from Mormon violence. The Mormons requested an investigating committee to inquire into the whole subject and suggest means necessary for future safety to each party.

Also they demanded military protection from the mobs and outlaws that infested the country. The Governor sent some troops to keep order. They were stationed about midway between Far West and Adam-on-Diamond. A committee was also appointed and sent to Gallatin to inquire into the recent disturbances. This committee had full power to send for witnesses, make arrests of persons accused of crime, and generally to do all things necessary for a fall and complete investigation of the entire affair. Many arrests were made at the request of the committee. The persons so arrested were taken before Justice Black, of Daviess County, and examined; witnesses were examined for both parties, and much hard and false swearing was done on both sides. After a long and fruitless examination the committee adjourned, leaving the military to look after matters until something would turn up to change the feeling of danger then existing. It was thought by the committee that all would soon become quiet and that peace would soon be restored. The Gentiles of the country were dissatisfied with the action of the committee, and were in no way disposed to accept peace on any terms; they determined that, come what would, the Mormons should be driven from the State of Missouri. Letters were written by the Gentiles around Far West to all parts of the State, and elsewhere, giving the most fearful accounts of Mormon atrocities. Some of the writers said it was useless to send less than three or four men for each Mormon, because the Mormons felt sure of Heaven if they fell fighting, hence they did not fear death; that they fought with the desperation of devils. Such reports spread like wildfire throughout Northern Missouri, and thence all over the States of the Mississippi Valley, and resulted in creating a feeling of the most intense hatred in the breasts of all the Gentiles against the Mormons. Companies of volunteers were raised and armed in every town through Northern Missouri, and commenced concentrating in the vicinity of the Mormon settlements. The troops sent by the Governor to guard the settlers and preserve order soon took part with the mob, and all show for legal protection was gone so far as Mormons were concerned. I had built a cabin in the valley of Adam-on-Diamond, at the point where the Prophet said Adam blessed his posterity after being driven from the Garden of Eden. The condition of the country being such that we could not labor on our farms, I concluded to go and hunt for wild honey. Several of my neighbors agreed to join me in my bee hunt, and we started with our teams, and traveled northeasterly until we reached the heavy timber at the three forks of Grand River. We camped on the middle fork of Grand River, and had fine success in securing honey. We had been out at camp only two or three days when we discovered signs of armed men rushing through the country. On the 3rd of October, 1838, we saw a large number of men that we knew were enemies to the Mormons, and on their way, as we supposed, to attack our people at the settlements. I concluded to go and meet them, and find out for certain what they were really intending to do. I was forced to act with caution, for, if they discovered that we were Mormons, our lives would be taken by the desperate men composing the mob who called themselves State volunteers.

I took my gun and carried a bucket on my arm and started out to meet the people, to learn their intentions. I met them soon after they had broken camp on Sunday morning. As soon as I saw them I was certain they were out hunting for Mormons. I concluded to pass myself off as an outsider, the better to learn their history. My plan worked admirably. I stood my ground until a company of eighteen men rode up to me, and said:

"You move early."

"Not d--d early, gentlemen; I am not moving any sooner then you are. What are you all doing in this part of the country, armed to the teeth as you are? Are you hunting for Indians?"

"No," said they, "but we wish to know where you are from, and what you are doing."

"I am from Illinois; there are four of us who have come out here to look up a good location to settle. We stopped on Marrowbone, and did think of staying there, until the settlers and Mormons got into a row at Gallatin, on election day. After that we concluded to strike out and see what this country looked like. I am now going to cut a bee tree that I found yesterday evening, and I brought my gun along so that if I met an old buck I could secure some venison, to eat with my honeycomb."

As I got through my statement, they all huddled around me, and commenced to relate the horrors of Mormonism. They advised me to have nothing to do with the Mormons, for said they, "As old Joe Smith votes, so will every Mormon in the country vote, and when they get into a fight, they are just the same way, they stick together; when you attack one of the crew you bring every one of them after you like a nest of hornets."

I said I had heard a little of the fuss at Gallatin, but did not suppose I had got the right of the story, and would be glad if they would tell me just how it was. I should like to learn the facts from an eye witness. Several of the men spoke up and said they were there and saw it all. They then told the story, and did the Mormons more justice than I expected from them.

They said, among other things, that there was a large rawboned man there, who spoke in tongues, and that when the fight commenced he

CHARGE OF THE DANITES

said, "Charge Danites," and if ever you saw men pitch in like devils, they did it there. Our men fell thick as hail wherever those Danites charged with their clubs.

They then said the Mormons must leave the country, and if we do not make them do so now, they will be so strong that we cannot compel them to go, unless we force them away; they will be so strong in a few years that they will rule the country as they please. That another band of men would come along soon, and they would then go through the Mormon settlements, and burn up every house, and lynch every d--d Mormon they could find. That the militia had been sent to keep order in Daviess County, but would soon be gone, and the work of destroying the Mormons in general would begin. I said, "Give them h--l, and if they have done as you say they have, pay them in their own coin."

The company then passed on, and I returned with a heavy heart to my friends. I advised taking an immediate start for home, and in a few minutes we were on our way. While coming up from home we had found four bee trees, that we left standing, intending to cut them down and get the honey as we went back. When we got on the prairie, which was about eight miles across, the men with me wanted to go and get the honey. I was fearful that the people I had met in the morning would attack the settlements, and I wanted to go directly home and let trees and honey alone.

While we were talking the matter over, a single black bird came to us apparently in great distress. It flew around each one of us, and would alight on the head of each one of our horses, and especially on my horses' heads, and it even came and alighted on my hat, and would squeak like it was in pain, and turn its feathers up, and acted like it wished to warn us of danger. Then it flew off towards the settlements where I wished to go. All admitted that they were strange actions for a bird, but they still insisted on going to out the bee trees. I was persuaded to go with them. We had gone a quarter of a mile further, when the black bird returned to us and went through the same performances as before, and again flew off toward the settlement. This was to me a warning to go home at once, that there was danger there to my family. I then proposed that we all join in prayer. We did so, and I prayed to the Author of our existence, and asked that if it was his will for as to go home at once, and if the black bird had been sent as a warning messenger, to let it return again, and I would follow it. We then traveled on some two miles, when the messenger returned the third time and appeared, if possible, more determined than before to turn us towards home. I turned my team and started, as straight as I could go, for Adam-on-Diamond. As we passed over the prairie we saw the smoke rising from many farms and houses in the vicinity of where we had left our bee trees. This smoke showed us that our enemies were at work, and that had we kept on in the course we were first intending to travel we would have fallen into the hands of the lawless mob and lost our lives. Before we reached home the news of the attack upon the settlements had reached there. It was also reported, and we afterwards learned that the report was true, that many of the Mormon settlers had been tied to trees and fearfully whipped with hickory withes, some of them being horribly mangled by the mob. This conduct on the part of the Gentiles roused every Mormon to action, and the excitement was very great. Joseph Smith, the Prophet, was sent for. In the meantime Col. White called together every man and boy that could carry arms. When the forces were assembled Col. White made a war speech. As he spoke he stood by his fine brown horse. There was a bear skin on his saddle. He had a red handkerchief around his head, regular Indian fashion, with the knot in front; bare headed, in his shirt sleeves, with collar open, showing his naked breast. He held a large cutlass in his right hand. His manner of address struck terror to his enemies, while it charged his brethren with enthusiastic zeal and forced them to believe they were invincible and bullet proof. We were about three hundred and seventy five strong. I stood near Col. White while he was speaking, and I judge of its effect upon others by the way it affected me.

While our Colonel was in the midst of his speech the aid-de-camp of the militia Colonel was sent with a dispatch to Col. White, to the effect that the militia had become mutinous and could no longer be controlled, but were going to join the mob; that the Colonel would disband his forms, and he would then go and report to the Governor the true condition of the country; that Col. White must take and make use of all the means in his power to protect the people from the mob, for the government officers were powerless to aid him. The aid did not deliver his message, for as he rode up close to where Col. White was standing speaking to his men, he stopped and listened a short time; then wheeled his horse and rode back to the militia camp and reported that Col. White had 15,000 men under arms, in battle array, and would be upon their camp in less than two hours; that he was then making a speech to the army, and that it was the most exciting speech he had ever listened to in his life; that he meant war and that of the most fearful kind; and that the only safety for their forces was in instant retreat. The soldiers broke camp and left in haste. I cannot say that the Colonel commanding the militia was alarmed, or that he fled through fear of being overcome, but it suited him to leave there, for he was anxious to prevent a collision between his troops and the men under Col. White.

The Prophet, Joseph Smith, when informed of the danger of the settlers from mob violence, sent Maj. Seymour Brunson, of Far West, with fifty men, to protect the settlers who lived on the two forks of the Grand River. Col. White kept his men in readiness for action. A strong guard was posted round the settlement; a point was agreed upon, to which place all were to hasten in case of alarm. This point of meeting was east of the town, under the bluffs, on the main road leading from Mill Port to Adam-on-Diamond. This road ran between the fields and bluff.

We expected to be attacked every hour. A few nights afterwards the alarm was given, and every man rushed to the field. When I reached the command, I found everything in confusion. The officer in command tried to throw two companies across the road, but the firing was heavy and constant from the opposing forces, who had selected a strong point for the purpose of attack and defense. The flash of the rifles, and the ringing reports that echoed through the hills at each discharge of the guns, added to the confusion, and soon forced the Mormons to take up their position in the fence corners and elsewhere, so they could be in a measure protected from the bullets of the enemy.

Soon there was order in our ranks, and we were prepared to dislodge our opponents or die in the attempt, when two men came at the full speed of their horses, shouting, "Peace, peace, cease firing, it is our friends," etc. Chapman Duncan, the Adjutant of Col. White, was the one who shouted peace, etc. We were then informed that the men we had taken for a part of the Gentile mob were no other than the command of Maj. Brunson, who had been out on the Three Forks of Grand River, to defend the settlers, and that he had been ordered back to the main body, or any of the Hosts of Israel; that they had intended to stop at Mill Port, but finding it deserted, they concluded to alarm the troops at Adam-on-Diamond, so as to learn whether they would fight or not. I admit that I was much pleased to learn that danger was over, and that we were facing friends and not enemies; yet I was mad to think any men would impose upon us in that way. The experiment was a dangerous one, and likely to be very serious in its consequences. The other men with me were equally mad at the insult offered by those who had been so foolish as to question our bravery.

By the efforts of our officers all was soon explained, and amid peals of laughter we returned to our homes.

The withdrawal of the State militia was the signal for the Gentiles and Mormons to give vent to the worst of their inclinations. The Mormons, at command of the Prophet, at once abandoned their homes, taking what could be carried with them, and hastened to either Far West or Adam-on-Diamond for protection and safety. Some few refused to obey orders, and they afterwards paid the penalty for disobedience by giving up their lives to the savage Gentiles who attacked and well nigh exterminated them. Armed men roamed in bands all over Caldwell, Carroll, and Daviess Counties; both Mormons and Gentiles were under arms, and doing injury to each other when occasion offered. The burning of houses, farms, and stacks of grain was generally indulged in by each party. Lawlessness prevailed, and pillage was the rule.

The Prophet, Joseph Smith, said it was a civil war; that by the rules of war each party was justified in spoiling his enemy. This opened the door to the evil disposed, and men of former quiet became perfect demons in their efforts to spoil and waste away the enemies of the Church. I then found that men are creatures of circumstances, and that the occasion calls forth the men needed for each enterprise. I also soon saw that it was the natural inclination of men to steal, and convert to their own use that which others possessed. What perplexed me most was to see that religion had not the power to subdue that passion in man, but that at the first moment when the restrictions of the Church were withdrawn, the most devout men in our community acted like they had served a lifetime in evil, and were natural born thieves.

But the men who stole then were not really honest, for I spotted every man that I knew to steal during the troubles in Missouri and Illinois, and I have found that they were never really converted, were never true Saints, but they used their pretense of religion as a cloak to cover their evil deeds. I have watched their rise and fall in the Church, and I know from their fate that honesty is the only true policy.

Being young, stout, and having plenty of property, I fitted myself out in first class style. I had good horses and plenty of the best of arms. I joined in the general patrol duty, and took part in daily raids made under either Major Brunson or Capt. Alexander McRay, now bishop of a Ward in Salt Lake City. I saw much of what was being done by both parties.

I also made several raids under Captain Jonathan Dunham, alias

Black Hawk. I remember one incident that was amusing at the time, as it enabled us to determine what part of our forces would fight on the field and face the enemy, and also those who preferred to fight with their mouths.

Early in the morning, while Maj. Brunson's men were marching along, shivering in the cold - for it was a dark, cloudy morning, late in October, 1838 - we saw a company of horsemen some three miles away. We concluded they were Missourians, and made for them at full speed. They halted and appeared willing to fight us when our command got within three hundred yards of them. Many of our *pulpit braves* found out all at once that they must stop and dismount, to fix their saddles or for some other reason. The remainder of us rode on until within one hundred and fifty yards of the other force, and were drawn up in line of battle. Maj. Brunson rode forward and hailed them, saying,

"Who are you?"

"Capt. McRay," was the reply. "Who are you?"

"Maj. Brunson."

They met and shook hands. Seeing this the pulpit braves rushed up in great haste and took their places in the ranks, and lamented because we did not have an enemy to overcome.

So it is through life - a coward is generally a liar; those men were cowards, and lied when they pretended they would like to fight. All cowards are liars, but many liars are brave men.

While I was engaged with the Mormon troops in ranging over the country, the men that I was with took a large amount of loose property, but did not while I was with them burn any houses or murder any men. Yet we took what property we could find, especially provisions, fat cattle and arms and ammunition. But still many houses were burned and much damage was done by the Mormons, and they captured a howitzer and many guns from the Gentiles. Frequent attacks were made upon the Mormon settlements. The Mormons made an attack on Gallatin one night, and carried off much plunder. I was not there with them, but I talked often with them and learned all the facts about it. The town was burnt down, and everything of value, including the goods in two stores, was carried off by the Mormons. I often escaped being present with the troops on their thieving expeditions, by loaning my horses and arms to others who liked that kind of work better than I did. Unless I had adopted that course I could never have escaped from being present with the Hosts of Israel in all their lawless sets, for I was one of the regular Host, and I could not escape going when ordered, unless I furnished a substitute, which sometimes was accepted, but not always. A company went from Adam-on-Diamond and burned the house and buildings belonging to my friend McBrier. Every article of moveable property was taken by the troops; he was utterly ruined. This man had been a friend to me and many others of the brethren; he was an honorable man, but his good character and former acts of kindness had no effect on those who were working, as they pretended, to build up the Kingdom of God. The Mormons brought in every article that could be used, and much that was of no use or value was hauled to Adam-on-Diamond. Men stole simply for the love of stealing. Such inexcusable acts of lawlessness had the effect to arouse every Gentile in the three Counties of Caldwell, Carroll and Daviess, as well as to bring swarms of armed Gentiles from other localities.

Lyman White, with three hundred men, was called to defend Far West. I went with his command. The night White reached Far West, the battle of Crooked River was fought. Captain David Patton, alias Fear Not, one of the *twelve apostles* was sent out by the Prophet with fifty men, to attack a body of Missourians, who were camping on the Crooked River. Captain Patton's men were nearly all, if not every one of them, Danites. The attack was made just before daylight in the morning. Captain Fear Not wore a white blanket overcoat, and led the attacking party. He was a brave, impulsive man. He rushed into the thickest of the fight, regardless of danger - really seeking it to show his men that God would shield him from all harm. But he counted, without just reason, upon being invincible, for a ball soon entered his body, passing through his hips, and cutting his bladder. The wound was fatal; but he kept on his feet, and led his men some time before yielding to the effects of the wound. The Gentiles said afterwards that Captain Patton told his men to charge in the name of Lazarus, "Charge, Danites, charge!" and that as soon as he uttered the command, which distinguished him, they gave the Danite Captain a commission with powder and ball, and sent him on a mission to preach to the spirits that were in prison. In this battle several men were killed and wounded on both sides. I do not remember all of the names of the Danites that were killed, but I do remember that a man by the name of Banion was killed, and one by the name of Jas. Holbrook was wounded. I knew a man by the name of Tarwater, on the Gentile side, that was cut up fearfully. He was taken prisoner. The Danites routed the Gentiles, who fled in every direction. The night being dark, Jas. Holbrook and another Danite met, and had a hand to hand fight, in which they cut each other fearfully with their swords before they discovered that they were friends. After the Gentiles retreated, the Mormons started for Far West, taking Tarwater along as a prisoner. After traveling several miles, they halted in a grove of timber, and released Tarwater, telling him he was free to go home. He started off, and when he was some forty yards from the Mormons, Parley P. Pratt, then one of the Twelve Apostles, stepped up to a tree, laid his gun up by the side of the tree, took deliberate aim, and shot Tarwater. He fell and lay still. The Mormons, believing he was dead, went on and left him lying where he fell. Tarwater came to, and reached home, where he was taken care of, and soon recovered from his wounds. He afterwards testified in court against the Mormons that he knew, and upon his evidence Parley P. Pratt was imprisoned in the Richmond jail, in 1839.

I must remind the reader that I am writing in prison, and am not allowed to have a book of reference, and as most of my private writings and journals have been heretofore delivered to the agents of Brigham Young, and all have been destroyed, or at least kept from me, I am forced to rely on my memory for names and dates, and if I make mistakes in either, this must be my excuse.

JOSEPH SMITH
(The Founder and first Prophet of the Mormon Church)

CHAPTER V

THE MORMON WAR IN MISSOURI

AFTER 1844, it was my habit to keep a journal, in which I wrote at length all that I considered worthy of remembering. Most of my journals, written up to 1860, were called for by Brigham Young, under the plea that he wished the Church historian to write up the Church history, and wished my journal to aid him in making the history perfect. As these journals contained many things not intended for the public eye, and especially very much concerning the crimes of Mormon leaders in Southern Utah and elsewhere, and all I knew of the Mountain Meadows Massacre, and what led to it, they were never returned to me. I suppose they were put out of the way, perhaps burned, for these journals gave an account of many dark deeds.

I was at Far West when the Danites returned. They brought Captain Patton with them. He died that night, and his death spread a mantle of gloom over the entire community. It robbed many of their fond hope that they were invincible. If *Fear Not* could be killed, who could claim immunity from the missiles of death, hurled by Gentile weapons?

I admit up to this time I firmly believed what the Prophet and his apostles had said on that subject. I had considered that I was *bullet proof*, that no Gentile ball could ever harm me, or any Saint, and I had believed that a Danite could not be killed by Gentile hands. I thought that one Danite could chase a thousand Gentiles, and two could put ten thousand to flight. Alas! my dream of security was over. One of our mighty men had fallen, and that by Gentile hands. My amazement at the fact was equal to my sorrow for the death of the great warrior apostle. I had considered that all the battles between Danites and Gentiles would end like the election fight at Gallatin, and that the only ones to be injured would be the Gentiles. We had been promised and taught by the Prophet and his priesthood that henceforth God would fight our battles, and I looked as a consequence for a bloodless victory on the side of the Lord, and that nothing but disobedience to the teachings of the priest-

hood could render a Mormon subject to injury from Gentile forces. I
believed as our leaders taught us, that all our sufferings and persecutions, were brought upon us by the all-wise God of Heaven, as chas-
tisement to bring us together in unity of faith and strict obedience to the
requirements of the Gospel; and the feeling was general, that all our sufferings were the result of individual sin, and not the fault of our leaders
and spiritual guides. We, as members of the Church, had no right to
question any act of our superiors; to do so wounded the Spirit of God,
and lead to our own loss and confusion.

I was thunderstruck to hear Joseph Smith, the apostle, say at the
funeral of Capt. Patton that the Mormons fell by the missiles of death
the same as other men. He also said that the Lord was angry with the
people, for they had been unbelieving and faithless; they had denied the
Lord the use of their earthly treasures, and placed their affections upon
worldly things more than they had upon heavenly things; that to expect
God's favor we must blindly trust him; that if the Mormons would wholly trust in God the windows of heaven would be opened and a shower
of blessings sent upon the people; that all the people could contain of
blessings would be given as a reward for obedience to the will of God
as made known to mankind through the Prophet of the ever living God;
that the Mormons, if faithful, obedient and true followers of the advice
of their leaders, would soon enjoy all the wealth of the earth; that God
would consecrate the riches of the Gentiles to the Saints. This and much
more he said to induce the people to obey the will of the priesthood. I
believed all he said, for he supported it by quotations from Scripture,
and if I believed the Bible, as I did most implicitly, I could not help
believing in Joseph Smith, the Prophet of God in these last days. Joseph
Smith declared that he was called of God and given power and authority from heaven to do God's will; that he had received the keys of the
holy priesthood from the apostles Peter, James and John, and had been
dedicated, set apart and anointed as the Prophet, seer and revelator; sent
to open the dispensation of the fullness of time, according to the words
of the apostles; that he was charged with the restoration of the house of
Israel, and to gather the Saints from the four corners of the earth to the
land of promise, Zion, the Holy Land (Jackson County), and setting up
the kingdom of God preparatory to the second coming of Christ in the
last days.

Every Mormon, if true to his faith, believed as fully in Joseph Smith
and his holy character as they did that God existed.

Joseph Smith was a most extraordinary man; he was rather large in stature, some six feet two inches in height, well built, though a little stoop shouldered, prominent and well developed features, a Roman nose, light chestnut hair, upper lip full and rather protruding, chin broad and square, an eagle eye, and on the whole there was something in his manner and appearance that was bewitching and winning; his countenance was that of a plain, honest man, full of benevolence and philanthropy and void of deceit or hypocrisy. He was resolute and firm of purpose, strong as most men in physical power, and all who saw were forced to admire him, as he then looked and existed.

In the sports of the day, such as wrestling, etc., he was over an average. Very few of the Saints had the strength needed to throw the Prophet in a fair tussle; in every gathering he was a welcome guest, and always added to the amusement of the people, instead of dampening their ardor. During the time that we were camping at Adam-on-Diamond, waiting to see what would be the result of the quarrel between our Church and the Gentiles, one Sunday morning (it had rained heavily the night before and the air was cold) the men were shivering over a few firebrands, feeling out of sorts and quite cast down. The Prophet came up while the brethren were moping around, and caught first one and then another and shook them up, and said, "Get out of here, and wrestle, jump, run, do anything but mope around; warm yourselves up; this inactivity will not do for soldiers." The words of the Prophet put life and energy into the men. A ring was soon formed, according to the custom of the people. The Prophet stepped into the ring, ready for a tussle with any comer. Several went into the ring to try their strength, but each one was thrown by the Prophet, until he had thrown several of the stoutest of the men present. Then he stepped out of the ring and took a man by the arm and led him in to take his place, and so it continued - the men who were thrown retiring in favor of the successful one. A man would keep the ring so long as he threw his adversary. The style of wrestling varied with the desires of the parties. The Eastern men, or Yankees, used square hold, or Collar and elbow; those from the Middle States side hold, and the Southern and Western men used breeches hold and old Indian hug or back hold. If a man was hurt he stood it without a murmur; it was considered cowardly and childish to whine when thrown down or hurt in the fall.

While the sport was at its height Sidney Rigdon, the mouthpiece of the Prophet, rushed into the ring, sword in hand, and said that he would not suffer a lot of men to break the Sabbath day in that manner. For a moment all were silent, then one of the brethren, with more presence of mind than the others, said to the Prophet, "Brother Joseph, we want you to clear us from blame, for we formed the ring by your request. You told us to wrestle, and now Brother Rigdon is bringing us to account for it."

The Prophet walked into the ring and said, as he made a motion with his hand: "Brother Sidney, you had better go out of here and let the boys alone; they are amusing themselves according to my orders. You are an old man. You go and get ready for meeting and let the boys alone." Just then catching Rigdon off his guard, as quick as a flash he knocked the sword from Rigdon's hand, then caught him by the shoulder, and said; "Now, old man, you *must* go out, or I will throw you down." Rigdon was as large a man as the Prophet, but not so tall. The prospect of a tussle between the Prophet and the mouthpiece of the Prophet, was fun for all but Rigdon, who pulled back like a crawfish, but the resistance was useless, the Prophet dragged him from the ring, bareheaded, and tore Rigdon's fine pulpit coat from the collar to the waist; then he turned to the men and said: "Go in, boys, and have your fun. You shall never have it to say that I got you into any trouble that I did not get you out of."

Rigdon complained about the loss of his hat and the tearing of his coat. The Prophet said to him: "You were out of your place. Always keep your place and you will not suffer; but you got a little out of your place and you have suffered for it. You have no one to blame but yourself." After that Rigdon never countermanded the orders of the Prophet, to my knowledge - he knew who was boss.

An order had been issued by the Church authorities commanding all of the members of the Mormon Church to leave their farms, and to take such property as they could remove, and go to one of the two fortified camps - that is Far West or Adam-on-Diamond. A large majority of the settlers obeyed, and the two camps were soon full of people who had deserted home again for the sake of the gospel.

There was a settlement on Log Creek, between three and five miles east from Far West. It was quite a rich settlement. A man named Haughn had just completed a good flouring mill on the creek. The morning after the battle of Crooked River, Haughn came to Far West to consult with the Prophet concerning the policy of the removal of the settlers on Log Creek to the fortified camps. Col. White and myself were standing by when the Prophet said to him: "Move in, by all means, if you wish to save your lives." Haughn replied that if the settlers left their homes all

of their property would be lost, and the Gentiles would burn their houses and other buildings. The Prophet said: "You had much better lose
your property than your lives, one can be replaced, the other cannot be
restored; but there is no need of your losing either if you will only do as
you are commanded." Haughn said that he considered the best plan was
for all of the settlers to move into and around the mill, and use the blacksmith's shop and other buildings as a fort in case of attack; in this way
he thought they would be perfectly safe. "You are at liberty to do so if
you think best," said the Prophet. Haughn then departed, well satisfied
that he had carried his point.

The Prophet turned to Col. White and said: "That man did not come
for counsel, but to induce me to tell him to do as he pleased; which I
did. Had I commanded them to move in here and leave their property,
they would have called me a tyrant. I wish they were here for their own
safety. I am confident that we will soon learn that they have been
butchered in a fearful manner."

At this time the Missourians had determined to exterminate the
whole of the Mormon people. Governor Lilburn W. Boggs issued orders
to that effect. I think General Clark was the officer in command of all
the Gentile forces. Gen. Atchison and Gen. Doniphan each commanded
a division of from three to eight thousand men, and they soon besieged
Far West. The Mormons fortified the town as well as they could, and
took special care to fortify and build shields and breastworks, to prevent
the cavalry from charging into the town. The Gentile forces were mostly camped on Log Creek, between the town of Far West and Haughn's
Mill, and about a mile from Far West, and about half a mile south of our
outer breastworks. Our scouts and picket guards were driven in, and
forced to join the main ranks for safety. The Mormon troops were
placed in position by the officers, so as to guard every point. Each man
had a large supply of bullets, with the patching sewed on the balls to
facilitate the loading of our guns, which were all muzzle loaders. The
Mormon force was about eight hundred strong, poorly armed; many of
the men had no guns; some had single barrel pistols, and a few had
homemade swords. These were all of our implements of war. So situated, we were still anxious to meet the enemy, and demanded to be led out
against our foes. Our men were confident that God was going to deliver the enemy into our hands, and so we had no fears. I was one of the
advance force, and as I lay behind some timber, with my cap box open,
and bullets lying on the ground by my side, I never had a doubt of being

able to defeat the Gentile army. The troops lay and watched each other two days, then the Gentiles made two efforts to force their way into the town by stratagem; but seeing our forces in order, they did not come within range of our guns. The Mormons stood in the ranks, and prayed for the chance of getting a shot; but all to no effect. The same evening we learned of the massacre at Haughn's Mill. The description of this massacre was such as to freeze the blood of each Saint, and force them to swear revenge should come someday.

HAUGHN'S MILL MASSACRE

was reported about as follows to us at Far West. When the Gentile mob attacked the Mormons at the mill the Mormons took shelter in the black-smith shop and other buildings. The mob took advantage of the banks of the creek and the timber, and very nearly surrounded the shop, which was built of logs, and served as a slaughterhouse instead of a shelter or protection. The mob, while protected as they were, shot down the Mormons at their leisure. They killed eighteen and wounded as many more; in fact they killed and wounded every one who did not run away during the fight and take refuge in the woods. After shooting down all that could be seen, the mob entered the blacksmith shop and there found a young lad who had secreted himself under the bellows. One of the men said, "Don't shoot; it is but a small boy." The reply was, "Nits will make lice; it is best to save them when we can." Thus saying, they shot the little fellow where he lay. There was an old man in the settlement by the name of McBride, who had been a soldier in the Revolutionary war; he was killed by being hacked to pieces with a corn-cutter while beg-ging for his life. The dead and wounded were thrown into a well all together. Several of the wounded were afterwards taken out of the well by the force that went from Far West, and recovered from their wounds. So great was the hatred of the mob that they saved none, but killed all who fell into their hands at that time. I received my information of the massacre from David Lewis, Tarleton Lewis, William Laney and Isaac Laney; they were Kentuckians, and were also in the fight, but escaped death. Isaac Laney was shot seven times, leaving thirteen ball holes in his person; five of the shots were nearly in the centre of the chest; one entered under the right arm, passed through the body and came out under the left arm; yet, strange as it appears, he kept his feet, so he informed me, and ran some three hundred yards to a cabin, where a woman raised a loose plank of the cabin floor, and he lay down and she replaced the boards.

The mob left, and in about two hours Laney was taken from under the cabin floor nearly lifeless. He was then washed, anointed with oil, the elders praying for his recovery, according to the order of the Holy Priesthood, and he was promised, through prayer and faith in God, speedy restoration. The pain at once left him, and for two weeks he felt no pain at all. He then took cold, and the wound in his hips pained him for some two hours, when the elders repeated their prayers and again anointed him, which had the effect desired. The pain left him, and never returned. I heard Laney declare this to be a fact, and he bore his testimony in the presence of many of the Saints. I saw him four weeks after the massacre and examined his person. I saw the wounds, then healed. I felt of them with my own hands, and I saw the shirt and examined it, that he had on when he was shot, and it was cut in shreds. Many balls, had cut his clothing, that had not touched his person.

The massacre at Haughn's Mill was the result of the brethren's refusal to obey the wishes of the Prophet. All the brethren so considered it. It made a deep and lasting impression on my mind, for I had heard the Prophet give the counsel to the brethren to come into the town. They had refused, and the result was a lesson to all that there was no safety except in obeying the Prophet.

Col. George M. Hinkle had command of the troops at Far West, under Joseph Smith. He was from Kentucky, and was considered a fair weather Saint. When danger came he was certain to be on the strong side. He was a fine speaker, and had great influence with the Saints.

Previous to the attack on Far West, Col. Hinkle had come to an understanding with the Gentile commanders that in case the danger grew great, they could depend on him, as a friend and one through whom they could negotiate and learn the situation of affairs in the camp of the Saints. When our scouts were first driven in, Col. Hinkle was out with them, and when they were closely pursued he turned his coat wrong side out and wore it so. This was a peculiar move, but at the time it did not cause much comment among his men, but they reported it to the Prophet, and he at once became suspicious of the Colonel. The Prophet, being a man of thought and cool reflection, kept this information within a small circle, as that was a bad time to ventilate an act of that kind. The Prophet concluded to make use of the knowledge he had gained of Hinkle's character, and use him to negotiate between the two parties. I do not believe that Joseph Smith had the least idea that he, with his little handful of men, could stand off that army that had come up against him. I know that now, but at that time was full of religious zeal and felt that the Mormon Hosts of Israel were invincible. Joseph wished to use Hinkle to learn the destiny of the Gentiles, so that he could prepare for the worst. Col. Hinkle was sent out by Joseph to have an interview with the Gentiles.

The Colonel returned and reported to Joseph Smith the terms proposed by the Gentile officers. The terms offered were as follows: Joseph Smith and the leading men of the Church, Rigdon, Lyman White, P. P. Pratt, Phelps and others, were to give themselves up without delay, the balance of the men to surrender themselves and their arms by ten o'clock the following day, the understanding being that all would be tried for *treason* against the Government, and for other offenses. The Prophet took advantage of this information, and had every man that was in imminent danger, leave the camp for a place of safety. The most of those in danger went to Illinois. They left at once, and were safe from all pursuit before the surrender took place, as they traveled north and avoided all settlements. When the brethren had left for Illinois, as just stated, Joseph Smith called all of his remaining troops together, and told them they were a good lot of fellows, but they were not perfect enough to withstand so large an army as the one now before them, that they had stood by him, and were willing to die for and with him, for the sake of the Kingdom of Heaven, that he wished them to be comforted, for God had accepted their offering, that he intended to, and was going to offer himself up as a sacrifice, to save their lives and to save the Church. He wished them all to be of good cheer, and pray for him, and to pray that he and the brethren that went with him might be delivered from their enemies. He then blessed his people in the name of the Lord. After this, he and the leading men, six in number went with him direct to the camp of the enemy. They were led by a Judas, Col. G.M. Hinkle. I stood upon the breastworks and watched them go into the camp of the enemy. I heard the yells of triumph of the troops, as Joseph Smith and his companions entered. It was with great difficulty that the officers could restrain the mob from shooting them down as they entered. A strong guard was then placed over them to protect them from mob violence.

The next morning a court martial was held, at which Joseph Smith and his six companions that had surrendered with him, were sentenced to be shot. The execution was to take place at eight o'clock the next morning. When the sentence of the court martial was announced to them, Col. Lyman White said "Shoot and be d--d." General Atchison and Col. Doniphan arrived with their divisions the same day, soon after the court martial had been held. Col. Doniphan, in particular, remonstrated against the decision. He said it was nothing more or less than cold blooded murder, and that every name signed to the decision was signed in blood, and he would withdraw his troops and have nothing to do in the matter, if the men were to be shot. General Atchison sustained Col. Doniphan, and said the wiser policy would be, in as much as they had surrendered themselves as prisoners, to place them in the Richmond jail, and let them take the due course of the law; let them be tried by the civil authorities of the land. In this way justice could be reached and parties could be punished according to law, and thus save the honor of the troops and the nation. This timely interposition and wise course on the part of Col. Doniphan and General Atchison, changed the course and prevented the hasty action of an infuriated mob, calling itself a court, men who were all the bitter enemies of Joseph Smith and his followers.

The next day a writing desk was prepared, with two secretaries or clerks; it was placed in the middle of the hollow square formed by the troops. The Mormons were marched in double file across the centre of the square, where the officers and men who had remained In Far West surrendered themselves and their arms to General Clark, Commander-in-Chief of the Missouri Militia, then in arms, against the Saints at Far West. I was among the number that then surrendered. I laid down a good Kentucky rifle, two good horse pistols and a sword. After stacking our arms we were marched in single file, between a double file of the militia, who stood in a line from the secretary desk, extending nearly across the square, ready to receive us, with fixed bayonets. As each man came up to the stand, he stepped to the desk and signed his name to an instrument recapitulating the conditions of the treaty, which were substantially as follows: We were to give a deed to all of our real estate, and to give a bill of sale of all our personal property, to pay the expenses of the war that had been inaugurated against us; that a committee of twelve should be appointed, one for Far West and one for Adam-on-Diamond, who were to be the sole judges of what would be necessary to remove each family out of the State, and all of the Mormons were to leave Missouri by the first of April, A.D. 1839, and all the rest of the property of the Mormons was to be taken by the Missouri troops to pay the expenses of the war. When the committee had examined into affairs and made the assignment of property that the Mormons were to retain, a pass would be given by the committee to each person as an evidence that he had gone through an investigation both as to his conduct and property. The prisoners at Far West were to be retained and not allowed to return home until the committee had reported and given the certificate that all charges had been met and satisfied. I remained a prisoner for nine days, awaiting the action of the committee. While such prisoner I witnessed many scenes of inhumanity, even more degrading than brutality itself. The mob of the militia was mostly composed of men who had been neighbors of the Mormons. This mob rifled the city, took what they wished, and committed many cruel and shameful deeds. These barbarous acts were done because they said the Mormons had stolen their goods and chattels, and while they pretended to search for stolen property they ravished women and committed other crimes at will. One day, while standing by a log fire, trying to keep warm, a man came up and recognized Riley Stewart, and said, "I saw you knock Dick Weldon down at Gallatin." With this he sprang and caught at an ax that had been stuck in a log; while trying to get the ax out, as it stuck fast in the log, Stewart ran; the man succeeded in getting the ax loose; he then threw it with all his force at Stewart; fortunately the ax struck him a glancing blow on the head, not killing him, but giving him a severe wound. When one of the mob saw a saddle, or bridle, or any article they liked, they took it and kept it, and the Mormon prisoners dared not say a word about it.

The night after he was wounded, Stewart broke through the guard, and escaped to his wife's people in Carroll County, fifty miles south of Far West. As soon as the citizens heard that Stewart had arrived, they notified his wife's brothers and father that an armed mob intended to take him out and whip him severely, and then tar and feather him. His friends notified him of the fact, and he attempted to make his escape, but the mob was on the watch. They caught him, and, holding two pistols at his head, forced him to take off his coat, kneel down, and receive fifty lashes. These were given him with such force that they cut through his linen shirt. After this whipping, he returned to Far West, and took his chances with the rest of us. One day a soldier of the mob walked up to a house near where I was standing. The house was occupied by an old widow woman. The soldier noticed a cow in the little shed, near the house. He said he thought that was a Danite cow; that he wanted to have the honor of killing a Danite, or something that belonged to a Danite. The old widow came to the door of her cabin, and begged him to spare her cow, saying it was her only dependence for milk, that she had no meat, and if her cow was killed, she must suffer. "Well, then," said he, "you can eat the cow for a change." He then shot the cow dead, and stood there and tantalized the old woman when she cried over her loss.

While we were standing in line, waiting our turns to sign the treaty, a large company of men, painted like Indians, rode up and surrounded us. They were a part of the men who were in the fight at the town of Gallatin, on the day of election. They tantalized us and abused us in every way they could with words. This treatment was hard to bear, but we were powerless to protect ourselves in any way.

CHAPTER VI

LEE LOCATES THE GARDEN OF EDEN

I HAD a fine gray mare that attracted the attention of many of the mob. I was allowed to take her to water, while closely guarded by armed men. One day as I took her to water I was spoken to by several men, who said they were sorry for a man like me, who appeared to be honest and peaceably disposed; that they knew that I and many honest men were deluded by Joseph Smith, the impostor. But they thanked God he would delude no more people; that he would certainly be shot; that I had better quit my delusion and settle down by the officer in command, who was then talking to me, in Carroll County, and make a home for my family; that I would never have peace or quiet while I remained with the Mormons. I heard him through. Then I said: "No man has deceived me. I am not deceived by Joseph Smith, or any other man. If I am deceived it is the Bible that has deceived me. I believe that Joseph Smith is a Prophet of God, and I have the Bible as my authority in part for this belief. And I do not believe that Joseph Smith will be shot, as you seem to think. He has not finished his work yet."

As I finished my remarks the officer became fearfully enraged, and said, "That is the way with all you d--d Mormons. You might as well try to move a mountain as to turn a Mormon from his delusion. Blow the brains out of this fool!" In an instant several guns were leveled on me. I imagined I already felt the bullets piercing my body. The soldiers would certainly have shot me down if the officer had not immediately countermanded his order, by saying, "Hold on, boys, he is not worth five charges of ammunition." I said, "Gents, I am your prisoner, unarmed and helpless, and I demand your protection. But if you consider there is any honor in treating a man, an American prisoner, in this way, you can do it."

As we returned to camp the man said, "We will make it hot for the Mormons yet before we are done with them, and if you have not got enough of them now, you will have before you are done with them; and you will remember my words when it is too late to serve you."

"I may," said I; "when I do I will own up like a little man. But until I am so convinced I will never turn my coat."

"Well," said he, "you are not so bad after all. I like a firm man, if he only has reason on his side."

The Mormons were forted, or barricaded, in the public school houses, and kept without any rations being issued to them. The grain fields and gardens that belonged to the Mormons were thrown open to the stock and wasted. Our cattle and other stock were shot down for sport and left for the wolves and birds of prey to devour. We were closely guarded, and not allowed to go from our quarters without a guard. We were nearly starved for several days, until I obtained permission to go out and bring in some of the cattle that the soldiers had killed for sport. The weather was cold and the snow deep, so the meat was good. I also got permission to gather in some vegetables, and from that time, while we remained prisoners, the men had plenty to eat, yet often it was of a poor quality. While a prisoner I soon learned that the loud and self-conceited men were of little account when danger stared them in the face.

Arrangements had been made to carry the treaty into effect. It was found necessary to send General Wilson with five hundred men to Adam-on-Diamond to compel the surrender, and signing of the treaty, as had been done at Far West, and the people of that place were to be treated just as we had been.

I was recommended to General Wilson by the officer who had ordered his men to blow my brains out, as a suitable man for a guide to Adam-on-Diamond. He said that I was as stubborn an a mule, but still there was something about me he respected. That he believed that I was honest, and certainly no coward. General Wilson said: "Young man, do you live at Adam-on-Diamond?" I said: "I cannot say that I do, but I did once, and I have a wife and child there that I would like to see; but as to a home I have none left." He said, "Where did you live before you came here?" "In Illinois," I answered. "You shall soon see your wife and child. I will start in the morning with my division for Adam-on-Diamond. You are at liberty to select two of your comrades and go with me as guides, to pilot us there. Be ready for an early start and report to my adjutant." "Thank you, sir, I will do as you request," said I.

I selected two good men, I think Levi Stewart was one, but I have really forgotten who the other man was. In the morning I was on hand in time. The day was cold and stormy, a hard north wind blowing, and the snow falling rapidly. It was an open country for thirteen miles, with eighteen inches of snow on the ground. We kept our horses in the lope until we reached Shady Grove timber, thirteen miles from Far West. There we camped for the night by the side of Waldo Littlefield's farm. The fence was burned for campfires, and his fields of grain were fed to the horses, or rather the animals were turned loose in the fields. After camp was struck I went to General Wilson and said, "General, I have come to beg a favor of you. I ask you in the name of humanity to let me go on to Adam-on-Diamond today. I have a wife and helpless babe there. I am informed our house has been burned, and she is likely out in this storm without a shelter. You are halfway there; the snow is deep, and you can follow our trail (it had then slackened up, or was snowing but little) in the morning; there is but one road to the settlement." He looked at me for a moment, and then said, "Young man, your request shall be granted, I admire your resolution." He then turned to his Aid, who stood trembling in the snow, and said,

"Write Mr. Lee and his two comrades a pass, saying that they have gone through an examination at Far West, and have been found innocent," etc. The Adjutant drew out his portfolio and wrote as follows: "I permit John D. Lee to remove from Daviess to Caldwell County, and to pass out of the State, as he has undergone an examination at Far West and was fully acquitted. Marrowbone Encampment, Caldwell County, Mo., Nov. 15, 1839.

"R. WILSON, Brigadier Gen.

"R. F. COCKEY, Aid-de-Camp"

After receiving my pass I thanked the General for his humane act, and with my friends made the journey, through the snow, to Adam-on-Diamond. As we neared home the sun shone out brightly. When I got in sight of where my house had been, I saw my wife sitting by a log fire in the open air, with her babe in her arms. Some soldiers had cut a large hickory tree for firewood for her, and had built her a shelter with some boards I had dressed to weatherboard a house, so she was in a measure comfortable. She had been weeping, as she had been informed that I was a prisoner at Far West, and would be shot, and that she need not look for me, for she would never see me again. When I rode up she was nearly frantic with delight, and as soon as I reached her side she threw herself into my arms and then her self possession gave way and she wept bitterly; but she soon recovered herself and gave me an account of her troubles during my absence.

The next evening, General Wilson and his command arrived and camped near my little shanty. I started at once to report to General Wilson. On my way to him I passed my friend McBrier, who had trusted me for some cattle. I still owed him for them. I told him why I had been unable to pay him, and wished him to take the cattle back, as I still had all of them except one cow that had died of the murrain; that it was an honest debt, and I wished to pay it. I asked him to go to my shanty with me, and said he could take what cattle were left, and a black mare that was worth $75, and an eight day clock that was worth $25, for my note. "I have not got your note," said he. "Who has it?" I asked him. "I do not know, I supposed you had it." I never saw it since I gave it to you." "Well," said he, "my house was burned, and all my property either burned or taken from me, and your note was in the house when it was burned." "Well," said I, "it matters not with me, if you will take the property and give me a receipt against the note, so that it cannot be collected the second time, I will settle the debt." He then said, "I thought you had been in the party that burned the house, and had taken your note, but I am now satisfied to the contrary, and that you are an innocent man. All I ask is for you to renew the note. The property of the Mormons will be held to pay their debts, and the expenses of the war, and I will get my pay in that way. You just renew the note, and that will settle all between us." I then renewed the note, after which he went with me to General Wilson. McBrier introduced me to a number of the soldiers as an honest Mormon. This worked well in my favor, and pleased me much, for it satisfied me more than ever that honesty was the best policy. I had done nothing that I considered wrong; there was no stolen property around my house. I did not have to run and hide, or screen any act of mine from the public gaze. My wife had been treated well personally, during my absence; no insults had been offered to her, and I was well pleased at that. I was treated with respect by Gen. Wilson and his men. True, I was associated with the people that had incurred the displeasure of the authorities, and my neighbors, who had committed crimes and larcenies, were then receiving fearful punishment for all they had done. The punishment, however, was in a great part owing to the fault of the people. When the Gentiles found any of their property that had been stolen, they became very abusive.

Every house in Adam-on-Diamond was searched by the troops for stolen property. They succeeded in finding very much of the Gentile property that had been captured by the Saints in the various raids they made through the country. Bedding of every kind and in large quantities was found and reclaimed by the owners. Even spinning wheels, soap barrels and other articles were recovered. Each house where stolen property was found was certain to receive a Missouri blessing from the troops. The men who had been most active in gathering plunder had fled to Illinois, to escape the vengeance of the people, leaving their families to suffer for the sins of the bleeding Saints. By the terms of the treaty all the Mormons were to leave Daviess County within fifteen days, but they were allowed to stay through the winter in Caldwell County; but all had to depart from Missouri before the first day of the next April. There were but few families that met with the kind treatment that mine did. The majority of the people were censured and persecuted as much as they were able to stand and live.

In justice to Joseph Smith I cannot say that I ever heard him teach or even encourage men to pilfer or steal little things. He told the people that in an open war the contending factions were justified in taking spoil to subsist upon during the war; but he did despise this little, petty stealing. He told the people to wait until the proper time came to take back their rights, "then," said he, "take the whole State of Missouri like men."

When the people at Adam-on-Diamond had signed the treaty, and complied with the stipulations, the committee of twelve commenced their duties. When it came my turn to take the property necessary to take me out of the State, I was told to fit myself out comfortably. I told them that I had a wife and one child, that I had two good wagons, one a heavy one horse wagon, with fills, and that I had a large mare that was equal to a common span, that the mare and wagon would do me, that I wanted some bedding and our clothing, and some other traps of little value; that I had a good milk cow that I wished to give to a friend who had lost all his cattle, and his wife had died a short time before, leaving a little babe that must have milk. I told them they could take the rest of my property and do with it as they did with that of the brethren. I was worth then in property, at a fair valuation, $4,000. The officers were astonished at me and said they did not wish to oppress a man who acted fairly. They told me to take my large wagon and two of my best horses, and all the outfit that I wanted. I thanked them for their kindness. I was permitted to give the cow to my friend and I had the privilege of taking such articles as I wished. I fitted up with just what would take me to Illinois, and left the remainder as a spoil for the enemies of the Church.

I did not regret the loss of my property; I gave it up as the price of my religious freedom; but I did feel cast down to think and know that I was associated with so many petty thieves, whose ambition never rose higher than the smoke of their corncob pipes. I was sorrowful to find that the perfection I had thought the people possessed, was not, in fact, a part of their natures.

I had long desired to associate myself with an honest people, whose motto should be promptness, punctuality, honesty - a people that feared God and worked righteousness, dealt justly, loved mercy and walked uprightly with each other before their God; where my property, my life, my reputation would be held sacred by them all, the same as if it was their own. For the society of such a people I was willing to forsake all earthly substance, and even to have my name cast out as evil and trodden under foot, if I could be found worthy to serve with such a blessed people, and thus earn the boon of eternal life. But I had found another class of people; they fell far short of the requisites that I had believed they possessed. When I found fault with having such characters in the Church I was told of the parable where Christ likened the kingdom of heaven to a net that was cast into the sea, which, when drawn to the shore, had in it all kinds of fish; the servants picked out the good and kept them for the Master's use, and the bad were cast back into the sea; that we could not expect anything different with the kingdom on earth; that it was a trick of the evil one to cause such persons to rush into the gospel net to harass and torment the Saints with their evil doings, but the time would come when forbearance would cease to be a virtue, then all those who worked iniquity or gave offense in the kingdom would be cut off and destroyed; that we must bear with them until the time came to correct the evil.

Before I speak of other things I will say a few words of the country we were then in. Adam-on-Diamond was at the point where Adam came and settled and blest his posterity after being driven from the Garden of Eden. This was revealed to the people through Joseph Smith, the Prophet. The Temple Block in Jackson County, Missouri, stands on the identical spot where once stood the Garden of Eden. When Adam and Eve were driven from the Garden they traveled in a northeasterly course until they came to a valley on the east side of Grand River. There they tarried for several years, and engaged in tilling the soil. On the east of the valley there is a low range of hills. Standing on the summit of the bluffs a person has a full view of the beautiful valley that lies below, dotted here and there with elegant groves of timber. On the top of this range of hills Adam erected an altar of stone, on which he offered sacrifice unto the Lord. There was at that time (in 1838) a pile of stone there, which the Prophet said was a portion of the altar on which Adam offered sacrifice. Although these stones had been exposed to the elements for many generations of time, still the traces remained to show the dimensions and design of the altar. After Adam had offered his sacrifice he went up the valley some two miles, where he blessed his posterity and called the place the Valley of Adam-on-Diamond, which, in the reformed Egyptian language, signifies Adam's Consecrated Land. It is said to be seventy five miles, in a direct course, from the Garden of Eden to Adam-on-Diamond. Those supposed ancient relics and sacred spots of earth are held sacred by the greater portion of the Latter Day Saints. To a casual observer it appears that this people are all the time chasing a phantom of some sort, which only exists in the brain of the fanatical followers. These things, and much more concerning the early days, were revealed to Joseph Smith.

On the 20th day of November, 1838, I took leave of my home, and the spot I considered sacred ground, on Adam-on-Diamond, and started as a banished person to seek a home in Illinois. We went to my farm on Shady Grove Creek, and staid over night. We found everything as we had left it, nothing had been interfered with. I killed a large hog and dressed it to carry with us to eat on the journey. The snow was fully twenty inches deep, weather very cold, and taken all in all, it was a disagreeable and unpleasant trip. We went to the settlement on Log Creek, and stopped with the family of Robert Bidwell. He had plenty of property. This man had good teams, and had reaped where he had not sown, and gathered where he had not strewn. He was engaged in removing families of his helpless brethren to Quincy, Illinois, who had not teams to move themselves, but who had a little money that he was after, and he got all they had. For some reason unexplained to me, he had been permitted to keep all of his property; none of it was taken by the troops. While at Bidwell's I bought a crib of corn, about two hundred bushels, for a pocket knife. I built a stable for my mare, and a crib for the corn, and hauled wood enough to do the whole family for the rest of the winter. I also attended to Bidwell's stock and worked all the time for him. They had five children, which made considerable work for the women folks; my wife worked for them all the time. During this time we had nothing but corn to eat. The hog I killed at my farm was diseased, and I had to throw the meat away. Notwithstanding our constant work for Bidwell's family, they never gave us a drop of milk or a meal of victuals while we remained there. Mrs. Bidwell fed six gallons of milk to their hogs each day. I offered to feed the hogs corn for milk, so we could have milk to eat with our boiled corn, but she refused the offer, saying they had all they needed. They did have provisions of every kind in abundance, but not a particle of food could we obtain from them. Prayer meetings were frequently held at their house. They had plenty of tallow, but Mrs. Bidwell would not allow a candle to be burned in the house unless some other person furnished it. One night at prayer meeting I chanced to speak upon the subject of covetousness, and quoted the twelfth chapter of Paul to the Corinthians, where he speaks of members of the Church of Christ being united. I was feeling badly to see so much of the covetousness of the world in some of the members of the Church, and I talked quite plainly upon the subject. The next morning Mrs. Bidwell came into our room and said that my remarks at the meeting the evening before were directed at her, and she wanted me to understand that if I did not like my treatment there, she wanted us to go where we would fare better. This inhuman and unwelcome language did not set well on an empty stomach, and was more than I could bear. I burst into tears. Yet I pitied the ungrateful woman. As soon as I could control my feelings I said, "Sister Bidwell, I will take you at your word. I will leave your house as soon as I can get my things into my wagon, but before I leave you, I wish to say a few words for you to ponder on when we are gone. In the first place, you and I profess to be members of the same Church; for the sake of our faith my family has been broken up and driven from a comfortable home, in this inclement season of the year. We came here seeking shelter from the stormy blasts of winter, until the severity of the weather was past, when we intended to leave this State. You have been more fortunate than your brethren and sisters who lived in Daviess County. You are allowed to live in your own house, but we are homeless wanderers. Now you drive us from the shelter of your roof, for a trivial offense, if offense it was. But I assure you that you are only angry because my words were the truth. Woe unto you who are angry and offended at the truth. As you do unto others, so will your Heavenly Father do unto you. In as much as you have done this unnatural act, you will yet be houseless and homeless - you will be one day dependent upon those that you now drive from your door."

At first she mocked me, but soon her tune changed and she commenced to cry. She then begged me not to get angry with what a woman said. I told her I could not undo what I had said - that I should start at once for Quincy, Illinois. We left the house of the stingy and selfish family, intending to go direct to Illinois. We traveled until we arrived at the house of a man by the name of Morris; they had a much smaller house than Bidwell's, but they would not listen to our continuing our journey during the severe cold weather. We accepted their invitation, and stayed there about two weeks. This family possessed the true Christian spirit and treated us while there as kindly as if we had been their own children. While staying with Brother Morris I attended several meetings at Far West. Old Father Smith, the father of the Prophet, lead the meetings. He also directed the exodus of the Saints from Missouri to Illinois. Thomas B. Marsh was at that time president of the Twelve Apostles, and I think Brigham Young was second and Orson Hyde the third on the roll. The great opposition to our people and Church caused the two pillars, Marsh and Hyde, to become weak kneed and turn over to the enemy. Col. G.M. Hinkle, Dr. Averard, Judge W.W. Phelps, and others of the *tall* men of the Church followed suit. I remember going with Levi Stewart to some of those fallen angels (in the days of our prosperity they had looked like angels to me) to inquire what to do and what was to be the future conduct of our people. G.M. Hinkle said that it was his opinion our *leaders*, Joseph Smith and those with him in prison, would be either hung or imprisoned for life, that the members of the Church would scatter to the four winds, and never gather again in this dispensation. We then went to Joseph's father and asked him for counsel. He told us that the Saints would gather again in Illinois. We asked him at what point. He said, "I do not know yet, but the farther north we go the less poisonous serpents we will find." He then advised us to attend private meetings and be set apart to the ministry. Public meetings could not be held by the terms of the treaty. We did attend private meetings, and I was ordained in the Quorum of Seventies, under the hands of Joseph Young and Levi Hancock. Stewart was ordained to the *lesser* priesthood, which gave him authority to preach and baptize, but not to confirm. The office that I held gave me authority to preach, baptize and confirm by the laying on of hands, for the reception of the Holy Ghost, and to ordain and set apart Elders, Priests, Teachers and Deacons, and to ordain a Seventy or High Priest, as the office of a Seventy belongs to the Melchisedek Priesthood; yet a Seventy or High Priest is generally ordained and set apart by the presidents of the several quorums. After we were ordained we attended a private feast and blessing meeting, at which my wife and I got our Patriarchal Blessing, under the hands of Isaac Morley, Patriarch. This office properly belongs to those that are ordained and set apart to that calling, to bless the fatherless and the widow especially, but he can bless others who ask it and pay one dollar for the blessing. Often the widow and the poor are blessed free, but this is at the option of the Patriarch.

My Patriarchal Blessing was in the following form: "Patriarchal Blessing of John D. Lee. By Isaac Morley, Patriarch. Caldwell County, Missouri, Dec. --, 1838. Brother John D. Lee: In the name of Jesus of Nazareth, and by virtue and authority of the Holy Priesthood, in me vested, I lay my hands upon thy head, and confer upon thee a Patriarchal or Father's Blessing. Thou art of Ephraim, through the loins of Joseph, that was sold in Egypt. And inasmuch as thou hast obeyed the requirements of the gospel of salvation; thy sins are forgiven thee. Thy name is written in the Lamb's Book of Life, never more to be blotted out. Thou art a lawful heir to all the blessings of Abraham, Isaac and Jacob in the new and everlasting covenant. Thou shalt travel until thou art satisfied with seeing. Thousands shall hear the everlasting gospel proclaimed from thy lips. Kings and princes shall acknowledge thee to be their father in the new and everlasting covenant. Thou shalt have a numerous posterity, who shall rise up and bless thee. Thou shalt have houses and habitations, flocks, fields and herds. Thy table shall be strewed with the rich luxuries of the earth, to feed thy numerous family and friends who shall come unto thee. Thou shalt be a counselor in Israel, and many shall come unto thee for instruction. Thou shalt have power over thine enemies. They that oppose thee shall yet come bending unto thee. Thou shalt sit under thine own vine and fig tree, where none shall molest or make thee afraid. Thou shalt be a blessing to thy family and to the Church of Jesus Christ of Latter-Day Saints. Thou shalt understand the hidden things of the kingdom of heaven. The spirit of inspiration shall be a light in thy path and a guide to thy mind. Thou shalt come forth in the morning of the first resurrection, and NO POWER shall hinder, except the shedding of innocent blood, or consenting thereto. I seal thee up to eternal life. In the name of the Father, and of the Son, and of the Holy Ghost, Amen, and Amen."

To a true believer in the faith of the Latter Day Saints a blessing of this kind, from under the hand of a Patriarch, was then, and is now, considered *next to a boon* of eternal life. We were taught to look upon a

Patriarch as a man highly favored of God, and that he possessed the gift of discerning of spirits and could read the *present* and *future* destiny of men. Of all this I then had no doubt.

Patriarchal blessings are intended to strengthen, stimulate and encourage true Saints, and induce them to press on to perfection while passing through this world of sorrows, cares and disappointments.

Having been ordained and blessed, my next step was to arm myself with the Armor of Righteousness, and in my weakness pray for strength to face a frowning world. I had put my hands to the plow and I was determined that, with God's help, I would never turn back to the sinful elements of the world, the flesh and the devil.

CHAPTER VII

THE SAINTS GATHER AT NAUVOO

ABOUT the middle of February, 1839, I started back for Fayette County, Illinois, with my family, in company with Levi Stewart and Riley Helm, two of my old Illinois neighbors. While traveling through Missouri we were kindly treated by most of the people; many of them requested us to stop and settle down by them. I refused to do so, for I knew there was no safety for a true Saint in that State, at that time. When we crossed the Mississippi River at Quincy, and touched Illinois soil, I felt like a new man, and a free American citizen again.

At this place I found many of the Saints who had preceded us, camped along the river. Some had obtained employment, all appeared happy in the faith and strong in the determination to build up the Kingdom. Here I parted with Ailey Helm, his team had given out, and he could go no farther. I gave him twenty five cents in money, all that I had in the world, and twelve pounds of nails, to buy food with until he could find aid from some other quarter. I had laid in enough provisions at Brother Morris' to last me until I could reach my old home again.

I started from Quincy by way of Mr. Vanleven's, the man I sold my cattle to when going to join the Saints. Without meeting with any remarkable adventures, I arrived at Vanleven's house and was kindly received by him. He had the money ready for me, and paid me in full all he owed on the cattle. I now saw that some honesty yet remained in the world. I took $200 and left the rest of it with my friend and banker, so that it would be safe in case I met another storm of oppression.

I then went to Vandalia, Illinois, and put up with my wife's sister's husband, Hickerson. He was in good circumstances, I left my wife with her sister, after laying in a supply of provisions for her and our child. I then commenced preparing for a mission. I did not know where I was to go, but I felt it my duty to go forth and give my testimony to the truth of the Gospel as revealed by Joseph Smith, the Prophet of the everlasting God. Stewart was to go with me; he had made arrangements for the comfort of his family, during his absence.

I started on my first mission about the 1st of April, 1839. I bade adieu to my little family and started forth, an illiterate, inexperienced person, without purse or scrip. I could hardly quote a passage of Scripture, yet I went forth to say to the world that I was a minister of the gospel, bearing a message from on high, with the authority to call upon all men to repent, be baptized for the remission of their sins, and receive the Holy Spirit by the laying on of hands. I had never attempted to preach a discourse in my life. I expected trials, and I had them to undergo many times.

Brother Stewart and myself started forth on foot, with our valises on our backs. We walked about thirty miles the first day, and as night was approaching, we called at a house for lodging. They had been having a log rolling there that day, and quite a number of people were around the house. We asked for lodging and refreshments. Our request was carried back to the supper room to the man of the house, and we stood at the gate awaiting the reply. Presently the man came out and said that no d--d Mormon preacher could stay in his house; and if we wished to save our scalps, we had better be making tracks lively. Brother Stewart took him at his word, and started off at a double quick. I followed, but more slowly. We made no reply to that man's remarks.

A mile further on we again called for lodging. The man could not keep us, as he was poor, and his family was sick; but he directed us to a house half a mile from the traveled road, where he said a man lived that was an infidel, but he would not turn a hungry man from his door. We went to the house, and asked for entertainment. The man said he never turned a man from his door hungry, but he had as soon entertain horse thieves as Mormon preachers; that he looked upon all Mormons as thieves, robbers and scoundrels. There was determination in his voice as he addressed us in this manner. He held his rifle in his hand while speaking. Then he said, "Walk in, gentlemen. I never turn the hungry away." He then addressed his wife, a very pretty, unassuming lady, and said, "Get these men some supper, for I suppose they feel pretty lank."

A good supper was soon on the table; but I could not eat. Stewart ate his supper, and soon was enjoying himself talking to the family. He was a great talker; liked to hear himself talk. They requested me to eat, but I thanked them and said rest would do me more good than eating. I soon retired, but did not sleep. I was humiliated; my proud spirit was broken and humbled; the rough words used toward me had stricken me to the heart. At daylight we were on our way again.

About ten o'clock we arrived at a little town, and went to the pump to get a drink. While there a woman came to the pump, and asked us if we were Mormon preachers. We told her we were out on that business, but had never preached yet. She invited us to her house, saying she owned the hotel; that she was a widow; she would inform the people of the town that we were there, and as it was the Sabbath, we could preach in her house; for she wished to hear the strange doctrine. We consented to remain, and went home with her and had something to eat. At eleven o'clock, A.M., I made my debut to quite an attentive audience.

I both quoted and made Scripture. I had been fasting and praying until I had become as humble as a child. My whole mind and soul were swallowed up in the Gospel. My most earnest desire was to be able to impart to others that knowledge that I had of the truths of the Gospel. When I began to speak I felt an electric thrill through my whole system. I hardly knew what I said, and the people said I spoke from inspiration; and none of the audience noticed my mistakes in quoting Scripture.

After dinner my companion, Stewart, proposed to travel on, and I agreeing with him, we left the town, although the people wished us to stay and preach again. I had but little confidence in myself, and concluded to preach but seldom, until I got over my timidity or man -fearing feeling that most new beginners are subject to. But I have now been a public speaker for thirty-five years, and I have not yet entirely gotten over that feeling.

We started for Cincinnati, and traveled two days and a half without food. My boots hurt my feet and our progress was quite slow. The third night we applied to a tavern keeper for lodging and food. He said we were welcome to stay in his house free, but he must have pay for what we eat. We sat in the hall all night, for we were much reduced by hunger and fatigue. That was a miserable night indeed. I reflected the matter over and over again, scrutinized it up one side and down the other. I could not see why a servant of God should receive such treatment - that if I was in the right faith, doing the will of God, that He would open up the way before me, and not allow me to perish under the sore trials then surrounding me. I had seriously considered the propriety of walking back to where the kind landlady had given us our last meal, but was soon comforted, for these words came into my mind, "He that putteth his hands to the plow, and then looketh back, is not fit for the Kingdom of Heaven;" "If ye were of the world, then the world would love its own, but because I have chosen you out of the world, the world persecuteth you;" "Ye, and all who live Godly in Christ Jesus, shall suffer persecution, while evil men and seducers shall wax worse and worse, deceiving and being deceived;" that the Son of God himself, when he entered upon the duties of *His* mission, was led into the wilderness, where He was tempted forty days and nights, and when he was hungry and asked for bread, he was told, substantially, that if his mission was of God, that God would feed him, that if hungry he could turn the stones to bread and eat. I remembered that similar sayings had been thrown into our teeth. These thoughts passed through my frame like electricity, or to use the language of one of the old prophets, it was like fire shut up in my bones; I felt renewed and refreshed from head to foot, and determined to trust in that Arm that could not be broken, to conquer and subdue the passions of my nature, and by the help of God to try and bring them in subjection to the will of the Spirit, and not of the flesh, which is carnal, sensual and devilish. I determined that there should be no lack on my part.

Daylight came at last, and we renewed our journey. I put a double guard over my evil passions that were sown thickly in my sinful nature. The passion most dreaded by me was the lust of the flesh; that I knew to be the worst enemy to my salvation, and I determined to master it. I have walked along in silence for hours, with my heart lifted up to God in prayer, pleading with Him to give me power over my passions and sinful desires, that I might conquer and drive from my mind those besetting sins that were continually warring with the Spirit, which, if cherished or suffered to remain, would wound and grieve the Spirit and drive it away. It is written, "My Spirit will not dwell in an unholy temple." Jesus said to his followers that they were the Temple of the Living God; that if they who had charge of those temples, or bodies, allowed them to become unholy, that he would destroy that body; but those who guarded their temples, and kept them pure and holy, that he and his Father would come and take up their abode and dwell with them as a constant companion forever, even unto the end; and would guide them in all truth and show them things past, present and to come. From day to day I have kept my mind in a constant strain upon this subject. Notwithstanding this the tempter was ever on the alert, and contested every inch of ground with me. Often, while I was in the most solemn reflections, the tempter would place before me some lovely female, possessing all the allurements of her sex, to draw my mind from the contemplation of holy things. For a moment humanity would claim the victory, but quick as thought I would banish the vision from my mind, and plead with God for strength and power to resist the temptations that were besetting me, and to enable me to cast aside the love of sinful pleasures. The words of the Apostle Paul were appropriate for me at that and in future time, when he declared that he died daily to crucify the deeds of the flesh; so it was with me. I was soon convinced that I could not serve two masters, God and Mammon. When I tried to please the one I was certain to displease the other. I found that I must give myself up wholly to God and His ministry, and conduct myself as a man of God, if I would be worthy of the name of a messenger of salvation. I must have the Spirit of God to accompany my words, and carry conviction to the honest in heart. In this way I grew in grace from day to day, and I have never seen the day that I regretted taking up my cross and giving up all other things to follow and obey Christ, my Redeemer and Friend.

But I do most sincerely regret that I have ever suffered myself to be captivated by the wiles of the devil, contrary to my better judgment. I regret that I have ever listened, or given the least credence, to the many monstrous absurdities that Brigham Young has introduced into the Mormon creed, and claimed, as the successor of Joseph Smith, to have coupled with the gospel of Jesus Christ. Brigham Young has introduced many things that have no affinity with the gospel whatever; but these new doctrines are contrary, in spirit and substance, to the gospel. They are at war with the doctrines of the Church, and antagonistic to the peace, safety, and happiness of the people known as Latter Day Saints. The whole study, aim, and design of Brigham Young is to disrobe the Saints of every vestige of their remaining constitutional rights, and take from them all liberty of thought or conscience. He claims, and has claimed, since he became the head of the Church, that the will and acts of the people must all be dictated by him. The people have no right to exercise any will of their own. In a word, he makes himself out to be as infallible as the God of the universe, and delights in hearing the apostles and elders declare to the people that he, Brigham Young, *is God*. He claims that the people are answerable to him as to their God. That they must obey his every beck and call. It matters not what he commands or requests the people to do, it is their duty to hear and obey. To disobey the will of Brigham Young is, in his mind, a sin against the Holy Ghost, and is an unpardonable sin to be wiped out only by blood atonement. The followers of Brigham Young are serfs, slaves, and willing instruments to carry out the selfish designs of the man that disgraces the seat once occupied by God's chosen Prophet, Joseph Smith.

I must now resume my narrative, but I will hereafter speak of Brigham Young more at length.

We left the *Fasting Hotel*, so I called it, and traveled to Hamilton, Ohio, then a neat little town. As we arrived in the center of the town, I felt impressed to call at a restaurant, kept by a foreigner. It was then noon. This was the first house we had called at since morning. As we entered, the proprietor requested us to unstrap our valises and sit down and rest, saying we looked very tired. He asked where we were from, and where we were going. We answered all his questions. He then offered us refreshments; we informed him that we had no money, and had eaten nothing for three days. He said it made no difference to him, that if we had no money we were more welcome than if we had plenty of it. We then eat a hearty meal, and he gave us a drink of cider. He then filled our knapsacks with buns, cheese, sausages, and other things, after which he bid us God speed. We traveled on with hearts full of gratitude to God, the bountiful Giver, who had opened the heart of the stranger who had just supplied our wants, and we felt grateful to and blessed the man for his generous actions. While passing through Cincinnati we were offered refreshments by a lady that kept an inn. We crossed the Ohio River at Cincinnati, and stopped over night at a hotel on the Kentucky side of the river. We then traveled through Kentucky and into Overton and Jackson Counties, Tennessee.

I now bear testimony, though many years have passed since then, that from the moment that I renewed my covenant to deny myself of all unrighteousness, and decided to live the life of a man devoted to God's work on earth, I have never felt that I was alone, or without a Friend powerful to aid, direct and shield me at all times and during all troubles.

I stopped with my friend Levi Stewart at the houses of his relatives in Overton and Jackson Counties, and preached several times. My friend Stewart was blessed with a large bump of self esteem. He imagined that he could convert all of his relations at once; that all he had to do was to present the gospel, and they would gladly embrace it. He appeared to forget that a prophet was not without honor, save in his own country and among his own kinfolks. Stewart, though I was his superior in the priesthood, if not in experience and ability, looked upon me as a cipher, fit for nothing. The rough treatment and slights that I received from him were more than humiliating to a man of fine feelings and a proud spirit, such as I possessed. I said nothing to him, but I poured out my soul in secret prayer to my Heavenly Father, asking him to open the door for my deliverance, so that my proud spirit, which was bound down, might have a chance to soar in a free element.

One Sunday we attended a Baptist meeting. We sat facing the preacher, but at the far side of the house. My mind was absorbed in meditating upon my future labors. Gradually I lost consciousness of my surroundings, and my whole being seemed in another locality. I was in a trance and saw future events. What I then saw was to me a reality, and I will describe it as such. I traveled, valise in hand, in a strange land, and among a people that I had never seen. I was kindly received by the people, and all, my wants were supplied without my having to ask for charity. I traveled on, going over a mountainous country. I crossed a clear, handsome river, and was kindly received by the family of the over of the ferry at the river. I stayed with this family for some days. I then recrossed the river and called at a house, where I asked for a drink of water, which was given to me. I held quite a conversation with two young women. They informed me that there was no minister in the neighborhood; also that their father had gone in pursuit of a Mormon preacher that had passed that way a few days before. A few days passed, and I saw myself in the midst of a large congregation, to whom I was preaching. I also baptized a large number and organized quite a flourishing branch of the Church there, and was in charge of that people. I was very popular with, and almost worshiped by my congregation. I saw all this, and much more, when my vision closed.

My mind gradually changed back, and I found myself sitting in the meeting house, where I had been just forty minutes before. This was an open day vision, in which the curtains of heaven were raised and held aside from futurity to allow me to look into the things which were to come. A feeling of heavenly rapture filled my being, so much so that, like the apostle who was caught up into the third heaven, I did not know whether I was in the body or out of it during my vision. I saw things that it would be unlawful for men to utter. While the vision lasted my soul was lighted up as if illuminated with the candle of God. When the vision closed, the hallowed influence gradually withdrew; yet leaving sufficient of its glorious influence upon my soul to justify me in feeling and knowing that I was then chosen of God as a servant in his earthly kingdom; and I was also made to know, by my sensations, that my vision was real, and would soon be verified in every particular.

At the close of the church services, we returned to our lodgings.

Stewart asked me if I was sick. I said, "No, I am not sick, but I feel serious; yet I am comfortable." That evening, after I had given some time to secret prayer, I retired to rest. Very soon afterwards the vision returned, though somewhat varied. I was in the midst of a strange people, to whom I was propounding the gospel. They received it with honest hearts, and looked upon me as a messenger of salvation. I visited from house to house, surrounded by friends and kindred spirits, with whom I had once been familiar in another state of existence. I was in the spirit, and communing with the host of spirits that surrounded me; and encouraged me to return to the body, and continue to act the part that my Master had assigned me. No person, except those who have entered by pureness of heart and constant communion with God, can ever enter into the joyous host, with whom I then, and in after life, held intercourse.

When I came to myself in the morning, I determined to travel until the end of time, to find the people and country that God had shown me in my first vision; and I made my arrangements to start forth again, knowing that God now went with me.

I started off the next morning, after having a talk with Brother Stewart. He tried to dissuade me from going, saying I had little experience, not sufficient to warrant my traveling alone, that we had better remain together where we were for a season, for we had a home there, and we could study and inform ourselves, more thoroughly before starting out among strangers. I told him that, in and of my own strength I was but a weak vessel; but my trust was in God, and unless He would bless my labors I could not accomplish much. That I was God's servant, engaged in His work, therefore I looked to Him for strength and grace sufficient to sustain me in my day of trial. That I trusted in the arm of God alone, and not in one of flesh.

I started off in a southwesterly course, over the Cumberland Mountains, and went about seventy miles through a heavily timbered country. I found many species of wild fruit in abundance along the way. Springs of pure, cold water were quite common. I passed many little farms and orchards of cultivated fruit, such as cherries, peaches, pears and apples. As I proceeded, the country became familiar to me, so much so that I soon knew I was on the very ground I had seen in my vision in the Baptist Church. I saw the place where I had held my first meeting, and my joy was great to behold with my eyes what I had seen through a glass darkly. I turned aside from the road, and beneath the spreading branches of the forest trees I lifted my heart with gratitude to God for what he had done for me. I then went to the house where I had seen the multitude assemble, and where I was preaching. I saw the two young ladies there that I had beheld in my vision. They appeared to me as though I had known them from infancy, they so perfectly accorded with those that I had seen while God permitted me to see into futurity. Yes, I saw the ladies, but their father was gone from home. I asked for a drink of water, and it was handed to me, as I had seen it done in my vision. I asked them if there had ever been any Mormon preachers in that country. They said there had not been any there. The young ladies were modest and genteel in behavior.

I passed on to the Cumberland River, was set over the river by the ferryman and lodged at his house. So far all was natural, it was part of what God had shown me; but I was then at the outer edge of my familiar scenery. I stayed about a week with the ferryman. His name was Vanleven, a relative of my friend and banker in Illinois. I made myself useful while there. I attended the ferry, and did such work as I could see needed attending to. I also read and preached Mormon doctrines to the family. On the fifth day after reaching the ferry, I saw five men coming to the ferry. I instantly recognized one of them as the man I had seen in my vision- the man that took me to his house to preach. My heart leaped for joy, for God had sent him in answer to the prayers I had offered to God, asking that the man should be sent for me. I crossed the men over and back again, and although I talked considerably to the man about what was uppermost in my mind, he said nothing about my going home with him. I was much disappointed. I retired for secret prayer, and asked God, in the name of His Son Jesus Christ, to aid me, to send the man whom I had seen in my vision back for me. Before I left my knees I had an evidence that my prayer was answered. The next morning at daylight I informed my friends that I must depart in search of my field of labor. They asked me to stay until breakfast, but I refused. One of the negroes put me over the river, and directed me how to cross the mountains on the trail that was much shorter than the wagon road. I stopped in a little cove and ate a number of fine, ripe cherries. I then went on until I reached what to me was enchanted ground. I met the two sisters at the gate, and asked them if their father was at home. "No, he is not at home," said the ladies, "he has gone to the ferry to see a Mormon preacher, and see if he can get him to come here and preach in this neighborhood," and then said I must have met him on the road. I told them that I had come over the trail, and said I was probably the man he had gone for. They replied, "Our father said that if you came this way, to have you stop and stay here until his return, and to tell you that you are welcome to preach at our house at any time." This was on Friday. I took out my pencil and wrote a notice that I would preach at that place on the following Sunday, at ten o'clock, A.M. I handed it to the girls. They agreed to have the appointment circulated. I passed on and preached at a place twelve miles from there, and returned in time for my appointment. When I arrived within sight of the place of meeting, I was filled with doubt and anxiety. I trembled all over, for I saw that a vast concourse of people had come to hear an inexperienced man preach the gospel. I went into the grove and again prayed for strength and assistance from my Father in Heaven, to enable me to speak His truth aright. I felt strengthened and comforted. As I arose from prayer, these words came into my mind, "Truth is mighty and will prevail."

I waited until the hour arrived for preaching; then I approached the place where I had once been in a vision. This meeting place was in a valley, near a bold, pure spring; on either side was a high, elevated country; in the centre of this valley there stood a large blacksmith and wagon shop, surrounded with a bower of brush wood, to protect the audience from the sun. This bower would seat one thousand people. In the centre of the bower they had erected a frame work or raised platform for a pulpit.

I took my place and preached for one hour and a half. My tongue was like the pen of a ready writer. I scarcely knew what I was saying. I then opened the doors of the Church for the admission of members. Five persons joined the Church, and I appointed another meeting for that night. I again preached, when two more joined the Church. The next day I baptized the seven new members. I then arranged to hold meetings at that place three times a week. I visited around the country, seeking to convert sinners, while not engaged at this place. The first converts were leading people in that county. Elisha Sanders and his wife and daughter were the first to receive the gospel. Sanders was a farmer; he had a large flouring mill, owned a wood yard, and was engaged in boatbuilding on the Cumberland River. Caroline C. Sanders had volunteered to publish the appointment of my first meeting, which I left with the daughters of Mr. Smith.

I labored at this place two months, and baptized twenty-eight persons, mostly the heads of families. I then organized them into a Branch of the Church. Brother Sanders fitted up a room very handsomely for me, in which I could retire for study, fast and secret prayer. I was made to feel at home there, and felt that God had quite fully answered my prayers. I had the knowledge that God's Spirit accompanied my words, carrying conviction to the hearts of sinful hearers, and gave me souls as seals to my ministry.

Brother Stewart soon preached himself out at his relatives' neighborhood. He heard of my success, and came to me. He said that the people where he had been preaching were an unbelieving set. I introduced him to the members of my congregation, and had him preach with me a few times, which gratified him very much. One Sunday we were to administer the Ordinance of Baptism. Several candidates were in attendance. Brother Stewart was quite anxious to baptize the people. I was willing to humor him. So I said, "My friends, Brother Stewart, a priest of the New Dispensation, will administer the Ordinance of Baptism." The people stood still; no one would go forward, or consent for him to baptize them. They said they would not be baptized until I would baptize them myself. I told them I would act if they desired it. So I baptized the people, and Brother Stewart was much offended with them. He had not yet learned that he that exalteth himself shall be cast down, and he that humbleth himself shall be exalted.

I then called on the people for a contribution, to get some clothing for Brother Stewart. I had concluded to have him return home, and wished to clothe him up before he started, for he was then quite in need of it. The contribution was more liberal than I expected.

I stayed there some three weeks after Brother Stewart had started for home. Then I made up my mind to go home and visit my family. Brother E. Sanders invited me to go to Gainsborough with him, where he presented me with a nice supply of clothing. Caroline C. Sanders presented me with a fine horse, saddle and bridle, and $12 in money. The congregation gave me $50, and I had from them an outfit worth over $300. I at first refused to accept the horse, but Miss Sanders appeared so grieved at this that I finally took it. I left my congregation in charge of Elder Julien Moses, and started for my family about the 1st of October, 1839. I promised to call on my flock the next Spring, or to send a suitable minister to wait upon them.

When I reached Vandalia, Illinois, I found my family well. God had raised up friends for them in my absence. The Saints were then gathering at Commerce, Hancock County, Illinois. I visited my sister's family that Fall; they then lived about one hundred miles north of Vandalia. I preached often through Central Illinois, and that Fall I baptized all of my wife's family, except her father. He held out and refused the gospel until he was on his death bed; then he demanded baptism, but being in a country place he died before an elder could be procured to baptize him. But by the rules of our Church a person can be baptized for the dead, and so he was saved to eternal life by the baptism of one of his children for the salvation of his soul.

CHAPTER VIII

LEE CONTINUES HIS MISSIONARY WORK

SHORTLY after my return to Illinois, I built a house for my family, and that Winter assisted my brother-in-law, Richard Woolsey, to do his work in the blacksmith shop. I sometimes visited my wife's sister Nancy and family. They lived on the Four-Mile Prairie, in Fayette County, Illinois. Nancy had married a man named Thomas Gatewood; he was known in that county as young *Tom*, as his father's name was Thomas. Nancy was the second wife of young Tom. His first wife left one child, a boy; he was quite a lad then, and very chubby. The people when speaking of the Gatewood family, would designate them in this way, "Old Tom," "Young Tom," and "Tom Body," and I understand this name stuck to them for many years.

During the Winter I entered into a trading and tracking business with G. W. Hickerson. We would go over the country and buy up chickens, butter, feathers, beeswax; coon skins, etc., and haul them to St. Louis, and carry back calicoes and other goods in payment for the articles first purchased. We made some money that way. While carrying on this trade I drew the remainder of my money from my friend, Vanleven, and began my preparations for again joining the Saints at Nauvoo. About the middle of April, 1840, 1 succeeded in securing a good outfit, and with my old friend Stewart, again joined the Saints at Nauvoo. I felt it to be God's will that I must obey the orders of the Prophet, hence my return to the society of the brethren.

Joseph Smith, and his two counselors, his brother Hyrum and Sidney Rigdon, had been released from jail in Richmond, Missouri, and were again at the head of the Church, and directing the energies of the brethren. It was the policy of Joseph Smith to hold the city lots in Nauvoo at a high price, so as to draw money from the rich, but not so high as to prevent the poor from obtaining homes. The poor who lost all their property in following the Church were presented with a lot free, in the center of the city. The Prophet told them not to sell their lots for less

WINTER IN ILLINOIS

than $800 to $1,000, but to sell for that when offered, then they could take a cheaper lot in the outskirts of the city, and have the money to fix up comfortably. All classes, Jews and Gentiles, were allowed to settle there, one man's money was as good as another. No restrictions were then placed on the people; they had the right to trade with any one that suited them. All classes attended meetings, dances, theatres, and other gatherings, and were permitted to eat and drink together. The outsiders were invited to join in all of our amusements. Ball was a favorite sport with the men, and the Prophet frequently took a hand in the sport. He appeared to treat all men alike, and never condemned a man until he had given him a fair trial to learn what was in him.

Among the first things done was the laying of the foundation of the Temple. When this was done each man was required to do one day's work in every ten days, in quarrying rock or doing other work for the Temple. A company was sent up the Mississippi River to the Pineries to get out lumber for the Temple and other public buildings. The money for city lots went into the Church treasury to purchase materials for the Temple, which could not be supplied by the Saints' own labor.

At the conference in April, 1840, the Prophet delivered a lengthy address upon the history and condition of the Saints. He reminded the brethren that all had suffered alike for the sake of the gospel. The rich and the poor had been brought to a common level by persecution; that many of the brethren were owing debts that they had been forced to contract in order to get out of Missouri alive. He considered it was unchristian-like for the brethren to demand the payment of such debts; that he did not wish to screen any one from the just payment of his debts, but he did think that it would be for the glory of the kingdom if the people would, of their own will, freely forgive each other for all their existing indebtedness, one to the other, then renew their covenants with Almighty God and with each other; refrain from evil, and *live their religion*; by this means, God's Holy Spirit would support and bless the people. The people were then asked if they were in favor of thus bringing about the year of Jubilee. All that felt so inclined were asked to make it known by raising their hands; every hand in the audience was raised. The Prophet then declared all debts of the Saints to and from each other, forgiven and wiped out. He then gave the following words of advice to the people: "I wish you all to know that because you were justified in taking property from your enemies while engaged in war in Missouri, which was needed to support you, there is now a different conditions of things existing. We are no longer at war, and you must stop stealing. When the right time comes we will go in force and take the whole State of Missouri. It belongs to us as our inheritance; but I want no more petty stealing. A man that will steal petty articles from his enemies, will, when occasion offers, steal from his brethren too. Now I command you that you that have stolen, must steal no more. I ask all the brethren to now renew their covenants and start anew to live their religion. If you will do this, and you will forgive my faults, I will forgive you your past sins." The vote was taken on this proposition, and resulted in the unanimous decision of the people to act as requested by the Prophet.

He then continued, saying that he never professed to be a perfect man. Said he, "I have my failings and passions to contend with the same as the greatest stranger to God has. I am tempted the same as you are, my brethren. I am not infallible. All men are subject to temptation, but they are not justified in yielding to their passions and sinful natures. There is a constant warfare between the two natures of man. This is the warfare of the Saints. It is written that the Lord would have a tried people - a people that would be tried as gold as tried by the fire, even seven times tried and purified from the dross of unrighteousness. The chances of all men for salvation are equal. True, some have greater capacity than others, yet the chances for improving our minds and subduing our passions by denying ourselves of all unrighteousness and cultivating the principles of purity are all the same; they are within the reach of every man; all have their free agency; all can lay hold of the promises of eternal life, if they will only be faithful and comply with God's will and obey the priesthood in these last days. Never betray any one, for God hates a traitor, and so do I," said the Prophet. Then he said, "Stand by each other; never desert a friend, especially in the hour or trouble. Remember that our reward consists in doing good acts and *not* in long prayers like the Scribes and Pharisees of old, who prayed to be seen of men. Never mind what men think of you, if your hearts are right before God. It is written, 'Do unto others as you would that others should do unto you.' The first commandment is, 'Thou shalt love the Lord thy God with all thy heart, mind and strength.' The second commandment is, 'Thou shalt love thy neighbor as thyself.' Upon these two hang all the law and the prophets." To more deeply impress these truths upon the minds of his people, the Prophet gave them an account of the man who fell among thieves and was relieved by the stranger, and he also taught us from the Scriptures, as well as by the revelations that he had received from God, that it is humane acts and deeds of kindness, justice and words of truth, that are accounted to man for righteousness; that prayers made to be heard by men, and hypocritical groans, are displeasing to God. The Prophet talked to us plainly, and fully instructed us in our duty and gave the long-faced hypocrites such a lecture that. much good was done. I had at that time learned to dread a religious fanatic, and I was pleased to hear the Prophet lay down the law to them. A fanatic is always dangerous, but a religious fanatic is to be dreaded by all men - there is no reason in one of them. I cannot understand how men will blindly follow fanatical teachers. I always demanded a reason for my belief, and hope I will never become a victim of fanaticism.

During the summer of 1840 I built a house and such other buildings as I required on my lot on Warsaw street, and was again able to say I had a *home*.

The brethren were formed into military companies, that year, in Nauvoo. Col. A. P. Rockwood was drill master. Rockwood was then a Captain, but was afterwards promoted to Colonel of the Militia or Host of Israel. I was then fourth corporal of a company. The people were regularly drilled and taught military tactics, so that they would be ready to act when the time came for returning to Jackson County, the promised land of our inheritance. Most of my wife's relatives came to Nauvoo that year, and settled near my house.

In 1841 I was sent on a mission through Illinois, Kentucky and Tennessee. I also visited portions of Arkansas. I traveled in company, on that mission, with Elder Franklin Edwards. I was then timid about speaking in towns or cities. I felt that I had not sufficient experience to justify me in doing so. My comrade had less experience than I had, and the worst of it, he would not study to improve his mind or permit me to study in quiet. He was negligent, and did not pay sufficient attention to secret prayer, to obtain that nearness to God that is so necessary for a minister to have if he expects his works to be blessed with Divine favor. I told him he must do better, or go home. He promised to do better; also agreed that he would do the begging for food and lodging, and I might do the preaching. I accepted the offer, and in this way we got along well and pleasantly for some time.

At the crossing of the Forkadeer River we staid over night with the ferryman, and were well entertained. When we left the ferry, the old gentleman told us that we would be in a settlement of Methodist people that evening, and that they were set in their notions, and hated Mormons

as bad as the Church of England hated the Methodists, and if we got
food or shelter amongst them, he would be mistaken. He said for us to
begin to ask for lodging by at least an hour by sun, or we would not get
it. In the after part of the day we remembered the advice of the morning
and stopped at every house. The houses were about half a mile apart. We
were refused at every house. The night came on dark and stormy, the
rain fell in torrents, while heavy peals of thunder and bright flashes of
lightning were constant, or seemed so to me. The timber was very
heavy, making the night appear darker than it would otherwise have
been. The road was badly cut up with heavy freight teams passing over
it, and the holes were full of water. We fell into many holes of mud and
water, and were soon well soaked. About ten o'clock we called at the
house of a Methodist class leader, and asked him for lodging and food.
He asked who we were. We told him that we were Mormon preachers.
As soon as he heard the name Mormon, he became enraged, and said no
Mormon could stay in his house. We started on. Soon afterwards we
heard him making efforts to set his dogs on us. The dogs came running
and barking, as a pack of hounds always do. Brother Edwards was much
frightened, but I told him not to be scared, I would protect him. So when
the dogs came near us I commenced to clap my hands and shouted like
the fox was just ahead of us; this caused the whole pack of dogs to rush
on and leave us in safety. In this way we escaped injury from the pack
of ten or more dogs that the Methodist had put on our trail. The next
house we came to we were again refused shelter or food. I asked for permission to sit under his porch until the rain stopped. "No" said he, "if
you were not Mormons, I would gladly entertain you, but as you are
Mormons I dare not permit you to stop around me." This made twenty
one houses that we had stopped at and asked for lodging, and at each
place had been refused, simply because we were Mormons. About midnight my partner grew very sick of his contract to do the begging, and
was resolved to die before he would ask for aid from such people again.
I told him I would have both food and lodging at the next place we
stopped. He said it was useless to make the attempt, and I confess that
the numerous refusals we had met with were calculated to dishearten
many a person, but I had faith in God. I had never yet gone to Him in
an humble and penitent manner without receiving strength to support
me, nor had he ever sent me emptyhanded from Him. My trust was in
God, and I advanced to the next house confident that I would not ask in
vain. As we approached the house we discovered that some negroes

were having a dance. I asked where their master was; they pointed out the house to me. We walked to the house, and up on the porch. The door was standing open, a candle was burning, and near the fire a woman was sitting holding a sick child on her lap. The man was also sitting near the fire. Our footsteps attracted their attention; our appearance was not inviting as we stood there wet, muddy and very tired. I spoke in a loud voice, saying, "Sir, I beseech you, in the name of Jesus Christ, to entertain us as servants of the living God. We are ministers of the gospel, we travel without purse or scrip; we preach without hire, and are now without money; we are wet, weary and hungry; we want refreshments, rest and shelter." The man sprang to his feet, but did not say a word. His wife said, "Tell them to come in." I said, "We will do you no harm, we are friends, not enemies." We were invited in. Servants were called, a good fire was made and a warm supper placed before us. After eating we were shown to a good bed. We slept until near ten o'clock in the morning. When we did awaken, our clothes were clean and dry, and a good breakfast was ready and waiting for us. In fact, we were as well treated as it was possible to ask for.

This family had lately come from the State of Virginia, intending to try that climate for a year, and then if they liked it, they intended to purchase land and stay there permanently. After breakfast, the gentleman said, "You had a severe time of it amongst the Christians yesterday and last night. As you are ministers, sent out to convert sinners, you cannot do better than to preach to these Christians, and seek to convert them." He offered to send word all over the settlement, and notify the people, if we would only stay there and preach that night. We accepted his offer, and remained that day; thus securing the rest that we so much needed, and thanking God for still remembering and caring for us, His servants.

Agreeably to arrangements, previously made, we preached in the Methodist meeting-house, to a very attentive audience, upon the subject of the first principles of the gospel; alluded to the treatment of Christ and his followers by the Pharisees and Sadducees, the religious sects of those days, and that we preached the same gospel, and fared but little better. This meeting house was built on the line between the Methodists and Universalists. Members from both persuasions were present. Our neighbor, who fed and cared for us, leaned to the latter faith. At the close of our remarks, the class-leader, who had set the hounds on our track, was the first to the stand to invite us home with him.

I told him that the claims of those who did not set their dogs on us, after they had turned us from their doors hungry, were first with me - that his claims with me were an after consideration. He said it was his negro boys that sent the hounds after us, but he would not be bluffed. He said that one of us had to go with him - that if I would not go Frank must go. I told him that Elder Edwards could use his own pleasure, but I would hold a meeting that night with those Universalist brethren, and thus we parted. Elder Edwards went to spend the night with the class-leader, and attended the meeting with the friends who had invited him home with them. I had a good time. Of their own accord they made up a collection of a few dollars, as a token of their regard for me. I was to meet Elder Edwards at the house of my friend, who took us in at midnight from the storm, by an hour by sun, to start on; but he did not put in his appearance for an hour or more. When he got within talking distance I saw by his features that he had been roughly dealt with. His first words were, "That is the wickedest old man that I ever met with, and if he don't repent God will curse him." That was enough, and I began to laugh. I conceived what he had to encounter the long night before. He said, "If the Lord will forgive me for going this time I will never go again, without you are along." I said to him, "Frank, experience teaches a dear school, yet fools will not learn at any other. I knew what treatment you would receive, and refused to go with him. If you had been a wise man you would have taken the hint and kept away from him."

We made our way through to Overton County, Tennessee. Here I advised my friend Edwards to return back to Nauvoo, and gave him money to pay his fare on a steamer, as he was cut out for anything but a preacher.

At Carlisle, the county seat of Overton County, I met with a young man, an elder, by the name of Dwight Webster. Though but little experienced, be was a man of steady habits and an agreeable companion. We held a number of meetings together in this part of the country. Webster and Moses had been companions together, and met with much opposition. Webster and I baptized several persons, and made a true friend of a wealthy merchant, named Armstrong, who welcomed us to his house and placed us under his protection. He also owned a large establishment in Louisville, Kentucky. He was an infidel, though an honorable and highminded gentleman. His wife Nancy, and her sister Sarah, were both baptized.

While here I received a letter from James Pace, one of my near neighbors in Nauvoo, requesting me to visit his brother, William Pace, and his

relatives in Rutherford County, Tenn. Elder A. 0. Smoot and Dr. David
Lewis succeeded us in this county and in Jackson County, Tenn., and
added many to those whom we had already baptized. We made our way
through to Stone River, preaching by the way, as opportunity occurred.
Here I handed my letter of introduction to William Pace, brother of my
neighbor James Pace, who received us very kindly and procured us the
liberty of holding forth in the Campbellite Chapel. Here we were
informed that the Campbellite preachers were heavy on debate, that
none of the other sects could stand before them, and they dare not meet
them in public or private discussion. I replied that my trust was in God,
that the message I had to bear was from Heaven - that if it would not
bear the scrutiny of man I did not want to stand by it, but if it was of
God, He would not suffer His servants to be confounded, if they were
only honorable and trusted in him.

Truth is mighty and will prevail; Error cannot stand before Truth. If
these men can overthrow the gospel which I preach, the sooner they do
it the better for me. I do not wish to deceive any one, or to deceive
myself. If any one can point on an error in the gospel which I preach, I
am willing to drop that error, and exchange it for truth.

The hour came, we both spoke. We spoke on the first principles of the
gospel of Christ, as taught by the Saviour and his apostles. Before sitting down I extended the courtesy to any gentleman that wished, to
reply or offer any remarks either for or against what we had set forth.
Parson Hall, the presiding Campbellite minister, was on his feet in a
moment and denounced us as impostors. He said we were holding forth
a theory that was fulfilled in Christ; that the canon of Scripture being
full, these spiritual gifts that were spoken of in the New Testament were
done away with, being no longer necessary; that as for the "Golden
Bible" (Book of Mormon), that was absurd in the extreme, as there were
to be no other books or revelations granted. He quoted the revelations
of St. John in his support, where it reads, "He that addeth to, or dimin-
isheth from the words of the prophecies and this Book, shall have the
plagues herein written added to his torment," or words to that effect. I
followed him in the discussion, and quoted John where it reads, "He that
speaketh not according to the law and the testimony hath no light in
him." I said that my authority and testimony were from the Bible, the
book of the law of the Lord, which all Christian believers hold as a
sacred rule of their faith and practice. To that authority I hoped my worthy friend would not object. I illustrated my position by further quota-

tions from the Scriptures, and when our meeting was over the people flocked around us in a mass, to shake hands with us and invite us to their houses - the Methodists, Baptists and Presbyterians especially. The planters in this county were mostly wealthy, and prided themselves on being hospitable and kind to strangers, especially to ministers of the gospel. We went from house to house and preached from two to three times a week. We saw that the seed had already been sown in honest hearts and we were near to them. Knowing the danger of being lifted up by self-approbation, I determined to be on my guard, to attend to secret prayer, and reading and keeping diaries. When at our friend Pace's house we would frequently resort to a lonely grove to attend to prayer and read to ourselves.

CHAPTER IX

MORMONISM - ITS DOCTRINES, AND HOW IT ORIGINATED

A SHORT time after the events narrated in the preceding chapter, it was arranged that Parson Hall and myself should bold another discussion at the Campbellite Chapel. Parson Hall did not want to meet me in the discussion, but he had to do so or lose his flock, as all the people had become interested in the subject of Mormonism.

We met at the appointed time, and chose two umpires to act as moderators of the meeting. The subject to be discussed was: "Are apostles, prophets, teachers, etc., together with the spiritual gifts spoken of, as recorded by the Apostle Mark in his 16th chapter, necessary to be in the Church now as they were then?" I took the affirmative, the Parson the negative; the discussion lasted six hours. In his closing speech Parson Hall became very abusive and denounced the Mormons to the lowest regions of darkness, and the Prophet, Joseph Smith, as a vile impostor. I replied to him and closed the discussion. It was agreed that the Old and New Testaments should be the only authorities to be quoted by us. The umpires refused to decide who had the best of the discussion. They said it rested with the people to decide for themselves. It was evident, however, that the people were with me. The principal topic of conversation was about this strange Mormon doctrine.

Parson Hall's flock was by no means satisfied with his course. He said this Mormon doctrine was the strongest Bible doctrine he ever heard of, and he feared the consequences of a further discussion of it. But this would not satisfy the people, who wanted to hear and learn more of it; so another discussion was agreed upon, in which Parsons Curlee and Nichols were to assist Parson Hall, and prompt him.

The subject was, "Is the Book of Mormon of Divine origin, and has it come forth in direct fulfillment of prophecy? And was Joseph Smith inspired of God?" I had the affirmative. We selected three judges; the hall was thronged. I felt the responsibility of my situation, but I put my trust in God to give me light and utterance to the convincing of the hon-

est and pure in heart. The discussion lasted many hours. I showed con-
clusively, both from the Old and New Testaments, that, in accordance
with scripture and prophecy, the ten tribes of Israel had been broken up
and scattered upon the face of the earth. That sure and indisputable evidence had been found and produced, by which it was certain that the
tribes of North American Indians were descendants from the ten tribes
of Israel. I showed that from many customs and rites, prevalent among
the Indians, that there could be no doubt, in any rational mind, but that
these tribes had sprung from the remnants of the scattered ten tribes of
Israel. The prophecies of the Old and New Testaments, the traditions
and history of the Indians, so far as known, their solemn religious rites
and observances, were conclusive evidence of this fact. And God has
repeatedly promised that, in His own good time, these tribes of Israel,
this chosen people, should be again gathered together, that a new and
further revelation should be given them, and to the whole world, and
that under this new dispensation Zion should be rebuilt, and the glory of
God should fill the whole earth; as the waters cover the mighty deep.

It should be as a sealed book unto them, which men deliver to one
that is learned, saying, "Read this book," and he saith, "I cannot, for it
is a sealed book." It is strange that a people, once so favored of God,
strengthened by His arm and counseled by his prophets and inspired
men, should have so far wandered and become so lost to all sense of
duty to God! But so it was, until, as the prophet says, the Book that
should come unto them, should speak to them out of the ground - out of
the dust of the earth; as a "familiar spirit, even out of the dust of the
earth." The Book that was to contain the divine revelation of God was
to come forth, written upon plates, in a language unknown to men." But
a man unlearned, not by his own power, but by the power of God, by
means of the Urim and Thummim, was to translate it into our language.
And this record, in due time, came according to God's will. It was found
deposited in the side of a mountain, or hill, called Cumorrah, written in
the reformed Egyptian language, in Ontario County, in the State of New
York. It was deposited in a stone box, put together with cement, air
tight. The soil about the box was worn away, until a corner of the box
was visible. It was found by Joseph Smith, then an illiterate lad, or
young man, who had been chosen of God as His instrument for making
the same known to men.

Joseph Smith was a young man of moral character, belonging to no
sect, but an earnest enquirer after truth. He was not permitted to remove

the box for a period of two years after he found it. The angel of God that had the records in charge, would not permit him to touch them. In attempting to do so, on one occasion, his strength was paralyzed, and the angel appeared before him and told him that that record contained the gospel of God, and an historical account of the God of Joseph on this land; that through their transgressions the records were taken away from them, and hid in the earth, to come forth at the appointed time, when the Lord should set His heart, the second time, to recover the remnant of His people, scattered through all nations; that the remnant of His people should be united with the stick of Judah, in the hands of Ephraim, and they should become one stick in the hands of the Lord. This is the Bible, which is the stick of Judah, that contained the gospel and the records of the House of Israel, till the Messiah came. The angel further informed him that when the Ten Tribes of Israel were scattered, one branch went to the north; that prior to the birth of Jesus Christ the other branch left Jerusalem, taking the records with them, of which the Book of Mormon is a part. The branch of the Ten Tribes which went north doubtless have a record also with them.

When these plates, containing the Book of Mormon and God's will, as therein revealed, were removed from Ontario County, New York, they were taken to Professor Anthon, of New York City, for translation. He replied that he could not translate them, that they were written in "a sealed language, unknown to the present age." This was just as the prophet Isaiah said it should be.

Do any of the present denominations counsel with the Lord? No, they deny revelation, and seek to hide their ways from Him. Upon all such He pronounces woe.

I do not wish to be considered as casting aspersions on any other sect. It is not my purpose to do so. The love that I have for truth, and the salvation of the human family, may cause me to offend, but if I do so it is because of my exceeding zeal to do good. Remember that the reproof of a friend is better than the smite of an enemy. Jesus said, "Woe unto you that are angry and offended because of the truth." It is not policy on your part to be offended on account of the truth. If your systems will not stand the scrutiny of men, how can they stand the test of the great judge of both the living and the dead? I place a greater value upon the salvation of my soul than I do upon all earthly considerations.

After my second discussion I began to baptize some of the leading members of the Campbellite Church. Among the first to be baptized were John Thompson and wife. Thompson was sheriff of Rutherford County, and was an influential man. Among others who were baptized were Wm. Pace and wife. Mrs. Pace was a sister of Parson Nichols, who assisted Parson Hall in his last discussion with me. Major D. M. Jarratt and wife, Mrs. Caroline Ghiliam, Major Miles Anderson, and others, were also baptized and received into the Church. My friend Webster, after being with me about a month, returned to visit and strengthen the branches of the Church established in Smith, Jackson and Overton Counties. I continued my labors here on Stone River and Cripple Creek about six months. During the most of this time I availed myself of the opportunity of studying grammar and other English branches. During my stay I lectured three times a week, on Wednesdays, Saturdays and Sunday afternoon. Sabbath forenoon I attended the meetings of other denominations. During this time I held four public discussions, in addition to those I had held with Parson Hall. I held two discussions with the Rev. James Trott, who had for fifteen years been a missionary to the Cherokee nation.

I held a closing debate in that settlement with the Rev. Mr. Cantrall, of the Campbellite faith. He came from a distance, at the request of friends, to endeavor to save the flock. After consultation with Parson Hall, and other members of the flock, they refused to submit to moderators or judges, neither were they willing to be confined to the Old and New Testaments for authority to disprove the doctrine that I defended. Their proposition was that Mr. Cantrall should speak first, bringing any argument he chose; when he had finished I was to conclude the debate, and the people were to judge for themselves who had the best of the argument. My friends would not consent to this arrangement, but I told them that they could have it their own way, that if the Rev. Cantrall wished to condescend to the platform of a blackguard, that in case of necessity I might meet him there, though I would prefer an honorable debate to slander and ridicule. This statement I made to the assembly prior to the Rev. gentleman's mounting the stand, with Parsons Hall, Curlee, Trott and Nichols as prompters.

They had provided themselves with a roll of pamphlets and newspapers, containing many of the low, dirty, musty, cunning, lying stories about Joe Smith's walking on the water, being a money digger, an impostor and a thousand such stories. Mr. Cantrall read and emphasized each story, as his prompters handed them to him. He occupied about two hours and a half in this manner, and about half an hour in trying to point

out discrepancies in the Book of Mormon. He spoke of the absurdities
of the boat that the Nephites built to cross the ocean in, from Asia to
America. That it was built tight, excepting a little hole on top, for air,
and that it would shoot through the water like a fish, and ridiculed such
an absurdity. He defied me to produce any such inconsistencies in the
Holy Bible. He said the Bible was a book of common sense, written by
men inspired of God. It was full of good works, and only pure characters, and nothing like the impostor Joe Smith. He challenged me again
to point out a single instance in the Bible which would compare with the
stories in the Book of Mormon. The idea of apostles and prophets and
supernatural gifts in the Church, as it was in the days of Christ, was
absurd. That the History of Nephi was absurd and a burlesque upon
common sense. That he hoped none of the people would be led away by
such nonsense and folly. I sat facing him during all his long harangue of
abuse and ridicule. When it came my turn to speak, I asked the reverend
gentleman to occupy my seat, that I did not want more than thirty minutes to reply. I said to the assembly that a sense of duty to the truth, and
to the cause I had espoused, alone prompted me to make any reply to
the long tirade of abuse and sarcasm they had been listening to. The
gentleman and his prompters had gathered quite an angry looking cloud
of pamphlets and newspaper slang and abuse, which culminated in a tornado of bolts of thunder, tapering off with wind, blixen and chinck-a-
pin bushes, without quoting a single passage of scripture to disprove my
position, or in support of their own. But on the contrary, he had become
an accuser of the brethren, speaking evil of things he knew not. The
spirit of persecution, hatred and malice is not the spirit of the meek and
lowly Saviour. The gentleman tells you that the day of perfection has
arrived, that Satan is bound in the gospel chain, that we have no need of
spiritual manifestations, that this is the reign of Christ. Now, I will say
if this is the millennial reign of Christ, and the devil is bound in the
gospel chain, I pity the inhabitants of the earth when he gets loose again.
After reading the description of the millennial reign, as it shall be, and
described by the prophet Isaiah, can any one be so stupid as to believe
that we are now living in that eventful day? Shame on a man who would
deceive and tamper with the souls of men! The gentleman who has told
you this don't believe it.

The gentleman has challenged me to produce anything from the
Bible equaling in strangeness the building of a boat like a fish, in which
the Nephites crossed the ocean from Asia to America. I call his attention

to the first chapter of the Book of Jonah. Here a very strange craft was used for three days and nights, in which to send a missionary to Nineveh. This craft was constructed after the manner of the boat spoken of in the Book of Mormon. If the Prophet was correct in the description of his craft, he too scooted through the water in the same way that the Nephites did in their boat. The Book of Mormon is nothing more or less than a book containing the history of a portion of the House of Israel, who left Jerusalem about the time of the reign of Zedekiah, King of Judah, and crossed the ocean to America; containing also the gospel which was preached to them on this continent, which is the same gospel as that preached by Christ and his Apostles at Jerusalem. The Bible and the Book of Mormon both contain a history of the different branches of the House of Israel, and each contains the gospel of Christ as it was preached unto them, the different branches of the house of Israel, and to all nations. Both testify of each other, and point with exactness to the dispensation of the fullness of time. The Book of Mormon does not contain a new gospel; it is the same gospel as that preached by Christ. That it is a mysterious book, is just what the Prophet said it should be, "a marvelous work, a wonder." But my friend says that it is too mysterious, too wonderful for human credence, and challenges me to point out anything told in the Bible that seems inconsistent with reason or our experience. Now, which is the most reasonable, that Nephi built a boat after the pattern mentioned in the Mormon Bible, directed by God how to build it, and crossed the ocean to this continent, or that Jonah was in the whale's belly for three days and three nights, and then made a safe landing? Or would it sound any better if Nephi had said that when he and his company came to the great waters, that the Lord had prepared great whales, two or more, to receive them and their outfit, and set them over on this side by that means? Nothing is impossible with God. If He saw fit to send Jonah on his mission in a whale's belly, I have no fault to find with Him for so doing. He has the right to do His own will and pleasure; and if he instructed Nephi how to fashion his boat, or Noah to build an ark against the deluge; or to cause Baalam's ass to speak and rebuke the madness of his master; or caused Moses to lead the children of Israel through the Red Sea, without any boat at all; or caused the walls of Jericho to fall to the ground, and the people to become paralyzed through the tooting of rams' horns; or empowered Joshua to cause the sun to stand still while he slaughtered his enemies; is any one of these things more wonderful than the other? Now any one of these instances that I have selected from the Bible, if found in the Book of Mormon, would be sufficient to stamp it with absurdity and everlasting contempt, according to argument of the gentlemen who oppose me; but when found in the Bible the story assumes another phase entirely. It is as the Saviour said of the Pharisees, "Ye strain at a gnat and swallow a camel." My opponent strains at a gnat, when found in the Book of Mormon, but if camels are found in the Bible he could swallow them by the herd. I cannot see why a big story, told in the Bible, should be believed any more readily than if found in the Book of Mormon. It is not my purpose to find discrepancies in the characters of the ancient prophets or inspired writers, but my opponent has challenged me to produce from the Bible a character of such disrepute as that of Joe Smith, the Mormon Prophet. Now I will say that of the characters that I shall mention, we have only their own history or account of what they did. Their enemies and contemporaries have long since passed away. But if their enemies could speak worse of them than they have of themselves, decency would blush to read their history. I will refer to only a few instances. Moses, the meek, as he is called, murdered an Egyptian that strove with an Israelite, and had to run away from his country for the offense. He was afterwards sent by God to bring the Israelites out of bondage.

Noah was a preacher of righteousness. He built the ark, and was saved through the deluge. His name has been handed down from posterity to posterity, in honorable remembrance, as one who feared God and worked righteousness. But we find him soon after the flood getting drunk, exposing his nakedness, and cursing a portion of his own posterity. Lot, whose family was the only God fearing family in Sodom and Gomorrah, rescued by the angel of God from the judgments that overwhelmed those cities, when only a short distance from Sodom became drunk and debauched his daughters.

Think of the conduct of David with Uriah's wife, and David was, we are told, a man after God's own heart. Also Judah, judge in Israel. Peter cursed and swore and denied his Master. The enemies of Christ said he was a gluttonous man and a wine bibber; a friend of publicans and sinners; that after the people at the marriage feast were well drunken, that he turned water into wine that they might have more to drink; that in the corn fields he plucked the ears of corn and ate them; that he saw an ass hitched, and without leave he took it and rode into Jerusalem; that he went into the Temple and overset the tables of the money changers and took cords and whaled them out, telling them they had made his Father's house a den of thieves. I am aware that all Christians justify the acts of Christ, because he was the Son of God. But the people at that time did not believe him to be the Son of God, any more than the gentleman does that Joseph Smith was the Prophet of God. I have alluded to these instances merely in refutation of the challenge imposed upon me by my opponent. But few seem to comprehend that man, in and of himself, is frail, weak, needy and dependent, although the Creator placed within his reach, as a free agent, good and evil, and has placed in the heart of every rational being a degree of light that makes us sensitive and teaches us right from wrong. As the Saviour says, "There is a light that lighteth every man that cometh into the world."

I have been obliged to abbreviate my argument very much, lest I tire my readers. I had scarcely closed speaking before my Reverend opponents were making for the door. They would have nothing more to do with the Mormon. Some were honest enough to acknowledge that Mormonism, as it was called, would stand the test; that it could not be disproved from the Bible, and that sooner or later all other creeds would have to give way to it, or deny the Bible, for the more it was investigated the more popular it would become, as it would expose the many weak points and inconsistencies of the different denominations. Others denounced it as an imposition, and warned their adherents to have nothing to do with it. This kind of talk from the pulpit only served to give Mormonism a new impetus. I soon baptized many converts, and organized branches in that and adjoining counties of over one hundred members.

CHAPTER X

LEE CASTS OUT DEVILS AND DOES OTHER WONDERFUL WORKS

A SHORT time after holding the discussion mentioned in the preceding chapter, Dr. A. Young, of Jackson County, Tenn., came to me and wished me to go with him, and join in a discussion with a couple of Campbellite preachers. At first declined, as the distance was nearly one hundred miles, and my labors in the ministry where I then was were pressing. I had more calls to preach than I could fill.

Dr. A. Young was made a bishop, and A. O. Smoot, a convert, was made an elder in the Church.

I finally consented to go and attend the discussion. On our arrival at the place agreed upon, I learned that all necessary arrangements had been made. The subject was, "Is the Book of Mormon of Divine authenticity, found in the Old and New Testaments, and is Joseph Smith Divinely inspired and called of God?" We had the affirmative. There was a large concourse of people assembled. The discussion lasted two days. At the close of the debate the judge decided that the Mormons brought forth the strongest reasonings and scriptural arguments, but that the other side had the best of the Mormons in sarcasm and abuse.

When I was about to leave Dr. Young exchanged horses with me, he keeping my pony, and giving me a very fine blooded black mare. I was then built up, so far as a good outfit for traveling was concerned. Dr. Young traveled with me as far as Indian Creek, Putnam County, twenty five miles southeast, as report said that a couple of Mormons had been "raising h--l" there, to use, their own words. So we concluded to visit the place and learn the facts. This was about the first of March. It was on Saturday that we arrived there. We rode at once to the Methodist Chapel. Here we found several hundred people assembled - the most distressed and horrified looking worshippers my eyes ever beheld. Their countenances and actions evinced an inward torture of agony. Some of them were lying in a swoon, apparently lifeless; others were barking like dogs; some singing, praying and speaking in tongues, their eyes red and distorted with excitement.

The chapel was situated in a yard surrounded with trees. I was so overcome with amazement and surprise that I had forgotten that I was on horseback. The first that I remember was that a man had led my horse inside the gate and was putting me off, saying, "Come, get down, you are a Mormon preacher; we are having fine times." I objected, but walked to the south end of the chapel, instead of going inside. A chair was set for me by some rational person, and I leaned my head upon my hands and commenced praying. I was a stranger, both to the people and to their religious exercises. I was puzzled, not knowing what to do in the situation. I saw a young woman, about eighteen years of age, of handsome form and features, in her stocking feet, her handsome black hair hanging down over her shoulders in a confused mass. She was preaching what she called Mormonism, and warning the multitude to repent and be baptized, and escape the wrath of God. In front of her stood a young Methodist minister, to whom she directed her remarks. He smiled at her. All of a sudden she changed her tack, and belted him right and left for making light of what she said. The next moment she confronted me, and said, "You are a preacher of the true Church, and I love you!" Thus saying, she sprang at me to embrace me with open arms. I stretched forth my hand and rebuked the evil spirit that was in her, and commanded it to depart in the name of the Lord Jesus, by virtue of the holy priesthood in me vested. At this rebuke she quailed, and turned away from me like a whipped child, and left the crowd and went home, ashamed of her conduct.

This occurrence gave me confidence in God, and in Him I put my trust still more than I had ever done before. It was now about sunset and we had had no refreshment since morning. I arose and informed the multitude that we would preach at that place on the morrow at ten o'clock. A merchant by the name of Marshbanks invited us home with him, some of the leading men accompanying us. They informed us that a couple of men, brothers, from West Tennessee, named William and Alfred Young, formerly members of the Baptist Church, who had joined the Mormons, had been there and preached; that they enjoyed spiritual gifts as the apostles anciently did, and had baptized the people into that faith, and had ordained John Young, Receiver of the Land Office there, a preacher; that he was an intelligent, well-educated man, but was now a fanatic, and many of their leading men were ruined and business prostrate, and all through that impostor, Joe Smith. They said he ought to be hung before he did any more harm; that their settlement was being ruined and all business stopped; that if any one would give John Young, or Mark Young, his father, who was formerly a Methodist class leader, their hand, or let them breathe in their face, he could not resist them, but would come under the same influence and join them. I told them that I had been a member of this Church for a number of years and had never seen or heard of anything of this kind.

The next morning, about day break, those two fanatics were at Marshbanks' house. They said they had a glorious time through the night, and had made a number of converts. I began to reason with them from the scriptures, but as soon as I came in contact with their folly, they began to whistle and dance, and jumped on to their horses and left.

Sometime after, on our way to the chapel my friend Marshbanks indulged in a great deal of abuse of Joe Smith. He told me that I could not be heard among the fanatics at the chapel, and that I had better return to his house and hold a meeting there.

I said to him, "In the name of the Lord Jesus Christ, I will preach there today, and not a dog will raise his voice against me, and you shall bear witness to it." He replied, "Very well. I will go with you and try and keep order." As we entered the chapel, the same scene of confusion prevailed that we observed the day before. Some were stretched on the floor, frothing at the mouth, apparently in the agonies of death. Others were prophesying, talking in tongues, singing, shouting and praying. I walked into the pulpit as a man having authority, and said, "In the name of Jesus Christ, and by virtue and authority of the Holy Priesthood invested in me, I command these evil spirits that are tormenting you, to be still, while I lay before you the word of life and salvation." As I spoke every eye was turned upon me and silence reigned; the evil spirits were subdued and made powerless. There were two Presbyterian ministers there who asked leave to take notes of my sermon, which I freely granted, telling them farther that they were at liberty to correct me if in anything I spoke not according to the Law and Testimony of Christ.

I preached a plain sermon on the first principles of the gospel of Christ, as taught by the apostles. I showed to them that the house of God was a house of order, and not confusion; that the Spirit of God brings peace, joy, light and complete harmony. The testimony of Jesus in the spirit of prophecy, and every person who has the Spirit of Jesus has the spirit of prophecy, and should and would do the will of Heaven; that one may have a gift of prophecy, another of tongues, another of interpretation - but let one speak at a time; that this fanaticism which they had witnessed during the last few days was not to be fathered upon Joseph Smith or upon the Mormons; that we had no affinity for such a religion, and that we discarded it as from beneath and not from God. Before I dismissed the meeting I asked my Presbyterian friends if they wished to reply to me. They said they did not; that they were much pleased with my remarks, and that they were scriptural and reasonable.

I then concluded to return to the Branch at Rutherford County and continue my labors there. A delegation came to me from the Assembly and said, "Mr. Lee, your discourse today has turned us up side down. You have convinced many of us that we are going astray. Do not, for mercy's sake, leave us in this situation. We are persuaded that many are honest hearted and will obey the truth." I replied, "My mission is to preach the truth, to call erring children of men to repentance." I appointed a meeting, and preached that evening at the house of David Young, a brother of Mark Young, the Methodist class leader, to a large body of inquiring minds. The following day we preached at the side of a clear running brook. After the preaching many demanded to be baptized. I went down into the water and baptized twenty-eight persons, among whom were two well educated young men. One was a nephew of Gov. Carlin, of Illinois; the other was F. McCollough, now a bishop at Alpine City, Utah.

Most of the leading families of Putnam County were converted, and I organized them into a Branch, and remained with them about ten days, teaching and instructing them, the better to establish them upon the true basis of order and equity, and to guard them against those fanatical influences that had been ruining the people of this neighborhood.

Elder Samuel B. Frost had been laboring in DeKalb County, East Tennessee, where he had baptized about thirty converts. As he passed on his return to Nauvoo, I sent for him to tarry with me a few days, and assist me, as Dr. Young had returned home. Such of the people who had been under the power of the spirit of darkness became alarmed, and dared not trust themselves away from us. We fasted and prayed three days and three nights, pleading with the Father, in the name of the Son, to give us power over those evil spirits.

And here I will say that up to the time of my witnessing what I have here narrated, I was skeptical on the subject of our power over evil spirits. I had heard of such manifestations, but had never seen them with my own eyes before. My experience here impressed me deeply, that we could attain such power, and showed me the stern necessity of living near to God, for man, in and of himself, is nothing but a tool for the tempter to play with.

As I said, the people durst not trust themselves away from us. One time we were in a large room, at Mark Young's house. I was sitting by a desk writing in my diary. Adolphus Young, the chairman of the delegation which had waited on me and requested me to remain with them and set them right, was walking to and fro across the room. As he came near me I noticed that his countenance changed, and as he turned from me he cast a fearful glance at me. I kept my eyes upon him as he walked away from me. When near the centre of the room he wilted down and exclaimed, "Oh! God have mercy on me." Without a word spoken, Elder Frost and myself sprang to him. Laying my hands upon him I commanded the evil spirits, by virtue of the Holy Priesthood, and in the name of Jesus Christ, to come out of him. As I spoke these words I felt as if a thousand darts had penetrated my mouth, throat and breast. My blood ran cold in my veins; my pulse stopped beating; in a word, I was terror stricken. I saw a legion of evil spirits in the vision of my mind. And what was still more, they had fastened their fangs in me and I was about to give up the contest, when another influence came to my relief, and said to my spirit: "Why yield to the powers of darkness? You hold the key over those evil spirits. They should be subject to your bidding the the name of Jesus, through faith." This last comforting influence relieved my fears, strengthened my faith, and gave me power to overcome the evil spirits. I was not more than a minute or two in this situation, but during that time I endured more agony, torture, and pain than I ever did in the same time before or since.

This may seem to be a fabulous story to my readers, many of whom will, no doubt, attribute it to fanaticism; nevertheless it is true. The man was restored, and bore record of the power of God to his deliverance, and was to the day of his death an honorable, good citizen.

I was never considered a long faced preacher, During my stay here I added to this Branch of the Church until it was more than fifty members strong. My friend, Elder Frost, agreed to wait in Overton County until I could revisit the Branch in Rutherford County, and set things in order there. Then I was to accompany him home to our families in Nauvoo, the City of Joseph. I ordained William Pace to the office of the lesser priesthood, to take charge of the Saints there. We also ordained Adolphus Young to preside over the Branch at Indian Creek, Putnam

County. After calling on Dr. A. Young, I joined my friend, Elder Frost, and drove to Nauvoo for him six jacks and jennets to exchange for land, that he might have a place to come to. We had a pleasant journey to Nauvoo, as the weather was fine. On arriving in the city I met my family, all in good health. I traded some of my stock with Hyrum Smith, the Prophet's brother, for land.

It was now June, 1842. In the summer and fall I built me a snug, two story brick house on Warsaw street, and made my family quite comfortable. I enclosed my ground and fixed things snug and nice. I then took a tour down through Illinois. H. B. Jacobs accompanied me as a fellow companion on the way. Jacobs was bragging about his wife and two children, what a true, virtuous, lovely woman she was. He almost worshiped her. But little did he think that, in his absence, she was sealed to the Prophet Joseph, and was his wife.

We raised up quite a Branch of the Church in Clinton County. Among others whom we baptized, were the Free sisters, Louisa and Emeline; also the Nelsons. Emeline Free was afterward sealed to Brigham Young, and her sister Louisa to myself. She is now Daniel H. Wells' first wife.

I also visited my relatives in Randolph County, the home of my youthful days. Here I baptized my cousin Eliza Conners, with whom I had been raised. I also baptized Esther Hall, the sister of my old friend Samuel Hall, with whom I lived when I was first married. I was kindly received in my own county.

But few, however, cared to investigate the principles of Mormonism, as the most of them were Catholics. In all my travels I was agent for our paper, the *Nauvoo Neighbor*, and collected means, tithings and donations for the building of the Temple. From here I returned home by steamboat.

Through the winter Joseph Smith selected forty men for a city guard, from the old tried veterans of the cause. I was the seventh man chosen. These men were also the lifeguard of the Prophet and Patriarch and of the twelve Apostles. My station as a guard was at the Prophet's mansion, during his life, and after his death my post was changed to the residence of Brigham Young, he being the acknowledged successor of the Prophet. From the time I was appointed until we started across the plains, when at home I stood guard every night, and much of the time on the road, one-half of the night at a time, in rain, hail, snow, wind and cold, to nourish, protect and guard, and give strength to the man that has proven to be the most treacherous, ungrateful villain on earth. In return for all of my faithfulness and fidelity to him and the cause that he taught, he has wantonly sacrificed me in a dastardly and treacherous manner. But I must not think or reflect too much upon so frail a being. He has contracted the debt himself, and sooner or later must atone for his own sins. "Vengeance is mine, saith the Lord, and I will repay." Such a base, vile, inhuman wretch, cannot long escape justice. However, I intend to speak more fully of this depraved man at the proper time and place in this narrative.

CHAPTER XI

DURING the winter of 1841, a letter was sent to the Prophet from the leading men and members of the Branch Church on Stone River, Tennessee, and Cripple Creek, Rutherford County, Tennessee, desiring him to send me back to labor in that country, as there was a wide field for preaching there.

They stated that I had so ingratiated myself among the people that no other man could command the influence and respect to do good that I could among them. This was enough. In the latter part of February I took leave of my family and entered upon my mission.

To refuse to comply with the call of the Prophet is a bad omen. A man so doing is looked upon with distrust, renders himself unpopular, and is considered a man not to be depended upon. At the time I started the river was blocked with ice. I traveled on foot, without purse or scrip, like the apostles of old, carrying out the motto of the Church, the bee of the desert, "Leave the hive emptyhanded and return laden." In this way I, as well as many other elders, brought in money, thousands of dollars, yearly to the Church, and I might say many hundreds of thousands, as the people among whom I traveled were mostly wealthy, and when they first received the love of the truth their hearts as well as their purses were opened, and they would pour out their treasures into the lap of the Bishop. All were taught that a liberal man deviseth liberal things, and by his liberality shall he live, and that he that soweth liberally shall reap bountifully, etc.

As I passed along my way, I strengthened the brethren of the various Branches, reminding them of their duties, especially of the necessity of building the Temple. That duty was more important than all others, for in that alone, when completed, they could attain to the highest exaltation of the Priesthood, together with all the spiritual gifts that belong thereto. When I arrived at my old home, the place of my childish days, I found Elder John Twist, who was waiting my arrival. We staid in that neighborhood a few days, and then started on again. My uncle was going on our way with a wagon for about one hundred miles, and we accompanied him. I passed through Kaskaskia, where I was born, but did not preach there, for my uncle was in a hurry to reach the point of his destination in Jackson County, where he was establishing a wood yard on the Mississippi River. Here we intended to take a steamer for Nashville, but no steamer would take us on board at the landing, for it was a bad one to bring boats up to. While staying at that place we preached to the people, and made our home with Mr. V. Hutcheson, and his sister Sarah, where we were treated very kindly. Finally a flat boat came in sight. We hailed it and went aboard. We were soon on good terms with the Captain and crew, and went with them to Memphis, Tennessee. At this place the Captain of the flat boat sold out his cargo, and then offered to pay our fare on a steamer from Memphis to Nashville. While we were in Memphis, General William Henry Harrison, then a candidate for President, arrived, and a great political meeting of the Whig party was held in the open air. After my friend Wm. Springer, the Captain of the flat boat, had sold his cargo and received his money, he invited my friend Twist and myself to go with him to a saloon. There were quite a number of men in the saloon, fiddling, eating, drinking and otherwise enjoying themselves. Captain Springer was not used to drinking. He soon got mellow, felt rich, and commenced throwing his money around in a careless manner. The saloonkeeper was a man with an eye to business, and was particularly interested in friend Springer. He treated him often and insisted on his drinking. I tried to get Springer to go to his boat, and took him by the arm and started off with him, when one of the crowd told me not to be so officious, that the man knew his own business and was capable of attending to it. I said nothing to him in reply, but I sent Twist in haste to the boat for the crew to come at once before Springer was robbed of his money. They came, but not any too soon for his benefit, as a row had commenced, with the design of going through him while it was going on. When the crew came, I started for the boat with Springer, the crew keeping back the crowd of drunken robbers. By acting in this way we saved him and his money too. Twist and myself refused all kinds of drinks that night. We were therefore sober and in good condition to protect the man who had favored us and been our friend. Next morning Springer wished to reward us, but we refused to let him do so.

I told him we had done nothing but our duty. We parted with him and his crew, and took passage in a new steamer that was owned in Nashville, and was then making its first trip from Nashville to New Orleans. The boat got into a race with the Eclypse, another fine boat. The Captain was a fine man. The crew were all negroes. One of the fire-men on our boat took sick, and was unable to do his work. I saw that the Eclypse was crowding us closely. I threw off my coat and took the negro's place as fireman. I saw a barrel of resin near by; I broke the head in with an ax and piled the resin in the fire. This soon had its effect, and our boat soon left the Eclypse far in the rear. The steamers parted at the mouth of, the Ohio. The Captain was so well pleased with my work that he gave Elder Twist and myself a free passage.

When we reached Nashville Elder Twist became homesick and left me, and returned to Nauvoo. I gave him $10 to pay his way home. I was thus left alone once more. I found the Branch at Nashville in a healthy condition, and much pleased to have me with them. I then visited the Branch in Putnam County, and preached to them, advising all to go to Nauvoo. I added several new members to the Church. By the next Spring that entire Branch had gone to Nauvoo. The Branch on Stone River also went to Nauvoo soon after I returned home. A delegation, headed by Captain John H. Redd, came to invite me to go and preach in the settlement where Captain Redd lived. They said I could not preach publicly, for my life would be in danger, as many of the citizens were very hostile to the Mormons and had run one man out of the neighbor-hood for practicing Mormonism, and Randolph Alexander had been run off for preaching Mormonism. Captain Redd was formerly a sea captain and a native of South Carolina. I told the delegation I would preach, pro-vided they gave general publicity to my appointment. They were star-tled at the proposal, and said my life would not be safe a moment if I undertook to preach in public. I told them to trust that to me. They returned home and gave general notice of when and where I would preach. At the appointed time I started for the place of meeting, which was twenty miles from Murfreesborough. I was met by a guard of ten men, headed by Captain Redd, who came to meet and protect me. The next day I preached to a large number of people. I spoke two hours to them, upon the subject of our free institutions and the constitutional rights of American citizens. I told them who I was and what I was; that I was a free American citizen; that I claimed the right of free speech as a free man; that I held myself open for investigation; that if the people wished me to set forth the tenets of our faith I would do so, otherwise I would leave; that if they did not desire to bear the truth they could make it manifest and I would leave their country. The vote was unanimous for me to tarry and preach to them. I preached there twice. My first sermon was upon the apostasy of the churches of the day and the necessity of a purer gospel, proving what I said by the Scriptures. I then followed up with the origin and authenticity of the Book of Mormon.

I was then induced to continue my sermons. I staid there and continued to do my Master's will. After the fourth sermon I commenced to baptize members. The first one that I baptized at that place was Parson John Holt, of the Christian faith. Then I baptized seven of the members of his church, then Captain Redd and his family. This unexpected success of the gospel created great excitement in that section of country. About ten miles from there lived two men, lieutenants in the militia company of Captain Bogardus, of Missouri fame and disgrace. These men had strayed into this section of the country, and were employed by two wealthy farmers, and were acting as overseers. They told fearful stories about the Mormons in Missouri, and gathered up a mob of about twenty five men and came with them, determined to tar and feather me if I preached again. Word reached the settlement of what was intended. The people came to me to ask what they should do. I told them to wait and let me manage the affair. The next day, Sunday, while I was preaching, one of the lieutenants, by the name of Dickey, made his appearance with ten men. He informed me of his design, and that I must quit preaching and leave for other parts of the country. "Not just yet," said I. At this he and his men made a rush for me. As they started the women next to the stand formed a circle around me. While thus surrounded I continued my sermon. I refuted the absurd stories of Dickey and his crew, and I then told the people there what I knew had been done at Far West by Lieut. Dickey and the members of Captain Bogardus' company. The mob tore down my stand, but could not get at me. Then they retired to consult Captain J. H. Redd then appointed a meeting to be held at his place that afternoon, and he told the people that he did not want any person to come into his yard unless they came intending to behave; that if there was any violence used there some one would get hurt. I preached at his house that afternoon. A fearful storm raged during most of the time, but this was fortunate, for it kept the mob away. While I was preaching a drunken wag interrupted me and called me a d--d liar. Captain Redd was sitting near me with two large pistols, which he called his peacemakers. This insult was not more than out of the fellow's mouth when Captain Redd caught him by the neck and rushed him out of the house into the rain. The coward begged hard for himself, but he was forced to go out and sit under a porch during the rest of the sermon. Captain Redd was a kind-hearted, generous man, but would not stand abuse. The next Sunday was a cloudy day, so the meeting was held within doors. Dickey had by this time raised his mob to about fifty men, and had made every arrangement to give me a warm reception. Two men who were intoxicated were selected to start the disturbance, or "open the ball," as they called it. I had just commenced speaking, when one of these men began to swear and use indecent language, and made a rush for me with his fist drawn. I at once made a Masonic sign of distress, when, to my relief and yet to my surprise, a planter rushed to my aid. He was the man who employed Dickey. He took the drunken men and led them out of the crowd, and sat by me during the rest of my sermon, thus giving me full protection. That man was a stranger to me, but he was a good man and a true Mason. His action put an end to mob rule at that place. After the meeting I baptized some ten persons.

Soon afterwards I was sent for by Col. Tucker, of Duck Creek, Marshall Co., to come there, a distance of thirty miles. I attended, and delivered three lectures, which were well received by all, the Colonel in particular. He was a wealthy Virginian, and pressed me warmly to make his house my home. His wife and family were favorably impressed. They were of the Presbyterian order, and two of her brothers were ministers of that faith. I remained here a few days, and left an appointment to preach on the following Saturday and Sunday. Before leaving I let the Colonel's lady have books on our faith, and returned to fill some appointments that I had made at Capt. Redd's. At the appointed time I returned to fill my appointments on Buckskin River.

Within half a mile of Col. Tucker's house was a Methodist chapel. At this place lived a New Light preacher, an old man, who invited me to stop with him. He informed me that Col. Tucker had become bitter against the Mormons on account of his wife believing in them, and that she wanted to be baptized. She had left word with him requesting me not to leave without baptizing her. This was something that I wished to avoid, so to prevent trouble I concluded not to go to Col. Tucker's at all. I filled my appointments, and returned to my Christian friend's house for refreshments, intending to make my way over the mountains that night, and thus avoid meeting Mrs. Tucker. I had just finished supper, and stepped to the door to start back, when I met Mrs. Tucker. She upbraided me for not calling to see her. I said to her that it was contrary to the rules of our faith for an elder to interfere in any man's family against the wish or will of the husband or parents; that she should keep quiet and the Lord would take the will for the deed. The more I tried to reconcile her, the more determined she became to be baptized. While I was talking with her a young man came to us and reported that Col. Tucker had ambushed himself, with a double barreled shotgun, near the place of baptizing, swearing vengeance against the man that attempted to baptize his wife.

I was in hopes to persuade her to return, but in vain. She said to me, "You have declared your mission is from Heaven, that you are a servant of God, and I believe it. Now I demand baptism at your hands. If you are a servant of God, don't shrink from your duty."

I looked at her for a moment, and said, "Woman, if you have faith enough to be baptized under these circumstances, I have faith enough to try it at least." Some ten personal friends who lived in the little village accompanied us to the water, a short distance above the usual place of baptizing, and attended during the performance of the ordinance. They advised her to return home immediately, with her two servants, and never let on as though anything had happened. We started to return to the house of my friend, carrying my boots in my hand. It was now dark. As I got to the top of a high fence, and cast my eyes about me, I luckily saw a man near me in the rear, with a double barreled shotgun in his hands, or what I supposed was such. He was within ten steps of me, or nearer. I at once recognized him to be Col. Tucker. Having heard of his threats, I was induced not to tempt him too far. I placed my hands on the fence and sprang over it, alighting on the other side, near a cross fence which separated the garden from a field of corn, to avoid a collision with him. As quick as thought I got on the opposite side of the fence, among the corn, which was at full height. I was within twenty feet of Tucker and could hear all that was said. I heard him rave, draw his shotgun down, and demand with oaths what they were doing there. Had they been baptizing his wife? I recognized the voice of the Parson's lady with whom I was stopping. She had the wet clothes of Mrs. Tucker.

"Tell me," demanded Tucker, "if my wife has been baptized, or I will blow your brains out." The reply was, "She has been baptized." "Where is that infernal Mormon preacher?" demanded the Colonel; "I will put a load of shot through him." "He is in that corn field," was the reply. The Colonel then raved the more. Finally some of his friends persuaded him to return home, and not disgrace himself. He pretended to do so, but it was only a feint to get me out, I feared. After waiting until all was quiet, I returned to the house of my friend, and passed through the door and went out on the porch. I sat down and was slipping off my socks, to put on dry ones, when I heard a rustling in the room behind me. The next moment Col. Tucker had his gun leveled on me, and it flashed. He then whirled the butt of it to fell me to the earth. Seeing my danger I sprang and caught him around the waist, with one of his arms in my grasp, which left him with only one arm loose. He said, "I have you now, d--n you, where I want you." He was a strong, muscular man, and, no doubt, supposed I would be no match for him. I ordered a young man that stood near by, to take his gun. I then gripped him with an iron hug, and sent him back into the room. The old gentleman with whom I was stopping, ordered him out of the house unless he would behave himself. He said he had invited me to his house, and felt that it was his duty to protect me. The Colonel replied that he would go if he could, that he never knew before that when he was in the hands of a Mormon, he was in a bear's clutches. I said, "I will take you out if it will accommodate you." Thus saying, I stepped out on the porch with him. I saw that he was will-ing to go. This gave me new courage. He said, "D--n you, let me go or I will blow your brains out when I get loose." I replied, "There is but one condition on which I will let you go, and that is that you will go home and be quiet and trouble me no more." He replied, "D--n you, I will settle with you for all this." I felt that a man who would treat a stranger as he had me, could not have the moral courage to back him in so shameful an act as the one he was engaged in. This was in the month of July, and it was very warm. I had hugged him closely, and he was growing weak. He said again, "Let me go, I am getting faint. I will be still if you will let go of me, and I will make it hot for you if you don't let me go." As he said this I renewed my grip upon him, and raising him up, said, "You have tried to take my life without cause, and still persist in doing so. If you don't behave I will throw you out of sight on this hard ground." I said this with an emphasis as though I meant it. As I was, as he supposed, in the act of dashing him to the ground, he begged of me, saying that if I would let him loose, he would go and trouble me no more. I let him fall to the ground, and handed him his gun, and let him live. When he got a little distance away he began threatening me, and said he would be revenged. After all had quieted down I retired to rest in the upper story of a friend's house.

About one o'clock in the morning I was awakened by the voice of a
female, which I recognized as the voice of Mrs. Tucker, in company
with two or three other ladies. She informed me that her husband was
bent on my destruction, and that he and ten men were way laying my
road, and advised me not to start in that direction; that her husband had
accused her of wetting the wads in his gun to save my life; but for me
to be of good cheer and put my trust in God, and that she had not regretted the steps she had taken. I thanked her for her kindness, and told her
that I wished her to return home and not come to see me any more; that
I was in the hands of God and He would protect me and deliver me safe;
that her visits to me would only make her husband more enraged at her.
They retired and I fell asleep.

At four o'clock I awoke, dressed myself, and ordered the servant to
saddle my horse. As the servant hitched my horse to the post, Tucker
and several men appeared upon the ground. Tucker told the servant that
he would cut him in two if he saddled my horse. I spoke to Tucker kindly, saluting him with the time of day. His reply was, "I have got you
now, d--n you." Thus saying, he ordered his nephew to bring Esquire
Walls immediately. After washing, I took my seat on the porch, and took
out my Bible to read. Tucker stood about ten steps from me to guard me
and my horse. My old friend, the New Light preacher, with whom I was
lodging, had a fine horse saddled for me and hitched on the south side
of the corn field. He advised me to pass down through the corn field
while I could do so without being detected, and thus get away out of the
county before a warrant could be issued for my arrest. Deliverance was
very tempting, yet I did not like the name of running away from trouble. It would convey the impression of fear, if not guilt, to most casual
observers. So I chose to face the music and abide the consequences.

A little after sunrise I saw Justice Walls coming, and some fifty men
with him. At this my heart leaped for joy. Among so many I was satisfied all were not against me, as many of them had attended lectures and
were favorably impressed with them. After a short interview with Col.
Tucker, Justice Walls informed me that Col. Tucker demanded from him
a warrant for my arrest, for having baptized his wife without his consent. I asked Col. Tucker if he ever forbid me to baptize his wife; if he
did not invite me to his house and invite me to stop there when I
returned; that I had not seen him, after this conversation, until after his
wife was baptized. That I had not urged her to be baptized; that she
came to me and demanded to be baptized. I told the Justice that I had

violated no law of Tennessee. The law allows a wife much greater privileges than being baptized without the consent of her husband; that she could sell one third of his real estate, and her deed would be good. The Justice said I was right, and told the Colonel it would be useless to issue a warrant without just cause. The Colonel then demanded a warrant for my arrest for assault and battery. He said I had abused his person, and that he was sore all over and scarcely able to walk. The Justice told the Colonel that it seemed to him that he was the one who had made the assault; that he snapped a loaded gun at me and had attempted to take my life, and that what I had done was in self-defense. He told Colonel Tucker he would talk with him again.

He then beckoned to me to follow him, and I did so. We went into a room by ourselves, when he said to me, "Parson Lee, you have many warm friends here. I have been very much interested in your lectures. I believe you to be honest and firm in your faith, and I will do all I can for you. Colonel Tucker is a desperate man when aroused. As a matter of policy, to humor him, I will give him a writ, but I will manage to delay the time to enable you to get out of the county. I will send for my law books, with instructions to delay in getting them here, and will argue with the Colonel that I must have my books here to examine the law. It is only four miles to the county line, when you will be all right. Then take the trail over the mountain, and they will not know which way you have gone. When you get into your county remember me on election day. This county and Rutherford County send three members to the Legislature. I am a candidate, and the vote of your friends in these counties will secure my election. When I send for my books you appear and bid us goodbye, as though you were not afraid of any man. Colonel Tucker has promised me he will use no violence if I will give him a writ." The Justice then gave me a token of the Brotherhood, and then walked out to confer with Colonel Tucker, and sent his nephew back for his books, instructing him to delay in getting them, so as to give me time to get out of the county, before an officer could overtake me. He told the Colonel to keep cool and he would soon have a writ for me. I went into the dining room and and down to breakfast, and ate a little as a blind. Then taking up my saddle-bags, bade them all goodbye.

I walked to my horse, that stood hitched where the servant had left him. As I left the house Justice Walls followed me as though he was very much surprised, and said, "Parson Lee, I hope you will tarry until this matter can be settled amicably." I told him that I had violated no law, that my ministerial engagements compelled me to leave, and that I should have done so before had not this unpleasant affair detained me; that I chose to serve God rather than fear the ire of man. Thus saying, I placed my saddle upon my horse. Colonel Tucker leveled his gun on me, and said, "D--n you, I knew you would run." I turned and eyed him and told him to put up his gun; that I had borne all I intended to from him; that if he attempted violence he would never trouble another man. At the same time the Justice told him to be careful, that he had made himself liable already. I mounted my horse and turned to the Colonel and told him he might guard that wood pile until the day of judgment, for all that I cared. He again raised his gun, but was prevented by the bystanders from shooting. I rode off leisurely, and when about seventy five yards away I stopped and watered my horse. Tucker again drew his gun on me, and I expected him to shoot every moment, but I durst not show fear. My road lay along the mountain for some two miles. When I passed a house I would walk my horse, and sing and seem to be wholly unconcerned, but when I was out of sight I put my horse on the keen jump, and was soon safe out of Marshall County and in Rutherford. Finding an out-of-the-way place, with good blue grass and plenty of shade, I got down from my horse and returned thanks to my Father in heaven for my deliverance.

In the afternoon I arrived at the house of Capt. Redd, where I generally made my home. The brethren all came to welcome me back, and I related to them my experience and deliverance. A short time after this James K. Polk and Col. Jones, both candidates for the office of Governor of Tennessee, and the candidates for the Legislature, including my friend Walls, met at Murfreesborough and held a political meeting. Walls related to me the sequel of what happened with Col. Tucker. When his nephew went for his law books he permitted his horse to get away, and was nearly ruined in the brush and grapevines while I was escaping. Col. Tucker did not blame the Justice at all, but rather sympathized with him in his misfortune. Mrs. Tucker still remained firm in her faith. The kindness of Justice Walls to me in my hour of peril was not forgotten. I spoke of it in all my meetings, and to my friends in private. And to this act of justice and humanity he owed his election, as he was elected by a majority of only five votes.

I visited the Branch on Stone River and made arrangements to return to my family at Nauvoo, the City of Joseph. The two Branches now numbered about sixty members. I organized a Branch west of

Murfreesborough, and ordained John Holt to the office of Elder. I baptized a young girl at Readysville, by the name of Sarah C. Williams, of rich parentage. She was about ten years old, and afterwards emigrated to Nauvoo, with the family of Wm. Pace. She was sealed to me in her fourteenth year, and is still with me. She is the mother of twelve children, and has been a true, faithful companion to me. I lectured at Murfreesborough for about ten days, and about the first of October, 1843, I took the steamer at Nashville for my home at Nauvoo, arriving there on the 14th of October.

CHAPTER XII

Upon my return home I found my family well. Work on the Temple was progressing finely, and every effort was being made to push it ahead. About this time John C. Bennett came on a visit to see the Prophet, and soon after joined the Church. At that time he wielded quite an influence in government affairs. He grew in the graces of the Prophet and became his right hand man. He endeavored, in connection with Stephen A. Douglass, to obtain a charter for the City of Nauvoo. Bennett organized the Nauvoo Legion, and was elected Major General. Through his influence, backed by Douglass, arms were obtained for the Legion from the government. A Free Mason's lodge, and the privileges of Masonry, were extended to the Legion. Judge Cleveland, of Springfield, Ill., was very friendly, and frequently visited the Prophet. A fine lodge was built in Nauvoo, and many were admitted as members. The brothers, Joseph and Hyrum Smith, held high positions in the brotherhood. I here became a member of the order and received three degrees.

The institution flourished during our stay in Nauvoo, and was frequently visited by the Grand Worshipful Master from Springfield, and lectures were had and a library established. I was Librarian of the order. I was also Wharf Master of the city, and held the position of Major in the Nauvoo Legion, and commanded the escort in the Fifth Infantry. I was made the general clerk and reader for the Seventies and issued the laws to that body. I held the office of a Seventy, and was collector of the delinquent military tax. The same Fall I was appointed on a committee, with Brigham Young as counselor, to build a hall for the Seventies, the upper story to be used for the Priesthood and the Council of Fifty. Previous to my being appointed on the committee two committees had been appointed, but had accomplished nothing, and we commenced without a dollar. My plan was to build it by shares, of the value of five dollars each. Hyrum Smith, the Patriarch, told me that he would give the

Patriarchal Blessing to any that labored on the foundation of the building. The Seventies numbered about four hundred and ninety men. I was
to create the material. That is, I would watch, and when I could get a
contract to take out lumber from the river, as rafts would land at the city,
I would take common laboring men, and the portion of the lumber that
we got for our pay we would pile up for the building. In this way we got
all the lumber needed. The brick we made ourselves, and boated the
wood to burn them and our lime from the island.

In the month of March, 1844, we had the building up on the west side
nearly two stories high. One day when the wall was built up nine feet
high and forty five feet long, and was of course green, a tornado came
that night and blew the wall down, breaking columns and joists below,
doing a damage of several thousand dollars. I was inclined to be down
in the lip, but Brigham Young laughed at me, and said it was the best
omen in the world; it showed that the Devil was mad, and knew that the
Seventy would receive the blessings of God in that house; and as they
were special witnesses to the nations of the earth, they would make his
kingdom quake and tremble; that when Noah was building the ark he
was mobbed three times, but he persevered, and finally they said, "Let
the d--d old fool alone, and see what he will accomplish." "Just so with
you; double your diligence and put her up again. If you do not you will
lose many a blessing."

I went to work again with as many men as could work to advantage.
We threw the wall down flat, and commenced a new one, another brick
thicker than the former. I borrowed fifty thousand brick, and made them
and returned them when the weather was fine. By the first of May we
had the Hall closed in.

I must now leave the building of the hall for other matters. During the
winter, Joseph, the Prophet, set a man by the name of Sidney Hay
Jacobs, to select from the Old Bible such scriptures as pertained to
polygamy, or celestial marriage, and to write it in pamphlet form, and to
advocate that doctrine. This he did as a feeler among the people, to pave
the way for celestial marriage. This, like all other notions, met with
opposition, while a few favored it. The excitement among the people
became so great that the subject was laid before the Prophet. No one
was more opposed to it than was his brother Hyrum, who denounced it
as from beneath. Joseph saw that it would break up the Church, should
he sanction it, so he denounced the pamphlet through the *Wasp*, a newspaper published at Nauvoo, by E. Robinson, as a bundle of nonsense

and trash. He said if he had known its contents he would never have permitted it to be published, while at the same time other confidential men
were advocating it on their own responsibility. Joseph himself said on
the stand, that should he reveal the will of God concerning them, that
they, pointing to President W. Marks, P. P. Pratt, and others, would shed
his blood. He urged them to surrender themselves to God instead of
rebelling against the stepping stone of their exaltation. In this way he
worked upon the feelings and minds of the people, until they feared that
the anger of the Lord would he kindled against them, and they insisted
upon knowing the will of Heaven concerning them. But he dared not
proclaim it publicly, so it was taught confidentially to such as were
strong enough in the faith to take another step. About the same time the
doctrine of "sealing" for an eternal state was introduced, and the Saints
were given to understand that their marriage relations with each other
were not valid. That those who had solemnized the rites of matrimony
had no authority of God to do so. That the true priesthood was taken
from the earth with the death of the Apostles and inspired men of God.
That they were married to each other only by their own covenants, and
that if their marriage relations had not been productive of blessings and
peace, and they felt it oppressive to remain together, they were at liberty to make their own choice, as much as if they had not been married.
That it was a sin for people to live together, and raise or beget children,
in alienation from each other. There should exist an affinity between
each other, not a lustful one, as that can never cement that love and
affection that should exist between a man and his wife. I will here mention that Orson Hyde and W.W. Phelps turned against Joseph in
Missouri, and forsook him in time of peril and danger, and even testified against him in the courts. After the troubles were over, and Joseph
was again in place in the midst of the Saints, they both wished to be
restored to fellowship and standing in the Church, confessing their
faults. Joseph laid the case before the Church, and said that if God could
forgive them he ought to, and would do so, and give them another
chance. With tears be moved that we would forgive them and receive
them back into fellowship. He then sent Elder O. Hyde and John E. Page
to Jerusalem, and to the land of Palestine, to dedicate that land for the
gathering of the Jews. Report said that Hyde's wife, with his consent,
was sealed to Joseph for an eternal state, but I do not assert the fact. I
also understood that Brigham Young's wife was sealed to Joseph. After
the death of Joseph, Brigham Young told me that Joseph's time on earth

was short, and that the Lord allowed him privileges that we could not have.

A difference arose between Joseph and Wm. Law, his second counselor, on account of Law's wife. Law said that the Prophet proposed making her his wife, and she so reported to her husband. Law loved his wife and was devoted to her, as she was an amiable and handsome woman, and he did not feel like giving her up to another man. He exposed the Prophet, and from that time became his enemy. His brother, Wilson Law, sided with him. They were Canadians, and wealthy and influential men. They, in connection with Foster and Higbee, who were on the wane in the faith, established a paper at Nauvoo, called the *Expositor*, in which they took about the same position that the *Salt Lake Daily Tribune* does. They set the Prophet up without mercy. They soon got after Brigham for trying to influence Martha Brotherton to be sealed to Joseph. Her father found it out and helped to expose them, which made it rather hot for them. The next move of the Prophet and his friends was to get the City Council to pass an ordinance declaring the *Expositor* to be a nuisance, and also Higbee's grocery, unless they would close them up.

John C. Bennett became suspected, and fears were entertained that he would join the faction. He was accused of selling offices in the military organization, to certain men who would help him win the good graces of some of the young sisters, and that he became intimate with Orson Pratt's wife, while Pratt was on a mission. That he built her a fine frame house, and lodged with her, and used her as his wife. Fearing that Bennett would assail the character of the Prophet, I brought him before the City Council, and had him make a statement, certifying that he knew nothing derogatory to the character of the Prophet, and that his behavior was that of a gentleman and a man of God. After this, Bennett was hauled up and dealt with, and severed from the Church. He said that the Prophet gave him permission to do as he had done with Mrs. Pratt. Joseph said Bennett was guilty of adultery, but that as a matter of policy he had not exposed him until after Bennett had made his statement.

Previous to this time, the Prophet had written a letter to Martin Van Buren, wishing to know his views in regard to the grievances and wrongs of the Mormon people, should he be elected President. He replied that he believed their cause was just, and that Congress had no right to interfere. That it was a State matter, and was left to the Executive. The Prophet addressed another letter to Wm. H. Harrison, on the same subject. His answer was but little more satisfactory. He then drew up a statement of his own, of the power and policy of the Government. A convention was called, and the Prophet was nominated as a candidate for the Presidency. He set forth his views in the *Nauvoo Neighbor*, a newspaper formerly known as the *Wasp*. He stated that if the people would elect him President it would be the salvation of the nation, but if otherwise, the Union would soon be severed. That the two political parties would continue to influence the people until it would end in a civil war, in which all nations would take part, and this nation would be broken up. At this convention, the Elders were assigned missions to different States. I was sent to stump the State of Kentucky, with ten elders to assist me.

Brigham Young said to me, "You had better shut up the Seventies Hall, and obey, perhaps, the last call of the Prophet." Things looked rather squally before I left, and but little prospect of growing better. I left Nauvoo on the 4th of May, 1844, with greater reluctance than I had on any previous mission. It was hard enough to preach the gospel without purse or scrip, but it was nothing compared to offering a man with the reputation that Joseph Smith had, to the people as a candidate for the highest gift of the nation. I would a thousand times rather have been shut up in jail, than to have taken the trip, but I dared not refuse.

About one hundred of us took the steamer Osprey, for St. Louis. Our mission was understood by all the passengers on board. I was not long waiting until the subject was brought up. I had made up my mind to banish all fear, and overcome timidity. I made the people believe that I felt highly honored to electioneer for a Prophet of God. That it was a privilege that few men enjoyed in these days. I endeavored to make myself agreeable by mixing with the passengers on the steamer. I told them that the Prophet would lead both candidates from the start. There was a large crowd on the boat, and an election was proposed. Judges and clerks were appointed and a vote taken. The Prophet received a majority of seventy-five, out of one hundred and twenty-five votes polled. This created a tremendous laugh, and we kept it up till we got to St. Louis. Here the most of us took the steamer Mermaid. The change of steamers afforded me a new field of labor. Here I met a brother of Gen. Atchinson, one of the commanders of the militia that served against the Church at Far West. He became very much interested in me, and when we parted at Smithland, Ky., he invited me to go home with him and preach in his neighborhood. My destination being Frankfort, I could not accept his invitation. I went to Lexington, by way of Georgetown, lecturing as I went. I finally went to the Capital, put up at a hotel, and endeavored to hire the State House to speak in, but found it engaged.

My funds were low, though my hotel bill was four dollars per day. After three days' trial I hired the Court House. The people said that no Mormon had ever been able to get a hearing, though several had attempted to do so. When evening came I had to light up the house and ring the bell. Elder S. B. Frost assisted me. Soon the hall was filled with none but juveniles, from ten to fifteen years of age. I understood the trick. They supposed I would leave, but to their surprise I arose and said I was glad to see them out in such great numbers; that I knew they had good parents, or they would not be here; that if they would take seats and be quiet we would sing them some of our Mormon songs. Elder Frost was a charming singer. We sung two or three songs. Our juvenile hearers seemed paralyzed. I then knelt down and prayed. By this time the hall was crowded with men, and I begged them not to crowd my little friends out. I then spoke about an hour and a half upon the constitutional rights of American citizens. I spoke of the character of the Southern people; that they were noted for their kind and generous treatment of strangers in particular, but that I feared, from the treatment I had received, that I had missed my way in Kentucky. My sires were of Southern birth; my father was a relative of the Revolutionary Lee, of Virginia; my uncle was from Lexington, Kentucky; that I came a stranger into their midst, and I felt confident that the right of speech would be extended to us; that we were ministers of the gospel, traveling without purse or scrip, dependent upon the generosity of the people for food and raiment, nor did we preach for hire; that if they wished, we would remain there and lecture, and if it met the approbation of the people they could have the gospel preached to them without money and without price. The first man that spoke up was a saddler; he said he was a poor man, but we were welcome to his house, giving the street and number. About twenty more responded in like manner, among them some of the most wealthy men of the county. We went home with a rich farmer, and continued our labors, having more calls than we could fill. We were sent for by a rich planter, who lived about twenty miles away. I was anxious to extend our labors as much as it was advisable.

On our way to the planter's we found it difficult to obtain dinner. The orthodox people did not like to associate with Mormons. I finally asked them to direct me to where some infidel or gambler lived. They wanted

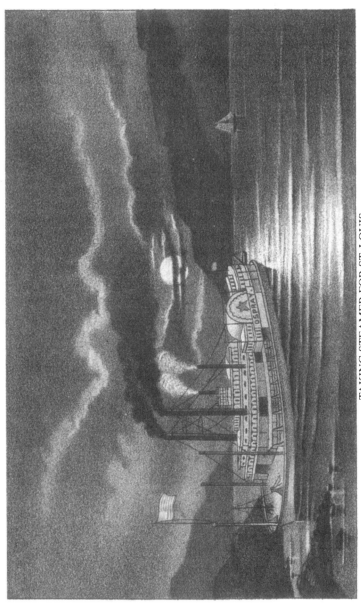

TAKING STEAMER FOR ST. LOUIS.

to know what on earth I wanted of them. I replied, "To get something to eat; that they were too liberal-minded to turn a stranger away from their door. That the Saviour ate with publicans and sinners, for the very reason that we do, for the religious scribes and pharisees would not feed him." They pointed us to the next house, where we went and were kindly received and entertained. The gentleman informed us that he belonged to no church, but that he had an interest in a church, and said we were welcome to preach there. He went and made an appointment for us to preach. We preached there and were received with the greatest kindness. I soon began to baptize, and calls came in on every side, when the papers brought us the news of the assassination of the Prophet Joseph, and his brother Hyrum.

We returned immediately to Frankfort, as I expected the Elders there, to learn what to do. We all retired to Maple Grove, on the Kentucky River, and kneeled in prayer, and asked the Lord to show us whether or not these reports were true. I was the mouth in prayer, but received nothing definite in answer to my prayer. I told the elders to follow their own impressions, and if they wished to do so, to return to Nauvoo. Each of them made his way back. I went and spent the evening with a Mr. Snow. He claimed to be a cousin of Erastus Snow, who was favorable to us. We spent the evening talking over the reported deed. The next morning, about ten o'clock, my mind was drawn out in prayer. I felt as though the solemnity of eternity was resting upon me. A heavenly, hallowed influence fell upon me, and continued to increase until I was electrified from head to foot. I saw a large personage enter the door and stand before me. His apparel was as white as the driven snow, and his countenance as bright as the noonday sun. I felt paralyzed, and was speechless and motionless. It remained with me but a moment, then receded back out of the door. This bright being's influence drew me from my chair and led me south about three hundred yards, into a plot of clover and blue grass, and stood over a persimmon tree, which afforded a pleasant shade. I fell prostrate upon my face upon the grass. While here I saw Joseph, the Prophet, and Hyrum his brother, the Patriarch, and their wounds by which they had been assassinated. This personage spoke to me in a soft, low voice, and said that the Prophet and Patriarch had sealed their testimony with their blood. That our mission was like that of the Apostles, and our garments were clear of the blood of the nation. That I should return to Nauvoo and wait until power was granted us from on high. That as the Priesthood fell upon the Apostle Peter, so should it rest with the twelve apostles of the Church for the present. And thus the vision closed, and I gradually returned back to my native element. Rising up I looked at my watch and saw that I had been there an hour and a quarter. Returning to the house my friend Snow asked me if I was ill. I replied in the negative. He said I was very pale, that he saw my countenance change while I sat in my chair; that when I went out of the door it seemed as though every drop of blood had left me, or been changed. I then told him that the reports in the papers were true, and the two Saints, the Prophet and the Patriarch, was no more. I asked him to take me to the landing, as I wished to take the evening packet, as my labors were done in this country for the present. He importuned me so hard that I told him what I had seen. He saddled a horse for me and one for himself, and we started, in company with several others, for the landing. When we were about to start on the steamer, Mr. Steele, a brother of the Captain, introduced me to the Captain. About eight persons demanded baptism, but I could not stop, but advised them to come to Nauvoo; among them was my friend Snow. I had a cabin passage free. When I reached Nauvoo, the excitement was at the highest point.

CHAPTER XIII

DEATH OF JOSEPH SMITH - SOME OF BRIGHAM YOUNG'S CRIMES

Joseph Smith, the Prophet, and Hyrum, his brother, were assassinated on the 24th day of June, 1844, at Carthage, Ill., about twenty miles from Nauvoo, while under the pledged faith of Gov. Ford, of Illinois. Gov. Ford had promised them protection if they would stand trial and submit to the judgment of the court. By his orders the Nauvoo Grays were to guard the jail while the prisoners awaited a trial.

The mob was headed by Williams and Sharp, editors of the *Nauvoo Signal*. When they approached the jail the guard made no resistance, but fell back. Stephen Markham, who had been to visit the prisoners an hour or so before they were killed, gave Joseph an Allen revolver. A part of the mob rushed up stairs, to the inner door of the prison, and burst it open and attempted to enter. Dr. Richards parried off the bayonets with his heavy cane. Joseph reached out his hand and fired off his six shots at the crowd, and wounded several mortally. Hyrum, who was trying to brace against the door, received a shot in the face near the nose. He said, "I am a dead man," and fell. John Taylor received a shot, but fortunately it struck his watch which saved his life. These four were in the prison. Taylor, however, received another shot and fell. Joseph left the door, sprang through the window, and cried out, "Oh, Lord, my God, is there no help for the widow's son!" as he sprang from the window, pierced with several balls. The crowd then left the door and ran around to the windows.

Dr. Richards covered Taylor with a straw bed. Several shots were fired at the bed, some of which cut his legs. Dr. Richards looked out of the window on the scene, and had several balls pass through his clothing, but received no injury. After Joseph fell he was set up against the well curb and shot again. A young man named Boggs rolled up his sleeves, and with a knife attempted to cut off his head. At this instant, many of the bystanders report that a flash of light encircled the Prophet, and the man who was advancing to cut off his head fell back. They all

DEATH OF JOSEPH SMITH

seemed frightened, and fled after perpetrating the horrid deed. A runner was sent to Nauvoo to acquaint Governor Ford with what had been done. The Governor was terror stricken, as it endangered his life, he being alone, without a guard, and at the mercy of the Mormons, had they chosen to take advantage of him while he was in Nauvoo. Governor Ford advised them to be quiet, and promised that he would see that their murderers should be prosecuted. He gave the Mormons a company of troops to go and bring their dead friends to Nauvoo. They were placed in rough oak plank boxes and brought to the city. There was great lamentation and mourning over them among the people. Joseph was a man dearly loved by the Saints, and blessed with direct revelation from God, and was an honorable, generous, high-minded man. The remains of the Prophet and his brother were laid in a sepulcher made of stone. The rough boards, which once enclosed them, were sawed in pieces and distributed among their friends, many of whom had canes made of the pieces, with a lock or the hair of the Prophet set in the top of them, and those canes are kept as sacred relics to this day.

But I must go back and speak of the cause of their arrest. While I was in Kentucky the printing press and the grocery of Higbee & Foster were declared nuisances, and ordered to be destroyed. The owners refused to comply with the decision of the City Council, and the Mayor ordered the press and type destroyed, which was done. The owner of the grocery employed John Eagle, a regular bully, and others, to defend it. As the police entered, or attempted to enter, Eagle stood in the door and knocked three of them down. As the third one fell the Prophet struck Eagle under the ear and brought him sprawling to the ground. He then crossed Eagle's hands and ordered them to be tied, saying that he could not see his men knocked down while in the line of their duty, without protecting them.

This raised the ire of those men, Higbee, Foster, and others, and they got out writs for the arrest of Joseph and others, and laid their grievances before the Governor. Joseph, knowing the consequences of such a move, concluded to leave for the Rocky Mountains, and lay out a country where the Saints would not be molested. He crossed over into Iowa, with a few faithful friends with him. These friends begged him to return and stand his trial; that the Lord had always delivered him, and would again. He told them that if he returned he would be killed, but that if he went away he would save his life and the Church would not be hurt; that he would look out a new country for them; that the Governor had also advised him to do so. These old grannies then accused him of cowardice, and told him that Christ had said he would never leave his brethren in trouble. He then asked them if his Emma wished him to return. They answered, "Yes." He then said it was all light before him, and darkness behind him, but he would return, though he felt like a sheep being led to the slaughter. The following day he crossed the river again to Illinois. He kissed his mother in particular, and told her that his time had come, and that he would seal his testimony with his blood. He advised his brother Hyrum not to go with him - that he would be a comfort to the churches when he, the Prophet, should be gone. Hyrum said, "No, my brother, I have been with you in life and will be with you in death!" The Prophet then called Gen. Dunham and had some private talk with him, and started for the jail at Carthage. Dunham said that the Prophet requested him to take his command and ambush it in a grove near Carthage, and watch the movements of the crowd, but Dunham dared not go contrary to tile orders of the Governor. He might have gone in the night time, as he knew that Joseph feared treachery.

About this time the settlements on Bear Creek and at Great Plains had a difficulty with the outsiders, and the settlements were broken up and the settlers driven to Nauvoo. The Mormons sought redress under the law. The sheriff tried to suppress the riot by a posse, but could not get a posse from the outsiders, and he was obliged to summon them from the Mormons. This made him unpopular and endangered his life, which rendered him powerless. Governor Ford tried to bring to justice those who had assaulted the Smiths, but public opinion was against him, and the mass of the people objected, hence nothing was done. Some of the leaders in the horrid deed were members of the Legislature, and though the disturbance was partially quelled, still the feeling of enmity continued to exist until the final breaking up of the Church.

Every exertion was made to push forward the completion of the Temple at Nauvoo.

Before proceeding further, we must learn who was to be the successor of the Prophet to lead the Church. It was then understood among the Saints that young Joseph was to succeed his father, and that right justly belonged to him. Joseph, the Prophet, had bestowed that right upon him by ordination, but he was too young at that time to fill the office and discharge its solemn duties. Some one must fill the place until he had grown to more mature age. Sidney Rigdon set up his claim, he being the second counselor to the Prophet. Rigdon had a few backers for his claims. A man by the name of Strong, who had been writing for the Prophet, set up his claim to the office, by forging an appointment from Joseph. Time passed on until the whole twelve got in from their missions, and a conference was held, and the several claimants came forward with their claims. Sidney Rigdon was the first who appeared upon the stand. He had been considered rather in the background for sometime previous to the death of the Prophet. He made but a weak claim. Strong did not file any. Just then Brigham Young arose and roared like a young lion, imitating the style and voice of Joseph, the Prophet. Many of the brethren declared that they saw the mantle of Joseph fall upon him. I myself, at the time, imagined that I saw and heard a strong resemblance to the Prophet in him, and felt that he was the man to lead us until Joseph's legal successor should grow up to manhood, when he should surrender the Presidency to the man who held the birthright. After that time, if he continued to claim and hold the position, he could not be considered anything else than an usurper, and his acts would not meet the approbation of Heaven. Hence the course of Brigham Young has been downward ever since. As soon as he got the reins of government in his hands, he swore that he would never suffer an officer to serve a writ on, or arrest him, as they had Joseph; that he would send them across lots to h--l, that dark and gloomy road whence no traveler ever returned. At that time I lived on Warsaw street, about one half of a mile east of the Temple.

He wished me to remove near to him, as I was one of the guards that were assigned to guard him. I had quite a comfortable brick house and lot, all in fine order, on Warsaw street. He told me to let him have my property on Warsaw street and he would buy me a house on the flat, nearer to him. I did so, and he bought out Samuel D. Frost, and sent him on a mission to Kentucky, where I had been laboring, taking his family with him. He had a nice little frame house. I moved into it and had it finished on the inside and made quite comfortable. Brigham at that time was living in a little log house, but was preparing to build a brick house. I renewed my labors on the Hall of the Seventies, and finished it in grand style. It was then dedicated, and the different quorums all had a picnic party in it, beginning with the first quorum, consisting of seventy seven men to each quorum. Brigham said this hall would be a creditable building in London. He called upon me to organize all the young men into Quorums of Seventy, and keep the records for them. He appointed me General Clerk and Recorder of the Seventies, and through me were to be issued the licenses of the quorums. This was to be my compensation for my services. Joseph Young was the senior president over all the quorums. My responsibility increased daily. I was offered the position of senior president, I to select my six counselors and my Quorum of Seventy, but I declined, as I did not want the responsibility. I held then all the offices I could fill. Having finished the hall, I was offered, or rather had a mission, to build Joseph Young, the head president of the Seventies, a neat brick dwelling. Calling upon the Seventies to assist me, I soon mustered all the help that was necessary, and made brick enough to build me a large dwelling house. Including my other buildings it was ninety feet front, two and a half stories high, with a good cellar. By the middle of July, 1845, I had both houses, the one for Joseph Young, and the one for myself, finished, ready for painting. During the Winter of 1844-5 a man by the name of Stanley took up a school, teaching the use of the broadsword. At the expiration of his term I opened three schools, of fifty scholars each, in the same exercise. I gave thirteen lessons in each school, receiving two dollars from each scholar. This made me six hundred dollars. I received twenty-five cents for each license that I issued. With these means I purchased paints and oils to finish my dwelling house. I became very popular among the Saints, and many of them donated labor and materials for my dwelling house. I had a handsome inclosure, with fine orchard, well of water, house finished and grained from top to bottom, and everything in the finest order. I was young, strong and athletic. I could drive ahead and work all day and stand guard half of the night, through all kinds of weather. My pay for all this was the honor and trust reposed in me. To guard the president and leading men of the Church was considered a great and mighty thing, and would not be exchanged by those holding that office for ten dollars a night. It was considered that this would qualify those performing that duty for any position of honor or trust. In 1845 I was present at a trial, when two young men named Hodges were indicted and tried for murdering an old man and his wife. The Hodges said that Brigham Young had sent them to rob the old people of their money, of which they were supposed to have a large amount.

When they went to rob the house they found the inmates ready for them, and one of them was wounded. Thinking then that they would be detected, they killed the old people, and robbed them of their money. One of the party became alarmed and reported on the two Hodges boys. Their older brother, Erwin Hodges, said that Brigham Young had gotten his brothers in this scrape, and that he could get them out of it, and that if he did not do so his (Brigham Young's) blood would atone for it. The same evening as Erwin was returning home, a little after dark, he was met by two men who had been waiting for him to come alone. After some little conversation, as Erwin was turning, he was struck over the head with a police club, and then stabbed four times over the heart. The murderers then fled, supposing him to be dead. He was, however, only stunned, and the bleeding revived him. He ran about one hundred and fifty yards, and fell near Brigham Young's gate. He called for water, and also for Brigham to lay his hands upon him. Some person asked him who had done the deed. He replied he thought they were his friends, and expired without finishing the sentence, or he was afraid to tell.

A neighbor came running to my house, knowing that Brigham was there, as he often came there to keep away from suspicious persons. I started home with Brigham, and while on the way, I remarked to him that it was a shocking affair. After a moment's hesitation, he replied that it was not any worse for Hodges to be killed than it would have been for him (Young) to have his blood shed. This answer recalled to my mind the threat that Erwin had made during the day, at the trial of his brothers, who were sentenced and hung at Burlington, Iowa. These men who turned away from the Church were the most bitter enemies to Brigham Young, and sought every opportunity to entrap him. They had a list of their most private friends to ensnare him, and find an occasion to arrest him with a warrant. This caused Brigham Young to keep hidden as much as possible. In the meantime, his "destroying angels" were dilligently on the watch, and every suspicious man was closely tracked up, and no strategy neglected to find out his business. If they were suspicious that any man wanted to serve a writ on his Honor, Brigham Young, they were careful never to let that man escape. Sometimes they would treat them with great kindness, and in that way decoy them to some out-of-the-way place, and "save" them, as they called it. They were not only on the track of officers, but all suspected characters who might come on to spy out what was going on; for instance, the consecrating of the stock of their enemies, by the Saints, and driving it in at night and butchering it, and distributing it among their friends. Joseph Smith in his lifetime said that a man who would steal from a Gentile, would steal from his brother if he could not steal from any one else; that he deprecated this petty thieving, and that the Saints should wait until the proper time, and then steal back the whole State of Missouri and get their homes back with interest. I knew of several men who were put out of the way in this manner, though I never saw any of them killed. Besides there were enough willing tools to do all this kind of dirty jobs without me, though it was entrusted to the police to do, they being sworn to secrecy. If any of them was caught in a scrape, it was the duty of the rest to unite and swear him out. It was claimed that the Gentiles had no right to administer an oath. I have heard men say they would swear a house full of lies to save one of the brethren. Whatever the police were ordered to do, they were to do and ask no questions. Whether it was right or wrong mattered not to them, they were responsible only to their leaders, and they were amenable only to God. I was a confidant among them, and they let me into the secret of all they did, and they looked to me to speak a good word for them with Brigham, as they were ambitious to please him and obtain his blessing. I knew that I was in their full confidence, and the captain of the police never asked me to do anything he knew I was averse to doing. Under Brigham Young, Hosea Stout was Chief of Police. They showed me where they buried a man in a lot near the Masonic Hall. They said they got him tight and were joking with him while some men were digging his grave. They asked him to go with them into a pit of corn, saying it was fully grown. They told him they had a jug of whisky cached out there. They led him to his grave, and told him to get down there, and hand up the jug, and he should have the first drink. As he bent over to get down, Rosswell Stevens struck him with his police cane on the back of the head and dropped him. They then tightened a cord around his neck to shut off his wind, and then they covered him up, and set the hill of corn back on his grave to cover up any tracks that might lead to his discovery.

Another man they took in a boat, about two o'clock at night, for a ride. When out in the channel of the river, the man who sat behind him struck him upon the head and stunned him. They then tied a rope around his neck and a stone to the other end of the rope, and sent him to the bottom of Mississippi River. There was another man whose name I have forgotten, who was a great annoyance to the Saints at Nauvoo. He generally brought a party with him when he came to the city, and could threaten them with the law, but he always managed to get away safely. They (the Saints) finally concluded to entrust his case to Howard Egan, a policeman, who was thought to be pretty long headed. He took a party of chosen men, or "destroying angels," and went to La Harpe, a town near the residence of this man, and watched an opportunity when he would pass along. They "saved" him, and buried him in a wash out at night. In a short time afterwards, a thunder storm washed the earth away and exposed the remains. They also told me of an attempt to rob an old man and one son who lived on the Bear River. Ebenezer Richardson, an old tried veteran and policeman, had charge of this mission. Four of them went near the residence of the old folks. Two of them went to the house to get lodgings and refreshments. The old gentleman told them that he was not prepared to entertain them, and directed them to a neighbor who lived a mile away. They insisted upon stopping, and said they were weary and would lie down upon their blankets. The fact was that the old man was suspicious of them and utterly refused to keep them. They then went away and counseled over the matter, and concluded to wait until they were all asleep, then burst in the door before they could have time to resist. The old man and his son being sure that they had come for the purpose of robbing them, had expected, and were waiting for their return. Each of them had a gun. Richardson and the party waited until about midnight, when they slipped carefully to the house and listened. All was still. Then Richardson and another man burst in the door. As the robbers were in the act of entering the house, the old man and his son both fired. Richardson's arm was broken just below the elbow; the other man received a slight wound. The reception was rather hot and they backed water and were glad to get away. Richardson wore a cloak to conceal his broken arm. The matter was kept a profound secret.

I was in Brigham Young's office about this time. His brother Joseph, and quite a number of others were present, when Brigham raised his hand and said, "I swear by the eternal Heavens that I have unsheathed my sword, and I will never return it until the blood of the Prophet Joseph and Hyrum, and those who were slain in Missouri, is avenged. This whole nation is guilty of shedding their blood, by assenting to the deed, and holding its peace." "Now," said he, "betray me, any of you who dare to do so!" Furthermore, every one who had passed through their endowments in the Temple, were placed under the most sacred obligations to avenge the blood of the Prophet, whenever an opportunity offered, and to teach their children to do the same, thus making the entire Mormon people sworn and avowed enemies of the American nation.

They teach the rising generation to look upon every Gentile or outsider, as their enemy, and never to suffer one of their number to be sen-

DISPOSING OF A CORPSE

tenced by a Gentile court. They have even gone so far as to teach them not to allow a Gentile judge to hang a Mormon dog. That they have no Agent to come into the territory, and to sit in judgment upon the Saints. That the Saints are to judge the world instead of the officers of the world judging them. I once thought that I never could be induced to occupy the position that I now do, to expose the wickedness and corruption of the man whom I once looked upon as my spiritual guide, as I then considered Brigham Young to be.

Nothing could have compelled me to this course save an honest sense of the duty I owe myself, my God, the people at large, and my brethren and sisters who are treading the downward path that will lead them to irretrievable ruin, unless they retrace their steps and throw off the yoke of the tyrant, who has long usurped the right of rule that justly belongs to the son of Joseph, the Prophet. I have been driven to the wall by circumstances beyond my control, and have been forced to resort to the first law of nature, self-protection. Perhaps this has served to open my eyes to a sense of duty. I confess I have been deeply steeped in fanaticism, even more so than I was aware of, until I felt the bitter pangs of its direful influence upon me.

I heard Mother Smith, the mother of Joseph the Prophet, plead with Brigham, Young, with tears, not to rob young Joseph of his birthright, which his father, the Prophet, bestowed upon him previous to his death. That young Joseph was to succeed his father as the leader of the Church, and it was his right in the line of the priesthood. "I know it," replied Brigham, "don't worry or take any trouble, Mother Smith; by so doing you are only laying the knife to the throat of the child. If it is known that he is the rightful successor of his father, the enemy of the Priesthood will seek his life. He is too young to lead this people now, but when he arrives at mature age he shall have his place. No one shall rob him of it." This conversation took place in the Masonic Hall at Nauvoo, in 1845. Several persons were then present.

In the meantime Brigham had sought to establish himself as the leader of this Church. Many years, however, passed away before he dared assume or claim to be the rightful successor of Joseph, the Seer, Prophet, and Revelator to the Church. When the time came, according to his own words, for Joseph to receive his own, Joseph came, but Brigham received him not. He said, as an excuse, that Joseph had not the true spirit. That his mother had married a Gentile lawyer, and had infused the Gentile spirit into him. That Joseph denied the doctrine of

A "BLOOD ATONED" VICTIM, NEAR NAUVOO

his father, celestial marriage. Brigham closed the door and barred him from preaching in the Tabernacle, and raised a storm of persecution against him. He took Joseph's cousin, George A. from using his influence in favor of Joseph as the leader of the people, which he otherwise would have done. He also ordained John Smith, the son of Hyrum the Patriarch, to the office of Patriarch to the Church, and his brother Joseph F, Smith, to the office of one of the Twelve Apostles, thus securing their influence and telling them that had young Joseph been willing to act in harmony with them, the heads of the Church, he could have had his place, but that he was too much of a Gentile ever to lead this people. Brigham said he had some hopes that David, a brother of young Joseph, when he became older, might occupy the place of his father, but Joseph never would. In this low, cunning, intriguing way he blinded the eyes of the people, and gained another advantage over them in establishing himself and family at the head of the Church, as the favored of the Lord. Strange as it may appear, yet it is true, that many of this people are blind to the intrigues of this heartless imposter. They suffer themselves to be bound in fetters and bondage, and surrender the last principle of manhood and independence, and make themselves slaves to that corrupt usurper and his profligate family, who have robbed the fatherless, and usurped the right to rule that belongs to another; and who has been trying to put his profligate sons at the head of this Church, to rule over this people.

Now let us for a moment divest ourselves of fanaticism, which is the result of ignorance, and look from the standpoint of justice and reason, and compare the conduct and character of the two families. Young Joseph, the legal heir of the Prophet, because he denies polygamy, or celestial marriage, is accused of not following in the footsteps of his father, which Brigham says renders him unworthy to be a leader of this people. How much better is Brigham's son, John W. Young? Has he followed in the footsteps of the Prophet? Every one acquainted with his heartless conduct must answer No! On the contrary, he turned away the bride of his youth, and his offspring by her, and also his other wives that were given him in the celestial order of marriage, and then took up with an actress from the stage! A woman not even of the faith of the Mormon Church.

Notwithstanding all this he is put forward by his father, Brigham, as his right-hand man, to guide the destinies of this Church and people. Oh! consistency, where art thou! and justice! where hast thou fled! Have this people lost their understanding? Does it require inspiration to detect the fraud and injustice at the bottom of this move? I think not. But it does require a great deal more fanaticism than I want to possess to make me believe that God or justice has anything to do with it. I am honest in saying that it is from beneath, and none but a depraved, heartless wretch, would stoop so low as to use religion as a cloak to dupe and deceive the people. To accomplish so corrupt a purpose he has robbed the rich and the poor of this people. He has made them pay tithes and tributes to himself. He has made himself rich and waxed fat, until he really imagines himself to be the Lord's vicegerent here on earth, and that no man has the right to interfere with him. He is above the law - he is the Lord's anointed! Oh! vain man, go hide thyself, and consider from whom thou hast received the succession, and through whose hard earnings thou hast been made rich.

I must not forget to make mention of the qualifications of young Briggy, the son of the present leader of the Church. He is considered by his father fully qualified to be his successor; to stand at the head of the Church and lead the Saints. This amiable son of the Prophet Brigham, while on a mission to England, concluded that he would measure arms with Queen Victoria and the Prince of Wales, by driving as many horses as she did to her carriage. This was a violation of law. The Queen very soon gave Prince Briggy to understand that she was the ruler of that kingdom; that if his father could measure arms with the President of the United States, his son could not do so with her. Prince Brig was shut up in jail, and there he was to remain until the fine for his offense was paid. I have been told that $26,000 were paid from the perpetual emigration fund for his release. This emigration fund is collected from the people for the gathering together of poor saints, but the liberty of this worthy young man was of more consequence then the gathering in of poor saints. Perhaps it is this ambitious act of the Prophet's son that has qualified him to act as a leader! How does the character of Smith's sons compare with that of Brigham Young's sons? The one were peaceable, law-abiding citizens, the others are spendthrifts and ambitious, regardless of law or order - just like their father, full of self-esteem, miserly and bigoted. I remember twenty years ago, among the first members of the Church, it was all the talk that young Joseph would soon take the leadership of the Church, as the rightful successor of his father, the Prophet. At that time it never was thought that Brigham Young intended to hold the place permanently, and establish himself and profligate family at the head of the Church, as he has done, to make slaves of the Saints, to keep and support himself and his worthless sons. The Saints have suffered themselves to be led step by step downward, lulled to sleep by false promises and phantoms that can never be realized. They are powerless, and having lost their self control, they cannot resist the charms by which the serpent captivates his victims and holds them fast under his influence. Oh! that I had the power of speech to touch the understanding of my brethren and sisters, to wake them from the stupor and lethargy that has overcome them, through the subtle cunning of the devil, that I fear has already made the bonds of many of them so strong they can never loose them.

But I must stop and take a retrospective view of things in Nauvoo, that I have not yet mentioned, trusting to my worthy friend Bishop to place these sentiments which I have just written in their proper place in my history. I have felt impressed to write them while I could do so, not knowing that I would have the liberty to bring up all the circumstances to that date.

CHAPTER XIV

INSIDE VIEW OF POLYGAMY AND THE DOCTRINE OF "SEALING"

IN THE Winter of 1845 meetings were held all over the city of Nauvoo, and the spirit of Elijah was taught in the different families as a foundation to the order of celestial marriage, as well as the law of adoption. Many families entered into covenants with each other - the man to stand by his wife and the woman to cleave unto her husband, and the children to be adopted to the parents. I was one of those who entered into covenants to stand by my family, to cleave to them through time and eternity. I am proud to say I have kept my obligations sacred and inviolate to this day. Others refused to enter into these obligations, but agreed to separate from each other, dividing their substance, and mutually dissolving their former relations on friendly terms. Some have mutually agreed to exchange wives and have been sealed to each other as husband and wife by virtue and authority of the holy priesthood. One of Brigham's brothers, Lorenzo Young, now a bishop, made an exchange of wives with Mr. Decker, the father of the Mr. Decker who now has an interest in the cars running to York. They both seemed happy in the exchange of wives. All are considered aliens to the commonwealth of Israel until adopted into the kingdom by baptism, and their children born unto them before the baptism of the parents are to be adopted to the parents, and become heirs to the kingdom through the law of adoption. But the children that are born to parents after the baptism of the parents are legal heirs to the kingdom.

This doctrine extends much further. All persons are required to be adopted to some of the leading men of the Church. In this, however, they have the right of choice, thus forming the links of the chain of priesthood back to the father, Adam, and so on to the second coming of the Messiah. Time will not allow me to enter into the full details of this subject. The ordinance of celestial marriage was extensively practiced by men and women who had covenanted to live together, and a few men had dispensations granted them to enter into plural marriages, which were taught to be the stepping stone to celestial exaltation. Without plural marriage a man could not attain to the fullness of the holy priest-

hood and be made equal to our Saviour. Without it he could only attain
to the position of the angels, who are servants and messengers to those
who attain to the Godhead.

These inducements caused every true believer to exert himself to
attain that exalted position, both men and women. In many cases the
women would do the "sparking," through the assistance of the first wife.

My second wife, Nancy Bean, was the daughter of a wealthy farmer,
who lived near Quincy, Illinois. She saw me on a mission and heard me
preach at her father's house. She came to Nauvoo and stayed at my
house three months, and grew in favor and was sealed to me in the
Winter of 1845. My third and fourth wives were sealed to me soon afterward, in my own house. My third wife, Louisa, is now the first wife of
D. H. Wells. She was then a young lady, gentle and beautiful, and we
never had an angry word while she lived with me. She and her sister
Emeline were both under promise to be sealed to me. One day Brigham
Young saw Emeline and fell in love with her. He asked me to resign my
claims in his favor, which I did, though it caused a great struggle in my
mind to do so, for I loved her dearly. I made known to Emeline
Brigham's wish, and even went to her father's house several times and
used my influence with her to induce her to become a member of
Brigham's family. The two girls did not want to separate from each
other; however, they both met at my house at an appointed time and
Emeline was sealed to Brigham, and Louisa was sealed to me. Amasa
Lyman officiated at the ceremony. At the same time Sarah C. Williams,
the girl that I had baptized in Tennessee, when but a child, at the house
of Wm. Pace, and who came to Nauvoo, stood up and claimed a place
in my family. She is yet with me and is the mother of twelve children.
She has been a kind wife, mother and companion. By Louisa I had one
son born, who died at the age of twelve. She lived with me about one
year after her babe was born. She then told me that her parents were
never satisfied to have one daughter sealed to the man highest in authority and the other below her. Their constant teasing caused us to separate,
not as enemies, however. Our friendship was never broken. Her change
made her more miserable than ever. After we got into Salt Lake Valley
she offered to come back to me, but Brigham would not consent to her
so doing. Her sister became a favorite with Brigham, and remained so
until he met Miss Folsom, who captivated him to a degree that he
neglected Emeline, and she died brokenhearted.

Plural marriages were not made public. They had to be kept still. A young man did not know when he was talking to a single woman. As far as Brigham Young was concerned, he had no wives at his house, except his first wife, or the one that he said was his first wife. Many a night have I gone with him, arm in arm, and guarded him while he spent an hour or two with his young brides, then guarded him home and guarded his house until one o'clock, when I was relieved. He used to meet his beloved Emeline at my house.

In the Spring of 1845 Rachel Andors was sealed to me - the woman who has stood by me in all my troubles. A truer woman was never born. She has been by me true, as I was to Brigham, and has always tried to make my will her pleasure. I raised her in my family from five years of age. She was a sister to my first wife. Her mother, Abigail Sheffer, was sealed to me for an eternal state. The old lady has long since passed away, and entered into eternal rest and joy.

But to resume the narrative of events at Nauvoo. In the year 1845 the building of the Temple was progressing. Through the Summer trouble was brewing among all the Saints, both in Illinois and Iowa. Many of my friends from Tennessee, and some from Kentucky, emigrated and joined us during that Summer and Fall, as well as some from other places. An effort was made to complete the Nauvoo House if possible, but finding the storm approaching too fast the work on the House was abandoned, and all hands put at work on the Temple. We were anxious to complete the Temple, in order that we might receive our promised blessings in it before we commenced our exodus across the plains in search of a home, we knew not where. Our time was limited, and our Christian friends who surrounded us, whose ire had been aroused to the highest pitch, were not likely to allow us to remain longer than our appointed time. The killing of the Smiths had aroused their friends to acts of violence, and many whose houses were burned and property destroyed, who had come to Nauvoo for protection and shelter, retaliated by driving in stock from the range to subsist upon. No doubt the stock of many an innocent man was driven away, and this served to bring others into trouble.

Thus things grew worse the longer the Saints remained at Nauvoo. It was an unfortunate matter, and much of the trouble that came upon the Church was brought on through the folly and fanaticism of the Saints. I have seen relentless cruelty practiced by those who directed this cattle stealing. I cannot call it anything else, though they called it getting back what had been taken from them. It caused many strangers to come to the city to look for traces of their cattle. A company was organized, called the "Whittlers." They had long knives, and when any of these strangers would come to town, they would gather around him, and whittle; none of them saying a word, no matter what question was asked. They would thus watch any stranger, gathering close to him, until they finally ran him out of town. I never took part in such low, dirty doings. I was taught from a child to respect all persons, as every spirit begets its like. I never did think any good came of such conduct. A man must respect himself, or he can never command others.

During the fall of 1845 companies were formed for making wagons for the contemplated move, as a great many of the Saints were poor, and had neither wagons nor teams. Teams were more easily obtained than wagons. People traded off their lots and loose property for teams. Many of the wagons had wooden hoops in place of tires, for the want of iron, though iron and everything else was at the lowest price. Common labor was only twenty five cents per day, but money was hard to get.

About the 1st of December, 1845, we commenced filling up the rooms for giving endowments. I assisted in putting up the stoves, curtains and other things. It was about fifteen days before we got everything ready. I must mention that when the doctrine of baptizing for the dead was first introduced, the families met together, down by the river side, and one of their number, of the order of the Melchisedek Priesthood, officiated. They were baptized in behalf of all they could remember, the men for the men, and the women for the women. But when the fount was ready in the Temple, which rested on the twelve carved oxen, they went and were baptized in it, after the same order, except that a clerk must make a record of it, and two witnesses must be present, and the name of the person baptized and for whom he or she was baptized, and the date of baptism, together with the name of the officiating elder, and the name of the clerk and witnesses entered in the register or record. All persons who are baptized must also be confirmed. Male and female alike pass through the same ceremony, and the fact entered in the record kept for that purpose.

This is done for all who have died without the knowledge of the gospel. As Jesus, while his body lay in the tomb, went and preached to the spirits, in the spirit world, the doctrine of his gospel to all who had died before hearing it, since the days of Noah, so through baptism for the dead, can our friends, and those who have gone before us, be made partakers of this new and last gospel sent to us, and receive its blessings and ed eternal reward. No person, however, is allowed the privilege of this baptismal fount, or their washings or anointings, unless they have paid their tithings promptly, and have a certificate to that effect. In many cases, also, where men require it, their just debts must be settled before they are allowed to be baptized, washed or anointed. In the order of Endowment, a list is made out the day previous, of those who wish to take their endowments. Every person is required to wash himself clean, from head to foot. Also to prepare and bring a good supply of food, of the best quality, for themselves and those who labor in the house of the Lord. In the latter about twenty-five persons are required in the different departments to attend to the washing, anointing, blessing, ordaining, and sealing. From twenty-five to fifty persons are passed through in twenty four hours.

I was among the first to receive my washings and anointings, and even received my second anointing, which made me an equal in the order of the Priesthood, with the right and authority to build up the kingdom in all the earth, and power to fill any vacancy that might occur. I have officiated in all the different Branches, from the highest to the lowest. There were about forty men who attained to that order in the Priesthood, including the twelve Apostles and the first presidency, and to them was entrusted the keeping of the records. I was the head clerk; Franklin D. Richards was my assistant clerk. My office was in room number one, at President Young's apartments.

I kept a record of all the sealings, anointings, marriages and adoptions.

I was the second one adopted to Brigham Young. I should have been his first adopted son, being the first that proposed it to him, but always ready to give preference to those in authority, I placed A. P. Rockwood's name first on the list. I also had my children adopted to me in the Temple. Brigham Young had his children adopted to himself, and we were the only ones, to my knowledge, that had our children so adopted at the Temple at Nauvoo. As time would not permit attending to all the people, the business was rushed through day and night.

Officers were on the alert to arrest Brigham Young. He often hid in the different apartments of the Temple. One day about sunset, an officer, knowing that he was in the Temple, waited for him to come out, as his carriage was waiting for him at the door. Brigham threw his cloak around Wm. Miller, who resembled Brigham in build and stature, and sent him to the carriage with Geo. D. Grant, his driver. As they got to the carriage, Grant said to Miller, "Mr. Young, are you ready to go?" As he spoke to him, the officer said: "Mr. Young, I have a writ for you. I want you to go with me to Carthage," twenty miles distant. Miller replied, "Shall I take my carriage?" The officer answered, "You may if you choose, and I will pay the bill."

Grant then drove Miller to Carthage, and the marshal took him to the hotel and supplied him with refreshments. After supper an apostate Mormon called in with the marshal to see him. When he saw Miller, he said to the marshal:

"By heavens! you are sold this time. That is not Brigham, that is Mr. Miller."

The marshal was a good deal nettled, and said to Miller:

"I am very much obliged to you."

Miller replied:

"You are quite welcome. I hope you will pay my bill as you agreed to do."

"Why did you deceive me?" demanded the marshal.

"I did not," replied Miller, "you deceived yourself. I said nothing to deceive you."

"All right," replied the marshal, "I will settle your bill, and you can return in the morning, if you choose."

This friendly warning gave Brigham to understand that it was time for him to get away, that many such tricks would not be wholesome.

In the Temple I took three more wives - Martha Berry, Polly Ann Workman and Delethea Morris, and had all my family sealed to me over the altar, in the Temple, and six of them received their second anointings, that is, the first six wives did, but the last three we had not time to attend to.

On the 10 of February, 1846, Brigham Young and a small company crossed the Mississippi River, on the ice, into Iowa, and formed an encampment on a stream called Sugar Creek. I crossed, with two wagons, with the first company. Brigham did this in order to elude the officers, and wait there until all who could fit themselves out could join him. Such as were in danger of being arrested were helped away first. Our police crossed over to guard the first Presidency. Those who were not liable to be arrested remained back and sent their teams forward. I took one of Brigham's wives, Emeline, in one of my wagons, with Louisa, her sister, as far as Florence or Rainsville. All of Brigham's wives, except the first, were taken by the brethren, as he did not at that time have the teams or means to convey his family across the plains, but was dependent on the brethren for help, though he had used every means in his power to raise an outfit.

Brigham called a council of some of the leading men. Among them was one Joseph L. Heywood and myself. Heywood was a merchant at Quincy, Illinois, and was doing a fair business before he joined the Mormon Church, and was considered an honorable man. When the Mormons were driven from Missouri many had occasion to bless him for his many kindnesses to them in their hour of trouble. At the council, after some conversation upon our present move, Brigham proposed to appoint a committee of men, against whom no charges could be brought, to return to Nauvoo and attend to the selling of the property of the Saints, and to see to fitting out the people and starting them forward. He proposed that I, A. W. Babbitt, Joseph L. Heywood and David S. Fulmer be that committee. Brother Heywood was asked to turn over his whole stock of goods to fit the first Presidency and the Apostles for the journey. This to Brother Heywood was a stunner. He replied that he was indebted to honorable men in the East for the most of his stock, and that he did not dare to defraud them; that he had been taught from childhood to deal honorably with all men. He was told by Brigham that he could raise the money to pay his Eastern creditors from the sales of the property at Nauvoo. This brother Heywood thought very doubtful, as the property of a deserted city would not be very valuable. Brigham then said that this was a case of emergency, and they must have the goods; that Brother Heywood must write to his creditors and tell them that owing to the trouble among the people business had fallen off, and that he could not pay them, but would in the future. Brigham told him if he failed to raise money from the sale of city property, as soon as the Church was established that he would raise the money for him to satisfy his creditors, and this would give him more influence than ever among the outside world. They finally persuaded Heywood to turn over his goods. If time permits I will hereafter tell how he came out of the matter. For all of my services for the leading men I never received a dollar. I have managed, however, to maintain my family in good style, to pay my tithing and live independently of help from the Church. I was called a shrewd trader and a good financier, and always had plenty.

I usually had some money on hand. These were considered by Brigham noble traits in my character. He would rather a person would give to him than beg from him.

CHAPTER XV

THE SAINTS MOVE WESTWARD

A FEW words in regard to the Prophet Joseph. He was tried twenty
one times for different offenses, and acquitted each time. One time
when he was visiting at Peoria, he was captured by four men from
Missouri, who started with him in a wagon, to take him to that State.
Two of them sat beside him with cocked pistols, punching him in the
side occasionally, and telling him that if he opened his mouth they
would blow his brains out. He was not arrested by any process of law,
but they were trying to kidnap him. Stephen H. Markham, an old tried
friend of Joseph, ran ahead to the town of Peoria, employed a lawyer,
got out a writ of habeas corpus, and had him set at liberty. When the
news reached Nauvoo, the Saints were in the wildest state of excitement. The Mormon steamer there was laden with troops, who hastened
to Peoria to rescue the Prophet. When they arrived there they found him
at liberty. This was in 1843. The same winter he organized what was
called the "Council of Fifty." This was a confidential organization. A
man by the name of Jackson belonged to it, though he did not belong to
the Church. This council was designated as a lawmaking department,
but no record was ever kept of its doings, or if kept, they were burned at
the close of each meeting. Whenever anything of importance was on
foot this council was called to deliberate upon it. The council was called
the "Living Constitution." Joseph said that no legislature could enact
laws that would meet every case, or attain the ends of justice in all
respects.

As a man, Joseph tried to be a law-abiding citizen, but he had a mot-
ley crew to manage, men who were constantly doing something to bring
trouble upon them. He often reproved them and some he disfellow-
shipped. But being of a forgiving disposition, when they would come
back to him and beg his forgiveness, his kind, humane heart could not
refuse them. He was often basely imposed upon.

I was standing with him one cold day, watching a couple of men who were crossing the river in a canoe. The river was full of ice, running swiftly. As they neared the shore the canoe upset, throwing them into the river. One of them got on a cake of ice, but the other made several attempts before he could do so. As quick as thought Joseph sent a runner to them with a bottle of whisky, saying, "Those poor boys must be nearly frozen." This man Jackson was standing near; said he, "By Heavens, he is the most thoughtful man on earth."

On another occasion, on the 4th of July, 1843, at a celebration, a number of toasts had been offered, when some one said, "Brother Joseph, suppose you give us a toast." Raising his glass, with water in it, in the place of spirits, he said, "Here is wishing that all the mobocrats of the nineteenth century were in the middle of the sea, in a stone canoe, with an iron paddle, that a shark might swallow the canoe, and the shark be thrust into the nethermost part of h--l, and the door locked, the key lost, and a blind man hunting for it."

But to return to our expedition across the plains. The snow lay about eight inches deep on the ground when the first company crossed the river. The plan of operation was this: We must leave Nauvoo, whether ready or not. All covenanted to help each other, until all were away that wanted to go. The teams and wagons sent to help others away were to be sent back as soon as a suitable place was found at which to make a settlement, and leave the poor, or rather those who had no teams to go on with. I was unwilling to start out with a part of my family, leaving the rest behind, and thought that now was the time to get them out before greater trouble commenced. I went into Brigham's tent and told him what I thought of the matter, and that I thought I could fit up teams ina few days and bring them all away. He replied that he had been thinking of the same thing. Said he:

"Go, I will give you five days in which to sell out and cross the river again, and bring me one hundred dollars in gold."

I informed the portion of my family that was with me of my intentions. My first wife was still at Nauvoo. I had the confidence of my family, and I was a man who seldom undertook anything that I did not carry out. I started back on foot, and crossed the river on the ice. I fell in with acquaintances about La Harpe, who were in trouble about a number of wagons and teams which they had purchased in the State. The devil was to pay generally. Some of the Gentiles who had lost cattle laid it to the Mormons in Nauvoo, and they were determined to take cattle from the Mormons until they got even. I had a brick house and lot on Parley street that I sold for three hundred dollars in teams. I told the purchaser that I would take seven wagons and teams, and before I went to sleep that night I had my entire outfit of teams. My large house, costing me $8000 (in Salt Lake City it would have been worth $50,000), I was offered $800 for. My fanaticism would not allow me to take that for it. I locked it up, selling only one stove out of it, for which I received eight yards of cloth. The building, with its twenty-seven rooms, I turned over to the committee, to be sold to help the poor away. The committee informed me afterwards that they sold the house for $12.50.

I was sitting with my family, and was telling them that I must get $500 in some way, but the Lord opened no way by which I could see where I could get it, and I had but five days in which to get out of Nauvoo. In an adjoining room was an old gentleman and his daughter, who rented the room of me. They were from Pennsylvania, and the old gentleman was wealthy. The daughter stepped into her father's room, and soon returned, saying that her father wished to see me. I went into his room. He gave me a seat and said, "You once did me a kindness that I have not repaid. Do you remember meeting me once, when coming from the Temple? I had been there with my wife and only child to get my washings and anointings. I was not admitted, because I was a stranger, and no one to vouch for me. I was returning with a heavy heart, when I met you. You returned with me and used your influence, vouched for us and procured our admittance. I obtained our endowments. I had a cancer on my breast at that time, that was considered incurable. From the hour I received our endowments it has never pained me and it is healing up. Now, I am thankful I have it in my power to do you a little favor in return." So saying, he lifted the lid of a box and counted out $500 in gold coin, saying that if it would help me I was welcome to it. I offered him a team, but he said he had money enough to buy his outfit, and support him while he lived, and that he felt thankful for an opportunity of returning my favor. This was to me an unexpected blessing from an honest heart. I wept with joyful gratitude; I had the means that I desired in my hands. The next morning I received my teams and wagons. All had to be fitted up for the journey. My family all went to work making tents and things needful for the journey. I sent my wagons to the Mormon wagon shop and told them to work night and day, and put them in the best order within three days, and I would give them $50 dollars in gold, which was $5 for a day and night's work, quite a difference from fifty cents, the usual price. They went to work in earnest, and as fast as a wagon was finished I had it loaded. In the meantime A. W. Babbitt was urging me to cross the river, as there was an officer in town looking for me. On the third day I started one of my ox teams across the river on the ice, and came near losing the whole outfit, by its breaking through the ice. I crossed no more teams that way. I then got a large wood boat and some twenty-five men to help me, and we cut through the ice across the river, so that the boat could be towed over. On the fourth day I had all of my effects at the river side. The day before, when I had crossed the team that had broken through the ice, I met an officer at the river side looking for me. He wanted to arrest me on the charge of lascivious cohabitation - having more wives than one. I told him that I had seen John D. Lee crossing the river the day before, and that one of his oxen broke through, and added that it was a pity he had not broken through also. I stepped into a saloon with the officer and we took a drink together. I then went with him into the wagon shop, and stepping in ahead of him, and tipping the wink to the men there, said,

"Have any of you seen John D. Lee today? Here is an officer looking for him."

They replied that he had crossed the river the day before. This satisfied the officer, and he went away. I bought oils and paints for my wagons, and five gallons of whisky to treat the boys who had helped me over the river. As we left the river, a heavy storm came up. It was so dark I could see nothing. I had four mule teams, and let them follow the road. We halted about a mile beyond the town of Montrose, and a man who lived there, named Hickenlooper, took us all in and attended to the animals. I went to sleep and did not wake until ten o'clock the next morning. This man had all the supplies we needed, flour, bacon, etc.; and I purchased my store of supplies from him. I learned that the company had moved on, and was camped at a place called Richardson's Point, forty-five miles from Montrose. Before reaching the encampment, I was met by Brigham Young, H. C. Kimball, and Dr. William Richards in their carriages, who bade me welcome. After we reached camp, a council was held, and I reported my success, and gave an account of my mission. When I had finished, Brigham asked me if I had brought him that hundred dollars. I replied I had, and handed it to him. He counted it, and then said,

"What shall I do with it?"

I replied, "Feed and help the poor."

He then prophesied, saying that I should be blessed, and means would come unto me from an unexpected source, that in time of need friends would be sent to my assistance.

The roads were in a bad condition, and we lay here a few days, during which time I painted and numbered my wagons. Myself, Geo. S. Clark, Levi Stewart and another man were appointed hunters, as there was much game in the country we had to pass through, turkey, deer and some elk.

From here we traveled to the Raccoon Fork of Grand River, in Iowa, about seventy-five miles. At the three forks of the Grand River we made a halt. In fact the rain had made the country impassable, and our provisions were running short. Here we found some wild hogs, and the men killed several. Brigham said that they were probably some of our hogs that had become scattered when we were driven out of Missouri. This was sufficient license for many to kill anything they could find.

While we lay here two men came to our camp, named Allen Miller and Mr. Clancy. They were traders to the Potawatomie Indians. Allen Miller had married one of my wives. They informed me that we could get everything we needed about fifty miles from there, near Grand River. We unloaded about seventeen wagons and selected out such articles as we could spare. I was appointed the Contracting Commissary, to do the purchasing for the companies. This was in April, 1846.

We started with those two men and the seventeen wagons, and drove to Miller's and made that headquarters, as he had provisions in abundance. The grass was like a meadow then. I had some horses and harness to exchange for oxen and cows. When we had turned out our stock for the day at Miller's, Mr. Clancy invited me home with him. On entering his house I found his partner, Patrick Dorsey, an Irishman, sick. Mr. Dorsey had been tormented with a pain in his eyes, in so much that he had rested neither day nor night, and was losing his sight. I asked him if he was a Catholic. He answered that he was. I knew their faith, as I was raised a Catholic and once believed in their doctrines. I asked him if he wished me to pray for him. He inquired if I was a minister, to which I replied that I was. He then said:

"Do pray with me, if you please, for I am in great distress."

I then laid my hands upon his head, and asked the Father, in the name of the Son, and by virtue of the holy priesthood in me vested, to stay his sufferings and heal him. The pain left him instantly, as he took his hat and walked with me to Miller's house. They were astonished to see him apparently without pain, and asked him what I had done for him. He

MORMONS LEAVING NAUVOO ON THEIR JOURNEY WESTWARD

answered:

"I was in great distress; a stranger laid hands upon my head, and prayed and made me whole; but who he was, or whence he came, I know not. But this I know, that I was almost blind, and now I see; I was sick, but now I am well."

This little occurrence created quite an excitement in the settlement, and nothing would do but I must preach the next evening. During the next day I made several trades. Evening came, and I preached at my friend Miller's. When I closed they made me up a purse of five dollars, and offered to load one of our wagons with provisions.

We remained here about a week and did finely in trading. On Sunday quite a large attendance, for a new country, turned out to hear me preach. I was weary and did not feel much like preaching. However I preached about an hour and a half. At the close of the service they made up ten dollars for me, and a Mr. Scott, a wealthy farmer, said that if I would drive my wagons to his establishment he would fill them all with flour, bacon, potatoes, etc. I had the use of my friend Miller's store to store away our traps, as I had more than we could take away. The people were anxious for me to stop there and take up a farm, make my home with them, and preach and build up a church. I told them I was bound for the Rocky Mountains. As for Mr. Dorsey, he offered me all he had, and wanted to know what to do to be saved. He gave me a history of his life. He told me he led a company of men from Carroll County, Missouri, when we were driven from the State. I reflected a little and gave him a list of city property at Nauvoo that I would turn out to him at one fourth its value, for such property as he wanted to turn out to me. He said he had twelve yoke of oxen and some twenty five cows, and other stock; four bee stands, three wagons, some six to eight hundred dollars' worth of bacon, flour, meal, soap, powder, lead, blankets, thirty rifles, guns, knives, tobacco, calicoes, spades, hoes, plows, harrows; also twelve feather beds and all of his improvements. He said he only wanted his carriage and a span of black horses, to take himself, wife and partner to Nauvoo. All the above property he turned over to me, and I gave him deeds to property in Nauvoo. He was to go back with our return teams, as Brigham had commenced making a settlement at the place where he was camped. He called the place Garden Grove. We returned to camp, laden with all our teams could haul, besides the three wagons that I had got from Dorsey. There was a great deal that we could not move away. I took a forty gallon cask of honey and a quantity of whisky and brandy from Dorsey. The bee stands, improvements and farming utensils I turned over for the use of the settlers that remained at Garden Grove.

This circumstance confirmed me in my oft-expressed opinion that much of the trouble that has followed this people has been created by wild, ignorant fanatics; for only a few years before these same people were our most bitter enemies, and when we came again and behaved ourselves, they treated us with the utmost kindness and hospitality.

I also made arrangements for all the labor needed by the company that was left, so that they could be planting crops and raising supplies while building houses to live in. The company left would be strengthened by others who would follow. All the borrowed teams were returned to bring others forward, and those who had teams of their own went on and made another settlement called Pisgah, and then went on to Council Bluffs, which was afterwards called Kanesville, in honor of Col. Thomas L. Kane. From this point I took a cargo of traps, consisting of feather beds, fine counterpanes, quilts, and such goods, and went down to Missouri, with a large number of wagons, to obtain a cargo of supplies, and beef cattle and cows. During my absence a call was made on the Mormons for five hundred men to go to Mexico, to defend the American flag. Col. Ethan Allen and Thos. L. Kane came to raise the required number of men. An express was sent back to Pisgah and Garden Grove to furnish their number. The ranks were nearly full before I reached camp. Dr. Richards said to me:

"I am glad you have returned. We want you for one of the Captains."

"All right," I answered, and started to enroll my name. Brigham Young called me back and said he could not spare me; that there were men enough to fill the bill without me. The battalion was filled, and Col. Allen, a United States officer, marched them to Fort Leavenworth, Kansas.

From Council Bluffs I returned to Missouri, to buy a drove of cattle for Brigham Young, Dr. Richards and others, they having received some money from England. I also loaded some twenty wagons with provisions and articles for trade and exchange. I also exchanged horses for oxen, as the latter were low and the former high in price. About the middle of August I returned, with about five hundred head of cattle.

While I was gone the camp had moved across the Missouri River, at a place called Cutler's Park. The cattle swam the river, but the provision train was still on the Iowa side of the river. A. Grant, and some other of

Brigham's men, teamsters and waiters, crossed back for a couple of loads of provisions for Brigham and some others. Without saying a word to me they loaded up from the train their supply of provisions. When I heard of it I was considerably ruffled, as this train was in my charge and I was responsible for it.

I went to Grant, who seemed to be the leader, and told him he had not acted the gentleman in interfering with what did not belong to him. We had some warm words, and had not other parties interfered we would have come to blows. He justified himself by saying that Brigham sent him. I told him I did not care who sent him - that there was a right way and a wrong way of doing things. The feeling grew bitter between us, and they accused me of doing many wrongful things in my office. Finally Brigham called us all together in the presence of the first Presidency and the Twelve Apostles, and we made our statements. My accusers said what they had to say, and then I replied. When Brigham had heard our statements he reproved my accusers sharply, and fully approved of all I had done. He then said we must not have any ill feeling, and directed us to shake hands and be friends. I was the first that arose to comply. We shook hands, and though we agreed to drop the matter, still the old spirit lingered, even after we had crossed the plains.

CHAPTER XVI

LEE GOES ON AN EXPEDITION TO SANTA FE

WE GOT into camp the next day. After striking camp I noticed that a tire was gone from one of the wagons. A few days afterwards the mother of my first wife went down to a stream near by, and caught a number of fine fish, and on her way back to the camp she found the missing tire. It had rolled nearly three hundred yards from the road, and was laying where it at last stopped. The people all began cutting hay and stacking it, so as to be prepared for feeding our stock during the winter.

One night in the latter part of September, I dreamed that Lieut. James Pace, of Co. E, Mormon Battalion, stood at my tent door, and said that Col. Allen, commanding the Mormon battalion, was dead. I saw him plainly in my dream, and after he gave the information, he started back to his camp, and a man went from our encampment with him. I saw him and his companion, and all they did on their way back to Santa Fe, their dangers from the Indians, said all that took place, etc.

The next evening I went, as was usual, with Brigham Young and Dr. Willard Richardson, the Church Historian, to attend a council meeting at Heber C. Kimball's camp. After the meeting was over, and we we were going back to our tents, I said to Brigham Young:

"We will find Lieut. Pace at my tent when we get there."

"How do you know that?" said he.

I then told him my dream, and we walked on. When we got in sight of my tent, there stood Lieut. James Pace, just as I had seen him in my dream. This did not surprise me, for I knew he would come. Brigham Young said:

"What on earth has brought you back?"

He replied, "Col. Allen is dead. The battalion is without a commander and I have returned by order of the other officers to report to you, and ask you who shall now lead us."

"Why did you not elect one of your Captains?" said Brigham Young.

"The officers prefer to let Col. Smith, of the United States Army, lead us, if you will consent to it. But some of our men object, so I came for orders from you," said Pace.

The matter was taken into consideration by Brigham Young until next morning. In the morning he came to me in my tent, and said:

"John, how would you like to go back with Brother Pace and get the remittances of the soldiers?"

I said nothing could be more objectionable than such a trip.

"My family is large, I have no houses for them; they are without provisions, and I have no means to shelter them from the winter storms. I have not sufficient hay cut to feed my stock through the winter. I must attend to keeping my stock in order or I will have nothing left to take me and my family over the plains next Spring. But," said I, "there is no one more willing to sacrifice, himself and his own interests for the benefit of the Church than I am."

He waited and heard me through; then he said, "Thus sayeth the Lord. You shall go, my son. Prosperity shall attend you during your absence, and you shall return in safety, not a hair of your head shall be hurt." I said, "It is sufficient to know your will, I will go; but who will take care of my family in my absence?"

He said, "I will see to your family, and attend to all you are interested in during your absence."

I was satisfied, and proceeded to carry out the will of Brigham Young. I had cut considerable hay in company with the brethren, but as it had to be divided, I considered I would not have much to my share, especially after I had to divide in Winter with the lazy poor, or poor devils. I never went much on this copartnership system of labor. There are always a number who will not work, and yet they are always present when there is a division to be made of the proceeds of the labor. Joseph Smith classed the poor in three divisions. He said, "There are three kinds of poor. The Lord's poor, the devil's poor, and the poor devils." I never objected to share with the Lord's poor, but when it came to dividing with the devil's poor and the poor devils too, it was rather more than I desired; it took away all the profits.

My outfit for the intended journey consisted of a snug light wagon, a span of good mules, a spyglass and such traps as a man needs on the plains. I also took Dr. Willard's dog with me to watch while I was asleep. I was ordered to keep my business secret from every one, for fear of being robbed on my return home. I was not allowed to even tell my wives where I was going, or how long I would be gone. I went to St.

Joseph, Mo., and put up at John Gheen's, and stayed there while fitting out for the trip. While there I met Luke Johnson, one of the witnesses to the Book of Mormon. I had a curiosity to talk with him concerning the same. We took a walk down on the riverbank, I asked him if the statement he signed about seeing the angel and the plates, was true. If he did see the plates from which the Book of Mormon was printed or translated. He said it was true. I then said, "How is it that you have left the Church? If the angel appeared to you, and you saw the plates, how can you now live out of the Church? I understand you were one of the twelve apostles at the first organization of the Church?"

"I was one of the twelve," said he, "I have not denied the truth of the Book of Mormon. But myself and several others were overtaken in a fault at Kirkland, Ohio - Wm. Smith, Oliver Cowdrey, one or two others, and myself. We were brought up for the offense before the Church authorities. Sidney Rigdon and Wm. Smith were excused, and the matter hushed up. But Cowdrey and myself were proceeded against and our choice given us to make a public confession, or be dropped from the Church. I refused to make the public confession unless Rigdon and Smith did the same. The authorities said that would not do, for Rigdon was counselor to the Prophet, and Wm. Smith was the brother of the Prophet, and also one of the twelve; but that if Cowdrey and I would confess, it would be a cloak for the other two. I considered this unjust and unfair. So I left the Church for that reason. But I have reflected over the matter much since that time, and I have come to the conclusion that each man is accountable for his own sins, also that the course I have been pursuing injures me alone, and I intend to visit the Saints and again ask to be admitted into the Church. Rigdon has gone to destruction, and Wm. Smith is not much better off today than I am."

This conversation was a great comfort to me. We went to Fort Leavenworth, where we learned that Colonel Smith had taken command of the battalion and had marched on with it. Lieut. Pace got another good horse here, and such oats and provisions as we needed. We then struck on after the command. We overtook the battalion about fifty miles below Bent's Fort. Our brethren were rejoiced to see us. Many had grievances to relate, and all had much to tell and inquire about. That morning they had buried one of the battalion named Phelps. The men said his death was caused by arsenic which the doctor had forced him to take. They claimed that Colonel Smith was a tyrant - that he was not the man that Colonel Allen had been. The command was on the march when we came up with it. There was a fifty mile desert before us, and little water on the route. Colonel Allen had allowed the men to pray with and for each other when sick and had not forced them to take medicine when they did not want it. But Colonel Smith deprived them of their religious rights and made them obey the doctor's orders at all times.The doctor examined the sick every morning and forced them to take medicine, or when they refused to take it they were compelled to walk, and when unable to walk and keep up with the others they were tied to the back end of the wagons, like they were animals. The doctor was generally called *Death*; he was know to all by that name. While traveling along Captain J. Hunt, of Company A, introduced Colonel Smith to me. I then invited them to ride in my wagon. They got in, and I soon introduced the subject of the treatment of the troops adopted by Colonel Allen, and spoke of its good influence over them. I said the men loved Colonel Allen, and would all have died for him, because he respected their religious rights. I said they were volunteers, and not like regular troops; that they were not used to regular military discipline, and felt that they were oppressed, and had lost confidence in their officers. I referred to the ill treatment of the men, and talked quite freely. Captain Hunt got very mad, and jumped out of the wagon. He said I talked like an insane man more than a man of sense. The Colonel said that he was willing to give up the command to the choice of the battalion. I said he had better keep it until we arrived at Santa Fe, but for his own sake he had better ease up on the boys a little. That evening Captain Hunt sent a delegation to me informing me that I was causing the command to mutiny, and I must stop it or he would have me put under arrest. I asked where he was going to find his men to put me under guard - that he could not find them in that command, and that if he doubted my word he had better try to arrest me. The Captain knew I was right, and so the matter ended. I then told them I would encourage the men to obedience until we reached Santa Fe. The troops were better treated after that.

On the march water was very scarce ; I saw a man offer $16 for a coffee pot of water one day on the desert. I walked most of the time, and let the sick ride in my wagon. When we reached the Spanish settlements we got pepper, onions, corn, sheep, goats and other articles of food. We reached Santa Fe in the midst of a snow storm. All the Mormons were pleased to find that honest Missourian, Colonel Doniphan, in command at that place. He had a kind, humane nature. The sick and disabled men of the battalion were sent to a Spanish town called Taos, under charge

MORMON FAMILY IN ARIZONA

THE BISHOP'S FAMILY AT 2 A.M.

of Captain Brant, for care and rest. Soon after reaching Santa Fe Colonel Philip St. John Cook took command of the battalion. The soldiers were paid off, and Howard Egan, who had accompanied me, was given one-half of the checks and money, donated by the soldiers for Brigham Young and Heber C. Kimball, and the remainder was given to me to carry back to winter quarters. I remained in camp ten days to recruit my animals, because I could not purchase an animal there for use. The army had taken everything fit to ride or walk.

I wished to have Lieut. Gully return with me, and it was necessary to obtain permission for him to resign before he could go with me. I went to see the commander and stated the situation to him, and asked that Lieut. Gully be allowed to resign. The General granted my request. The Lieutenant had been acting Commissary of Subsistence, and had to make up his papers before he could start. I waited until he was ready to go with me. I also took Russell Stevens with me, as he had been discharged on account of ill health. While thus waiting I was troubled with Egan considerably, for he was drunk every day, and I feared he would be robbed. I had Stevens watch him most of the time. By closely guarding him I kept him and the money safe. General Doniphan said I should have a guard with me, and he would send one back to protect us through the Indian country, but animals could not be procured. I then took the necessary trouble and procured as good a team as I could to start back with. With the consent of the General I got a large mule, after much trouble, to work with one of my own. While we were in camp at Santa Fe the Doctor was robbed. His trunk was stolen, carried out of the camp, and broken open. Two gold watches and some money were taken from it. Two mules were also stolen the same night. I knew nothing of this, nor who did it, until long afterwards. After we had started home Stevens had the mules. He brought them to camp and said they were his. I think Stevens and Egan robbed the Doctor, but they never acknowledged it to me. About the 11th of October, 1846, we started for home over a wilderness twelve hundred miles wide, nearly every foot of it infested with Indians. We camped in the mountains at Gold Springs, where little particles of gold can be seen on the bottom of the streams. Egan and Stevens did not join us until we had gone fifty miles from Santa Fe. They had the Doctor's mules and a Spanish horse with them when they joined us. When we had traveled ninety miles I discovered that one of my mules was failing. The little flesh that was on them was soft and would not last, for we had not fed them any grain. It was difficult to recruit our mules on the grass, for it is very short generally, and the immense herds of buffalo ranging over the country keep the grass short. At the last Spanish town we passed through I sent Egan to buy a couple of mules. That night Egan and Stevens came to camp with two poor, miserable looking little mules. I said:

"What on earth have you brought these poor brutes for?"

Egan said, "We cabbaged them; it was the best we could do."

I told him that I was on a mission of duty, and trusted in God, and I would not permit him to bring stolen articles to the camp. I then sent him back with the mules at once. I said, "My trust is in God, and not in the devil. We will go on, and you take back the mules, and leave them where you got them." He did as I directed. At Moro Station, on the Moro River, the last camp we would find until we reached the eastern side of the plains, we found a large, fat mule, that belonged to the Government. Lieutenant Gully gave the station keeper, a young man, a receipt for the mule, and we took it with us, as we were, in one sense, in Government employ. We were carrying a mail, and on general business for the Government. This was a large, fine, gentle mule. I called her Friendship. When the other animals grew weak, I fastened the double tree back to the axle, and thus Friendship hauled the wagon fully three hundred miles. At the Cimerone Springs we met a company of traders from St. Louis, with a train of thirty-eight wagons. One of their wagons was loaded with pitch pine wood for cooking purposes. It was then raining, and a regular plains storm was coming on. These storms are sometimes very destructive. A train had been overtaken at this same place a year before, and nearly all of the animals belonging to the train perished. I counted one hundred and ninety skeletons of mules that had died in that storm.

Many of the men also died at that time. The storm had taken place ten days earlier in the season than the one then threatening us. We were all invited to the camp by the Captain; the other men went, but I staid in the wagon to write up my account of the trip, which I was obliged to keep by order Brigham Young. Captain Smith then came to my wagon and gave me a drink of fine brandy. He invited us to take supper and break-fast with him, which we did. He asked me if I was not afraid to travel in such a small company, and said the Indians were all on the war path, and committing depredations all along the road, that he had a large train, yet did not consider himself safe. I answered, "My trust is in God, not in numbers." This led to a conversation on religious subjects. When I told

him who I was, and fully stated my belief to him, he was much interested in the new doctrine. At supper he had every thing to eat that could
be desired. The Captain put up a large tent over my wagon to protect it
from the storm and wind. The next morning the storm was over and we
made an early start. The Captain gave me a large cheese, a sack of butter crackers, some sardines, and many articles which were of great value
to us on our long, cold journey over the plains. He also gave me his
name, age, and place of residence in St. Louis, writing it in a little blank
book which he gave me. He then gave me five dollars in gold, shook
hands with me, and said, "Remember me in coming days," and we parted.

At the crossing of the Arkansas River, we met several companies of
Missouri troops. They informed us that Captain Mann, with three companies of troops, had been attacked by a large body of Southern Pawnee
and Cheyenne Indians, that they fought three hours, when the troops
were defeated and lost seven men killed, with quite a number wounded.
That three of the men had come for help. That Captain Mann had lost
all of his animals except the three that the messengers escaped with.
That the men only had a small supply of ammunition, and shot it all
away before they retreated. Reinforcements had gone to their assistance
and would bring in the command. They insisted upon us stopping with
them, saying it was madness for us to attempt to go on. I told them that
my trust was in God, and my business was urgent and we could not stop.
We went on twelve miles, when we met the troops bringing in the
wounded, and the remnant of the men who had been engaged with Capt.
Mann, in the late Indian fight; they also insisted upon our returning with
them. They said there were eight hundred mounted Indians not more
than two miles back, following up the rear guard, and that we would all
be certainly massacred unless we returned with them. I must admit that
the prospect looked dark. Still I felt impressed to go on. Along this river,
while it runs in nearly a level country and with no timber in a hundred
miles, yet there are many washes that sometimes ran out perhaps a mile
from the river. Often these washes, which were quite deep, caused the
road to run around them, thus forcing a person to travel a couple of
miles to gain two hundred yards in distance. It was near one of these
washes that we met the last body of troops. We stopped at the point
where the road turned back to the river. My comrades were in doubt
what to do. I felt that the danger was great. While debating the matter
over in my mind, my whole dream that I had the night when I saw Lieut.

Pace at my tent door, came fresh before me. I at once saw the whole situation. While studying upon this matter I heard a voice - an audible voice say:

"John, leave the road and follow me." The voice appeared to be about twenty feet in front of me, and the same distance from the earth. I was startled, for I could see no one who could have spoken thus to me. I said to Lieut. Gully:

"Did you hear that voice?"

"No," said he.

"What shall we do?" I asked.

He said, "You are entrusted with this mission, follow your impressions and all will be right."

From that moment I felt an invisible power that led me out into the plain, away from all roads or trails. We went along about half a mile, when we came to a low basin, which entirely hid us from the road. This basin contained about one acre of ground, and was covered with good grass. I felt it my duty to stop there, and did so. It was then about one o'clock, P.M. Soon after stopping we saw a cloud of dust made by a large herd of buffaloes running from the river where they had gone for water and had been frightened by Indians. We did not see the Indians, for we were perfectly protected by our position. We staid there and let our animals eat grass for about one hour and a half. We then started on again, following my *invisible guide*, in an easterly direction, over a country entirely strange to me. We traveled on until after dark, when we came to a deep wash which my guide directed me to follow down to the river. I did so, and came to the very spot where the Indians had attacked Captain Mann that morning. Fragments of the train lay scattered all over the plain. Our mules were much frightened, perhaps at the smell of the blood. We watered our animals, and filled our canteens with water. The night was still and the least noise would echo and re-echo through the river canyons, until it made the place more than horrid for people in our situation. We traveled on until near midnight, when we turned out our animals, tied the dog to the wagon tongue, to give us a guard, then all lay down and slept until daylight. We never camped near watering places, nor near the road. Our reasons for camping away from water, and at least half a mile from the road, were to avoid the Indians. We never had a fire at night.

The next day we found a large, fat young mule, with all its harness on. It had evidently been frightened during the battle and broke away from the command It was fully forty miles from the battle ground. I was much in need of fresh animals, for mine were nearly given out. The finding of this mule, as we did, gave me renewed confidence in God, and strengthened my belief that he was leading us.

The next day we traveled on in the same direction. The heavy rains had made the grass good. Buffalo were constantly in sight. We followed our course three days, when we struck the road again at a stream called Walnut Creek. Here we found a large Indian encampment, but the Indians were evidently out on a buffalo hunt. We crossed the creek and camped, concluding to cook our supper and let our animals eat and rest. It was no use trying to escape from the Indians, for I knew they had seen us and could capture us if they wished to do so. I concluded the best plan was to appear to be perfectly easy and without fear. Soon after camping, a band of over fifty warriors surrounded us. I offered to shake hands with them but they refused. I then offered them pine and needles and some calico that I had purchased to trade to the Spaniards. They took my proffered gifts and dashed them on the ground. I began to feel that although we had been delivered from many former dangers, our time had at last come. I remarked to Lieut. Gully, who was a true and faithful man:

"Pray in your heart to God, and ask him to turn away the ire of these people. They have been abused by large parties of white men and soldiers. They think we are of that class, and that we are only friendly because we are in their power, but if they know who we are, that we have been sent to preach the gospel to them, and to learn them its truths through the Book of Mormon, they would die sooner than see us hurt." I saw an elderly looking Indian turn and speak to a noble looking young warrior. They talked some time, and would occasionally turn and point to me. Then they all dismounted and came nearer to us. The old man raised his voice and talked in a loud tone, and in a rapid manner to his men, for about five or ten minutes. The young warrior then turned to us and spoke in plain English, very much to our surprise. He said:

"Young man, this is my father. He is the head chief of the Osage Indians. I have been educated in the East. We came here with the intention of scalping you all. This tribe has been abused by what my father calls the palefaces, though he wishes to be friendly with them. When a small part of this nation comes in contact with a larger force of palefaces, they are shot and abused, but when the Indians have the advantage the palefaces are always wanting to be friends. We thought you were of that class, but now my father is satisfied you are good men. I have read the Book of Mormon to him and to our tribe. I got the book from a preacher, who was in the Cherokee Nation. my father wishes me to say to you that you shall not be hurt. It you wish any dried buffalo meat you can have all that you want. Do not be afraid, we will not harm you, but you had better remain here until morning, for you may fall in with some of my father's braves, who will not know who you are, and they will attack you. If you stay until morning, I will go with you until you are out of danger." I replied that my business was urgent, and we must go on, that we had letters from the Mormon battalion to their friends at home, and must go on at once. The young man then told the chief what I said. The chief then said, through the young warrior:

"If you cannot stay, I will send word to the other others not to hurt you. They may not see you, as they are away from the road, but I will send some hunters out to tell them to let you pass in safety." I then thanked them very kindly, and told them I was raised among the Delawares and Cherokees, that when a child, I used to play with them before they were removed to this country, and that I was still their friend. They then asked if we wanted any dried meat, I told them no, that I would prefer some fresh meat. I saw a buffalo near by, and asked them to kill it, and bring me some of the meat. One of the Indians rode for the buffalo at the full speed of his horse. The well trained horse stopped, when near the buffalo, and the Indian shot it down, then jumped from his horse and out out a piece of the hump, and returned with it before we were ready to start. I then give the Indians what trinkets we had, and started on again. It was now after sunset.

Here was another manifestation of the providence of Almighty God. I felt so grateful for our deliverance that I could not restrain my tears of gratitude. I care not what people may call me. I know there is a just God, and a rewarder of those that diligently seek Him. I know that my Redeemer liveth and I shall see Him for myself and not for another. Though the day of my execution is near at hand - four days only are given me to continue the history of my life - (this is March the 19th, 1877) - my trust is in that Arm that cannot be broken. Though men may err, and cruelly betray each other unto death, my life may be taken from this earth, but nevertheless the hope of my calling in Christ Jesus, my Lord, is the same with me. I am *sure that I shall rest in peace*. I must not suffer my feelings to overcome me, or destroy the thread of my narrative. I wish to continue while time affords me a moment here, *that my history may live* when I am *no more.*

The next day only two Indians came to us, but they could not talk English, and we could not speak their tongue, so we had no conversation. I am certain from the actions of the two Indians that the old chief had kept his word with us and notified his tribe to let us go on in safety. On reaching the Pawnee Fork, a tributary of the Arkansas River, we found Captain Bullard's train of thirty wagons. They lay by all day in search of eight of their mules, that had been stampeded by the Indians, although they had been picketed and closely guarded. The company could not find a trace of them. The men were a rough, boisterous set, and, while our animals were very weary, I concluded it was still best to go further before camping. It was then raining, but that made the traveling better, for the country was quite sandy. We camped late that night at Ash Creek. We now felt that we were over the worst of our dangers, but we still had sufficient of trials before us to keep it from being a pleasure trip. Next morning our riding animals were unable to travel. They refused to go on. I again went to God in prayer and laid our case before Him, and asked that He would open up the way for our deliverance. That night I dreamed that I was exceedingly hungry and had little to eat, when five ears of large, solid corn were handed me by a person, who said, "This will do you until you get to where there is plenty." The ears of corn were of different colors; one ear was jet black, but perfectly sound; one was red, and one was yellow. I was much pleased with the corn and felt that there was not much danger of suffering now. The next morning our animals still looked fearfully bad; only two of our riding animals could raise the trot. Lieut. Gully said unless God soon sent us some fresh animals we would have to give up.

"We will not give up," said I. "God has protected us thus far and we must still trust in Him - in the eleventh hour of our trouble He will aid us. We will find help today."

"I hope so," said he.

He then said, "Have you been dreaming again?"

I related to him my dream about the corn, and said I thought the ears of corn meant mules. After prayer (we always kneeled in prayer, night and morning) we started on our way. The mules could hardly travel. We made about six miles, when we saw fresh tracks made by shod animals, that appeared to be dragging long ropes and pins. The tracks were following the road, going in the same direction that we were traveling. We had a long down grade before us. The plain was dotted here and there with herds of buffalo. I halted and took up my spyglass, and took a careful survey of the country. My efforts were rewarded by the sight of a number of mules feeding among the buffalo. We went on until we arrived as near them as we could get without leaving the road. We called a halt, turned our mules loose, then took out the oilcloth that I had to feed the mules on, and took a little of the grain we had left, and put it on the cloth. The strange mules saw it, and came running up to us to get a feed of grain. We then got hold of the ropes that were on the necks of four of the mules, and tied them together. There was a black mare mule that was quite shy, but I finally caught the rope that was on her neck. The mule at once came at me with her ears turned back and mouth open. She caught me by the arm and bit me severely, then turned and ran away. Lieutenant Gully said:

"Let her go, she will kill some of us."

"No, we will not let her go, we need all the mules," said I.

I again caught her, and she made for me again, but I caught the rope near the end where it was fastened to an iron pin, and struck her a blow with the pin, which knocked her down. I then placed my knee on her neck, and caught her by the nose with my hands. I held her this way until a bridle was put on her, after which we were able to manage her easily. I then hitched this wild mule to the wagon by the side of Friendship. We then had fresh riding animals, and turned our jaded ones loose, and drove them before us. At Kane Creek we lost the mule that I got from the soldiers at Santa Fe. It drank more of the alkali water than was good for it, so we left it on the plains and went our way. We saw so many fresh Indian signs around there that we knew we had no time to stay attending sick mules. A few nights afterwards I saw a large body of Indians among the cedars on a mountain, not far off, but our lucky star was guiding us, for soon after that we met three hundred soldiers, with whom we camped that night. The force was so strong that the Indians did not attack us. Next day we met soldiers very frequently, and every few hours we would meet a body of troops from that time until we reached Fort Leavenworth. It was storming very hard when we got to St. Joseph, Missouri. We put up at a hotel, but before our animals were in the stable, Egan was gone, and I could not find him that night, yet we searched for him very diligently. I was fearful that he would be robbed, but he happened to meet some honest men who put him in bed, and kept him and his money in safety until morning, when we found him.

After leaving St. Joseph, where we had purchased a lot of supplies, we started for winter quarters, and had to go through from six to ten feet of snow, the whole distance. We reached our friends in safety. I had two hundred dollars that the soldiers had made me a present of. I took three of the mules we had found on the way, and divided the others between my companions. We reached winter quarters, now called Florence, on the 15th day of December, 1846. The snow was deep, my family all living in tents, and in a suffering condition; but I must report first, as it is usual to pay homage to the man of God, Brigham Young, then attend to my family, but when I saw my family exposed to the pelting storms of Winter, while all others had comfortable log houses, I was angry. I cannot say I was disappointed, for it was not the first time that Brigham Young and others in authority had broken their promises made to me. My family received me as they always did, with open arms and thankful hearts.

CHAPTER XVII

LEE IS TREATED BADLY BY THE "BRETHREN"

I HAD brought home with me about all that my team could haul of supplies, clothing, groceries, etc., which soon made my family comfortable. I had met President Young and shaken hands with him, but had not made my report or delivered the money to him. The next morning the president called to see me, and notified me that the council would meet at nine o'clock at Dr. Richards', and for me to be there and make my report. He appeared greatly ashamed at the manner my family had been treated. I said:

"President Young, how does this compare with your promises to me, when I trusted all to you? I took my life in my hands and went into that Indian country, on that perilous trip, a distance of two thousand two hundred miles, through savage foes, to carry out your orders. I have found things as I feared they would be. When I started I asked you to care for my family, and you promised all that I asked of you. Now I see all my family exposed to the storm; they, of all the camp, are without houses. My best cattle have been butchered and eaten, but not by my family. The choice beef has been given to your favorites, and the refuse given to my wives and children." The President replied:

"Brother John, I am ashamed of the conduct of this people. I have mentioned the situation of your family several times, but the brethren did not feel like building houses for others until they had their own houses completed. I was intending this very day to call a meeting and have the brethren turn out and build houses for your family. Do not blame me, Brother John, for I have done the best that I could." Then putting his hand on my shoulder, he said: "Don't feel bad about it. You will live through, and the day will come when we can look back and see what we have endured for the Kingdom of Heaven's sake and will rejoice that we have passed through it." Then he wound up by saying, "Lord bless you, Brother John. You can now begin and make your family more comfortable than nine tenths of these people, for it does not take you long to put thing in shape. Come, cheer up, and you shall have $100 of the money for your services, and you can make a thousand out of it." But this, like all his other promises, fell to the ground, for I never got a cent of the money.

I met the council, and made my report, and handed over the checks for the money sent home by the soldiers. I received blessings without end, but all of them to come in the future, and also on condition that I remained faithful to the end.

Allow me to jump from 1847 to 1877, just thirty years and let the future tell my experience of that time, and what my prospects are today. As I said, my promise, blessings were all to be received in the future, and that too upon condition that I remained faithful to the end. I was adopted by Brigham Young, and was to seek his *temporal* interests here, and in return he was to seek my *spiritual* salvation, I being an heir of his family, and was to share his *blessings* in common with his other heirs. True to my pledges, I have at all times tried to do his bidding. I have let him direct my energies in all things. And now the time has come for me to prepare to receive my reward. An offering must be made, and I must prepare the wood and build the altar; then, as Abraham of old did with his son Isaac, be placed upon the altar as the sacrifice. But the Lord, or Abraham, had a ram tied in the thicket, when the hand of the Lord stretched forth and staid the fatal blow. But I doubt whether *my father Brigham* has been as thoughtful as Abraham was, I think not; I must meet my fate without murmuring or complaining. I must tamely submit, and *be true to the end.* I must not speak a word against the Lord's anointed, for if I do, I must lose the blessings promised for all that I have done. If I endure firm to the *end,* I will receive the martyr's crown, and my son will represent me here on earth, and carry on *my work* for an eternal state. This, to me, appears to be a hard way to receive my pay. I would rather lose the debt and begin anew, if I could. But it is now too late for escape from the fate that awaits me. It is said that experience teaches a dear school, and that fools will learn at no other. I fear that I have paid a little too much for mine.

My first duty was to build some comfortable houses for my family. Soon afterwards I was sent to St. Joseph to cash the checks and purchase some goods to supply the wants of the people. I was directed to purchase a lot of salt and potatoes from a Frenchman at Trading Point. I did so, and bought $300 worth on credit and sent them back to the settlement. I had to borrow the money from Mrs. Armstrong to pay the $300 debt. But she was afterwards sealed to me, and it was then all in the family, and I never asked Brigham Young for it and he never offered to pay it. He owes it to me yet. On that trip to St. Joseph I bought $1,500 worth of goods, such as were needed at the settlement. I advanced $700 of my own money and the remainder was from the money sent home by the Mormon Battalion. I took the goods back and we opened a store at winter quarters. A. P. Rockwood acted as chief clerk and salesman. We sold the goods at a great advance. What cost us seven cents at St. Joseph, we sold at *sixty-five* cents, and everything was sold at a similar profit. I kept the stock up during the Winter and did a good business. One drawback was this: many of the families of the men who were in the Mormon Battalion had no money, and we had to let them have goods on credit, but I had to stand the loss myself, for few of the men ever paid a dollar due me when they returned. Andrew Little was in the battalion, and at the request of Brigham Young I let his family have $258 worth of goods, and Brigham said I should have my money when Little returned, but I never got any of it. Little was also an adopted son of Brigham Young, and consequently did about as he pleased. James Pace, Thomas Woolsey, and a few others of the soldiers, paid me when they returned, for what I had advanced their families, but the majority never paid. When I returned from Santa Fe I found David Young, his wife and two daughters, lying sick and helpless; really in want. I took care of them and supplied them with food and such articles, as they required, until the death of the father, mother and one son, which took place in a short time - a few months after my return home. I had baptized this family in Putnam County, Tennessee, and felt a great interest in them. The two girls were sealed to me while we staid at winter quarters, and became members of my family. They are both still living. By them I have three sons and daughters. They were sealed to me in 1847. I was also sealed to Nancy Armstrong the same evening that I took the Young girls to wife. A few evenings afterwards I was sealed to Emeline Woolsey. She was my thirteenth wife. Nancy Armstrong's maiden name was Gibbons. She was the wife of a wealthy merchant by the name of Armstrong, who owned a large establishment in Louisville, Kentucky, and another Carlisle, Kentucky, at which places he did business as wholesale and retail dealer in dry goods. I became acquainted with the family at Carlisle, Overton County, Tennessee, while preaching there. The people of Carlisle were bitter enemies of the Mormon Church, and a mob threatened to tar and feather me one night, when Armstrong took me home with him and protected me. He was not a believer in any religion, but I always considered him a high-minded, honorable man. I afterwards stopped at his house often. His wife and sister Sarah were believers in the Mormon faith, but as Mr. Armstrong was not, I advised his wife not to become a member of the Church, and refused to baptize her until such time as her husband would consent to it. Elder Smoot afterwards baptized Sarah Gibbons and Nancy Armstrong.

Brother Smoot had taken his wife with him on the mission, and she laid the plan to get Sarah to go to Nauvoo. A wagon was sent to take Sarah Gibbons' goods to Nauvoo, and in it Mrs. Armstrong sent her valuable clothing and jewelry, amounting to some two thousand dollars. She intended to join the Saints at the first chance. A few months after Sarah had gone Mrs. Armstrong got the consent of her husband that she might pay a visit to her sister and the Church at Nauvoo; he fitted her up in fine style, sending two serving maids to wait on her. Soon after she left home, the friends of Armstrong advised him to stop his slaves at St. Louis, if he wanted to keep them, for his wife would never return to him. Armstrong stopped the slaves, and his wife went on to Nauvoo, where she staid until the Saints left that place after the death of the Prophet. I am satisfied that Smoot laid the plan to get Mrs. Armstrong to Nauvoo, so he could be sealed to her and get her property. Sarah Gibbons was sealed to Elder Smoot, but Mrs. Armstrong would not consent to take him as her husband, but she lived in the family until she got disgusted with Smoot's cruel treatment of her sister. She loaned him nearly all her money and he never paid it back; he wanted the rest of it, but she refused to let him have it; he then refused to take her with him across the plains. She told her griefs to my wife Rachel, and Rachel brought about the marriage between her and myself.

Mrs. Armstrong said to Rachel that I was the first man on earth to bring the gospel to her, and that she had always had a great regard for me since she first saw me, but that I appeared to treat her coldly. Rachel told her that I always spoke kindly of her, and that the reason I had not been more friendly, was because I had thought she wanted to become a member of Brother Smoot's family; that she had heard me speak of her in terms of praise many times. Finally she came to my house and I asked her in the presence of my wives, if she wished to become a member of my family. She said she did. My wives advised me to be sealed to her, and as the matter was agreeable all round, I did so. Brigham Young sealed her and the Young girls to me. She was a true, affectionate woman. My whole family respected her. She was forty-eight years of age when she was sealed to me, and she was a true wife until her death. In all matters of this kind I tried to act from principle and not from passion. Yet I do not pretend to say that all such acts were directed by principle, for I know they were not. I am not blind to my own faults. I have been a proud, vain man, and in my younger days I thought I was perfection. In those days I did not almost make due allowance for the failings of the *weaker vessels*. I then expected perfection in all women. I know now that I was foolish in looking for that in anything human. I have, for slight offenses, turned away good meaning young women that had been sealed to me and refused to hear their excuses, but sent them away heartbroken. In this I did wrong. I have regretted the same in sorrow for many years. Two of the young women so used, still have warm hearts for me, notwithstanding my unnatural conduct toward them. They were young and in the prime of life when I sent them from me. They have since married again, and are the mothers of nice families. They frequently send letters to comfort me in my troubles and afflictions, but their kind remembrances only serve to add to my self-reproach for my cruel treatment of them in past years. I banished them from me for less offenses than I had myself been guilty of. Should my history ever fall into the hands of Emeline Woolsey or Polly Ann Workman, I wish them to know that, with my last breath, I ask God to pardon me for the wrong I did them, when I drove them from me, poor young girls as they were.

President Young built a grist mill during the Winter, and ground meal for the people, charging a heavy toll for all that the mill ground. In the Spring I was ordered to go out and preach, and raise thirty-three wagons and the mules and harness to draw them. I succeeded in getting thirty of the teams. Brigham Young told me to go again, that he asked for thirty three teams, not for thirty. I went again, and preached so that I soon had the other teams. I then turned the whole outfit over to Brigham Young, so he could send his pioneers out to look up a new home for the Saints. I then offered to go with the company, but Brigham Young said:

"I cannot spare you; I can spare others better than you."

He then directed me to take my family and a company, and go and raise corn for the people. He said:

"I want you to take a company, with your family, and go up the river, and open up a farm, and raise grain and vegetables to feed the needy, and the soldiers' families, for we cannot depend on hauling our substance from Missouri, to feed so many as we have on our hands. I want so much grain raised that all will be supplied next Winter, for we must feed our animals grain if we wish them to cross the plains next Spring. There is an old military fort about eighteen miles above here, where the land was once farmed, and that land is in good condition for farming now. We will leave Father Morley in charge of the various settlements. Brother Heber C. Kimball will send some of his boys and make another farm this side of there."

Then turning to Father Morley, he said:

"I want John to take charge of the farming interests and the settlement, at my place, and you must counsel and advise with him from time to time. I want you and all the brethren to understand that the land nearest the settlement is to be divided between John and his wives, for they are all workers, and the others are to go further for their land."

I said that kind of an arrangement would not give satisfaction to the people, and that there were some of his adopted sons now jealous of me, and I feared the consequences, and preferred that the land be divided nearer equal.

He said, "Who are they that are jealous of you?"

I named several persons to him. In reply he said, naming a man, he would work all day under the shade of a tree. Another, he said, could work all day in a half bushel. Then he said:

"Such men will do but little; let them go to some outside place for their land. I want those who will work to have the best land. Let each family have an acre near by for a garden and truck patch. And now, Father Morley, I want you to see that John and his family have all the cleared land that they can tend, for I know they will raise a good crop, and when it is raised we can all share it with him. I want a company to follow Brother Lee, about the first of May, when the grass is good, of such men as can fit themselves out comfortably. My brother, John Young, will lead them, and Jedde Grant will be the Captain."

Then he turned to me and said:

"Brother John D., I want you to fit my brother John out. If he needs oxen let him have them, and I will pay them back again; see that he gets a good outfit. When he leaves here Father Morley will take charge of the Church. I want the Brethren to do as John D. tells them; he carries a good influence wherever he goes; no evil reports follow him from his field of labor; all respect him, and that is good evidence to me that he carries himself straight."

I then settled up my business at the winter quarters. President Young was indebted to the firm $285; of course he had not the money to settle the account, and he was just starting to look out a resting place for the Saints. His first adopted son, A. P. Rockwood, our salesman, could not spare a dollar to help his Father, Brigham Young, so the loss of that sum of money fell on me.

I told my adopted father, Brigham Young, that he was welcome to the $285. Before he left for the new land of promise, he said to me,

"My son John, what shall I do for you?"

I said, "Select me an inheritance when you find the resting place."

"I will remember you. May Heaven bless you. I bless you. Be a good boy. Keep an account of how each man, under your charge, occupies his time, while I am gone."

He then said I was to have half of all the improvements that were made, and half of the crop that was raised by the company that I fitted out with teams, seed and provisions. The pioneer company started April 1st, 1847. We moved to our new location, and called it Summer Quarters. We laid out a fort to protect us from the Indians, as they were troublesome. We then laid off our land. I found out that if I obeyed orders, it would require all the cleared land for my family, so I took and laid off three acres for each family - there were thirty-seven families for gardens, and I took the balance. Although I had given each family three times as much land, for a garden and truck patch, as Brigham Young had ordered, still the people found a great deal of fault with me. Mrs. Armstrong had some money left, and she told me to take it, and send for supplies and seed corn. I did take it, and sent four teams to Missouri for seed corn and provisions, and then put all hands to work building the fort, putting the land in order for the crop, etc. About the first of May, thirty-eight warriors of the Oto tribe came to our camp. They were in full paint, and on the warpath. They came in on the yell, and at full speed. It was just after daylight; I was laying the foundation of a house when they came to me. I threw logs against them the same as if I did not see them, but most of the brethren kept out of sight. The Indians began to build a fire in my garden, and one of them raised his gun to shoot one of my oxen, which the boys were then driving up. The majority of the Indians then formed a half circle, holding their bows fully sprung, and commenced a regular war dance. We were told not to shoot Indians, but to take sticks and whale them when they commenced any depredations. As the Indian took the leather-casing from his gun, so that he could shoot, I rushed at him with a heavy club, with the intention of knocking down as many of them as I could. I could speak their language some, so I told them I would kill them all if they shot my ox. They saw that I meant what I said. Then the two chiefs held out their hands, and yelled to the warrior not to shoot. He lowered his gun and returned to the crowd, but he was very angry. The other Indians seemed amazed, and stood as if they were paralyzed. Old man A. K. Knight followed me with a club, and stood by me all the time. Joseph Busby said:

"Hold on, Brother Lee, they outnumber us."

"Outnumber h--l," said I, "there are not Indians enough in their whole nation to make me stand by and see them shoot down my oxen before my eyes." Busby then ran into the house to load my gun, but he was so frightened he could not get the powder in the gun, so my wife, Rachel, loaded it for him. I looked around to see how things were, and I saw *seven of my wives* standing with guns in their hands, ready to shoot if I was attacked.

I succeeded in driving the whole band of Indians away from the settlement.

Sometime after the Indians had gone away an old chief returned and brought an ax, that he said one of his braves had stolen. I gave him a little ammunition and some bread, and he left me as a friend. My firm stand saved the settlement at that time and secured it from molestation in the future. The Indians never bothered us at Summer Quarters again. In the Fall they made us a friendly visit, and called me a Sioux Captain. Near our settlement there was an abundance of wild game - deer, turkey, prairie chickens, ducks, geese, brant, squirrels, etc., which gave us much of our food during our stay there. We worked diligently and raised an abundant crop of corn and vegetables. We built good, comfortable houses, and made the floors and roofs of basswood, which was abundant, near by, and worked easily. In July the people were nearly all sick. The fever and ague were nearly a contagion. Other diseases were not uncommon. In August and September seventeen of our people died. During those months we had hardly a sufficient number of well people to attend to the sick. The most of my family were very sick. My little son, Heber John, the child of my first wife, Agathe Ann, died; also David Young, Sr., the father of my two wives, Polly and Louisa; also their brother, David Young, Jr. I also lay at the point of death for some time. I was in a trance about one hour and a half. While in this condition my wives, Rachel A. and Nancy G., stood over me like guardian angels, and prayed

INDIAN WAR DANCE

constantly for me. My spirit left the body and I was taken into another sphere, where I saw myriads of people - many of whom I was acquainted with and had known on earth. The atmosphere that they dwelt in was pure and hallowed. Pain and sorrow were unknown, or at least were not felt there. All was joy and peace. Each spirit was blest with all the pleasure its ability enabled it to comprehend and enjoy. They had full knowledge of the earthly doings and also of the sphere where they were so blest. The glory of God shone upon them, and the power of Heaven overshadowed them all, and was to them a perfect shield from all temptations and dangers. I was anxious to remain there, but the spirits told me that I must return to the body and remain in it until my appointed time for death - that my work on earth was not yet finished. I obeyed, but did so with great reluctance, and once more entered the body, then apparently lifeless upon the bed of sickness. After taking possession of the body again I lay some time in deep thought, contemplating the majesty of God's works. I then spoke to my faithful nurses, and told them of what I had done, heard and witnessed. I soon recovered from my sickness, but my life was for some time a misery to me. I longed to join that angelic host that I had so lately visited in their mansions of glory and pleasure, where I knew I was to go when I could escape from this body of earthly material. This feeling of anxiety to go to my eternal rest was greatly strengthened by the bitter, malignant actions of men who acted like demons toward me and mine. Every species of intrigue and meanness was resorted to by some of the brethren to injure and torment me. They were jealous of me and anxious to provoke me to violence. Everything that envy and hatred could suggest was tried, to break up and scatter my family. Finally they reported to Father Morley that nothing but a change of rulers in the settlement would bring peace again.

Father Morley came, with several Elders, and called a meeting, at which he heard all the parties state their grievances against me. He then told them that they had brought nothing against me that reflected upon me as presiding officer; that I had acted well and for the best interest of the entire people; that all the trouble was from the wrong acts of the people.

One of the brethren, C. Kennedy, proposed a change. He wanted a High Priest to preside instead of a Seventy. I was tired of my position and consented to the change. A man by the name of Fuller was selected by Kennedy to rule over the people. Father Morley put the question to a vote of the people, and said that all who wished for a change of rulers should hold up their hands. Only two hands were raised. Then he said that all who wished me to remain in charge should raise their hands, when every person present but two voted that I should still be the ruler of that people at Summer Quarters. Father Morley then called upon the two brethren who voted against me to get up and tell what they had against me. They could give no good reason for wanting a change. They said they never lived by a better neighbor or kinder hearted man than I was, but that I was too kind; that I let the people run over me; that they voted for a change believing it would tend to unite the people and satisfy those who had been raising the fuss and finding fault.

Father Morley told them it was wrong to vote against a good man for such reasons. He then talked to the people on the principles of their religion for some time, and advised them to forsake their evil ways, for they were going in a way that led to hell, etc.

This ended my troubles for a short time, but I soon found out that my enemies had only let go their hold so they could spit on their hands and get a better one. They next asked to be allowed to organize a police force for the protection of the settlement, This was to be entirely separate from me. I granted their request. It was next decided to build an estray pound. A meeting was called and it was agreed that each man should build fence in proportion to the amount of stock that he owned, and that the public corral should be used for the estray pound. But no stock should be put into the pound until all the fencing was done, the gates set up, etc. I at once completed my fencing, but the grumblers had no time to work; they were kept busy finding fault. (This whole thing was a subterfuge to bother me; there was no need of a pound, as our cattle were all herded in day time and corralled at night. But I submitted, for I knew I could live by their laws as well as they could.) One evening soon after that, as the cattle were being driven up for the night, one of my oxen ran through a brush fence and got into a patch of corn. The herdsman ran him out in a moment. Instead of holding the herder responsible for the damage, or coming to me to make a complaint and demanding pay for the damage, they took my ox out of the corral, and, contrary to the vote of the people, took and tied him up to Wm. Pace's private corral. I was the only man there who had made his fence, as ordered by the meeting. I did not know that they had my ox tied up (for the work had not been done yet to justify putting any stock in the pound). Next morning I sent some of my boys out to yoke up my oxen, when they returned and informed me that one of my oxen was missing. I soon found the ox, and demanded its release. I was told I must pay $20 before I could have the ox, and that I must pay it in *money*. I saw this was done to worry me, so I sent word that I would pay in any kind of property that I had. They refused everything but money or butter. I had neither to spare, and they well knew it. I was still weak from my recent sickness, but I walked over and had a talk with Wm. Pace and tried to reason with him, but all to no purpose. I told him he should take pay for damage done by stock in the kind of property that the stock injured, but no, I must pay money or butter, or lose my ox. I reflected a moment and concluded that forbearance had ceased to be a virtue; that unless I defended my rights I would soon be without anything worth protecting. I then walked into the yard and untied the ox, and told my boy to drive him home. Pace stood by the gate with a large cane, but made no resistance; in fact he was not a bad man, but was being misled by bad company. Kennedy, Busby, Dunn, and others, were a little way off. They saw me, and came running to me. Charles Kennedy was the bully of the camp, and the leader of those against me. He came up and said, "If I had been here you would not have turned that ox out. I would have switched you if you had tried it."

I said, "Kennedy, I have lost property enough through the police without your oppressing me any more."

I had lost ten head of mules just before that by the dishonesty of the police. I then said I lost my mules by the failure of the police to do their duty, and I would not be imposed on in this way any more. He then shoved his fist under my nose. I parried his blow, and told him that he would do well to keep at a proper distance from me. He again made a pass at me. I then threw down my hat and said:

"If you attempt that again you must take what follows."

He came at me the third time, and as he did so I aimed to spoil his face, but he dropped his head as I struck, and the blow took effect on his eyebrow, and badly sprained my thumb. We were on a little knoll, full of the stumps of small trees that had been cut down. Kennedy caught hold of me and commenced shoving me back. I knew that my strength would not last long. I did not wish to risk having a tussle among the stumps. So I backed out towards the cleared ground. I fastened my left hand in his long black hair to steady myself, and as I reached the flat ground, I suddenly sprang back, breaking his hold, by tearing my shirt. I then jerked him forward to an angle of forty-five degrees and planted my fist square in his face; stepping back, and drawing him after me, I kept gradually feeding him in the face with my fist, the blood spurting from him all over me. The crowd saw their bully getting the worst of it, so they ran in to help him. Brother Teeples caught me around the arms, to prevent me from striking any more. My Rachel, who was standing by, called to her brother, James Woolsey, and he came and took hold of Kennedy and separated us.

I was very sorry that this fight took place, for I was forced to admit that I had fearfully punished the bully, his face was badly bruised. This suited the people; I had shown *violence*, and now they could lay a charge against me that they thought would stand.

I was at once cited to appear before the High Council, and be dealt with according to the rules of the Church, for a breach of the peace and unchristian conduct. The whole people were not against me, only a few; but there were enough of them to keep up a constant broil. They then began consecrating my property to their own use; killed my cattle, and ate them, and stole nearly everything that was loose. They stole wheat from my granaries, had it ground and eat it, and bragged about it. Kennedy, by the evil influences he commanded, induced my young wife, Emeline, to leave me and go to his house, and she went with his family to Winter Quarters. That was the reason that I turned her away and refused to take her back again. She repented and wished to come back, but I would not take her again. Similar influences were brought to bear on all of my family, but without much success. Such horrid treatment was not calculated to bind me to such a people, whose only aim appeared to be to deprive me of every comfort and enjoyment that made life endurable. I was in great trouble; in place of friends I had found enemies. There was a great struggle in my mind to decide what I should do. I looked upon those of my family that remained true and shared my persecutions, and knew that if I left the Church I could not keep and live with them; that if I left I must part with all but my first wife and her children - to do so was worse than death. I did not know what to do.

I finally appeared before the High Council to meet my accusers, who had formed a combination to destroy me. I had but few friends to defend me, and they were in a measure powerless. They dared not speak their mind in my behalf. Father Morley was true to me to the last, though he was becoming unpopular on account of having so long supported me. Lieut. Samuel Gully was another true friend of mine; he said he would never turn against me until I had done something wrong, even if

Brigham Young should desire him to do so. This at once lost him his influence in the council. The most willful and damnable lies were brought up against me. Many things which had been said and done in moments of amusement and jocularity were brought up, as if I had said and done the things for wicked purposes. Everything that could be discovered or invented to injure me was laid to my charge. All who were against me had a full chance to talk. Then Aaron Johnson, who was there, but not a member of the council, was called upon to fill a vacancy occasioned by the absence of some member. He made a speech to the council, and showed them where I had acted well; he then voted for my acquittal. James W. Cummings, who had been a member of the council when I was first tried in the Summer, and who then took my part, now thought he would make himself popular with the people, so he volunteered his evidence and gave false evidence against me. This man's action was very wrong and uncharitable. I had been more than a brother to him in the past; I had supplied his family with food many times when they would have suffered but for the help I gave them. This man is still a pet of Brigham Young's. The result of that trial was that I was ordered to confess that I had been in fault, and that I was alone to blame, and must ask the people to forgive me. If I refused I was to be cut off from the Church. To a man in my situation it was equivalent to death to be cut off from the Church; my wives would be taken from me, my property consecrated to the Church, and I turned adrift, broken and disgraced, and liable to suffer death at the hand of any brother of the Church who wished to take my life, either to save my soul or for purposes of revenge.

I replied that in justice to myself I could not make such a confession, but that, if nothing else would do, I would say, as the council demands me to say, I would make the confession. I was told that this would not do; that no whipping of the devil around a stump would do them; my confession must be full and unconditional. What the result would have been I cannot say, for just then a messenger returned, saying President Young was near at hand, on his return with the pioneers who had gone out with him to look for a resting place for the Saints. This stopped all further proceedings. The majority of the people rushed forth to meet Brigham Young.

I returned home, conscious of my own innocence and willing that the people should have the first show to talk to the president and give him their side of the case. I did this in part so I could tell how much he could be stuffed. The people told their story and misrepresented me in every way; they told him how I had divided the land, and said that I and Father Morley both said that he had ordered me and my family to take the cleared land. This Brigham Young flatly denied, and he never told a meaner lie in his life than that one, for he had insisted upon my taking much more of it than I did. He accused Father Morley and myself of being liars.

After that there was nothing left undone by many of the people that would irritate or injure me or my family. My property was stolen, my fences broken down, and everything that mean men could imagine or work up by acting in combination in studying deviltry was done to make life a burden to me. I had raised over seven thousand bushels of corn, and every one had a good crop. I had a large lot filled up in the husk, and I let my cattle run to it so as to keep them fat during the Winter, that I might drive them over the plains in the Spring. The rotten hearted police took advantage of my position, and drove my cattle from my own cornpile and put them into the estray pound, and charged me fifty dollars for thus illegally putting my cattle in the pound. I offered to put all the corn I had into their hands as security, until I could have a meeting called to examine into the charge. I wanted my cows at home, for we needed the milk. I had a large family, and many little children that would suffer without milk. Half the men in the settlement offered to go my security for the payment of the fifty dollars, if a meeting decided that I should pay it; but all to no purpose. The police wanted the milk themselves, and so they kept my cows. I sent Lieutenant Gully to Brigham Young with a statement of the case, but he paid no attention to it. Gully was well acquainted with Brigham Young, and was a fine man too. He insisted on giving Brigham the story in full, and demanded that he should go in person and see to the matter. But the president was immovable.

Things stood this way until Emeline, one of Brigham's wives, took the matter to heart, and begged him to go and see about the affair, and asked him to bring her to my house, to visit her sister Louisa, then one of my wives. He came, but said little of the trouble, and soon left again.

Two days afterwards I wrote Brigham Young a kind letter, and invited him to come to my house and eat a turkey dinner with me. I sent this by L. Stewart. He met Brigham on his way to my house and gave him my letter. I did not expect he would come to see me, but he was there. He treated me most kindly. When suppertime came he said to one of my wives,

"Sister, I have come for a bowl of good milk, but skim the cream off."
She replied, "We have no milk."

"How is that?" said he. "I thought Brother John always had milk."

I then told him that the police had my cows in the pound.

He said, "What on earth are they doing with your cows?"

I then told him the whole story in a few words. He scarcely waited to hear me, but called to his carriage driver, George D. Grant, and said, "Come, George, I will go and see about this matter."

He returned quite soon, saying, "Your cows will soon be here, and I do not think the police will meddle with them again."

He then asked me where my turkey was. I told him my friend Kennedy had robbed me of all my turkeys, but perhaps I could borrow one from him. I then sent Brother Gully to ask Kennedy to loan me a couple of fat turkeys; that I had President Young at my house and wanted them for his supper. He sent back word that President Young was welcome to all the turkeys he wanted, at his house. I then told President Young I would go out hunting and get him a nice one for dinner the next day. I went out that night with Gully and hunted some time, but the snow was a foot deep or more, and a crust had frozen on the top of it, so it was difficult hunting. At last we found a large drove of turkeys at roost in the tall cottonwood timber. I shot two of them by star light; one fell in the river, and we lost it, but the other fell dead at the roots of the tree. This was a very large and fat turkey. I considered it would do, and we returned home with it. We had been gone only a little over an hour. Brigham Young staid at my house while I was gone. We sat by the fire and talked until near midnight. I unbosomed myself to him; I told him of all my ill treatment, and asked him if I had failed in any respect to perform the duties of my mission that he gave me before he started with the pioneers across the plains. I told him of the great crop we had raised; that we had it in abundance to feed the poor and for every purpose; so much in fact that there was no sale for it. He said,

"You have done well, and you shall be blessed for it."

I said I hoped my blessings would be different from what I had been receiving. He replied,

"Jesus has said, in this world you shall have tribulation, but in Me you shall have peace - that is, if you bear these things patiently, without murmuring."

NOTE - The time having arrived for John D. Lee to start to the place of execution, he laid down his pen and left his manuscript just as I have given it to the reader. Fate decreed that his autobiography should be left in this unfinished state, but fortunately he had previously dictated a full confession to me, embracing all the principal events of his life from the time that his autobiography closed up to his death; which, being added to his own manuscript, makes his life complete. The confession is given just as he dictated it to me, without alteration or elimination, except in a few cases where the ends of justice might have been defeated by premature revelations.

Extracts from this confession have heretofore been given to the press, but the entire confession has not been published anywhere except in this book.

WM. W. BISHOP

CHAPTER XVIII

LAST CONFESSION AND STATEMENT OF JOHN D. LEE

WRITTEN AT HIS DICTATION AND DELIVERED TO WILLIAM W. BISHOP, ATTORNEY FOR LEE, WITH A REQUEST THAT THE SAME BE PUBLISHED

A S A DUTY to myself, my family, and mankind at large, I propose to give a full and true statement of all that I know and all that I did in that unfortunate affair, which has cursed my existence, and made me a wanderer from place to place for the last nineteen years, and which is known to the world as the MOUNTAIN MEADOWS MASSACRE.

I have no vindictive feeling against any one; no enemies to punish by this statement; and no *friends* to shield by keeping back, or longer keeping secret, any of the facts connected with the Massacre.

I believe that I must tell all that I do know, and tell everything just as the same transpired. I shall tell the truth and permit the public to judge who is most to blame for the crime that I am accused of committing. I did not act alone; I had many to assist me at the Mountain Meadows. I believe that most of those who were connected with the Massacre, and took part in the lamentable transaction that has blackened the character of all who were aiders or abettors in the same, were acting under the impression that they were performing a religious duty. I know *all* were acting under the orders and by the command of their Church leaders; and I firmly believe that the most of those who took part in the proceedings, considered it a religious duty to unquestioningly obey the orders which they had received. That they acted from a sense of duty to the Mormon Church, I never doubted. Believing that those with me acted from a sense of religious duty on that occasion, I have faithfully kept the secret of their guilt, and remained silent and true to the *oath* of secrecy which we took on the bloody field, for many long and bitter years. I have never betrayed those who acted with me and participated in the crime for which I am convicted, and for which I am to suffer death.

My attorneys, especially Wells Spicer and Wm. W. Bishop, have long tried, but tried in vain, to induce me to *tell all I knew* of the massacre and the causes which led to it. I have heretofore refused to tell the tale. Until the last few days I had intended to die, if die I must, without giving one word to the public concerning those who joined willingly, or unwillingly, in the work of destruction at Mountain Meadows.

To hesitate longer, or to die in silence, would be unjust and cowardly. I will not keep the secret any longer as my own, but will tell all I know.

At the earnest request of a *few* remaining friends, and by the advice of Mr. Bishop, my counsel, who has defended me thus far with all his ability, notwithstanding my want of money with which to pay even his expenses while attending to my case, I have concluded to write facts as I know them to exist.

I cannot go before the Judge of the quick and the dead without first revealing all that I know, as to what was done, who ordered me to do what I did do, and the motives that led to the commission of that unnatural and bloody deed.

The immediate orders for the killing of the emigrants came from those in authority at Cedar City. At the time of the massacre, I and those with me, acted by virtue of positive orders from Isaac C. Haight and his associates at Cedar City. Before I started on my mission to the Mountain Meadows, I was told by Isaac C. Haight that his orders to me were the result of full consultation with Colonel William H. Dame and all in authority. It is a new thing to me, if the massacre was not decided on by the head men of the Church, and it is a new thing for Mormons to condemn those who committed the deed.

Being forced to speak from memory alone, without the aid of my memorandum books, and not having time to correct the statements that I make, I will necessarily give many things out of their regular order. The superiority that I claim for my statement is this:

ALL THAT I DO SAY IS TRUE AND NOTHING BUT THE TRUTH

I will begin my statement by saying, I was born on the 6th day of September, A.D. 1812, in the town of Kaskaskia, Randolph County, State of Illinois. I am therefore in the sixty fifth year of my age.

I joined the Mormon Church at Far West, Mo., about thirty-nine years ago. To be with that Church and people I left my home on Luck Creek, Fayette County, Illinois, and went and joined the Mormons in Missouri, before the troubles at Gallatin, Far West and other points, between the Missourians and Mormons. I shared the fate of my brother Mormons, in being mistreated, arrested, robbed and driven from Missouri in a destitute condition, by a wild and fanatical mob. But of all this I shall speak in my life, which I shall write for publication if I have time to do so.

I took an active part with the leading men at Nauvoo, in building up that city. I induced many Saints to move to Nauvoo, for the sake of their souls. I traveled and preached the Mormon doctrine in many States. I was an honored man in the Church, and stood high with the Priesthood, until the last few years. I am now cut off from the Church for *obeying the orders* of my superiors, and doing so without asking questions - for doing as my religion and my religious teachers had taught me to do. I am now used by the Mormon Church as a scapegoat to carry the sins of that people. My life is to be taken, so that my death may stop further enquiry into the acts of the members who are still in good standing in the Church. Will my death satisfy the nation for all the crimes committed by Mormons, at the command of the Priesthood, who have used and now have deserted me? Time will tell. I believe in a *just God*, and I know the day will come when others must answer for their acts, as I have had to do.

I first became acquainted with Brigham Young when I went to Far West, Mo., to join the Church, in 1837. I got very intimately acquainted with all the great leaders of the Church. I was adopted by Brigham Young as one of his sons, and for many years I confess I looked upon him as an inspired and holy man. While in Nauvoo I took an active part in all that was done for the Church or the city. I had charge of the building of the "Seventy Hall"; I was 7th Policeman. My duty as a policeman was to guard the residence and person of Joseph Smith, the Prophet. After the death of Joseph and Hyrum I was ordered to perform the same duty for Brigham Young. When Joseph Smith was a candidate for the Presidency of the United States I went to Kentucky as the chairman of the Board of Elders, or head of the delegation, to secure the vote of that State for him. When I returned to Nauvoo again I was General Clerk and Recorder for the Quorum of the Seventy. I was also head or Chief Clerk for the Church, and as such took an active part in organizing the

Priesthood into the order of Seventy after the death of Joseph Smith.

After the destruction of Nauvoo, when the Mormons were driven from the State of Illinois, I again shared the fate of my brethren, and partook of the hardships and trials that befell them from that day up to the settlement of Salt Lake City, in the then wilderness of the nation. I presented Brigham Young with seventeen ox teams, fully equipped, when he started with the people from Winter Quarters to cross the plains to the new resting place of the Saints. He accepted them and said, "God bless you, John." But I never received a cent for them - I never wanted pay for them, for in giving property to Brigham Young I thought I was loaning it to the Lord.

After reaching Salt Lake City I stayed there but a short time, when I went to live at Cottonwood, where the mines were afterwards discovered by General Connor and his men during the late war.

I was just getting fixed to live there, when I was ordered to go out into the interior and aid in forming new settlements, and opening up the country. I then had no wish or desire, save that to know and be able to do the will of the Lord's anointed, Brigham Young, and until within the last few years I have never had a wish for anything else except to do his pleasure, since I became his adopted son. I believed it my duty to obey those in authority. I then believed that Brigham Young spoke by direction of the God of Heaven. I would have suffered death rather than have disobeyed any command of his. I had this feeling until he betrayed and deserted me. At the command of Brigham Young, I took one hundred and twenty-one men, went in a southern direction from Salt Lake City, and laid out and built up Parowan. George A. Smith was the leader and chief man in authority in that settlement. I acted under him as historian and clerk of the Iron County Mission, until January 1851. I went with Brigham Young, and acted as a committee man, and located Provo, St. George, Fillmore, Parowan and other towns, and managed the location of many of the settlements in Southern Utah.

In 1852, I moved to Harmony, and built up that settlement. I remained there until the Indians declared war against the whites and drove the settlers into Cedar City and Parowan, for protection, in the year 1853.

I removed my then numerous family to Cedar City, where I was appointed a Captain of the militia, and commander of Cedar City Military Post.

I had commanded at Cedar City about one year, when I was ordered to return to Harmony, and build the Harmony Fort. This order, like all other orders, came from Brigham Young. When I returned to Harmony and commenced building the fort there, the orders were given by Brigham Young for the reorganization of the military at Cedar City. The old men were requested to resign their offices, and let younger men be appointed in their place. I resigned my office of Captain, but Isaac C. Haight and John M. Higbee refused to resign, and continued to hold on as Majors in the Iron Militia.

After returning to Harmony, I was President of the civil and local affairs, and Rufus Allen was President of that Stake of Zion, or head of the Church affairs.

I soon resigned my position as President of civil affairs, and became a private citizen, and was in no office for some time. In fact, I never held any position after that, except the office of Probate Judge of the County (which office I held before and after the massacre), and member of the Territorial Legislature, and Delegate to the Constitutional Convention which met and adopted a constitution for the State of Deseret, after the massacre.

I will here state that Brigham Young honored me in many ways after the affair at Mountain Meadows was fully reported to him by me, as I will more fully state hereafter in the course of what I have to relate concerning that unfortunate transaction.

Klingensmith, at my first trial, and White, at my last trial, swore falsely when they say that they met me near Cedar City, the Sunday before the massacre. They did not meet me as they have sworn, nor did they meet me at all on that occasion or on any similar occasion. I never had the conversations with them that they testify about. They are both perjurers, and bore false testimony against me.

There has never been a witness on the stand against me that has testified to the whole truth. Some have told part truth, while others lied clear through, but all of the witnesses who were at the massacre have tried to throw all the blame on me, and to protect the other men who took part in it.

About the 7th of September, 1857, I went to Cedar City from my home at Harmony, by order of President Haight. I did not know what he wanted of me, but he had ordered me to visit him and I obeyed. If I remember correctly, it was on Sunday evening that I went there. When I got to Cedar City, I met Isaac C. Haight on the public square of the town. Haight was then President of that Stake of Zion, and the highest man in the Mormon priesthood in that country, and next to Wm. H. Dame in all of Southern Utah, and as Lieutenant Colonel he was second to Dame in the command of the Iron Military District. The word and command of Isaac C. Haight were at law in Cedar City, at that time, and to disobey his orders was certain death; be they right or wrong, no Saint was permitted to question them, their duty was obedience or death.

When I met Haight, I asked him what he wanted with me. He said he wanted to have a long talk with me on private and particular business. We took some blankets and went over to the old Iron Works, and lay there that night, so that we could talk in private and in safety. After we got to the Iron Works, Haight told me all about the train of emigrants. He said (and I then believed every word that be spoke, for I believed it was an impossible thing for one so high in the Priesthood as he was, to be guilty of falsehood) that the emigrants were a rough and abusive set of men. That they had, while traveling through Utah, been very abusive to all the Mormons they met. That they had insulted, outraged, and ravished many of the Mormon women. That the abuses heaped upon the people by the emigrants during their trip from Provo to Cedar City, had been constant and shameful; that they had burned fences and destroyed growing crops; that at many points on the road they had poisoned the water, so that all people and stock that drank of the water became sick, and many had died from the effects of poison. That these vile Gentiles publicly proclaimed that they had the very pistol with which the Prophet, Joseph Smith, was murdered, and had threatened to kill Brigham Young and all of the Apostles. That when in Cedar City they said they would have friends in Utah who would hang Brigham Young by the neck until he was dead, before snow fell again in the territory. They also said that Johnston was coming, with his army, from the East, and they were going to return from California with soldiers, as soon as possible, and would then desolate the land, and kill every d--d Mormon man, woman and child that they could find in Utah. That they violated the ordinances of the town of Cedar, and had, by armed force, resisted the officers who tried to arrest them for violating the law. That after leaving Cedar City the emigrants camped by the company, or cooperative field, just below Cedar City, and burned a large portion of the fencing, leaving the crops open to the large herds of stock in the surrounding country. Also that they had given poisoned meat to the Corn Creek tribe of Indians, which had killed several of them, and their Chief, Konosh, was on the trail of the emigrants, and would soon attack them.

All of these things, and much more of a like kind, Haight told me as we lay in the dark at the old Iron Works. I believed all that he said, and, thinking that he had full right to do all that he wanted to do, I was easily induced to follow his instructions.

Haight said that unless something was done to prevent it, the emigrants would carry out their threats and rob every one of the outlying settlements in the South, and that the whole Mormon people were liable to be butchered by the troops that the emigrants would bring back with them from California. I was then told that the Council had held a meeting that day, to consider the matter, and that it was decided by the authorities to arm the Indians, give them provisions and ammunition, and send them after the emigrants, and have the Indians give them a *brush*, and if they killed part or all of them, so much the better.

I said, "Brother Haight, who is your authority for acting in this way?"

He replied, "It is the *will of all in authority*. The emigrants have no pass from any one to go through the country, and they are liable to be killed as common enemies, for the country is at war now. No man has a right to go through this country without a written pass."

We lay there and talked much of the night, and during that time Haight gave me very full instructions what to do, and how to proceed in the whole affair. He said he had consulted with Colonel Dame, and every one agreed to let the Indians use up the whole train if they could. Haight then said:

"I expect you to carry out your orders."

I knew I had to obey or die. I had no wish to disobey, for I then thought that my superiors in the Church were the mouthpieces of Heaven, and that it was an act of godliness for me to obey any and all orders given by them to me, without my asking any questions.

My orders were to go home to Harmony, and see Carl Shirts, my son-in-law, an Indian interpreter, and send him to the Indians in the South, to notify them that the Mormons and Indians were at war with the *"Mericats"* (as the Indians called all whites that were not Mormons) and bring all the Southern Indians up and have them join with those from the North, so that their force would be sufficient to make a successful attack on the emigrants.

It was agreed that Haight would send Nephi Johnson, another Indian interpreter, to *stir up* all the other Indians that he could find, in order to have a large enough force of Indians to give the emigrants a good *hush*. He said, "These are the orders that have been agreed upon by the council, and it is in accordance with the feelings of the *entire people*."

I asked him if it would not have been better to first send to Brigham Young for instructions, and find out what he thought about the matter.

"No" said Haight, "that is unnecessary, *we are acting by orders*. Some of the Indians are now on the warpath, and all of them must be sent out; all must go, so as to make the thing a success."

It was then intended that the Indians should kill the emigrants, and make it *an Indian massacre*, and not have any whites interfere with them. No whites were to be known in the matter, it was to be all done by the Indians, so that it could be laid to them, if any questions were ever asked about it. I said to Haight:

"You know what the Indians are. They will kill all the party, women and children, as well as the men, and you know we are sworn not to shed innocent blood."

"Oh h--l" said he, "there will not be one drop of *innocent* blood shed, if every one of the d--d pack are killed, for they are the worse lot of outlaws and ruffians that I ever saw in my life."

We agreed upon the whole thing, how each one should act, and then left the iron works, and went to Haight's house and got breakfast.

After breakfast I got ready to start, and Haight said to me:

"Go, Brother Lee, and see that the instructions of those in authority are obeyed, and as you are dutiful in this, so shall your reward be in the kingdom of God, for God will bless those who willingly obey counsel, and make all things fit for the people in these last days."

I left Cedar City for my home at Harmony, to carry out the instructions that I had received from my superior.

I then believed that he acted by the direct order and command of William H. Dame, and others even higher in authority than Colonel Dame. One reason for thinking so was from a talk I had only a few days before, with Apostle George A. Smith, and he had just then seen Haight, and talked with him, and I knew that George A. Smith never talked of things that Brigham Young had not talked over with him beforehand. Then the Mormons were at war with the United States, and the orders to the Mormons had been all the time to kill and waste away our enemies, but lose none of our people. These emigrants were from the section of country most hostile to our people, and I believed then as I do now, that it was the will of every true Mormon in Utah, at that time, that the enemies of the Church should be killed as fast as possible, and that as this lot of people had men amongst them that were supposed to have helped kill the Prophets in the Carthage jail, the killing of all of them would be keeping our oaths and avenging the blood of the Prophets.

In justice to myself I will give the facts of my talk with George A. Smith.

In the latter part of the month of August, 1857, about ten days before the company of Captain Fancher, who met their doom at Mountain Meadows, arrived at that place, General George A. Smith called on me at one of my homes at Washington City, Washington County, Utah Territory, and wished me to take him round by Fort Clara, via Pinto Settlements, to Hamilton Fort, or Cedar City. He said,

"I have been sent down here by the old Boss, Brigham Young, to instruct the brethren of the different settlements not to sell any of their grain to our enemies. And to tell them not to feed it to their animals, for it will all be needed by ourselves. I am also to instruct the brethren to prepare for a *big fight*, for the enemy is coming in large force to attempt our destruction. But Johnston's army will not be allowed to approach our settlements from the east. God is on our side and will fight our battles for us, and deliver our enemies into our hands. Brigham Young has received revelations from God, giving him the right and the power to call down the curse of God on all our enemies who attempt to invade our territory. *Our greatest danger* lies in the people of California - a class of reckless miners who are strangers to God and his righteousness. They are likely to come upon us from the south and destroy the small settlements. But we will try and outwit them before we suffer much damage. The people of the United States who oppose our Church and people are a mob, from the President down, and as such it is impossible for their armies to prevail against the Saints who have gathered here in the mountains."

He continued this kind of talk for some hours to me and my friends who were with me.

General George A. Smith held high rank as a military leader. He was one of the twelve apostles of the Church of Jesus Christ of Latter Day Saints, and as such he was considered by me to be an inspired man. His orders were to me sacred commands, which I considered it my duty to obey, without question or hesitation.

I took my horses and carriage and drove with him to either Hamilton Fort or Cedar City, visiting the settlements with him, as he had requested. I did not go to hear him preach at any of our stopping places, nor did I pay attention to what he said to the leaders in the settlements.

The day we left Fort Clara, which was then the headquarters of the Indian missionaries under the presidency of Jacob Hamblin, we stopped to noon at the Clara River. While there the Indians gathered around us in large numbers, and were quite saucy and impudent. Their chiefs asked me where I was going and who I had with me. I told them that he was a big captain.

"Is he a Mericat Captain?"

"No," I said, "he is a Mormon."

The Indians then wanted to know more. They wanted to have a talk.

The General told me to tell the Indians that the Mormons were their friends, and that the Americans were their enemies, and the enemies of the Mormons, too; that he wanted the Indians to remain the fast friends of the Mormons, for the Mormons were all friends to the Indians; that the Americans had a large army just east of the mountains, and intended to come over the mountains into Utah and kill all of the Mormons and Indians in Utah Territory; that the Indians must get ready and keep ready for war against all of the Americans, and keep friendly with the Mormons and obey what the Mormons told them to do - that this was the will of the Great Spirit; that if the Indians were true to the Mormons and would help them against their enemies, then the Mormons would always keep them from want and sickness and give them guns and ammunition to hunt and kill game with, and would also help the Indians against their enemies when they went into war.

This talk pleased the Indians, and they agreed to all that I asked them to do.

I saw that my friend Smith was a little nervous and fearful of the Indians, notwithstanding their promises of friendship. To relieve him of his anxiety I hitched up and started on our way, as soon as I could do so without rousing the suspicions of the Indians.

We had ridden along about a mile or so when General Smith said,

"Those are savage looking fellows. I think they would make it lively for an emigrant train if one should come this way."

I said I thought they would attack any train that would come in their way. Then the General was in a deep study for some time, when he said,

"Suppose an emigrant train should come along through this southern country, making threats against our people and bragging of the part they took in helping kill our Prophets, what do you think the brethren would do with them? Would they be permitted to go their way, or would the brethren pitch into them and give them a good drubbing?"

I reeflected a few moments, and then said,

"You know the brethren are now under the influence of the late reformation, and are still red-hot for the gospel. The brethren believe the government wishes to destroy them. I really believe that any train of emigrants that may come through here will be attacked, and probably all destroyed. I am sure they would be wiped out if they had been making threats against our people. Unless emigrants have a pass from Brigham Young, or some one in authority, they will certainly never get safely through this country."

My reply pleased him very much, and he laughed heartily, and then said,

"Do you really believe the brethren would make it lively for such a train?"

I said, "Yes, sir, I know they will, unless they are protected by a pass, and I wish to inform you that unless you want every train captured that comes through here, you must inform Governor Young that if he wants emigrants to pass, without being molested, he must send orders to that effect to Colonel Wm. H. Dame or Major Isaac C. Haight, so that they can give passes to the emigrants, for *their passes will insure safet*y, but nothing else will, except the positive orders of Governor Young, as the people are all bitter against the Gentiles, and full of religious zeal, and anxious to avenge the blood of the Prophets."

The only reply he made was to the effect that on his way down from Salt Lake City he had had a long talk with Major Haight on the same subject, and that Haight had assured him, and given him to understand, that emigrants who came along without a pass from Governor Young could not escape from the territory.

We then rode along in silence for some distance, when he again turned to me and said,

"Brother Lee, I am satisfied that the brethren are under the full influence of the reformation, and I believe they will do just as you say they will with the wicked emigrants that come through the country making threats and abusing our people."

I repeated my views to him, but at much greater length, giving my reasons in full for thinking that Governor Young should give orders to protect all the emigrants that he did not wish destroyed. I went into a full statement of the wrongs of our people, and told him that the people were under the blaze of the reformation, full of wild fire and fanaticism, and that to shed the blood of those who would *dare to speak* against the

GEORGE A. SMITH

Mormon Church or its leaders, they would consider doing the will of God, and that the people would do it as willingly and cheerfully as they would any other duty. That the apostle Paul, when he started forth to persecute the followers of Christ, was not any more sincere than every Mormon was then, who lived in Southern Utah.

My words served to cheer up the General very much; he was greatly delighted, and said,

"I am glad to hear so good an account of our people. God will bless them for all that they do to build up His Kingdom in the last days."

General Smith did not say one word to me or intimate to me, that he wished *any emigrants* to pass in safety through the Territory. But he led me to believe then, as I believe now, that he did want, and expected every emigrant to be killed that undertook to pass through the Territory while we were at war with the government. I thought it was his *mission* to prepare the people for the bloody work.

I have always believed, since that day, that General George A. Smith was then visiting Southern Utah to prepare the people for the work of exterminating Captain Fancher's train of emigrants, and I now believe that he was sent for that purpose by the direct command of Brigham Young.

I have been told by Joseph Wood, Thomas T. Willis, and many others, that they heard George A. Smith preach at Cedar City during that trip, and that he told the people of Cedar City that the emigrants were coming, and he told them that they must not sell that company *any grain or provisions* of any kind, for they were a mob of villains and outlaws, and the enemies of God and the Mormon people.

Sidney Littlefield, of Panguitch, has told me that he was knowing to the fact of Colonel Wm. H. Dame sending orders from Parowan to Maj. Haight, at Cedar City, to *exterminate the Fancher outfit*, and to kill every emigrant without fail. Littlefield then lived at Parowan, and Dame was the Presiding Bishop. Dame still has all the wives he wants, and is a great friend of Brigham Young.

The knowledge of how George A. Smith felt toward the emigrants, and his telling me that he had a long talk with Haight on the subject, made me certain that it was the wish of the Church *authorities* that Fancher and his train should be *wiped out*, and knowing all this, I did not doubt then, and I do not doubt it now, either, that Haight was acting by full authority from the Church leaders, and that the orders he gave to me were just the orders that he had been directed to give, when he ordered me to raise the Indians and have them attack the emigrants.

I acted through the whole matter in a way that I considered it my religious duty to act, and if what I did was a crime, it was a crime of the Mormon Church, and not a crime for which I feel individually responsible.

I must here state that Klingensmith was not in Cedar City that Sunday night. Haight said he had sent Klingensmith and others over towards Pinto, and around there, to stir up the Indians and force them to attack the emigrants.

On my way from Cedar City to my home at Harmony, I came up with a large band of Indians under Moquetas and Big Bill, two Cedar City Chiefs; they were in their war paint, and fully equipped for battle. They halted when I came up and said they had had a big talk with Haight, Higby and Klingensmith, and had got orders from them to follow up the emigrants and kill them all, and take their property as the spoil of their enemies.

These Indians wanted me to go with them and command their forces. I told them that I could not go with them that evening, that I had orders from Haight, the *big Captain*, to send other Indians on the warpath to help them kill the emigrants, and that I must attend to that first; that I wanted them to go on near where the emigrants were and camp until the other Indians joined them; that I would meet them the next day and lead them.

This satisfied them, but they wanted me to send my little Indian boy, Clem, with them. After some time I consented to let Clem go with them, and I returned home.

When I got home I told Carl Shirts what the orders were that Haight had sent to him. Carl was naturally cowardly and was not willing to go, but I told him the orders must be obeyed. He then started off that night, or early next morning, to stir up the Indians of the South, and lead them against the emigrants. The emigrants were then camped at Mountain Meadows.

The Indians did not obey my instructions. They met, several hundred strong, at the Meadows, and attacked the emigrants Tuesday morning, just before daylight, and at the first fire, as I afterwards learned, they killed seven and wounded sixteen of the emigrants. The latter fought bravely, and repulsed the Indians, killing some of them and breaking the knees of two war chiefs, who afterwards died.

The news of the battle was carried all over the country by Indian runners, and the excitement was great in all the small settlements. I was notified of what had taken place, early Tuesday morning, by an Indian who came to my house and gave me a full account of all that had been done. The Indian said it was the wish of all the Indians that I should lead them, and that I must go back with him to the camp.

I started at once, and by taking the Indian trail over the mountain, I reached the camp in about twelve miles from Harmony. To go round by the wagon road it would have been between forty and fifty miles.

When I reached the camp I found the Indians in a frenzy of excitement. They threatened to kill me unless I agreed to lead them against the emigrants, and help them kill them. They also said they had been told that they could kill the emigrants without danger to themselves, but they had lost some of their braves, and others were wounded, and unless they could kill all the "*Mericats*," as they called them, they would declare war against the Mormons and kill every one in the settlements.

I did as well as I could under the circumstances. I was the only white man there, with a wild and excited band of several hundred Indians. I tried to persuade them that all would be well, that I was their friend and would see that they had their revenge, if I found out that they were entitled to revenge.

My talk only served to increase their excitement, and being afraid that they would kill me if I undertook to leave them, and I would not lead them against the emigrants, so I told them that I would go south and meet their friends, and hurry them up to help them. I intended to put a stop to the carnage if I had the power, for I believed that the emigrants had been sufficiently punished for what they had done, and I felt then, and always have felt that such wholesale murdering was wrong.

At first the Indians would not consent for me to leave them, but they finally said I might go and meet their friends.

I then got on my horse and left the Meadows, and went south.

I had gone about sixteen miles, when I met Carl Shirts with about one hundred Indians, and a number of Mormons from the southern settlements. They were going to the scene of the conflict. How they learned of the emigrants being at the Meadows I never knew, but they did know it, and were there fully armed, and determined to obey *orders*.

Amongst those that I remember to have met there, were Samuel Knight, Oscar Hamblin, William Young, Carl Shirts, Harrison Pearce, James Pearce, John W. Clark, William Slade, Sr., James Matthews, Dudley Leavitt, William Hawley, (now a resident of Fillmore, Utah

Territory), William Slade, Jr., and two others whose names I have forgotten. I think they were George W. Adair and John Hawley. I know they were at the Meadows at the time of the massacre, and I think I met them that night south of the Meadows, with Samuel Knight and the others.

The whites camped there that night with me, but most of the Indians rushed on to their friends at the camp on the Meadows.

I reported to the whites all that had taken place at the Meadows, but none of them were surprised in the least. They all seemed to know that the attack was to be made, and all about it. I spent one of the most miserable nights there that I ever passed in my life. I spent much of the night in tears and at prayer. I wrestled with God for wisdom to guide me. I asked for some sign, some evidence that would satisfy me that my mission was of Heaven, but I got no satisfaction from my God.

In the morning we all agreed to go on together to Mountain Meadows, and camp there, and then send a messenger to Haight, giving him full instructions of what had been done, and to ask him for further instructions. We knew that the original plan was for the Indians to do all the work, and the whites to do nothing, only to stay back and plan for them, and encourage them to do the work. Now we knew the Indians could not do the work, and we were in a sad fix.

I did not then know that a messenger had been sent to Brigham Young for instructions. Haight had not mentioned it to me. I now think that James Haslem was sent to Brigham Young, as a sharp play on the part of the authorities to protect themselves, if trouble ever grew out of the matter.

We went to the Meadows and camped at the springs, about half a mile from the emigrant camp. There was a larger number of Indians there then, fully three hundred, and I think as many as four hundred of them. The two Chiefs who were shot in the knee were in a bad fix. The Indians had killed a number of the emigrants' horses, and about sixty or seventy head of cattle were lying dead on the Meadows, which the Indians had killed for spite and revenge.

Our company killed a small beef for dinner, and after eating a hearty meal of it we held a council and decided to send a messenger to Haight. I said to the messenger, who was either Edwards or Adair, (I cannot now remember which it was), "Tell Haight, for my sake, for the people's sake, for God's sake, send me help to protect and save these emigrants, and pacify the Indians."

The messenger started for Cedar City, from our camp on the Meadows, about 2 o'clock P.M.

We all staid on the field, and I tried to quiet and pacify the. Indians, by telling them that I had sent to Haight, the Big Captain, for orders, and when he sent his order I would know what to do. This appeared to satisfy the Indians, for said they,

"The Big Captain will send you word to kill all the Mericats." Along toward evening the Indians again attacked the emigrants. This was Wednesday. I heard the report of their guns, and the screams of the women and children in the corral.

This was more than I could stand. So I ran with William Young and John Mangum, to where the Indians were, to stop the fight. While on the way to them they fired a volley, and three balls from their guns cut my clothing. One ball went through my hat and cut my hair on the side of my head. One ball went through my shirt and leaded my shoulder, the other cut my pants across my bowels. I thought this was rather warm work, but I kept on until I reached the place where the Indians were in force. When I got to them, I told them the Great Spirit would be mad at them if they killed the women and children. I talked to them some time, and cried with sorrow when I saw that I could not pacify the savages.

When the Indians saw me in tears, they called me "Yaw Guts," which in the Indian language means "cry baby," and to this day they call me by that name, and consider me a coward.

Oscar Hamblin was a fine interpreter, and he came to my aid and helped me to induce the Indians to stop the attack. By his help we got the Indians to agree to be quiet until word was returned from Haight. (I do not know now but what the messenger started for Cedar City, after this night attack, but I was so worried and perplexed at that time, and so much has happened to distract my thoughts since then, that my mind is not clear on that subject.)

On Thursday, about noon, several men came to us from Cedar City. I cannot remember the order in which all of the people came to the Meadows, but I do recollect that at this time and in this company Joel White, William C. Stewart, Benjamin Arthur, Alexander Wilden, Charles Hopkins and -- Tate, came to us at the camp at the springs. These men said but little, but every man seemed to know just what he was there for. As our messenger had gone for further orders, we moved our camp about four hundred yards further up the valley on to a hill, where we made camp as long as we staid there.

I soon learned that the whites were as wicked at heart as the Indians, for every little while during that day I saw white men taking aim and shooting at the emigrants' wagons. They said they were doing it to keep in practice and to *help pass off the time.*

I remember one man that was shooting, that rather amused me, for he was shooting at a mark over a quarter of a mile off, and his gun would not carry a ball two hundred yards. That man was Alexander Wilden. He took pains to fix up a seat under the shade of a tree, where he continued to load and shoot until he got tired. Many of the others acted just as wild and foolish as Wilden did.

The wagons were corralled after the Indians had made the first attack. On the second day after our arrival the emigrants drew their wagons near each other and chained the wheels one to the other. While they were doing this there was no shooting going on. Their camp was about one hundred yards above and north of the spring. They generally got their water from the spring at night.

Thursday morning I saw two men start from the corral with buckets, and run to the spring and fill their buckets with water, and go back again. The bullets flew around them thick and fast, but they got into their corral in safety.

The Indians had agreed to keep quiet until orders returned from Haight, but they did not keep their word. They made a determined attack on the train on Thursday morning about daylight. At this attack the Clara Indians had one brave killed and three wounded. This so enraged that band that they left for home that day and drove off quite a number of cattle with them. During the day I said to John Mangum,

"I will cross over the valley and go up on the other side, on the hills to the west of the corral, and take a look at the situation."

I did go. As I was crossing the valley I was seen by the emigrants, and as soon as they saw that I was a white man they ran up a *white* flag in the middle of their corral, or camp. They then sent two little boys from the camp to talk to me, but I could not talk to them at that time, for I did not know what orders Haight would send back to me, and until I did know his orders I did not know how to act. I hid, to keep away from the children. They came to the place where they had last seen me and hunted all around for me, but being unable to find me, they turned and went back to the camp in safety.

While the boys were looking for me several Indians came to me and asked for ammunition with which to kill them. I told them they must not hurt the children - that if they did I would kill the first one that made the attempt to injure them. By this act I was able to save the boys.

It is all false that has been told about little girls being dressed in white and sent out to me. There never was anything of the kind done.

I staid on the west side of the valley for about two hours, looking down into the emigrant camp, and feeling all the torture of mind that it is possible for a man to suffer who feels merciful, and yet knows, as I then knew, what was in store for that unfortunate company if the Indians were successful in their bloody designs.

While I was standing on the hill looking down into the corral, I saw two men leave the corral and go outside to cut some wood; the Indians and whites kept up a steady fire on them all the time, but they paid no attention to danger, and kept right along at their work until they had it done, and then they went back into camp. The men all acted so bravely that it was impossible to keep from respecting them

After staying there and looking down into the camp until I was nearly dead from grief, I returned to the company at camp. I was worn out with trouble and grief; I was nearly wild waiting for word from the authorities at Cedar City. I prayed for word to come that would enable me to save that band of suffering people, but no such word came. It never was to come.

On Thursday evening John M. Higbee, Major of the Iron Militia, and Philip K. Smith, as he is called generally, but whose name is Klingensmith, Bishop of Cedar City, came to our camp with two or three wagons, and a number of men all well armed. I can remember the following as a portion of the men who came to take part in the work of death which was so soon to follow, viz.: John M. Higbee, Major and commander of the Iron Militia, and also first counselor to Isaac C. Haight; Philip Klingensmith, Bishop of Cedar City; Ira Allen, of the High Council; Robert Wiley, of the High Council; Richard Harrison, of Pinto, also a member of the High Council; Samuel McMurdy, one of the counselors of Klingensmith; Charles Hopkins, of the City Council of Cedar City; Samuel Pollock; Daniel McFarland, a son-in-law of Isaac C. Haight, and acting an Adjutant under Major Higbee; John Ure, of the City Council; George Hunter, of the City Council; and I honestly believe that John McFarland, now an attorney-at-law at St. George, Utah, was there - I am not positive that he was, but my best impression is that he was there: Samuel Jukes; Nephi Johnson, with a number of Indians under his command; Irvin Jacobs; John Jacobs; E. Curtis, a

Captain of Ten; Thomas Cartwright of the City Council and High Council; William Bateman, who afterwards carried the flag of truce to the emigrant camp; Anthony Stratton; A. Loveridge; Joseph Clews; Jabez Durfey; Columbus Freeman, and some others whose names I cannot remember. I know that our total force was fifty-four whites and over three hundred Indians.

As soon as these persons gathered around the camp, I demanded of Major Higbee what orders he had brought. I then stated fully all that had happened at the Meadows, so that every person might understand the situation.

Major Higbee reported as follows: "It is the orders of the President, that all the emigrants must be *put out of the way*. President Haight has counseled with Colonel Dame, or has had orders from him to put all of the emigrants out of the way; none who are old enough to talk are to be spared."

He then went on and said substantially that the emigrants had come through the country as our enemies, and as the enemies of the Church of Jesus Christ of Latter-Day Saints. That they had no pass from any one in authority to permit them to leave the Territory. That none but friends were permitted to leave the Territory, and that as these were our sworn enemies, they must be killed. That they were nothing but a portion of Johnston's army. That if they were allowed to go on to California, they would raise the war cloud in the West, and bring certain destruction upon all the settlements in Utah. That the only safety for the people was in the utter destruction of the whole rascally lot.

I then told them that God would have to change my heart before I could consent to such a wicked thing as the wholesale killing of that people. I attempted to reason with Higbee and the brethren. I told them how strongly the emigrants were fortified, and how wicked it was to kill the women and children. I was ordered to be silent. Higbee said I was resisting authority.

He then said, "Brother Lee is afraid of shedding innocent blood, Why, brethren, there is not a drop of innocent blood in that entire camp of Gentile outlaws; they are set of cutthroats, robbers and assassins; they are a part of the people who drove the Saints from Missouri, and who aided to shed the blood of our Prophet Joseph and Hyrum, and it is our orders from all in authority, to get the emigrants from their stronghold, and help the Indians kill them."

I then said that Joseph Smith had told us never to betray any one.

That we could not get the emigrants out of their corral unless we used treachery, and I was opposed to that.

I was interrupted by Higbee, Klingensmith and Hopkins, who said it was the orders of President Isaac C. Haight to us, and that Haight had his orders from Colonel Dame and the authorities at Parowan, and that all in authority were of one mind, and that they had been sent by the council at Cedar City to the Meadows to counsel and direct the way and manner that the company of emigrants should be disposed of.

The men then in council, I must here state, now knelt down in a prayer circle and prayed, invoking the Spirit of God to direct them how to act in the matter.

After prayer, Major Higbee said, "Here are the orders," and handed me a paper from Haight. It was in substance that it was the orders of Haight to *decoy* the emigrants from their position, and kill all of them that could talk. This order was in writing. Higbee handed it to me and I read it, and then dropped it on the ground, saying,

"I cannot do this."

The substance of the orders were that the emigrants should be decoyed from their stronghold, and all exterminated, so that no one would be left to tell the tale, and then the authorities could say it was done by the Indians.

The words *decoy* and *exterminate* were used in that message or order, and these orders came to us as the orders from the Council at Cedar City, and as the orders of our military superior, that we were bound to obey. The order was signed by Haight, as commander of the troops at Cedar City.

Haight told me the next day after the massacre, while on the Meadows, that he got his orders from Colonel Dame.

I then left the council, and went away to myself, and bowed myself in prayer before God, and asked Him to overrule the decision of that Council. I shed many bitter tears, and my tortured soul was wrung nearly from the body by my great suffering. I will here say, calling upon Heaven, angels, and the spirits of just men to witness what I say, that if I could then have had a thousand worlds to command, I would have given them freely to save that company from death.

While in bitter anguish, lamenting the sad condition of myself and others, Charles Hopkins, a man that I had great confidence in, came to me from the Council, and tried to comfort me by saying that he believed it was all right, for the brethren in the *Priesthood* were all united in the thing, and it would not be well for me to oppose them.

I told him the Lord must change my heart before I could ever do such an act willingly. I will further state that there was a reign of terror in Utah, at that time, and many a man had been put out of the way, on short notice, for disobedience, and I had made some narrow escapes.

At the earnest solicitation of Brother Hopkins, I returned with him to the Council. When I got back, the Council again prayed for aid. The council was called the City Counselors, the Church or High Counselors; and all in authority, together with the private citizens, then formed a circle, and kneeling down, so that elbows would touch each other, several of the brethren prayed for divine instructions.

After prayer, Major Higbee said, "I have the evidence of God's approval of our mission. It is God's will that we carry out our instructions to the letter."

I said, "My God! this is more than I can do. I must and do refuse to take part in this matter."

Higbee then said to me, "Brother Lee, I am ordered by President Haight to inform you that you shall receive a crown of Celestial glory for your faithfulness, and your eternal joy shall be complete." I was much shaken by this offer, for I had full faith in the power of the Priesthood to bestow such rewards and blessings, but I was anxious to save the people. I then proposed that we give the Indians all of the stock of the emigrants, except sufficient to haul their wagons, and let them go. To this proposition all the leading men objected. No man there raised his voice or hand to favor the saving of life, except myself.

The meeting was then addressed by some one in authority, I do not remember who it was. He spoke in about this language: "Brethren, we have been sent here to perform a duty. It is a duty that we owe to God, and to our Church and people. The orders of those in authority are that all the emigrants must die. Our leaders speak with inspired tongues, and their orders come from the God of Heaven. We have no right to question what they have commanded us to do; it is our duty to obey. If we wished to act as some of our weakkneed brethren desire us to do, it would be impossible; the thing has gone too far to allow us to stop now. The emigrants know that we have aided the Indians, and if we let them go they will bring certain destruction upon us. It is a fact that on Wednesday night, two of the emigrants got out of camp and started back to Cedar City for assistance to withstand the Indian attacks; they had reached Richards' Springs when they met William C. Stewart, Joel

White and Benjamin Arthur, three of our brethren from Cedar City. The men stated their business to the brethren, and as their horses were drinking at the Spring, Brother Stewart, feeling *unusually* full of zeal for the glory of God and the upbuilding of the Kingdom of God on earth, shot and killed one of the emigrants, a young man by the name of Aden. When Aden fell from his horse, Joel White shot and wounded the other Gentile; but he, unfortunately got away, and returned to his camp and reported that the Mormons were helping the Indians in all that they were doing against the emigrants. Now the emigrants will report these facts in California if we let them go. We must kill them all, and our orders are to get them out by treachery if no other thing can be done to get them into our power."

Many of the brethren spoke in the same way, all arguing that the orders must be carried out.

I was then told the plan of action had been agreed upon, and it was this: The emigrants were to be decoyed from their stronghold under a promise of protection. Brother William Bateman was to carry a flag of truce and demand a parley, and then I was to go and arrange the terms of the surrender. I was to demand that all the children who were so young they could not talk should be put into a wagon, and the wounded were also to be put into a wagon. Then all the arms and ammunition of the emigrants should be put into a wagon, and I was to agree that the Mormons would protect the emigrants from the Indians and conduct them to Cedar City in safety, where they should be protected until an opportunity came for sending them to California.

It was agreed that when I had made the full agreement and treaty, as the brethren called it, the wagons should start for Hamblin's Ranch with the arms, the wounded and the children. The women were to march on foot and follow the wagons in single file; the men were to follow behind the women, they also to march in single file. Major John M. Higbee was to stand with his militia company about two hundred yards from the camp, and stand in double file, open order, with about twenty feet space between the files, so that the wagons could pass between them. The drivers were to keep right along, and not stop at the troops. The women were not to stop there, but to follow the wagons. The troops were to halt the men for a few minutes, until the women were some distance ahead, out into the cedars, where the Indians were hid in ambush. Then the march was to be resumed, the troops to form in single file, each soldier to walk by an emigrant, and on the right-hand side of his man, and the soldier was to carry his gun on his left arm, ready for instant use. The march was to continue until the wagons had passed beyond the ambush of the Indians, and until the women were right in the midst of the Indians. Higbee was then to give the orders and words, "Do Your Duty." At this the troops were to shoot down the men; the Indians were to kill all of the women and larger children, and the drivers of the wagons and I were to kill the wounded and sick men that were in the wagons. Two men were to be placed on horses near by, to overtake and kill any of the emigrants that might escape from the first assault. The Indians were to kill the women and large children, so that it would be certain that no Mormon would be guilty of shedding *innocent blood* - if it should happen that there was any innocent blood in the company that were to die. Our leading men all said that there was no innocent blood in the whole company.

The council broke up a little after daylight on Friday morning. All the horses, except two for the men to ride to overtake those who might escape, and one for Dan McFarland to ride as Adjutant, so that he could carry orders from one part of the field to another, were turned out on the range. Then breakfast was eaten, and the brethren prepared for the work in hand.

I was now satisfied that it was the wish of all of the Mormon priesthood to have the thing done. One reason for thinking so was that it was in keeping with the teachings of the leaders, and as Utah was then at war with the United States we believed all the Gentiles were to be killed as a war measure, and that the Mormons, as God's chosen people, were to hold and inhabit the earth and rule and govern the globe. Another, and one of my strongest reasons for believing that the leaders wished the thing done, was on account of the talk that I had with George A. Smith, which I have given in full in this statement. I was satisfied that Smith had passed the emigrants while on his way from Salt Lake City, and I then knew this was the train that he meant when he spoke of a *train* that would make threats and ill treat our people, etc.

The people were in the full blaze of the reformation and anxious to do some act that would add to their reputation as zealous Churchmen.

I therefore, taking all things into consideration, and believing, as I then did, that my superiors were *inspired* men, who could not go wrong in any matter relating to the Church or the duty of its members, concluded to be obedient to the wishes of those in authority. I took up my cross and prepared to do my duty.

Soon after breakfast Major Higbee ordered the two Indian inter-preters, Carl Shirts and Nephi Johnson, to inform the Indians of the plan of operations, and to place the Indians in ambush, so that they could not be seen by the emigrants until the work of death should commence.

This was done in order to make the emigrants believe that we had sent the Indians away, and that we were acting honestly and in good faith, when we agreed to protect them from the savages.

The orders were obeyed, and in five minutes not an Indian could be seen on the whole Meadows. They secreted themselves and lay still as logs of wood, until the order was given for them to rush out and kill the women.

Major Higbee then called all the people to order, and directed me to explain the whole plan to them. I did so, explaining just how every per-son was expected to act during the whole performance.

Major Higbee then gave the order for his men to advance. They marched to the spot agreed upon, and halted there. William Bateman was then selected to carry a flag of truce to the emigrants and demand their surrender, and I was ordered to go and make the treaty after some one had replied to our flag of truce. (The emigrants had kept a white flag flying in their camp ever since they saw me cross the valley.)

Bateman took a white flag and started for the emigrant camp. When he got about half way to the corral, he was met by one of the emigrants, that I afterwards learned was named Hamilton. They talked some time, but I never knew what was said between hem.

Brother Bateman returned to the command and said that the emi-grants would accept our terms, and surrender as we required them to do.

I was then ordered by Major Higbee to go to the corral and negotiate the treaty, and superintend the whole matter. I was again ordered to be certain and get all the arms and ammunition into the wagons. Also to put the children and the sick and wounded in the wagons, as had been agreed upon in council. Then Major Higbee said to me:

"Brother Lee, we expect you to faithfully carry out all the instruc-tions that have been given you by our council."

Samuel McMurdy and Samuel Knight were then ordered to drive their teams and follow me to the corral to haul off the children, arms, etc.

The troops formed in two lines, as had been agreed upon, and were standing in that way with arms at rest, when I left them.

I walked ahead of the wagons up to the corral. When I reached there

I met Mr. Hamilton on the outside of the camp. He loosened the chains from some of their wagons, and moved one wagon out of the way, so that our teams could drive inside of the corral and into their camp. It was then noon, or a little after.

I found that the emigrants were strongly fortified; their wagons were chained to each other in a circle. In the centre was a rifle-pit, large enough to contain the entire company. This had served to shield them from the constant fire of their enemy, which had been poured into them from both sides of the valley, from a rocky range that served as a breastwork for their assailants. The valley at this point was not more than five hundred yards wide, and the emigrants had their camp near the center of the valley. On the east and west there was a low range of rugged, rocky mountains, affording a splendid place for the protection of the Indians and Mormons, and leaving them in comparative safety while they fired upon the emigrants. The valley at this place runs nearly due north and south.

When I entered the corral, I found the emigrants engaged in burying two men of note among them, who had died but a short time before from the effect of wounds received by them from the Indians at the time of the first attack on Tuesday morning. They wrapped the bodies up in buffalo robes, and buried them in a grave inside the corral. I was then told by some of the men that seven men were killed and seventeen others were wounded at the first attack made by the Indians, and that three of the wounded men had since died, making ten of their number killed during the siege.

As I entered the fortifications, men, women and children gathered around me in wild consternation. Some felt that the time of their happy deliverance had come, while others, though in deep distress, and all in tears, looked upon me with doubt, distrust and terror. My feelings at this time may be imagined (but I doubt the power of man being equal to even imagine how wretched I felt). No language can describe my feelings. My position was painful, trying and awful; my brain seemed to be on fire; my nerves were for a moment unstrung; humanity was overpowered, as I thought of the cruel, unmanly part that I was acting. Tears of bitter anguish fell in streams from my eyes; my tongue refused its office; my faculties were dormant, stupefied and deadened by grief. I wished that the earth would open and swallow me where I stood. God knows my suffering was great. I cannot describe my feelings. I knew that I was acting a cruel part and doing a damnable deed. Yet my faith in the godliness of my leaders was such that it forced me to think that I was not sufficiently spiritual to act the important part I was command-ed to perform. My hesitation was only momentary. Then feeling that duty compelled *obedience to orders*, I laid aside my weakness and my humanity, and became an instrument in the hands of my superiors and my leaders. I delivered my message and told the people that they must put their arms in the wagon, so as not to arouse the animosity of the Indians. I ordered the children and wounded, some clothing and the arms, to be put into the wagons. Their guns were mostly Kentucky rifles of the muzzle-loading style. Their ammunition was about all gone - I do not think there were twenty loads left in their whole camp. If the emi-grants had had a good supply of ammunition they never would have sur-rendered, and I do not think we could have captured them without great loss, for they were brave men and very resolute and determined.

Just as the wagons were loaded, Dan. McFarland came riding into the corral and said that Major Higbee had ordered great haste to be made, for he was afraid that the Indians would return and renew the attack before he could get the emigrants to a place of safety.

I hurried up the people and started the wagons off towards Cedar City. As we went out of the corral I ordered the wagons to turn to the left, so as to leave the troops to the right of us. Dan McFarland rode before the women and led them right up to the troops, where they still stood in open order as I left them. The women and larger children were walking ahead, as directed, and the men following them. The foremost man was about fifty yards behind the hindmost woman.

The women and children were hurried right on by the troops. When the men came up they cheered the soldiers as if they believed that they were acting honestly. Higbee then gave the orders for his men to form in single file and take their places as ordered before, that is, at the right of the emigrants.

I saw this much, but about this time our wagons passed out of sight of the troops, over the hill. I had disobeyed orders in part by turning off as I did, for I was anxious to be out of sight of the bloody deed that I knew was to follow. I knew that I had much to do yet that was of a cruel and unnatural character. It was my duty, with the two drivers, to kill the sick and wounded who were in the wagons, and to do so when we heard the guns of the troops fire. I was walking between the wagons; the hors-es were going in a fast walk, and we were fully half a mile from Major Higbee and his men, when we heard the firing. As we heard the guns, I

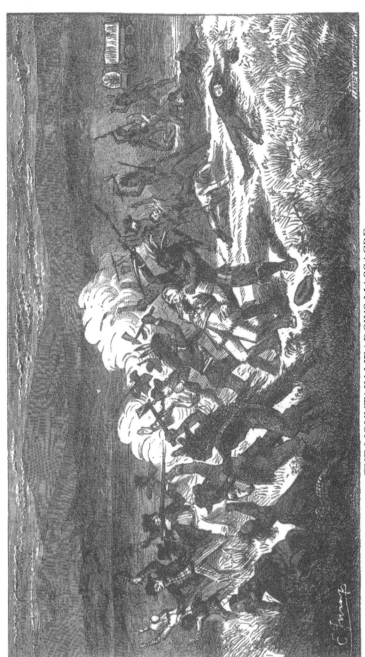

THE MOUNTAIN MEADOWS MASSACRE

ordered a halt and we proceeded to do our part.

I here pause in the recital of this horrid story of man's inhumanity, and ask myself the question, is it honest in me, and can I clear my conscience before my God, if I screen myself while I accuse others? No, never! Heaven forbid that I should put a burden upon others' shoulders, that I am unwilling to bear my just portion of. I am not a traitor to my people, nor to my former friends and comrades who were with me on that dark day when the work of death was carried on in God's name, by a lot of deluded and religious fanatics. It in my duty to tell facts as they exist, and I will do so.

I have said that all of the small children were put into the wagons; that was wrong, for one little child, about six months old, was carried in its father's arms, and it was killed by the some bullet that entered its father's breast; it was shot through the head. I was told by Haight afterwards, that the child was killed by accident, but I cannot say whether that is a fact or not. I saw it lying dead when I returned to the place of slaughter.

When we had got out of sight, as I said before, and just as we were coming into the main road, I heard a volley of guns at the place where I know the troops and emigrants were. Our teams were then going at a fast walk. I first heard one gun, then a volley at once followed.

McMurdy and Knight stopped their teams at once, for they were ordered by Higbee, the same as I was, to help kill all the sick and wounded who were in the wagons, and to do it as soon as they heard the guns of the troops. McMurdy was in front; his wagon was mostly loaded with the arms and small children. McMurdy and Knight got out of their wagons; each one had a rifle. McMurdy went up to Knight's wagon, where the sick and wounded were, and raising his rifle to his shoulder, said: "*O Lord, my God, receive their spirits, it is for thy Kingdom that I do this.*" He then shot a man who was lying with his head on another man's breast; the ball killed both men.

I also went up to the wagon, intending to do my part of the killing. I drew my pistol and cocked it, but somehow it went off prematurely, and I shot McMurdy across the thigh, my pistol ball cutting his buckskin pants. McMurdy turned to me and said:

"Brother Lee, keep cool, you are excited; you came very near killing me. Keep cool, there is no reason for being excited."

Knight then shot a man with his rifle; he shot the man in the head. Knight also brained a boy that was about fourteen years old. The boy came running up to our wagons, and Knight struck him on the head with the butt end of his gun, and crushed his skull. By this time many Indians reached our wagons, and all of the sick and wounded were killed almost instantly. I saw an Indian from Cedar City, called Joe, ran up to the wagon and catch a man by the hair, and raise his head up and look into his face; the man shut his eyes, and Joe shot him in the head. The Indians then examined all of the wounded in the wagons, and all of the bodies, to see if any were alive, and all that showed signs of life were at once shot through the head. I did not kill any one there, but it was an accident that kept me from it, for I fully intended to do my part of the killing, but by the time I got over the excitement of coming so near killing McMurdy, the whole of the killing of the wounded was done. There is no truth in the statement of Nephi Johnson, where he says I cut a man's throat.

Just after the wounded were all killed I saw a girl, some ten or eleven years old, running towards as, from the direction where the troops had attacked the main body of emigrants; she was covered with blood. An Indian shot her before she got within sixty yards of us. That was the last person that I saw killed on that occasion.

About this time an Indian rushed to the front wagon, and grabbed a little boy, and was going to kill him. The lad got away from the Indian and ran to me, and caught me by the knees; and begged me to save him, and not let the Indian kill him. The Indian had hurt the little fellow's chin on the wagon bed, when he first caught hold of him. I told the Indian to let the boy alone. I took the child up in my arms, and put him back in the wagon, and saved his life. This little boy said his name was Charley Fancher, and that his father was Captain of the train. He was a bright boy. I afterwards adopted him, and gave him to Caroline. She kept him until Dr. Forney took all the children East. I believe that William Sloan, alias Idaho Bill, is the same boy.

After all the parties were dead, I ordered Knight to drive out on one side, and throw out the dead bodies. He did so, and threw them out of his wagon at a place about one hundred yards from the road, and then came back to where I was standing. I then ordered Knight and McMurdy to take the children that were saved alive (sixteen was the number, some say seventeen, I say sixteen), and drive on to Hamblin's ranch. They did as I ordered them to do. Before the wagons started, Nephi Johnson came up in company with the Indians that were under his command, and Carl Shirts I think came up too, but I know that I then considered that Carl Shirts was a coward, and I afterwards made him suffer for being a coward. Several white men came up too, but I cannot tell their names, as I have forgotten who they were.

Knight lied when he said I went to the ranch and ordered him to go to the field with his team. I never knew anything of his team, or heard of it, until he came with a load of armed men in his wagon, on the evening of Thursday. If any one ordered him to go to the Meadows, it was Higbee. Every witness that claims that he went to the Meadows without knowing what he was going to do, has lied, for they all knew, as well as Haight or any one else did, and they all voted, every man of them, in the Council, on Friday morning, a little before daylight, to kill all the emigrants.

After the wagons, with the children, had started for Hamblin's ranch, I turned and walked back to where the brethren were. Nephi Johnson lies when he says he was on horseback, and met me, or that I gave him orders to go to guard the wagons. He is a perjured wretch, and has sworn to every thing he could to injure me. God knows what I did do was bad enough, but he has lied to suit the leaders of the Church, who want me out of the way.

While going back to the brethren, I passed the bodies of several women. In one place I saw six or seven bodies near each other; they were stripped perfectly naked, and all of their clothing was torn from their bodies by the Indians.

I walked along the line where the emigrants had been killed, and saw many bodies lying dead and naked on the field, near by where the women lay. I saw ten children; they had been killed close to each other; they were from ten to sixteen years of age. The bodies of the women and children were scattered along the ground for quite a distance before I came to where the men were killed.

I do not know how many were killed, but I thought then that there were some fifteen women, about ten children, and about forty men killed, but the statement of others that I have since talked with about the massacre, makes me think there were fully one hundred and ten killed that day on the Mountain Meadows, and the ten who had died in the corral, and young Aden killed by Stewart at Richards' Springs, would make the total number one hundred and twenty-one.

When I reached the place where the dead men lay, I was told how the orders had been obeyed. Major Higbee said, "The boys have acted admirably, they took good aim, and all of the d--d Gentiles but two or three fell at the *first fire*."

He said that three or four got away some distance, but the men on horses soon overtook them and cut their throats. Higbee said the Indians did their part of the work well, that it did not take over a minute to finish up when they got fairly started. I found that the first orders had been carried out to the letter.

Three of the emigrants did get away, but the Indians were put on their trail and they overtook and killed them before they reached the settlements in California. But it would take more time than I have to spare to give the details of their chase and capture. I may do so in my writings hereafter, but not now.

I found Major Higbee, Klingensmith, and most of the brethren standing near by where the largest number of the dead men lay. When I went up to the brethren, Major Higbee said,

"We must now examine the bodies for valuables."

I said I did not wish to do any such work.

Higbee then said, "Well, you hold my hat and I will examine the bodies, and put what valuables I get into the hat."

The bodies were all searched by Higbee, Klingensmith and Wm. C. Stewart. I did hold the hat a while, but I soon got so sick that I had to give it to some other person, as I was unable to stand for a few minutes. The search resulted in getting a little money and a few watches, but there was not much money. Higbee and Klingensmith kept the property, I suppose, for I never knew what became of it, unless they did keep it. I think they kept it all.

After the dead were searched, as I have just said, the brethren were called up, and Higbee and Klingensmith, as well an myself, made speeches, and *ordered* the people to keep the matter a secret from the *entire* world. Not to tell their wives, or their most intimate friends, and we pledged ourselves to keep everything relating to the affair a secret during life. We also took the most binding oaths to stand by each other, and to always insist that the massacre was committed by Indians alone. This was the advice of Brigham Young too, as I will show hereafter.

The men were mostly ordered to camp there on the field for that night, but Higbee and Klingensmith went with me to Hamblin's ranch, where we got something to eat, and staid there all night. I was nearly dead for rest and sleep; in fact I had rested but little since the Saturday night before. I took my saddle blanket and spread it on the ground soon after I had eaten my supper, and lay down on the saddle blanket, using my saddle for a pillow, and slept soundly until next morning.

I was awakened in the morning by loud talking between Isaac O. Haight and William H. Dame. They were very much excited, and quarreling with each other. I got up at once, but was unable to hear what they were quarreling about, for they cooled down as soon as they saw that others were paying attention to them.

I soon learned that Col. Dame, Judge Lewis of Parowan, and Isaac C. Haight, with several others, had arrived at the Hamblin ranch in the night, but I do not know what time they got there.

After breakfast we all went back in a body to the Meadows, to bury the dead and take care of the property that was left there.

When we reached the Meadows we all rode up to that part of the field where the women were lying dead. The bodies of men, women and children had been stripped entirely naked, making the scene one of the most, loathsome and ghastly that can be imagined.

Knowing that Dame and Haight had quarreled at Hamblin's that morning, I wanted to know how they would act in sight of the dead, who lay there as the result of their orders. I was greatly interested to know what Dame had to say, so I kept close to them, without appearing to be watching them.

Colonel Dame was silent for some time. He looked all over the field, and was quite pale, and looked uneasy and frightened. I thought then that he was just finding out the difference between giving and executing orders for wholesale killing. He spoke to Haight, and said:

"I must report this matter to the authorities."

"How will you report it?" said Haight.

Dame said, "I will report it just as it is."

"Yes, I suppose so, and implicate yourself with the rest?" said Haight.

"No," said Dame. "I will not implicate myself, for I had nothing to do with it."

Haight then said, "That will not do, for you know a d--d sight better. You ordered it done. Nothing has been done except by your orders, and it is too late in the day for you to order things done and then go back on it, and go back on the men who have carried out your orders. You cannot *sow pig* on me, and I will be d--d if I will stand it. You are as much to blame as any one, and you know that we have done nothing except what you ordered done. I know that I have obeyed orders, and by G-d I will not be lied on."

Colonel Dame was much excited. He choked up, and would have gone away, but he knew Haight was a man of determination, and would not stand any foolishness.

As soon as Colonel Dame could collect himself, he said:

"*I did not think there were so many of them, or I would not have had anything to do with it.*"

I thought it was now time for me to chip in, so I said:

"Brethren, what is the trouble between you? It will not do for our chief men to disagree."

Haight stepped up to my side, a little in front of me, and facing Colonel Dame. He was very mad, and said:

"The trouble is just this: Colonel Dame *counseled* and *ordered* me to do this thing, and now he wants to back out, and go back on me, and by G-d, he shall not do it. He shall not lay it *all* on me. He cannot do it. He must not try to do it. I will *blow him to h--l* before he shall lay it all on me. He has got to stand up to what he did, like a little man. He knows he ordered it done, and I dare him to deny it."

Colonel Dame was perfectly cowed. He did not offer to deny it again, but said:

"Isaac, I did not know there were so many of them."

"That makes no difference," said Haight, "you ordered me to do it, and you have got to stand up for your *orders*."

I thought it was now time to stop the fuss, for many of the young brethren were coming around. So I said:

"Brethren, this is no place to talk over such a matter. You will agree when you get where you can be quiet, and talk it over."

Haight said, "There is no more to say, for he knows he ordered it done, and he has got to stand by it."

That ended the trouble between them, and I never heard of Colonel Dame denying the giving of the orders any more, until after the Church authorities concluded to offer me up for the sins of the Church.

We then went along the field, and passed by where the brethren were at work covering up the bodies. They piled the dead bodies up in heaps, in little gullies, and threw dirt over them. The bodies were only lightly covered, for the ground was hard, and the brethren did not have sufficient tools to dig with. I suppose it is true that the first rain washed the bodies all out again, but I never went back to examine whether it did or not.

We then went along the field to where the corral and camp had been, to where the wagons were standing. We found that the Indians had carried off all of the wagon covers, and the clothing, and the provisions, and had emptied the feathers out of the feather beds, and carried off all the ticks.

After the dead were covered up or buried (but it was not much of a burial) the brethren were called together, and a council was held at the emigrant camp. All the leading men made speeches; Colonel Dame, President Haight, Klingensmith, John M. Higbee, Hopkins and myself. The speeches were first - thanks to God for delivering our enemies into our hands; next, thanking the brethren for their zeal in God's cause; and then the necessity of always saying the Indians did it alone, and that the Mormons had nothing to do with it. The most of the speeches, however, were in the shape of exhortations and commands to keep the whole matter secret from every one but Brigham Young. It was voted unanimously that any man who should divulge the secret, or tell who was present, or do anything that would lead to a discovery of the truth, should suffer death.

The brethren then all took a most solemn oath, binding themselves under the most dreadful and awful penalties, to keep the whole matter secret from every human being, as long as they should live. No man was to know the facts. The brethren were sworn not to talk of it among themselves, and each one swore to help kill all who proved to be traitors to the Church or people in this matter.

It was then agreed that Brigham Young should be informed of the whole matter, by some one to be selected by the Church council, after the brethren had returned home.

It was also voted to turn all the property over to Klingensmith, as Bishop of the Church at Cedar City, and he was to take care of the property for the benefit of the Church, until Brigham Young was notified, and should give further orders what to do with it.

CHAPTER XIX

CONFESSION CONTINUED AND CONCLUDED, MARCH 16, 1877, SEVEN DAYS PRIOR TO HIS EXECUTION

COLONEL DAME then blest the brethren and we prepared to go to our homes. I took my little Indian boy, Clem, on the horse behind me, and started home. I crossed the mountains and returned the same way I had come.

When I got in about two miles of Harmony, I overtook a body of about forty Indians, on their way home from the massacre. They had a large amount of bloody clothing, and were driving several head of cattle that they had taken from the emigrants.

The Indians were very glad to see me, and said I was their Captain, and that they were going to Harmony with me as my men. It was the orders from the Church authorities to do everything we could to pacify the Indians, and make them the fast friends of the Mormons, so I concluded to humor them.

I started on and they marched after me until we reached the fort at Harmony. We went into the fort and marched round inside, after which they halted and gave their whoop of victory, which means much the same with them as the *cheers* do with the whites. I then ordered the Indians to be fed; my family gave them some bread and melons, which they eat, and then they left me and went to their tribe.

I will here state again that on the field, before and after the massacre, and again at the council at the emigrant camp, the day after the massacre, orders were given to keep everything secret, and if any man told the secret to any human being, he was to be killed, and I assert as a fact that if any man had told it then, or for *many years afterwards, he would have died*, for some *"Destroying Angel"* would have followed his trail and sent him over the *"rim of the basin."*

From that day to this it has been the understanding with all concerned in that massacre, that the man who divulged the secret should die; he was to be killed, wherever he was found, for treason to the men who killed the emigrants, and for his *treason to the Church*. No man was at liberty to tell his wife, or any one else, nor were the brethren permitted to talk of it *even among themselves*. Such were the *orders* and *instructions*, from *Brigham Young* down to the lowest in authority. The orders to lay it all to the Indians, were just as positive as they were to keep it all secret. This was the counsel from all in authority, and for years it was faithfully observed.

The children that were saved were taken to Cedar City, and other settlements, and put out among different families, where they were kept until they were given up to Dr. Forney, the Agent of the United States, who came for them.

I did not have anything to do with the property taken from the emigrants, or the cattle, or anything else, for some three months after the massacre, and then I only took charge of the cattle because I was ordered to do so by Brigham Young.

There were eighteen wagons in all at the emigrant camp. They were all wooden axles but one, and that was a light iron axle; it had been hauled by four mules. There were something over five hundred head of cattle, but I never got the half of them. The Indians killed a large number at the time of the massacre, and drove others to their tribes when they went home from Mountain Meadows. Klingensmith put the Church brand on fifty head or more, of the best of the cattle, and then he and Haight and Higbee drove the cattle to Salt Lake City and sold them for goods that they brought back to Cedar City to trade on.

The Indians got about twenty head of horses and mules. Samuel Knight, one of the witnesses on my trial, got a large sorrel mare; Haight got a span of average American mules; Joel White got a fine mare; Higbee got a good large mule; Klingensmith got a span of mules. Haight, Higbee and Allen each took a wagon. The people all took what they wanted, and they had divided and used up much over half of it before I was put in charge.

The first time I heard that a messenger had been sent to Brigham Young for instructions as to what should be done with the emigrants, was three or four days after I had returned home from the Meadows. Then I heard of it from Isaac C. Haight, when became to my house and had a talk with me. He said:

"We are all in a muddle. Haslem has returned from Salt Lake City, with orders from Brigham Young to let the emigrants pass in safety."

In this conversation Haight also said:

"I sent an order to Higbee to save the emigrants, after I had sent the orders for killing them all, but for some reason the message did not reach him. I understand the messenger did not go to the Meadows at all."

I at once saw that we were in a bad fix, and I asked Haight what was to be done. We talked the matter over again.

Haight then told me that it was the orders of the Council that I should go to Salt Lake City and lay the whole matter before Brigham Young. I asked him if he was not going to write a report of it to the Governor, as he was the right man to do it, for he was in command of the militia in that section of country, and next to Dame in command of the whole district. I told him that it was a matter which really belonged to the military department, and should be so reported.

He refused to write a report, saying:

"You can report it better then I could write it. You are like a member of Brigham's family, and can talk to him privately and confidentially. I want you to take all of it on yourself that you can, and not expose any more of the brethren than you find absolutely necessary. Do this, Brother Lee, as I order you to do, and you shall receive a celestial reward for it, and the time will come when all who acted with us will be glad for the part they have taken, for the time is near at hand when the Saints are to enjoy the riches of the earth. And all who deny the faith and doctrines of the Church of Jesus Christ of Latter-Day Saints shall be slain - the sword of vengeance shall shed their blood; their wealth shall be given as a spoil to our people."

At that time I believed everything he said, and I fully expected to receive the celestial reward that he promised me. But now I say, *Damn all such "celestial rewards"* as I am to get for what I did on that fatal day.

It was then preached every Sunday to the people that the Mormons were to conquer the earth at once, and the people all thought that the millennium had come, and that Christ's reign upon earth would soon begin, as an accomplished fact.

According to the orders of Isaac C. Haight, I started for Salt Lake City to report the whole facts connected with the massacre, to Brigham Young. I started about a week or ten days after the massacre, and I was on the way about ten days. When I arrived in the city I went to the president's house and give to Brigham Young a full, detailed statement of the whole affair, from first to last - only I took rather more on myself than I had done.

He asked me if I had brought a letter from Haight, with his report of the affair. I said:

"No, Haight wished me to make a verbal report of it, as I was an eye witness to much of it."

I then went over the whole affair and gave him as full a statement as it was possible for me to give. I described everything about it. I told him of the orders Haight first gave me. I told him everything. I told him that "Brother McMurdy, Brother Knight and myself killed the wounded men in the wagons, with the assistance of the Indians. We killed six wounded men."

He asked me many questions, and I told him every particular, and everything that I knew. I described everything very fully. I told him what I had said against killing the women and children.

Brigham then said:

"Isaac (referring to Haight) has sent me word that if they had killed every man, woman and child in the outfit, there would not have been a drop of innocent blood shed by the brethren; for they were a set of murderers, robbers and thieves."

While I was still talking with him, some men came into his house to see him, so he requested me to keep quiet until they left. I did as he directed.

As soon as the men went out, I continued my recital. I gave him the names of every man that had been present at the massacre. I told him who killed various ones. In fact I gave him *all the information there was to give.*

When I finished talking about the matter, he said:

"This is the most unfortunate affair that ever befell the Church. I am afraid of treachery among the brethren that were there. If any one tells this thing so that it will become public, it will work us great injury. I want you to understand now, that you are *never* to tell this again, not even to Heber C. Kimball. *It must* be kept a secret among ourselves. When you get home, I want you to sit down and write a long letter, and give me an account of the affair, charging it to the Indians. You sign the letter as Farmer to the Indians, and direct it to me as Indian Agent. I can then make use of such a letter to keep off all damaging and troublesome inquiries."

I told him that I would write the letter. (I kept my word; but, as an evidence of his treachery, that same letter that he *ordered me* to write, he has given to Attorney Howard, and he has introduced it in evidence against me on my trial.)

Brigham Young knew when he got that letter just as well as I did, that it was not a true letter, and that it was only written according to his orders to throw the public off of the right trail. He *knew* that it was written simply to cast all the blame on the Indians, and to protect the brethren. In writing that letter I was still obeying my orders and earning that Celestial reward that had been promised to me.

He then said, "If only men had been killed, I would not have cared so much; but the killing of the women and children is the sin of it. I suppose the men were a hard set, but it is hard to kill women and children for the sins of the men. This whole thing stands before me like a horrid vision. I must have time to reflect upon it."

He then told me to withdraw and call next day, and he would give me an answer. I said to him,

"President Young, the people all felt, and I know that I believed I was obeying *orders*, and acting for the good of the Church, and in strict conformity with the oaths that we have all taken to avenge the blood of the Prophets. You must either sustain the people for what they have done, or you must release us from the oaths and obligations that we have taken."

The only reply he made was,

"Go now, and come in the morning, and I will give you an answer."

I went to see him again in the morning. When I went in, he he seemed quite cheerful. He said,

"I have made that matter a subject of prayer. *I went right to God with it*, and asked Him to take the horrid vision from my might, *if it was a righteous thing* that my people had done in killing those people at the Mountain Meadows. God answered me, and *at once the vision was removed*. I have evidence from God that He has overruled it all for good, and the action was a righteous one and well intended.

The brethren acted from pure motives. The only trouble is they acted a *little prematurely*; they were a *little* ahead of time. I *sustain you* and all of the brethren for what they did. All that I fear is treachery on the part of some one who took a part with you, but we will look to that."

I was again cautioned and commanded to keep the whole thing as a sacred secret, and again told to write the report as Indian Farmer, laying the blame on the Indians. That ended our interview, and I left him, and soon started for my home at Harmony.

Brigham Young was then satisfied with the purity of my motives in acting as I had done at the Mountain Meadows. Now he is doing all he can against me, but I know it is nothing but cowardice that has made him turn against me as he has at last.

When I reported my interview with Young to Haight, and gave him Brigham's answer, he was well pleased; he said that I had done well. He again enjoined secrecy, and said it must never be told.

I remember a circumstance that Haight then related to me about Dan. McFarland. He said:

"Dan will make a bully warrior."

I said, "Why do you think so?"

"Well," said he, "Dan came to me and said, 'You must get me another knife, because the one I have got has no good stuff in it, for the edge turned when I cut a fellow's throat that day at the Meadows. I caught one of the devils that was trying to get away, and when I cut his throat it took all the edge off of my knife.' I tell you that boy will make a *bully* warrior."

I said, "Haight, I don't believe you have any conscience."

He laughed, and said, "Conscience be d--d, I don't know what the word means."

I thought over the matter, and made up my mind to write the letter to Brigham Young and lay it all to the Indians, so as to get the matter off of my mind. I then wrote the letter that has been used in the trial. It was as follows: .

LETTER OF JOHN D. LEE TO BRIGHAM YOUNG

HARMONY, WASHINGTON CO., U. T.,
November 20th, 1857

To His Excellency, Gov. B. Young, Ex-Officio and Superintendent of Indian Affairs:

DEAR SIR: My report under date May 11th, 1857, relative to the Indians over whom I have charge as farmer, showed a friendly relation between them and the whites, which doubtless would have continued to increase had not the white *mans* been the first aggressor, as was the case with Capt. Fancher's company of emigrants, passing through to California about the middle of September last, on Corn Creek, fifteen miles south of Fillmore City, Millard County. The company there poisoned the meat of an ox, which they gave the Pah Vant Indians to eat, causing four of them to die immediately, besides poisoning a number more. The company also poisoned the water where they encamped, killing the cattle of the settlers. This unguided policy, planned in wickedness by this company, raised the ire of the Indians, which soon spread through the southern tribes, firing them up with revenge till blood was in their path, and as the breach, according to their tradition, was a national one, consequently any portion of the nation was liable to atone for that offense.

About the 22d of September, Capt. Fancher and company fell victims to their *wrath*, near Mountain Meadows; their cattle and horses were shot down in every direction, their wagons and property mostly committed to the flames. Had they been the only ones that suffered we would have less cause of complaint. But the following company of near the same *size* had many of their men shot down near Beaver City, and had it not been for the interposition of the citizens at that place, the whole company would have been *massacred* by the enraged Pah Vants. From this place they were protected by military force, by order of Col. W.H. Dame, through the territory, besides providing the company with interpreters, to help them through to the *Los Vaagus*. On the Muddy, some three to five hundred Indians attacked the company, while traveling, and drove off several hundred head of cattle, telling the company that if they fired a single gun that they would kill every soul. The interpreters tried to regain the stock, or a portion of them, by presents, but in vain. The Indians told them to mind their own business, or their lives would not be safe. Since that occurrence no company has been able to pass without some of our interpreters to talk and explain matters to the Indians.

Friendly feelings yet remain between the natives and settlers and I have no hesitancy in saying that it will increase so long an we treat them kindly, and deal honestly toward them. I have been blest in my labors the last year. Much grain has been raised for the Indians.

I herewith furnish you the account of W.H. Dame, of Parowan, for cattle, *wagons*, etc.

Furnished for the benefit of the Chief Owanup, (ss.) for
    Two yoke of oxen, $100 each, one wagon and chains

$75. Total	$275.00
Two cows $30 ea, for labor $80, ...	140.00
Total	$415.00

P.K. Smith, Cedar City, Iron County,

For two yoke cattle $100 each, and Mo. 2 Weekses Band................	$200 00
One cow $35, do one *wagon* $80, total, ...	115.00
Total	$315.00

Jacob Hamblin's account for the benefit of Talse Gobbeth
    Band, Santa Clara, Washington Co., (ss.)
Two yoke of cattle, $100 each, do one *wagon*, two chains,

$100, total	$300.00
Two cows $35 each, total	70.00
Total...	$370.00

Henry Barney's account for the benefit of Tennquiches
    Band, Harmony, (ss.)

For two yoke cattle $100, ...	$200.00
Do one *wagon* $100, do one plough $40, total................	140.00
Do four cows at $35 each, total	140.00
For labor in helping to secure crops, etc	40.00
Total	$520.00

For my services the last six months, and for provisions,

clothing, etc	$600.00
Sum Total	$2,220.00

From the above report you will see that the wants of the Natives have increased commensurate with their experience and practice in the art of agriculture.

With sentiments of high consideration,

I am your humble servant,

JOHN D. LEE,

Farmer to Pah Utes Indians.

Gov. B. Young, Ex-officio, and Superintendent of Indian affairs.

I forwarded that letter, and thought I had managed the affair nicely.

I put in the expense account of $2,220, just to show off, and to help Brigham Young to get something from the Government. It was the way his Indian farmers all did. I never gave the Indians one of the articles named in the letter. No one of the men mentioned had ever furnished such articles to the Indians, but I did it this way for safety. Brigham Young never spent a dollar on the Indians in Utah, while he was Indian Agent. The only money he ever spent on the Indians was when we were at war with them. Then they cost us some money, but not much.

Brigham Young, well knowing that I wrote that letter just for the protection of the brethren, used it to make up his report to the Government about his acts as Indian Agent. I obeyed his orders in this, as I did the orders of Haight at the Mountain Meadows, and I am now getting my pay for my falsehood. I acted conscientiously in the whole matter, and have nothing to blame myself for, except being so silly as to allow myself to be duped by the cowardly wretches who are now seeking safety by hunting me to the death.

The following winter I was a delegate to the Constitutional Convention, that met in Salt Lake City to form a constitution, preparatory to the application of Utah for admission into the Union. I attended during the entire session, and was often in company with Brigham Young at his house and elsewhere, and he treated me all the time with great kindness and consideration.

At the close of the session of the Convention, I was directed by Brigham Young to take charge of all the cattle, and other property taken from the emigrants, and take care of it for the Indians. I did as I was ordered. When I got home I gathered up about two hundred head of cattle, and put my brand on them, and I gave them to the Indians, as they needed them, or rather when they demanded them. I did that until all of the emigrant cattle were gone.

This thing of taking care of that property was an unfortunate thing for me, for when the Indians wanted beef, they thought they owned everything with my brand on it. So much so, that I long since quit branding my stock. I preferred taking chances of leaving them unbranded, for every thing with my brand on was certain to be taken by the Indians. I know that it has been reported that the emigrants were very rich. That is a mistake. Their only wealth consisted in cattle and their teams. The people were comfortably dressed in Kentucky jeans and lindsey, but they had no fine clothing that I ever saw.

They had but few watches. I never owned or carried one of the watches taken from the emigrants in my life, or had anything to do with any of their property, except to take care of the cattle for the Indians, as ordered to do by Brigham Young, as I have before stated in this confession.

There is another falsehood generally believed in Utah, especially among the Mormons. It is this. It has generally been reported that Brigham Young was anxious to help Judge Cradlebaugh arrest all the guilty parties. There is not one word of truth in the whole statement. Brigham Young knew the name of every man that was in any way implicated in the Mountain Meadows Massacre. He knew just as much about it as I did, except that he did not see it, as I had seen it.

If Brigham Young had wanted one man, or fifty men, or five hundred men arrested, all he would have had to do would have been to say so, and they would have been arrested instantly. There was no escape for them if he ordered their arrest. Every man who knows anything of affairs in Utah at that time knows this is so.

It is true that Brigham made a great parade at the time, and talked a great deal about bringing the guilty parties to justice, but he did not mean a word of it - not a word. He did go South with Cradlebaugh, but he took good care that Cradlebaugh caught no person that had been in the massacre.

I know that I had plenty of notice of their coming, and so did *all the brethren*. It was one of Brigham Young's cunning dodges to blind the government. That this is true I can prove by the statement of what he did at Cedar City while out on his trip with Judge Cradlebaugh to *investigate* the matter and *arrest* (?) the guilty parties.

Judge Cradlebaugh and his men were working like faithful men to find out all about it, but they did not learn very much. True, they got on the right track, but could not learn it all, for Brigham Young was along to see that they *did not learn the facts*.

While at Cedar City, Brigham preached one night, but none of the Judge's party heard him. In his sermon, when speaking of the Mountain Meadows Massacre, he said:

"Do you know who those people were that were killed at the Mountain Meadows? I will tell you who those people were. They were fathers, mothers, brothers, sisters, uncles, aunts, cousins and children of those who killed the Saints, and drove them from Missouri, and afterwards killed our Prophets in Carthage jail. These children that the government has made such a stir about, were gathered up by the government and carried back to Missouri, to St. Louis, and letters were sent to their relatives to come and take them; but their relations wrote back that they did not want them - that they were the children of thieves, outlaws and murderers, and they would not take them, they did not wish anything to do with them, and would not have them around their houses. Those children are now in the poor house in St. Louis. And yet after all this, I am told that there are many of the brethren who are willing to inform upon and swear against the brethren who were engaged in that affair. I hope there is no truth in this report. I hope there is no such person here, under the sound of my voice. But if there is, I will tell you my opinion of you, and the fact so far as your fate is concerned. Unless you repent at once of that *unholy* intention, and *keep the secret* of all that you know, you will die a *dog's* death, and be *damned*, and go to hell. I do not want to hear of any more *treachery among my people*."

These words of Brigham Young gave great comfort to all of us who were out in the woods keeping out of the way of the officers. It insured our safety and took away our fears.

There has been all sorts of reports circulated about me, and the bigger the lie that was told the more readily it was believed.

I have told in this statement just what I did at the Mountain Meadows Massacre. The evidence of Jacob Hamblin is false *in toto*. Hamblin lied in every particular, so far as his evidence related to me.

It is my fate to die for what I did; but I go to my death with a certainty that it cannot be worse than my life has been for the last nineteen years.

FACTS THAT I KNOW TO BE FACTS

As I have been in some respects a prominent man in the Mormon Church, the public may expect from me a statement of facts concerning other crimes and other things besides the Mountain Meadows Massacre. I do know some *facts* that I will state.

I could give many things that would throw light on the doings of the Church, if I had my journals, but as I said, nearly all of my journals have been made way with by Brigham Young; at least I delivered them to him and never could get them again.

I have delivered to my Counsel, Wm. W. Bishop, such journals as I have, and shall leave the one that I am now keeping in prison, when I am released by death from the necessity of writing down my thoughts from day to day, and he can make such use of it as he thinks best.

My statement of outside matters must be brief, but such an they are, the public can rest certain of this thing, *they are true*.

As many people think that Brigham Young cut me off from the Church, and refused to recognize me a short time after the massacre, I will relate a circumstance that took place ten years after all the facts were known by him.

In 1867 or 1868, I met President Brigham Young and suite, at

Parowan, seventy miles from Washington, the place where a part of my family resided. Lieut. James Pace was with me. The Prophet said to me, that he wanted uncle Jim Pace to go with me and prepare dinner for him and his suite at Washington, within three days. We were to go by my herd on the plains and in the valleys, and take several fat kids along and have a good dinner for them by the time they got there.

His will was our pleasure. We rode night and day, and felt thankful that we were worthy of the honor of serving the Prophet of the Living God. We did not consider the toil or loss of sleep a sacrifice, in such a laudable undertaking.

The time designated for dinner was one o'clock. The company arrived at eleven o'clock, two hours ahead of time. The Prophet drove up in front of Bishop Covington's house, on the same block where I lived; he halted about five minutes there, instead of driving direct to my house according to the previous arrangement. Then he turned his carriage around and got out with Amelia, his beloved, and went into the Bishop's house, leaving his suite standing in the streets. The peevish old man felt his dignity trampled on, because I was not present to the minute to receive him with an escort, to welcome and do homage to him upon entering the town.

As soon as I learned of his arrival I hastened to make apologies.

The Prophet heard my excuses, and said his family and brethren, all except himself and wife, could go to my house to dinner, that he would not eat until about two o'clock.

He then whispered to me and said, "Cut me a chunk off the breast of the turkey, and a piece of the loin of one of the fat kids, and put some rich gravy over it, and I will eat it at 2 P.M."

At two o'clock I again made his will my pleasure, and carried his dinner to him as requested, when he did me the honor of eating it. The rest of the company went to my house and took dinner.

Among my guests that day were George A. Smith, Bishop Hunter, John Taylor, W. Woodruff, several of the Prophet's sons and daughters, and many others. At dinner, George A. Smith and others of the Twelve Apostles laughed about the anger of Brigham, and said if the Old Boss had not got miffed, they would have lost the pleasure of eating the fat turkey. The party enjoyed themselves very much that day, and had many a laugh over the Prophet's anger robbing him of an excellent dinner.

I had part of my family at Washington, but I also had quite a family still living at Harmony, where several of my wives were staying.

The next morning the Prophet came to me and asked me if I was going to Harmony that night. I told him I did intend going.

"I wish you would go," said he, "and prepare dinner for us."

He then gave me full instructions what to prepare for dinner, and how he wanted his meat cooked, and said the company would be at my house in Harmony the next day at one o'clock, P.M.

I at once proceeded to obey his instructions. I rode to Harmony through a hard rainstorm, and I confess I was proud of my position. I then esteemed it a great honor to have the privilege of entertaining the *greatest man living*, the Prophet of the Lord.

My entire family at Harmony were up all night, cooking and making ready to feed and serve the Lord's anointed, and his followers.

I killed beeves, sheep, goats, turkeys, geese, ducks and chickens, all of which were prepared according to instructions, and were eaten by Brigham Young and his party the next day.

Prompt to time, the Prophet, the president of the Church and his suite, and an escort on horseback, came into the Fort. There were seventy-three carriages, besides the escort. I entertained the entire party, giving them dinner, supper and breakfast.

In 1858 Governor Young called upon me to go and locate a company of cotton growers, of which Joseph Ham was captain. This company was sent out by Governor Young and the leading men of Salt Lake City, to test the growing of cotton on the Santa Clara and Rio Virgin bottoms. In obedience to counsel, I located the company at the mouth of the Santa Clara River, about four miles south from where St. George now stands.

In 1859 or 1860, the first trip that ex-Gov. Young took from Salt Lake City to Southern Utah, he went by way of Pinto, Mountain Meadows, Santa Clara and Washington. I was then at Washington, building a grist mill, some two miles west of the town, when he came along.

I was sitting on a rock about thirty steps from the road. His carriage was in the lead, as was usual with him when traveling. When he came opposite where I was sitting, he halted and called me to his carriage, and bid me get in. I did so. He seemed glad to see me, and asked where I lived. I told him I lived on the same block that Bishop Covington did, that he would pass my door in going to the Bishop's, as I then thought he would put up with the Bishop, and not with a private person.

In crossing the creek, on the way into town, the sand was heavy. I went to jump out and walk. He objected, saying,

"Sit still. You are of more value than horseflesh yet."

When we neared my residence, he said:

"Is this where you live, John?"

I said, "It is," pointing at the same time to the east end of the block, and said, "That is where the Bishop lives."

The old man made no reply, but continued on. Then he said, "You have a nice place here. I have a notion to stop with you."

I said, "You are always welcome to my house."

Then he said to the company, which consisted, I think, of seventy three carriages, "Some of you had better scatter round among the brethren."

About half the company did so. The rest, with the Prophet, stayed at my house.

The next day, the whole company went on to Toquerville, twenty miles from my residence. I went with them to that place. In the evening all went to St. George, and held a two days' meeting. At the close of the meeting, the Prophet called me to the stand, and said,

"John, I will be at New Harmony on Wednesday next." (By way of explanation, I will here say, the town of Harmony changed its location three times. The first fort was built at the crossing of the north fork of Ash Creek, in 1852, and was abandoned in 1853, during the war with the Ute Indians. In 1855, a new site was selected, four miles northwest of Harmony No. 1, and an adobe fort was built two hundred feet square, and twenty two feet high. In 1860, Harmony No. 2 was demolished by a rainstorm, which continued twenty-eight days without stopping. At once after that, a site was selected at the head of Ash Creek, where a new settlement was started, which was called New Harmony.) "I want you to go and notify the Saints, and have a *Bowery* built, and prepare for our reception."

Jas. H. Imday was then president of that place, and was at the meeting. I here again tried to make the will of the Prophet my pleasure. I traveled all night, and reported the orders of the Prophet to the people.

Great preparations were made for his reception. A committee of arrangements was appointed, also a committee to wait on his Honor. Also an escort of fifteen men was selected to accompany this committee. They went out fifteen miles, where they met the Prophet and his followers and made a report of our proceedings. He thanked them, and said, "I am going to stop with Brother John D.," as he often called me. I took no part in the proceedings except to report the will of the Prophet to the people. I went on horseback alone, and met the president, as he is now called. I met him a mile or more outside of the town. As I rode up he halted, and said,

"*John*, I am going to stop with you."

I replied, "You know you are always welcome."

He then drove to the center of the town and halted; then he said,

"John, where do you live?"

I pointed across the field about half a mile.

Said he, "Have they fenced you out? You take the lead, and we will break a road to your house."

It being his will, we started and went to my house, sixteen carriages going along with us. Quite a number of the president's company had gone by Kanab, to Cedar City, to hold meetings in the settlements they would go through. The arrangements of the committee were treated with indifference, if not contempt by the president and his party. All the company but one carriage went to my house, that one stopped at James Pace's. During their stay at my house all were friendly. Brigham Young asked me to go with them to Cedar City, which I did.

In 1870, sometime in the Fall, I went from Parowan, by way of Panguich, up the Sevier River with Brigham Young, on a trip to the Pariah country. On this trip I was appointed a road commissioner, with ten men to go ahead, view out and prepare the road for the president and his company to travel over.

While at Upper Kanab, I had a private interview with the Prophet, concerning my future destination. Brigham said he thought I had met with opposition and hardships enough to entitle me to have rest the balance of my life. That I had best leave Harmony, and settle in some of those good places farther South; build up a home and gather strength around me, and after a while we would cross over into Arizona Territory, near the San Francisco Mountains, and there establish the order of Enoch, or United Order. We were to take a portable steam saw mill to cut lumber with which to build up the Southern settlements, and I was to run the mill in connection with Bishop L. Stewart. This I then considered an additional honor shown me by the Prophet.

From Upper Kanab, I was sent across the mountains to Lower Kanab, to Bishop Stewart's, to have him carry supplies to the Prophet and company. I had to travel sixty miles without a trail, but I was glad of a chance to perform any duty that would please the Prophet. I again met the company, and went with the party to Toquerville, where I closed arrangements with President Young about the saw mill. All was understood and agreed upon, and we parted in a very friendly manner.

About two weeks after leaving President Young and party at Toquerville, I was notified that I had been suspended from the Church.

The following Spring, I visited the Prophet at St. George, and asked him why they had dealt so rashly with me, without allowing me a chance to speak for myself; why they had waited seventeen years and then cut me off; why I was not cut off at once if what I had done was evil.

He replied, "I never knew the facts until lately."

I said, "President Young, you know that is not true. You know I told the whole story to you a short time after it happened, and gave you a full statement of everything connected with the massacre, and I then put more on myself then I was to blame for; and if your late informants have told you a story different from the one that I gave you soon after the massacre, when I reported the facts to you by order of Major Haight, they have lied like h--l, and you know it. I did nothing designedly wrong on that occasion. I tried to save that company from destruction after they were attacked, but I was overruled and forced to do all that I did do. I have had my name cast out as evil, but I know I have a reward awaiting me in Heaven. I have suffered in silence, and have done so to protect the brethren who committed the deed. I have borne the imputation of this crime long enough, and demand a rehearing. I demand that all the parties concerned be brought forward and forced by you to shoulder their own sins. I am willing to bear mine, but I will not submit to carry all the blame for those who committed the massacre."

The reply he made was this

"Be a man, and not a baby. I am your friend, and not your enemy. *You shall have* a rehearing. Go up to the office and see Brother Erastus Snow, and arrange the time for the hearing."

I did so. We arranged the time of meeting. It was agreed that if the telegraph wires were working, all parties interested were to be notified of the meeting, and required to be present at St. George, Utah, on the following Wednesday, at 2 P.M.

All parties agreed to this, and after talking over the whole thing, I again parted with President Young, in a very friendly manner.

I went to Washington and staid at my house and with my family there. The next morning I started for Harmony, to visit my family there, and make arrangements for the rehearing that was to me of the greatest of importance. I then considered that if I was cut off from the Church I had better be dead; that out of the Church I could find no joys worth living for.

Soon after I left Washington, Erastus Snow, one of the twelve apostles, arrived at my house and asked for me. My family told him that I had gone to Harmony to arrange for the new hearing and trial before the Church authorities. He appeared to be much disappointed at not meeting me, and told my family that Brigham Young had reconsidered the matter, and there would be no rehearing or investigation; that the order cutting me off from the Church would stand; that he would send a letter to me which would explain all the matter, and that the letter would reach Harmony about as soon as I did.

On the next Tuesday night an anonymous letter was left at my house by one of the sons of Erastus Snow, with orders to hand it to me. The letter read an follows:

"JOHN D. LEE, of Washington:

"*Dear Sir*: If you will consult your own interest, and that of those that would be your friends, you will not press an investigation at this time, as it will only serve to implicate those that would be your friends, and cause them to suffer with, or inform upon you. Our advice is to make yourself scarce, and keep out of the way."

There was no signature to the letter, but I knew it came from apostle Snow, and was written by orders of Brigham Young.

When I read the letter I knew I had nothing to hope for from the Church, and my grief was as great as I could bear. To add to my troubles, Brigham Young sent word to my wives that they were all divorced from me and could leave me, if they wished to do so. This was the greatest trouble that I ever had in my life, for I loved all my wives.

As the result of Brigham's advice, eleven of my wives deserted me, and have never lived with me since that time. I gave them all a fair share of the property that I then owned. I afterwards lost my large ferry-boat at my ferry on the Colorado River. Brigham Young was anxious to have the ferry kept in good condition for passing the river, for he did not know what hour he might need it, so he sent parties who put in another boat, which I afterwards paid him for.

I visited Brigham Young at his house in St. George in 1874, and never was received in a more friendly manner. He could always appear the saint when be was meditating treachery to one of his people. He then promised to restore me to membership in a short time.

Soon afterwards I was arrested (on or about the 9th of November, 1874), and taken to Fort Cameron, in Beaver County, Utah Territory, and placed in prison there. A few days after my arrest I was visited in prison by General George A. Smith, Orson Hyde, Erastus Snow, A. F. McDonald, and many other leaders of the Church. They each and all told me to stand to my integrity, and all would come out right in the end.

At this time the Prophet was stopping with Bishop Murdock, in Beaver City. My wife Rachel went at night to see him and have a talk about my ease. He received her with the utmost kindness, saying:

"Sister Rachel, are you standing by Brother John?"

"Yes, sir, I am," was her reply.

"That is right," said he. "God bless you for it. Tell Brother John to stand to his integrity to the end, and not a hair of his head shall be harmed."

This kindness was continued by the Churchmen until I was released on bail, in May, 1875.

And I will here say, I did not believe, until I was released on bail, that any member of the Church would desert me. I had every confidence that Brigham Young would save me at last. I knew then, as I know now, that he had the power, and I thought he had the will, to save me harmless. No man can be convicted in Utah if Brigham Young determines to save him, and I had his solemn word that I should not suffer. But now, when it is too late for me to help myself, I find I am selected by him as a victim, to be offered up to keep the Gentiles from prosecuting any of his pets for murder or other crimes.

When I gained my freedom after nearly two years of imprisonment, I found that some of the good Saints had been tampering with my wife Emma, to get the ferry out of my hands. The "One-Eyed Pirate," as the *Tribune* calls him, told her that I was not a brother in the Church, and had tried to alienate her affections from me.

Up to this time I had always tried to make the will of the Priesthood my pleasure, but this last act of their kindness towards a brother who had been in prison for nearly two years, began to shake my faith in the anointed of the Lord.

The loss of the ferry - for I virtually lost control of it by their treachery - was a great blow to me in my destitute condition. I then felt that the time was near approaching when they would sacrifice and tell me to screen their acts and cover up their own sins.

When I came before the court, on the 11th day of September, 1876, I was met with the same hypocritical smile and whisper, as on other occasions, and told to "Stand to your integrity. Let the will of the Lord's anointed be your pleasure. My mouth is sealed, but I know you will come out all right."

So they talked to me, the leaders of the Church and its prominent men, all telling me the same thing, while at the same time those low, deceitful, treacherous, cowardly, dastardly sycophants and serfs had combined to fasten the rope around my neck. No doubt they thought they could lull me to sleep, until they could kill and make a scapegoat of me, to atone for the sins of the whole Church, which fully endorsed this treacherous treatment, as has been established by the oaths given by the false, treacherous, sneaking witnesses who came on the stand by order and command of the Church, to consummate the vile scheme formed for my destruction

This last act of their charitable kindness let me out with them. All that I have made by making their will my pleasure, and yielding myself to their wishes, is the loss of my reputation, my fortune, my near and dear supposed friends, my salvation, and *my all*. My life now hangs on a single thread.

But is there no help for the widow's son? I can no longer expect help from the Church, or those of the Mormon faith. If I escape execution, it will be through the clemency of the nation, many of whose noble sons will dislike to see me sacrificed in this way. I acknowledge that I have been slow to listen to the advice of friends, who have warned me of the danger and treachery that awaited me. Yet I ask pardon for all the ingratitude with which I received their advice. When the people consider that I was ever taught to look upon treachery with horror, and that I have never permitted one nerve or fibre of this old frame to weaken or give way, notwithstanding the fact that I have been cut loose, and cast off and sacrificed by those who from their own standpoint, and according to their own theory, should have stood by me to the last, they may have some compassion for me. Perhaps all is for the best.

As it now stands, I feel free from all the obligations that have hitherto sealed my mouth, so far as the deeds of which I stand accused are concerned. I now consider myself at liberty to, and I now will state all the facts in the case, with which I am familiar. I am no traitor; I am only acting just to my own reputation. I am not sorry for the stand which I have taken, or my long silence.

Jacob Hamblin, commonly called "Dirty Fingered Jake," when called
as a witness, gave as a reason for his long silence, concerning what he
says I told him, that he was waiting for the right time to come, and he
thought it had come now.

This reminds me of a circumstance that was related by Joseph Knight
and John Lay, who were missionaries to the Indians under President
Jacob Hamblin, at his headquarters at Santa Clara Fort, in 1859. In the
Fall of 1859 two young men, on their way to California, stopped at the
fort to recruit their jaded animals, and expecting that while doing so
they might be so fortunate as to meet with some train of people going
to the same place, so they would have company to San Bernardino, the
young men staid at the fort some two months, daily expecting a company to pass that way, but still no one came. Hamblin assured them that
they could go through the country with perfect safety. At the same time
he had his plans laid to take their lives as soon as they started. The
Indians around the fort wanted to kill the men at once, but Hamblin
objected, and told the Indians to wait until the men got out on the desert
- that if they would wait *until the right time came* they might then kill
the men.

At last these young men started from the fort. Hamblin had told the
Indians that the right time had come, and that he wanted the Indians to
ambush themselves at a point agreed on near the desert, where the men
could be safely killed. The Indians obeyed Hamblin's orders, and as the
men came to the place of ambush the Indians fired upon them, and succeeded in killing one of the men. The other returned the fire, and shot
one of Hamblin's right-hand men or pet Indians through the hand; this
Indian's name was Queets, which means left-handed. By wounding this
Indian he managed to escape, and returned to the fort, but doing so with
the loss of the pack animals, provisions and the riding animal of his
partner that lay dead upon the desert. The survivor stayed with Mr. Judd
for a few days, when a company of emigrants passed that way, and with
them he succeeded in making his escape from the death that Hamblin
had planned for him.

Hamblin was at Salt Lake City when the Mountain Meadows
Massacre took place, and he pretends to have great sympathy with and

sorrow for their fate. I can only judge what he would have done towards the massacre if he had been at home by what he did to help the next train that passed that way. When this train was passing through the settlements, Hamblin made arrangements with Nephi Johnson and his other interpreters (all of them were tools for Hamblin) how and where to receive this company of the large herd of stock that belonged to the train. They had a large number of horses and cattle, more than five hundred head in all. Several interpreters were sent on ahead of the train. One of these was Ira Hatch. They were ordered by Hamblin to prepare the Indians to make a raid upon the stock, and these men and Indians obeyed orders then the same as my brethren and I did with the first company. About 10 o'clock, A.M, just after the train had crossed the Muddy, or a few miles beyond it on the desert, at the time and place as agreed on by Hamblin, and just as he had ordered it to be done, over one hundred Indians made a dash on the train and drove all the stock off to the Muddy.

The emigrants fired at the Indians, but the treacherous Nephi Johnson was acting as a guide, interpreter and friend to the whites; in fact that was how he came to be along with them - was to pretend to aid them and protect them from Indians, but in fact he was there by order of Hamblin, to make the Indian raid on the stock a success.

Nephi Johnson rushed out and told the emigrants that if they valued their own lives they must not fire again, for if they did so he could not protect them from the cruelty of the savages - that the Indians would return and massacre them the same as they did the emigrants at Mountain Meadows.

The acting of Johnson and the other interpreters and spies that were with him, was so good that after a consultation the emigrants decided to follow his advice. The final conclusion was, that as Johnson was friendly with the Indians, and could talk their language, he should go and see the Indians, and try and get the stock back.

The emigrants waited on the desert, and Johnson went to the Indians, or pretended to do so. After a few hours he returned, and reported that the Indians were very hostile, and threatened to attack the train at once; that he was afraid he could not prevent it, and the only chance for the emigrants was in their instant departure; that as the emigrants would be gaining a place of safety, he would, at the risk of his life, make an effort to keep the Indians back, and pacify them. Also that he would report to Hamblin as soon as possible, and raise a force of men at the fort, and get back the stock, if it could be done, and would write to the company, giving an account of his success, so they would get his letter at San Bernardino, and if he recovered the stock, the emigrants could send back a party to receive it, and drive it to California.

Under the circumstances, the company adopted his plan, and he left them on the desert, with all their loose stock gone; but the danger was over, for the stock was what Hamblin and Johnson had been working for.

Johnson returned and ordered the Indians to drive the stock to the Clara. The Indians acted like good Mormons, and obeyed orders. Hamblin gave them a few head of cattle for their services in aiding him to steal the drove. The remainder of the cattle and horses the *secret keeper*, Hamblin, took charge of for the benefit of the Mission. As the cattle became fat enough for beef, they were sold or butchered for the use of the settlers. Some were traded to other settlements for sheep and other articles. In this way Hamblin used all of the stock stolen from the Dukes Company, except some forty head.

In order to keep up an appearance of honesty and fairness, Hamblin wrote a letter to Capt. Dukes, in the fall of 1860, saying that he had recovered a small portion of the company's stock from the Indians, by giving them presents, and that some of the stock had been traded to the settlers by the Indians. This letter was to be confirmed by all the missionaries and settlers, when the stock was to be called for by the former owners. No one was to give information that would lead to the discovery of the stock.

This was always the way when the Mormons committed a crime against the Gentiles. All the brethren were to help keep the secret. Some of the Dukes Company came back to Hamblin's for their cattle and horses, and after three weeks' diligent search among the *secret keepers*, they succeeded in getting about forty head of cattle, and returned with them to California. Several of the settlers were severely censured for giving the little information that was given, which led to the recovery of that small portion of the large herd of cattle and horses that the Saints, Hamblin and Johnson, had stolen by the help of the Indians, and the efforts of the brethren.

THE MORMON METHOD OF DISPOSING OF SUSPECTED PERSONS

In the Winter of 1857-8 John Weston took an Irishman, that had been

INDIANS IN AMBUSH

stopping with him as his guest several days, on a hunt, and when he got him in the brush and timber four miles west of Cedar City, he cut the throat of the Irishman and left the body unburied. A son of Weston said that his father received orders to kill the man because Isaac C. Haight considered him a spy.

Near the same time, Philip Klingensmith laid in ambush to kill Robert Keyes (now a resident of Beaver City, Utah Territory), while Keyes was irrigating in his field. Klingensmith wanted to kill Keyes because Keyes refused to give false testimony when requested to do so by Klingensmith, who was then Bishop of the Church. When Keyes came within a few feet of the hiding place of Klingensmith, this "holy" man raised his gun and took deliberate aim at Keyes' heart, but the cap burst without exploding the powder, and so Keyes escaped.

After the Massacre, when Haight learned that Brigham Young did not fully approve of the deed, he then sought to screen himself, Higbee and Klingensmith, by putting me between them and danger. He reported that I was the big captain that planned, led and executed it; that the honor of each a noble deed for the avenging of the blood of the Prophets would lead to honor, immortality and eternal life in the kingdom of God; that I must stand to my integrity; that no man would ever be hurt. In this way it soon became a settled fact that I was the actual butcher and leader in that awful affair. Year by year that story has gained ground and strength, until I am now held responsible, and am to die, to save the Church. However, this is a regular trick of the Church leaders - use a man as long an he is of any use, and then throw him aside.

As I have stated in other places in my writings, the people in Utah who professed the Mormon religion were at and for some time before the massacre full of wildfire and fanatical zeal anxious to do something to build up the Kingdom of God on earth and to waste away the enemies of the Mormon religion. At that time it was a common thing for small bands of people on their way from California to pass through by way of Cedar City on their journey. Many of these people were killed simply because they were Gentiles. When a Gentile came into a town he was looked upon with suspicion, and most of the people considered every stranger a spy from the United States army. The killing of Gentiles was considered a means of grace and a virtuous deed.

I remember an affair that transpired at the old distillery in Cedar City, just before the massacre. I was informed of it when I went to Cedar City, by the chief men there, and I may say I know it to be true. The facts are as follows: Three men came to Cedar City one evening; they were poor, and much worn by their long journey. They were on their way to California. They were so poor and destitute that the authorities considered they were dangerous men, so they reported that they were spies from Johnston's army, and ordered the brethren to devise a plan to put them out of the way, decently and in order. That the will of God, as made known through Haight and Klingensmith, might be done, these helpless men were coaxed to go to the old distillery and take a drink. They went in company with John M. Higbee, John Weston, James Haslem and Wm. C. Stewart, and I think another man, but if so I have forgotten his name. The party drank considerable, and when the emigrants got under the influence of the whisky the brethren attacked them, and knocked the brains out of two of the men with the king bolt of a wagon. The third man was very powerful and muscular; he fought valiantly for his life, but after a brief struggle he was overcome and killed. They were buried near Cedar City.

This deed was sustained by all the people there. The parties who did the killing were pointed out as true, valiant men, zealous defenders of the faith, and as fine examples for the young men to pattern after.

ATTEMPT TO ASSASSINATE LIEUTENANT TOBIN

Sometime in the Fall of 1857, not long after the Mountain Meadows Massacre, it was decided by the authorities at Salt Lake City that Lieut. Tobin must be killed. Tobin had left a train at Salt Lake, joined the Church there, and afterwards married a daughter of General Charles C. Rich, one of the Twelve Apostles. Tobin was quite a smart man, and soon after his marriage he was sent to England on a mission.

While preaching in England, it was reported that he had committed adultery there, and he was ordered home. On his arrival in Salt Lake he was cut off from the Church, and I think his wife was taken from him by order of the Church. He made several efforts to get out of the Territory. Finally he got with a company en route for California, and left Salt Lake, intending to go to California, to escape the persecutions that were being forced upon him by the Church authorities. After he had been gone a few days the "Destroying Angels" were put on his trail, with orders to kill him without fail before they returned. Two desperate fanatics were selected, who knew nothing but to obey orders. Joel White and John Willis were the parties.

They started on the trail, determined to kill Tobin when they could find him. They had no cause to find fault with him; he had never injured them, but he had in some way fallen under the ban of the Church, and his death had been decreed. These vile tools of the Church leaders were keeping their oaths of obedience to the Priesthood, and were as willing to shed blood at the command of the Prophet or any of the apostles, as ever Inquisitor was to apply the rack to an offending heretic in the dungeons of the Inquisition. In fact Mormonism is Jesuitism refined and perfected.

White and Willis overtook the company that Lieut. Tobin was traveling with, at a point at or near the crossing or the Magottsey. They found where he was sleeping, and going right up to him as he lay on the ground, rolled up in his blanket, they shot him several times, and at last thinking him dead, they concluded to shoot him once more to make certain that he would not escape. So they put a pistol right up against his eye, and fired; the ball put out his eye, but did not kill him.

The "angels" made their escape and returned to Salt Lake City, and reported that *their orders were obeyed.*

Severely wounded as he was, Lieut. Tobin recovered, and was when I last heard from him in the Union army.

POWER OF THE PRIESTHOOD

At Parowan, in 1855 or 1856, there was a case that for a while shook my faith in the Church, but I soon got over it and was like others, satisfied that all was done for the glory of God, but that I was so sinful that I could not understand it.

There was a man living there by the name of Robert Gillespie. He was a member of the Church, had one wife, and owned a fine property. Gillespie wanted to be *sealed* to his sister-in-law, but for some reason his request was denied. He had known of others obtaining wives by committing adultery first and then being sealed to avoid scandal. So he tried it, and then went to the apostle George A. Smith, and again asked to be sealed to the woman; but George A. had a religious fit on him, or something else, so he refused to seal him or let him be sealed, giving as his reason for refusing, that Gillespie had exercised the rights of sealing without first obtaining orders to do so. A warrant was issued and Gillespie arrested and placed under guard, he was also sued in the Probate Court, before James Lewis, Probate Judge, and a heavy judgment was rendered against him, and all his property was sold to pay the fine and costs. The money was put into the Church fund and Gillespie was broken up entirely and forced to leave the Territory in a destitute condition.

Many such cases came under my observation. I have known the Church to act in this way and break up and destroy many, very many men. The Church was then, and in that locality, supreme. None could safely defy or disobey it. The Church authorities used the laws of the land, the laws of the Church, and Danites and "Angels" to enforce their orders, and rid the country of those who were distasteful to the leaders. And I say as a fact that there was *no escape* for any one that the leaders of the Church in Southern Utah selected as a victim.

WOODWARD'S WIFE

The fate of old man Braffett, of Parowan, was a peculiar one, and as it afterwards led me into trouble, I will give the story briefly, to show the power of the Priesthood and the peculiarity of the people there.

Old man Braffett lived at Parowan, and in the Fall of 1855 a man by the name of Woodward came to Braffett's house and stopped there to recruit his teams before crossing the deserts. Woodward had two wives. He had lived in Nauvoo, and while there had been architect for the Nauvoo House. While Woodward and his family were stopping with Braffett, one of his wives concluded that she would be damned if she went to live in California - leaving the land of the Saints - and she asked to be divorced from Woodward and sealed to Braffett. At first Braffett refused to take her, but she was a likely and healthy woman. She made love to the old man in earnest, and finally induced him to commit adultery with her. The parties were discovered in the act by old Mrs. Braffett, and she was not so firm in the faith as to permit her husband to enjoy himself without making a fuss about it. The authorities were informed of Braffett's transgressions, and he was arrested and taken before the Probate Judge and tried for the sin of adultery. He made a bill of sale of some of his property to me, for which I paid him before his trial. After hearing the case, the Probate Judge fined him $1,000, and ordered him to be imprisoned until the fine and costs were paid. Ezra Curtis, the then marshal at Parowan, took all of Braffett's property that could be found and sold it for the purpose of paying the fine, but the large amount of property which was taken was sold for a small sum, for the brethren would not bid much for property taken from one who had broken his covenants.

Being unable to pay the fine, the old man was ordered to be taken to Salt Lake City, to be imprisoned in the prison there. I was selected to take him to Salt Lake. I took the old man there, and after many days spent in working with Brigham Young and his apostles, I succeeded in securing a pardon from Brigham for the old man.

Braffett was put to work at Salt Lake by Brigham Young. He dared not return home at that time. His property was all gone, and he was ruined.

The part I took to befriend the old man made several of the brethren at Parowan mad at me, and they swore they would have revenge against me for interfering where I was not interested. I staid in Salt Lake some time, and when I started home there were quite a number or people along. All the teams were heavily loaded; the roads were bad, and our teams weak. We all had to walk much of the time. After we had passed the Sevier River the road was very bad. My team was the best in the whole company, and I frequently let some of the women who were in the party ride in my wagon. One evening, just about dark, I was asked by a young woman, by the name of Alexander, to let her ride, as she was very tired walking. I had her get in the wagon with my wife Rachel, and she rode there until we camped for the night. I got into the wagon after dark and drove the team. We had ridden along this way an hour or so, when Rachel said she was going to ride a while in the next wagon, which was driven by my son-in-law, Mr. Dalton. Soon after Rachel got out of the wagon, a couple of my enemies rode by. I spoke to them, and they rode on. As soon as these men reached the camp they reported that I had been taking improper privileges with Miss Alexander. I was at once told to consider myself under arrest, and that as soon as we reached Parowan I would be tried by the council for violating my covenants. I was surprised and grieved at the charge, for I was innocent, and the young woman was a very fine and virtuous woman, and as God is soon to judge me, I declare I never knew of her committing any sin. But she had to suffer slander upon her good name simply because she was befriended by me.

When we reached Parowan there was a meeting called by the Priesthood to try me. This council was composed of the President of that Stake of Zion and his two Counselors, the High Council, the City Council and the leading men of Parowan. It was a general meeting of the authorities, Church and civil, at Parowan. The meeting was held in a chamber that was used for a prayer circle. It was called a circle room, because the people met there to transact private business and to hold prayer in a circle, which was done in this way. All the brethren would kneel in a circle around the room, near enough to each other for their arms to touch, so that the *influence* would be more powerful. When the meeting was called to order all the lights were put out, and I was taken into the room and placed on trial. The charge was stated to me and I was ordered to confess my guilt. I told them I was innocent; that I had committed no crime - in fact had not thought of wrong. I told the truth, just as it was. I was then ordered to stand one side.

The young woman was then brought into the room, and as she came in a pistol was placed to my head and I was told to keep silent. She was questioned and threatened at great length, but not all the threats that they could use would induce her to tell a falsehood. She insisted that I was entirely innocent.

Next her father, an old man, was introduced and questioned. He told the council that he had diligently inquired into the matter, and believed I was innocent.

Neither the young woman nor her father knew who was in the room. All they knew was that they were being examined before the secret tribunal of Utah, and that a false oath in that place would ensure their death.

When the evidence had been received and the witnesses retired; the candles were again lighted. Then speeches were made by most of the men present, and every one but two spoke in favor of my conviction. Without taking a vote the meeting adjourned, or rather left that place and went somewhere else to consult. I was left in the dark, the house locked and guards placed around the building. I was told that my fate would soon be decided, and I would then be informed what it was to be. I knew so well the manner of dealing in such cases that I expected to be assassinated in the dark, but for some reason it was not done.

Next morning some food was brought to me, but I was still kept a prisoner and refused the liberty of consulting with any friends or any of my family.

Late that day I looked out of the window of the chamber where I was confined, and saw a man by the name of John Steel. He was first counselor to the President of that Stake of Zion. I called to him and asked him to secure my freedom. After stating the case to him he promised to see what could be done for me, and went off. Through his exertions I was soon released. I was told to go home and hold myself subject to orders - that my case was not yet decided.

I went home, but for months I expected to be assassinated every day, for it was the usual course of the authorities to send an "Angel" after all men who were *charged* or *suspected* of having violated their covenants. Nothing further was done about the case, but it was held over me as a means of forcing me to live in accordance with the wishes of the Priesthood and to prevent me from again interfering with the Church authorities when they saw fit to destroy a man, as they destroyed old man Braffett, and I believe it did have the effect to make me more careful who I befriended.

In 1854 (1 think that was the year) there was a young man, a Gentile, working in Parowan. He was quiet, and orderly, but was courting some of the girls. He was notified to quit, and let the girls alone, but he still kept going to see some of them. This was contrary to orders. No Gentile was at that time allowed to keep company with or visit any Mormon girl or woman. The authorities decided to have the young man killed, so they called two of Bishop Dames' Destroying Angels, Barney Carter and old man Gould, and told them to take that cursed young Gentile "*over the rim of the basin.*" That was a term used by the people when they killed a person.

The destroying angels made some excuse to induce the young man to go with them on an excursion, and when they got close to Shirts' mill, near Harmony, they killed him, and left his body in the brush.

The Indians found the body, and reported the facts to me soon afterwards. I was not at home that night, but Carter and Gould went to my house and staid there all night. Rachel asked them where they had been. They told her they had been on a mission to take a young man, a Gentile, *over the rim of the basin*, and Carter showed her his sword, which was all bloody, and he said he used that to help the Gentile over the *edge*. Rachel knew what they meant when they spoke of sending him "over the rim of the basin." It was at that time a common thing to see parties going out of Cedar City and Harmony, with suspected Gentiles, to send them "over the rim of the basin," and the Gentiles were *always killed.*

This practice was supported by all the people, and every thing of that kind was done by *orders* from the *Council*, or by orders from some of the Priesthood. When a Danite or a destroying angel was placed on a man's track, that man died, certain, unless some providential act saved him, as in Tobin's case; he was saved because the "angels" believed he was dead.

The Mormons nearly all, and I think every one of them in Utah, previous to the massacre at Mountain Meadows, believed in *blood atonement*. It was taught by the leaders and believed by the people that the Priesthood were inspired and could not give a wrong order. It was the belief of all that I ever heard talk of these things - and I have been with the Church since the dark days in Jackson County - that the authority that ordered a murder committed, was the only responsible party, that the man who did the killing was only an *instrument*, working by command of a superior, and hence could have no ill will against the person killed, but was only acting by authority and committed no wrong. In other words, if Brigham Young or any of his apostles, or any of the Priesthood, gave an order to a man, the act was the act of the one giving the order, and the man doing the act was only an instrument of the person commanding - just as much of an instrument as the knife that was used to cut the throat of the victim. This being the belief of *all good* Mormons, it is easily understood why the orders of the Priesthood were so blindly obeyed by the people.

Another circumstance came to my knowledge soon after it was done that will speak for itself. Not far from the time of the Mountain Meadows massacre, there was an emigrant who claimed to be a Mormon, but I never knew whether he was one or not, that worked a number of months for Captain Jacob Huffine, at Parowan. This man wanted his pay; it was not convenient to pay him; he insisted on being paid, but not getting his wages, he determined to leave there. He started away from the settlement at Summit, about seven miles from Parowan. The Indians of Parowan were sent for and ordered to overtake and kill the man. They did so, and shot him full of arrows. The man called to the Indians and told them that he was a Mormon and they must not kill him.

The Indians replied by saying,

"We know you, you are no Mormon, you are a Mericat; the Mormons told us to kill you."

They then beat his head with rocks, and cut his throat, then went back to Parowan and reported what they had done.

I was told all about this by the Indians. But I never inquired into the facts, for I then believed, and still have reasons to think the man was killed by *authority*. He had offended in some way, and his death was like that of many others, the result of orders from the Priesthood.

KILLING OF ROSMOS ANDERSON, ETC.

William Laney, of Harrisburg, Utah Territory, had formed the acquaintance of the family of Aden while on a mission to Tennessee, and he was saved from a mob who threatened his death because he was a Mormon preacher. When Fancher's train reached Parowan, Mr. Laney met young Aden and recognized him as the son of the man who had saved his life. Aden told him that he was hungry, that he and his comrades had been unable to purchase supplies from the Mormons ever since they left Salt Lake City, and that there appeared to be a conspiracy that had been formed against that train by which the Mormons had agreed to starve the emigrants. Laney took young Aden to his house, gave him his supper, and let him sleep there that night. The next day Laney was accused by leading men with being unfaithful to his obligations. They said he had supported the enemies of the Church and given aid and comfort to one whose hands were still red with the blood of the Prophets. A few nights after that the Destroying Angels, who were doing the bidding of Bishop Dame, were ordered to kill William Laney to save him from his sins, he having violated his endowment oath and furnished food to a man who had been declared an outlaw by the Mormon Church. The "Angels" were commanded by Barney Carter, a son-in-law of Wm. H. Dame, who now lives in Los Angeles County, California. The Angels called Laney out of the house, saying that Bishop Dame wished to see him. As Laney passed through the gate into the street, he was struck across the back of the head with a large club by Barney Carter. His skull was fractured somewhat and for many months Laney lay at the point of death, and his mind still shown the effect of the injury he then received, for his brain, has never quite settled since. I have frequently talked with Laney about this matter, but as he was fully initiated into the mysteries of the Church, he knows that he will yet be killed if his life can be taken with safety, if he make public the facts connected with the conspiracy to take his life. He is still strong in the Mormon faith, and almost believes that Dame had the right to have him killed. At the time Carter attempted to take the life of Laney, the Mormon Church was under the blaze of the reformation, and punishment by death was the penalty for refusing to obey the orders of the Priesthood.

RACHEL

EMELINE

LEE'S FAVORITE WIVES

One of the objects of the reformation was to place the Priesthood in possession of every secret act and crime that had been committed by a man of the Church. These secrets were obtained in this way: a meeting would be called; some Church leader would make a speech, defining the duties that the people owed to the Priesthood, and instructing the people why it was necessary that the Priesthood should control the entire acts of the people, and it was preached that to keep back any fact from the knowledge of the Priesthood was an unpardonable sin. After one or more such discourses, the people were called upon by name, commanded to rise from their seats, and standing in the midst of the congregation, to publicly confess all their sins. If the confession was not full and complete, it was also made the duty of the members of the Church, or any one of them who knew that the party confessing had committed a crime, which he had not divulged, it was then to be made public by the party knowing the same. Unless the party then confessed, a charge was preferred against him or her for a violation of covenants, and unless full confession and repentance immediately followed, the sinful member was to be slain for the remission of his sins, it being taught by the leaders and believed by the people that the right thing to do with a sinner who did not repent and obey the council, was to take the life of the offending party, and thus save his everlasting soul. This was called "Blood Atonement." The members who fully confessed their sins were again admitted into the Church and rebaptized, they taking new covenants to obey any and all orders of the Priesthood, and to refuse all manner of assistance, friendship or communication with those who refused a strict obedience to the authorities of the Church.

The most deadly sin among the people was adultery, and many men were killed in Utah for that crime.

Rosmos Anderson was a Danish man who had come to Utah with his family to receive the benefits arising from an association with the "Latter Day Saints." He had married a widow lady somewhat older than himself, and she had a daughter that was fully grown at the time of the reformation. The girl was very anxious to be sealed to her stepfather, and Anderson was equally anxious to take her for a second wife, but as she was a fine-looking girl, Klingensmith desired her to marry him, and she refused. At one of the meetings during the reformation Anderson and his stepdaughter confessed that they had committed adultery, believing when they did so that Brigham Young would allow them to marry when he learned the facts. Their confession being full, they were rebaptized and received into full membership. They were then placed under covenant that if they again committed adultery, Anderson should suffer death. Soon after this a charge was laid against Anderson before the Council, accusing him of adultery with his stepdaughter. This Council was composed of Klingensmith and his two counselors; it was the Bishop's Council. Without giving Anderson any chance to defend himself or make a statement, the Council voted that Anderson must die for violating his covenants. Klingensmith went to Anderson and notified him that the orders were that he must die by having his throat cut, so that the *running of his blood* would atone for his sins. Anderson, being a firm believer in the doctrines and teachings of the Mormon Church, made no objections, but asked for half a day to prepare for death. His request was granted. His wife was ordered to prepare a suit of clean clothing, in which to have her husband buried, she being directed to tell those who should inquire after her husband that he had gone to California.

Klingensmith, James Haslem, Daniel McFarland and John M. Higbee dug a grave in the field near Cedar City, and that night, about 12 o'clock, went to Anderson's house and ordered him to make ready to obey the council. Anderson got up, dressed himself, bid his family goodbye, and without a word of remonstrance accompanied those that he believed were carrying out the will of the "Almighty God." They went to the place where the grave was prepared; Anderson knelt upon the side of the grave and prayed. Klingensmith and his company then cut Anderson's throat from ear to ear and held him so that *his blood ran into the grave.*

As soon as he was dead they dressed him in his clean clothes, threw him into the grave and buried him. They then carried his bloody clothing back to his family, and gave them to his wife to wash, when she was then instructed to say that her husband was in California. She obeyed their orders.

No move of that kind was made at Cedar City, unless it was done by order of the "Council" or of the "High Council." I was at once informed of Anderson's death, because at that time I possessed the confidence of all the people, who would talk to me confidentially, and give me the particulars of all crimes committed by order of the Church. Anderson was killed just before the Mountain Meadows massacre. The killing of Anderson was then considered a religious duty and a just act. It was justified by all the people, for they were bound by the same covenants, and the least word of objection to thus treating the man who had broken his covenant would have brought the same fate upon the person who was so foolish as to raise his voice against any act committed by order of the Church authorities.

Brigham Young knew very well that I was not a man who would willingly take life, and therefore I was not ordered to do his bloody work. I never took part in any killing that was desired or ordered by the Church, except the part I took in the Mountain Meadows Massacre. I was well known by all the members of the Church as one that stood high in the confidence of Brigham Young, and that I was close-mouthed and reliable. By this means I was usually informed of the facts in every case where violence was used in the section of country where I resided. I knew of many men being killed in Nauvoo by the Danites. It was then the rule that all the enemies of Joseph Smith should be killed, and I know of many a man who was quietly put out of the way by the orders of Joseph and his Apostles while the Church was there.

It has always been a well understood doctrine of the Church that it was right and praiseworthy to kill every person who spoke evil of the Prophet. This doctrine had been strictly lived up to in Utah, until the Gentiles arrived in such great numbers that it became unsafe to follow the practice, but the doctrines still believed, and no year passes without one or more of those who have spoken evil of Brigham Young being killed, in a secret manner.

Springfield, Utah, was one of the hotbeds of fanaticism, and I expect that more men were killed there, in proportion to population, than in any other part of Utah. In that settlement it was *certain death* to say a word against the authorities, high or low.

In Utah it has been the custom with the Priesthood to make eunuchs of such men as were obnoxious to the leaders. This was done for a double purpose: first, it gave a perfect revenge, and next, it left the poor victim a living example to others of the dangers of disobeying counsel and not living as ordered by the Priesthood.

In Nauvoo it was the orders from Joseph Smith and his apostles to beat, wound and castrate all Gentiles that the police could take in the act of entering or leaving a Mormon household under circumstances that led to the belief that they had been there for immoral purposes. I knew of several such outrages while there. In Utah it was the favorite revenge of old, worn out members of the Priesthood, who wanted young women sealed to them, and found that the girl preferred some handsome young man. The old priests generally got the girls, and many a young man was unsexed for refusing to give up his sweetheart at the request of an old and failing, but still sensual apostle or member of the Priesthood.

As an illustration I will refer to an instance that many a good Saint knows to be true.

Warren Snow was Bishop of the Church at Manti, San Pete County, Utah. He had several wives, but there was a fair, buxom young woman in the town that Snow wanted for a wife. He made love to her with all his powers, went to parties where she was, visited her at her home, and proposed to make her his wife. She thanked him for the honor offered, but told him she was then engaged to a young man, a member of the Church, and consequently could not marry the old priest. This was no sufficient reason to Snow. He told her it was the will of God that she should marry him, and she must do so; that the young man could be got rid of, sent on a mission or dealt with in some way so as to release her from her engagement - that, in fact, a promise made to the young man was not binding, when she was informed that it was contrary to the wishes of the authorities.

The girl continued obstinate. The "teachers" of the town visited her and advised her to marry Bishop Snow. Her parents, under the orders of the counselor of the Bishop, also insisted that their daughter must marry the old man. She still refused. Then the authorities called on the young man and directed him to give up the young woman. This he steadfastly refused to do. He was promised Church preferment, celestial rewards, and everything that could be thought of - all to no purpose. He remained true to his intended, and said he would die before he would surrender his intended wife to the embraces of another.

This *unusual* resistance of authority by the young people made Snow more anxious than ever to capture the girl. The young man was ordered to go on a mission to some distant locality, so that the authorities would have no trouble in effecting their purpose of forcing the girl to marry as they desired. But the mission was refused by the still contrary and unfaithful young man.

It was then determined that the rebellious young man must be forced by harsh treatment to respect the advice and orders of the Priesthood. His fate was left to Bishop Snow for his decision. He decided that the young man should be castrated; Snow saying, "When that is done, he will not be liable to want the girl badly, and she will listen to reason when she knows that her lover is no longer a man."

It was then decided to call a meeting of the people who lived true to counsel, which was to be held in the schoolhouse in Manti, at which place the young man should be present, and dealt with according to Snow's will. The meeting was called. The young man was there, and was again requested, ordered and threatened, to get him to surrender the young woman to Snow, but true to his plighted troth, he refused to consent to give up the girl. The lights were then put out. An attack was made on the young man. He was severely beaten, and then tied with his back down on a bench, when Bishop Snow took a bowie-knife, and performed the operation in a most brutal manner, and then took the portion severed from his victim and hung it up in the schoolhouse on a nail, so that it could be seen by all who visited the house afterwards.

The party then left the young man weltering in his blood, and in a lifeless condition. During the night he succeeded in releasing himself from his confinement, and dragged himself to some haystacks, where he lay until the next day, when he was discovered by his friends. The young man regained his health, but has been an idiot or quiet lunatic ever since, and is well known by hundreds of both Mormons and Gentiles in Utah.

After this outrage old Bishop Snow took occasion to get up a meeting at the schoolhouse, so as to get the people of Manti, and the younger woman that he wanted to marry, to attend the meeting. When all had assembled, the old man talked to the people about their duty to the Church, and their duty to obey counsel, and the dangers of refusal, and then publicly called attention to the mangled parts of the young man, that had been severed from his person, and stated that the deed had been done to teach the people that the counsel of the Priesthood must be obeyed. To make a long story short, I will say, the young woman was soon after forced into being sealed to Bishop Snow.

Brigham Young, when he heard of this treatment of the young man, was very mad, but did nothing against Snow. He left him in charge as Bishop at Manti, and ordered the matter to be hushed up. This is only one instance of many that I might give to show the danger of refusing to obey counsel in Utah.

It frequently happened that men would become dissatisfied with the Church or something else in Utah, and try to leave the Territory. The authorities would try to convince such persons that they ought to remain, but if they insisted on going, they were informed that they had permission to do so. When the person had started off, with his stock and property, it was nearly always the rule to send a lot of Danites to steal all the stock and run it off into the mountains; so that in the majority of cases the people would return wholly broken up and settle down again as *obedient* members of the *Church*. It was a rare thing for a man to escape from the territory with all of his property, until after the Pacific Railroad was built through Utah. It was the general custom to rob the persons who were leaving the country, but many of them were killed, because it was considered they would tell tales that should not be made public, in the event of their reaching Gentile settlements.

Brigham Young discouraged mining at all times, and when any man found any metal he was ordered to keep it a secret. The people were taught to believe that the Latter-Day Saints would soon own all the wealth of the earth, and that no people but Mormons would be alive in a few years. That when the earth was conquered and the truths of Mormonism were universally acknowledged, the people would then have all the wealth they desired. Gold would be as plenty as silver, silver as plenty as brass, brass as plenty as stone, and stone as plenty as wood. That this gold, silver and other metals and precious stones would then be used for beautifying places of worship, and to make holy vessels of, and each man was to have all the wealth he could use or enjoy, if he was only faithful in these last days.

As a matter to satisfy the public, I will give the following facts connected with my personal history:

When I moved to Nauvoo, I had one *wife* and *one chil*d. Soon after I got there, I was appointed as the Seventh Policeman. I had superiors in office, and was sworn to secrecy, and to obey the orders of my superiors, and not let my left hand know what my right hand did. It was my duty to do as I was ordered, and not to ask questions. I was instructed in the *secrets* of the Priesthood to a great extent, and taught to believe, as I then did believe, that it was my duty, and the duty of all men to obey the leaders of the Church, and that no man could commit sin so long as he acted in the way that he was directed by his Church superiors. I was one of the Life Guard of the Prophet Joseph Smith.

HOW I FIRST HEARD OF THE DOCTRINE OF POLYGAMY

One day the Chief of Police came to me and said that I must take two more policemen that he named, and watch the house of a widow woman named Clawson. She was the mother of H. B. Clawson, of Salt Lake City. I was informed that a man went there nearly every night about ten o'clock, and left about day light. I was also ordered to station myself and my men near the house, and when the man came out we were to knock him down and castrate him, and not to be careful how hard we hit, for it would not be inquired into if we killed him.

I did not believe that the Chief of Police knew just what he was doing. I felt a timidity about carrying out the orders. It was my duty to report all *unusual* orders that I received from my superiors on the police force, to the Prophet Joseph Smith, or in his absence, to Hyrum, next in authority. I went to the house of the Prophet to report, but he was not at home. I then called for Hyrum, and he gave me an interview. I told him the orders that I had received from the Chief, and asked him if I should obey or not. He said to me,

"Brother Lee, you have acted wisely in listening to the voice of the Spirit. It was the influence of God's Spirit that sent you here. You would have been guilty of a great crime if you had obeyed your Chiefs orders."

Hyrum then told me that the man that I was ordered to attack was Howard Egan, and that he had been sealed to Mrs. Clawson, and that their marriage was a most holy one; that it was in accordance with a *revelation* that the Prophet had recently received direct from God. He then explained to me fully the doctrines of polygamy, and wherein it was permitted, and why it was right.

I was greatly interested in the doctrine. It accorded exactly with my views of the Scripture, and I at once accepted and believed in the doctrine as taught by the revelations received by Joseph Smith, the Prophet. As a matter of course I did not carry out the orders of the Chief. I had him instructed in his duty, and so Egan was never bothered by the police.

A few months after that I was sealed to my second wife. I was sealed to her by Brigham Young, then one of the Twelve. In less than one year after I first learned the will of God concerning the marriage of the Saints, as made known by Him in a revelation to Joseph Smith, I was the husband of *nine wives*.

I took my wives in the following order: first, Agathe Ann Woolsey; second, Nancy Berry; third, Louisa Free (now one of the wives of Daniel H. Wells); fourth, Sarah C. Williams; fifth, old Mrs. Woolsey (she was the mother of Agathe Ann and Rachel A. I married her for her soul's sake, for her salvation in the eternal state); sixth, Rachel A. Woolsey (I was sealed to her at the same time that I was to her mother); seventh, Andora Woolsey (a sister to Rachel); eighth, Polly Ann

Workman; ninth, Martha Berry; tenth, Delethea Morris. In 1847, while
at Council Bluffs, Brigham Young sealed me to three women in one
night, viz., eleventh, Nancy Armstrong (she was what we called a
widow. She left her first husband in Tennessee, in order to be with the
Mormon people); twelfth, Polly V. Young; thirteenth, Louisa Young
(these two were sisters). Next, I was sealed to my fourteenth wife,
Emeline Vaughn. In 1851, I was sealed to my fifteenth wife, Mary Ann
Groves. In1856, I was sealed to my sixteenth wife, Mary Ann Williams.
In 1858, Brigham Young gave me my seventeenth wife, Emma
Batchelder. I was sealed to her while a member of the Territorial
Legislature. Brigham Young said that Isaac C. Haight, who was also in
the Legislature, and I, needed some young women to renew our vitali-
ty, so he gave us both a dashing young bride. In 1859 I was sealed to my
eighteenth wife, Teressa Morse. I was sealed to her by order of Brigham
Young. Amasa Lyman officiated at the ceremony. The last wife I got
was Ann Gordge. Brigham Young gave her to me, and I was sealed to
her in Salt Lake by Heber C. Kimball. This was my nineteenth, but, as
I was married to old Mrs. Woolsey for her soul's sake, and she was near
sixty years old when I married her, I never considered her really as a
wife. True, I treated her well and gave her all the rights of marriage. Still
I never count her as one of my wives. That is the reason that I claim *only
eighteen true wives.*

After 1861 I never asked Brigham Young for another wife. By my
eighteen real wives I have been the father of sixty-four children. Ten of
my children are dead and fifty four are still living.

This is all I care to say about my own acts or the affairs of my family.

I have but little more to say.

To the jurymen who tried me, I say I have no unkind feelings. The
evidence was strong against me, and with that, and the instructions of
the court as they were given, the jury could do nothing but convict.

To the officers who have had me in charge during my confinement I
return my thanks for their personal kindness. I give them the thanks of
an old man, who is about to leave this earth and go to another sphere of
existence.

The few guardsmen who misused me I forgive, for they were not
conscious of their own wickedness.

If I have sinned and violated the laws of my country, I have done so
because I have blindly followed and obeyed the orders of the Church

leaders. I was guided in all that I did which is called criminal, by the orders of the leaders in the Church of Jesus Christ of Latter-Day Saints. I have never knowingly disobeyed the orders of the Church since I joined it at Far West, Missouri, until I was deserted by Brigham Young and his slaves.

I have selected Wm. W. Bishop as the person that I wish to publish my life and confessions, so that the world may know just what I did do, and why I acted as I have done. I have delivered Mr. Bishop all of the manuscripts and private writings that are in my possession, and wish him to have all that I may hereafter write. I have assigned him all my writings, and he is the only person on earth who has a right to publish my life or my confessions.

To my attorneys, one and all, who have given me their valuable services, I return my kindest thanks, and regret that poverty prevents my paying them for what they have done for me.

To my family I say, may God pour rich blessings upon you, one and all. I ask you to live here on earth so that you can justly claim a seat in the realms of bliss after life's troubles are ended.

To my enemies I say, *judge not, that ye be not judged.* In life you were often unjust to me. After I am dead remember to be charitable to one who never designedly did a wrong.

CONCLUSION OF THE CONFESSION OF JOHN D. LEE

Written in prison at Fort Cameron, near Beaver City, Utah Territory. Delivered to Hon. Sumner Howard by John D. Lee, on the field of execution, just before the sentence of death was carried into effect.

Forwarded to Wm. W. Bishop, by Hon. Sumner Howard, according to the last request of John D. Lee.

CAMP CAMERON, MARCH 13TH, 1877

Morning clear, still and pleasant. The guard, George Tracy, informs me that Col. Nelson and Judge Howard have gone. Since my confinement here, I have reflected much over my sentence, and as the time of my execution is drawing near, I feel composed, and as calm as the summer morning. I hope to meet my fate with manly courage. I declare my innocence. I have done nothing designedly wrong in that unfortunate and lamentable affair with which I have been implicated. I used my utmost endeavors to save them from their sad fate. I freely would have given worlds, were they at my command, to have averted that evil. I wept and mourned over them before and after, but words will not help them, now it is done. My blood cannot help them, neither can it make that atonement required. Death to me has no terror. It is but a struggle, and all is over. I much regret to part with my loved ones here, especially under that odium of disgrace that will follow my name; that I cannot help.

I know that I have a reward in Heaven, and my conscience does not accuse me. This to me is a great consolation. I place more value upon it than I would upon an eulogy without merit. If my work is done here on earth, I ask my God in Heaven, in the name of His Son Jesus Christ, to receive my spirit, and allow me to meet my loved ones who have gone behind the veil. The bride of my youth and her faithful mother, my devoted friend and companion, N. A., also my dearly beloved children, all of whom I parted from with sorrow, but shall meet them with joy - I bid you all an affectionate farewell. I have been treacherously betrayed and sacrificed in the most cowardly manner by those who should have been my friends, and whose will I have diligently striven to make my pleasure, for the last thirty years at least. In return for my faithfulness and fidelity to his and *his cause,* he has sacrificed me in a most shameful and cruel way. I leave them in the hands of the Lord to deal with them according to the merits of their crimes, in the final restitution of all things.

TO THE MOTHERS OF MY CHILDREN

I beg of you to teach them better things than to ever allow themselves to be let down so low as to be steeped in the vice, corruption and villainy that would allow them to sacrifice the meanest wretch on earth, much less a neighbor and a friend, as their father has been. Be kind and true to each other. Do not contend about my property. You know my mind concerning it. Live faithful and humble before God, that we may meet again in the mansions of bliss that God has prepared for His faithful servants. Remember the *last words* of your most true and devoted friend on earth, and let them sink deep into your tender aching hearts; many of you I may never see in this world again, but I leave my blessing with you. FAREWELL.

I wish my wife Rachel to take a copy of the above, and all my family to have a copy of the original. My worthy attorney, W.W. Bishop, will please insert it in my record or history, should I not be able to write up my history to the proper place, to speak of my worthy friend Wm. H. Hooper. Please exonerate him from all blame or censure of buying the stock of that unfortunate company, as there is *no truth* in the accusation whatever. He is a noble, highminded gentleman. And let it appear also of Bishop John Sharp, honorably, for the nobleness of the man who advanced me money in the time of trouble, and if my history meet with the favor of the public, pay those two gentlemen. My friends Hoge and Foster, as well as yourself and Spicer, some. You understand our agreement.

JOHN D. LEE

CHAPTER XX

ARREST OF JOHN D. LEE BY WM. STOKES, DEPUTY UNITED STATES MARSHAL

WISHING to give a correct account of the arrest of John D. Lee, by William Stokes, Deputy United States Marshal for the District of Utah, I wrote a letter to Mr. Stokes, on the 28th day of March, 1877, asking him to give the full facts, as many contradictory statements relating thereto had been in general circulation. The following letter was written by Mr. Stokes, and I know from the general character of the writer that the same is true in every particular. I give the letter in the language of the writer. It explains itself:

UNITED STATES MARSHAL'S OFFICE, DISTRICT OF UTAH, }
BEAVER CITY, UTAH, April 1st, 1877

WM. W. BISHOP, PIOCHE, NEVADA:

My Dear Sir: Yours of the 28th of March at hand and contents noted. As requested, I send you all the facts of the arrest of John D. Lee, from the time the warrants were placed in my hands until I arrested him and brought him to Beaver City. I tell it in my own way, and you can use it as you see proper.

About the first of October, 1874, warrants were placed in my hands for the arrest of Lee, Haight, Higbee, Stewart, Wilden, Adair, Klingensmith and Jukes (the warrant for the arrest of Dame not being placed in my hands at that time). I received instructions from General George R. Maxwell, United States Marshal for the District of Utah, that Lee was the most important one of all those indicted, and that he wanted him arrested first, if possible, but that it was a dangerous undertaking, for he was satisfied by what he could learn that he would never be taken alive. He wanted me to take him alive, if possible, but not at too great a risk; that he did not want to give me any plan of operations or particular instructions how to act, as he believed that I knew more about that kind of business than he did, and that he did not wish to give any officer under him any plans when he was sure, as he was in this case, that it would be laying a plan to have one of his own officers killed.

I took the case in hand, thinking at that time that I would have to go to Lee's place on the Colorado River. I was arranging for that trip.

On the 28th day of October, 1874, I started south from Beaver City, to summon jurors for the November term of the District Court for the Second Judicial District of Utah Territory, to be held at Beaver City. I also intended to procure a guide, if I could do so, and go to the Colorado River to make the arrest.

When I reached Parowan I learned that it was currently reported that Lee had come from the Colorado River, and was then in the southern counties of Utah. He was supposed to be at Harmony, because it was known that he had some accounts due him there, which he was then probably collecting, in the shape of provisions, to take back with him to the river.

I at once started on again, on my way south, determined to attempt to arrest him at Harmony, and to do so alone, for I did not know where reliable aid could be had. I considered there was no time to lose, and that I was taking no more chances to attempt the arrest alone than I would be taking if I found him at the Colorado River, at his stronghold, even if backed by a strong force.

On my way I met Thomas Winn. I told him what I was intending to do. I told him I was going to arrest Lee. Winn said he considered it almost madness, as it was reported that several of Lee's sons were with him, and all well armed. He kindly volunteered to go with me and take even chances.

We finally decided that he should go to Iron City and get help, as there were then several men there that we could depend on. He was to get these men and be at Harmony by daylight on the morning of the 30th of October. I was to go to Harmony and get there soon after dark the night of the 29th of October, and make the arrest, if I thought I could do so and get away in safety in the cover of the night. If not, I was to find out where he was, and wait for assistance.

When I got to Hamilton's Fort, eight miles south of Cedar City, I learned that Lee had left Harmony and gone back to the Colorado River, by the way of Toquerville, and was then several days ahead of me. I then sent a boy out on the Iron City road to stop Winn and send him back.

I proceeded on my way and summoned my jurors. I could hear nothing of Lee in the southern country. On my way back I stopped at

Thomas Winn's house, and got him to go over on the Sevier River, to see if Lee had not gone by the way of Panguitch, and stopped there to lay in more supplies.

Winn started on the 5th day of November, and took Franklin R. Fish with him. They pretended to be looking for stock. They were to report to me at Parowan, on the night of the 7th of November. I returned to Beaver City, and made my returns.

On the morning of November 7th, I started for Parowan to meet my men, Winn and Fish.

That same day Brigham Young went from Beaver to Parowan. He passed me near the Buck Horn Springs. I have no doubt but that he thought I was there to assassinate him, for he had four of the best fighting men of Beaver City with him as a guard. They were armed with Henry rifles, and as they came up to me, the guard rode between me and their beloved Prophet's carriage; but they had no reason for alarm. Brigham Young was not the man that I was after at *that* time.

I met Winn and Fish at Red Creek. As they were coming out of Little Creek Canyon, Winn remarked:

"*Your man is there!*"

I was very much surprised, as I had but little hope of finding Lee nearer than the Colorado River, but I found he was at the town of Panguitch, and was liable to leave at any time.

As the men had found that Lee had made every thing ready for a start, we rode on to Parowan, where I arranged my plan of action. Fish was to go back over the mountains to Panguitch that night, with instructions to come out and meet us, in case Lee should start away from Panguitch; otherwise he was to remain there and have Lee located, so that he could guide us to where he was, when we should arrive the next morning. I was to start back toward Beaver City on Sunday morning, the 8th day of November. I was to go on in that way until I had passed Red Creek settlement, and then go up Little Creek Canyon. The others who were to go as my assistants, were Thomas Winn, Thomas LaFevre, Samuel G. Rodgers and David Evans (Franklin R. Fish having gone the night before). They were to go into the mountains in different places, and all to meet near Thompson's Mill on Little Creek.

We followed this plan, and met at the mill. We then went over the mountains towards Panguitch.

The snow on the way would average fully two feet in depth, and the night was very cold. We stopped at a place about three miles from

Panguitch for the night. I then sent David Evans into Panguitch to see Franklin R. Fish, and find out if all was right, and then he was to report to us before daylight next morning, when we got near the town. Long before daylight we saddled our horses and started on, for the night was bitter cold. We had no blankets with us, and dared not build much fire, for fear it would alarm Lee and notify him or his friends that we were there. We reached the place where David Evans was to meet us, some time before daylight; he was not there. We waited until after the sun was up, but still Evans did not come. Then thinking that my plans had been found out in some way, and that my two men, Fish and Evans, were captured, and more than likely *blood atoned*, I concluded to act quickly and effectually.

We mounted our horses and dashed into the town at full speed. We found Evans, and learned that Fish had not been able to locate Lee, but knew that he was in town. I then ordered my men to go to different parts of the town, and to keep a good lookout, and not to let any wagon go out of town until they had searched the wagon. I inquired of the citizens about Lee, but could learn nothing from them about him. Some said they never knew him, others that they never heard of such a man, had not even heard the name. The citizens soon came crowding around in disagreeable numbers. I saw I must resort to strategy, or I and my friends were in danger; so in order to disperse the crowd, I took out my book and pencil and took down the names of those around me. I then summoned them to assist me in finding and arresting John D. Lee. They each and all had some excuse, but I refused to excuse any of them and ordered them to go and get their arms and come back and aid me. This worked well, for in less than five minutes there was not a Mormon to be seen on the streets of Panguitch. About this time I rode near Thomas Winn, when he said,

"I believe I have Lee spotted. I asked a little boy where Lee's wife lived, and he showed me the house."

This was something to work on. I then rode around to the house that Winn had pointed out to me. As I turned the street corner, I saw a woman looking into a log pen, and when she saw me, she turned back towards the house, then turned and walked back to the pen, and appeared to be talking to some one in the pen. She seemed to be very much excited. I rode by the house and around the lot, and while doing so I saw a little girl go out and look into the pen for a little while; she then took up a handful of straw and went back into the house. I, like

WILLIAM STOKES

(The Dep'y U.S. Marshal who arrested Lee)

Winn, was then satisfied that Lee was in that pen. I then told Winn to keep the place in sight, but not appear to be watching it, while I was getting ready to search for Lee. I soon afterwards met Samuel Lee. I took down his name and ordered him to assist me in searching for and arresting John D. Lee.

"John D. Lee is my father, sir," said he.

I told him it made no difference to me if he was his grandmother, that I was going to search the house and wanted him with me.

He said he was going down to the threshing machine to see his brother Al, and started off.

I drew my revolver and told him to stop.

He walked right along, looking back over his shoulder at me all the time. I then spurred my horse and went in front of him. He said,

"You can shoot and be d--d. I am not heeled, but I am going down to see my brother Al."

While we were talking, Alma Lee came up and asked what was up.

Sam said, "This is the officer come to arrest father."

Al said, "H--l! is that all! I thought there was a dog fight, I saw so many gathered around here."

He then took Sam one side and talked to him for a time. Sam soon came back and said he was ready to go with me.

I then dismounted and had Winn do the same. I first went into the house, where I found several women. I searched the house thoroughly, but found no one in it that I wanted. I then said to Sam,

"We will go over to this other house."

Sam very cheerfully said, "All right, come on," and started out ahead of me.

When I got into the yard I stopped, saying, "Hold on; here is a corral out here, let us examine it."

At this Sam came to a standstill, and was very much excited. I was then very certain that my man was there. I had to urge Sam considerably to get him to go up to the corral with me. Henry Darrow, one of Lee's sons-in-law, followed us. I took a circle around the corral, and then walked up to the log pen, which was used for a chicken house. This pen was about seven feet wide, nine feet long, and four feet high in the clear. There was a hose close to the ground, just about large enough for a man to crawl through. I first went to this hole and looked through into the pen, but I could see nothing but some loose straw in the back end of the pen. I then discovered a little hole between the top logs, near the back end, where the straw covering was off. I went to this hole and put my eye down to it, and I then saw one side of Lee's face, as he lay on his right side; his face was partly covered with loose straw. I waited a few seconds, until Winn came near enough for him to hear me without my speaking over a whisper. I then said,

"There is some one in that pen."

Darrow said, "I guess not."

I said. "I am certain there is a person in there."

By this time Winn was in position and was holding his Henry rifle ready for instant use. Winn and myself were alone. All my other men were in other parts of the town. Just then I saw Fish coming. I then said,

"Mr. Lee, come out and surrender yourself. I have come to arrest you."

He did not move. I repeated this several times, but no move was made by Lee. I then looked around to see if any of my men were coming. I saw that Fish was sitting on his horse fight in front of the door, and had his gun in his hand. I motioned my hand for him to come to me, but he remained still and kept watch of the house, as if he was going to shoot, or expected danger from that quarter. His action rather surprised me, for he was a brave man, and quick to obey orders. I then looked at the house to see what was attracting his attention, and I soon saw there was enough there to claim his full time. I saw two guns pointed through the logs of the side of the house and aimed directly at me, and Fish was watching the people who held those guns. That looked like business. I instantly drew two pistols from my overcoat pocket, taking one in each hand. Up to this time I had not drawn a pistol. I put one pistol through the crack in the roof of the pen, with the muzzle in eighteen inches of Lee's head. I then said to Winn,

"You go in there and disarm Lee, and I promise you that if a single straw moves, I will blow his head off, for my pistol is not a foot from his head."

Winn said, "All right," and was going into the pen. Darrow then commenced to beg me not to shoot. Lee also spoke and said,

"Hold on boys, don't shoot, I will come out."

He then commenced to turn over to get out of the pen, at the same time putting his pistol (which he had all the time held in his hand and lying across his breast) into the scabbard. I said to Winn, "Stand back and look out, for there is danger from the house."

Darrow continued to beg us not to shoot, saying, "Lee is an old man," etc. I told Darrow that I would not hurt a hair of Lee's head if he surrendered peaceably, but that I was not going to die like a dog, nor would I permit Lee to get away alive. Lee came out of the pen, and after straightening up, he said, very coolly, "Well, boys, what do you want of me?"

I said: "I have a warrant for your arrest, and must take you to Beaver with me."

I then took out the warrant and read it to him. When I got to that portion of the warrant which read "charged with murder," he said,

"Why didn't they put it in wholesale murder? They meant it."

He then asked me to show him the pistol that I put through the pen and pointed at his head. He said,

"It was the queerest looking pistol that I ever saw. It looked like a man's hand with the fingers cut off short."

I showed it to him. It was a dragoon pistol, with the barrel cut off short. He laughed when he saw it, and was not at all excited.

We then went to the house. The women seemed wild with excitement, some of them crying and all unreasonable in their language. Lee told his family to be quiet, and did all that he could to pacify them. He said he considered that the time had come when he could get a fair trial, etc.

I then sent and bought some wine, and took a pitcher of the liquid into the house to the women. They all took a drink. When I got to one of his daughters, who was crying bitterly, she took the glass and said,

"Here is hoping that father will get away from you, and that if he does, you will not catch him again till h--l freezes over."

I said, "Drink hearty, Miss."

By the time all the family had taken a drink, a large number of people had gathered around the house. I think fully one hundred and fifty Mormons were there. I turned to one of my men and told him to try and find some place where we could get something to eat. Lee heard me, and at once apologized for not thinking to ask us to have something to eat before that time. "But," said he, "the women folks have been making so much fuss that I have thought of nothing."

He then ordered breakfast for us all. His sons gathered around him and told him that if he did not want to go to Beaver, to say so, and they would see that he didn't go. Lee then took me one side and told me what his friends proposed, and wanted to know what answer he should give them. I thought he did this to see if there was any chance to frighten me.

LEE SURRENDERS

I told him to tell the boys to turn themselves loose; that I knew I had no friends in that place, except those who came with me, but we were well armed, and when trouble commenced we would shoot those nearest to us at the first, and make sure of them, and then continue to make it lively while we lasted.

Lee said he did not want anything of that kind to happen, and would see that the boys behaved themselves - that he thought the time had come for him to have a fair and impartial trial, and he would go with me.

I then hired a team from Lee, and hired his son-in-law to drive it. We started from Panguitch soon after breakfast. We put two of our animals in the team, making a four horse team - Darrow drove. Lee and Rachel, one of his wives, and two of my men rode in the wagon. It was about 11, A.M., on Monday, the 7th day of November, 1874, when we left Panguitch with John D. Lee as a prisoner. We reached Fremont Springs that night at about 11 o'clock, and camped there until daylight. The roads were so bad that we had been twelve hours in making thirty miles. The night was dark and cold, and having no blankets with us we could not sleep, and to add to the discomfort, we had nothing to eat.

We left Freemont Springs at daylight, and reached Beaver about 10 o'clock, A.M., November 10th, 1874. We had been twenty four hours without food. Lee and Rachel had fared better than we had, for they had a lunch with them. When we reached Beaver the people were almost thunderstruck with astonishment to know that John D. Lee had been arrested.

After the arrest Lee was in my custody the greater portion of the time that he was in prison. He never gave any trouble to me or his guards. He never tried to escape, but at all times assisted the guards to carry out the instructions that they had received from the officers.

This is a hasty sketch, but I trust will answer your purpose. Hoping you will meet with that success which you so richly deserve, I remain your most obedient servant,

WILLIAM STOKES

CHAPTER XXI

A JURY was sworn to try the case on Thursday, September 14, 1876, after which the court adjourned until the 15th.

Friday morning, September 15, 1876. The court met. Present, Hon. Jacob S. Boreman, Judge; Sumner Howard, United States Attorney; Presley Denney, Deputy United States Attorney; James R. Wilkins, Clerk; John D. Lee, the defendant on trial, with his attorneys, Wells Spicer, J. C. Foster, and Wm. W. Bishop; Wm. Nelson, United States Marshal, and the Deputies, Wm. Stokes, Franklin Brown and Edward Keisel.

The parties having announced themselves ready for trial, the following proceedings were had:

James R. Wilkins, Clerk, read the indictment against Lee, impleaded with others, to the jury, and stated the plea of the defendant.

Sumner Howard stated the case to the jury, on behalf of the people.

William W. Bishop stated the case for the defendant.

On motion of Sumner Howard, the court appointed A. S. Patterson, Esq., as official court reporter in the trial of this cause, when the following proceedings were had:

DEPOSITION OF BRIGHAM YOUNG

MR. HOWARD: If the Court please, I now propose to offer in evidence the deposition of Brigham Young; also the affidavit of Geo. A. Smith; also a letter written by John D. Lee to Brigham Young; also the report of Brigham Young to the Department of Indian Affairs, and also the proclamation of Brigham Young. These papers have been submitted to the attorneys for the defense, and they consent to their introduction. I now file them and place them in evidence to save time.

MR. BISHOP: May it please your Honor, while we deny that these documents are legal evidence of the fact in the indictment as charged, we still consent to the same being introduced, because we once came so near being placed in jail for offering the same papers, especially the deposition of Brigham Young and the affidavit of George A. Smith, as evidence at the former trial of this defendant. We wish to see what lengths the prosecution will go in this court, to convict the defendant on trial by law or without law. Our opinions as lawyers were against the admission of the evidence, but our client insists that the evidence be admitted. Contrary to our best judgment, we have consented. Let the evidence go in, and with it all besides that the authorities of the Church at Salt Lake City have unearthed for the perusal of our Brother Howard. We now know we are fighting the indictment, and also the secret forces and powers of the Mormon Church.

Mr. Howard then introduced the following documentary evidence:

TERRITORY OF UTAH, ⎫
BEAVER COUNTY ⎬ SS
⎭

In the Second Judicial District Court
The People, etc.
vs.
John D. Lee, Wm. H. Dame,   ⎫ Indictment for Murder
Isaac C. Haight, *et al.*   ⎬ September 16th, 1875

Questions to be propounded to Brigham Young on his examination as a witness in the case of John D. Lee and others, on trial at Beaver City, this 30th day of July, 1875, and the answers of Brigham Young to the interrogatives hereto appended, were reduced to writing, and were given after the said Brigham Young had been duly sworn to testify the truth in the above entitled cause, and are as follows:

First - State your age, and the present condition of your health, and whether in its condition you could travel to attend in person, at Beaver, the court now sitting there? If not, state why not.

Answer - To the first interrogatory, he saith:

I am in my seventy-fifth year. It would be a great risk, both to my health and life, for me to travel to Beaver at this present time. I am, and have been for some time, an invalid.

Second - What offices, either ecclesiastical, civil, or military, did you hold in the year 1857?

Answer - I was the Governor of this Territory, and ex-officio, Superintendent of Indian Affairs, and the President of the Church of Jesus Christ of Latter-Day Saints, during the year 1857.

Third - State the condition of affairs between the Territory of Utah and the Federal Government, in the Summer and Fall of 1857.

Answer - In May or June, 1857, the United States mails for Utah were stopped by the Government, and all communication by mail was cut off, an army of the United States, was en route for Utah, with the ostensible design of destroying the Latter-Day Saints, according to the reports that reached us from the East.

Fourth - Were there any United States judges here during the Summer and Fall of 1857?

Answer - To the best of my recollection there was no United States judge here in the latter part of 1857.

Fifth - State what you know about trains of emigrants passing through the territory to the West, and particularly about a company from Arkansas, en route for California, passing through this city in the Summer or Fall of 1857?

Answer - As usual, emigrants' trains were passing through our Territory for the West. I heard it rumored that a company from Arkansas, en route to California, had passed through the city.

Sixth - Was this Arkansas company of emigrants ordered away from Salt Lake City by yourself or any one in authority under you?

Answer - No, not that I know of. I never heard of any such thing, and certainly no such order was given by the acting Governor.

Seventh - Was any counsel or instructions given by any person to the citizens of Utah not to sell grain or trade with the emigrant trains passing through Utah at that time? If so, what were those instructions and counsel?

Answer - Yes, counsel and advice were given to the citizens not to sell grain to the emigrants to feed their stock, but to let them have sufficient for themselves if they were out. The simple reason for this was that for several years our crops had been short, and the prospect was at that time that we might have trouble with the United States army, then en route for this place, and we wanted to preserve the grain for food. The citizens of the Territory were counseled not to feed grain to their own stock. No person was ever punished or called in question for furnishing supplies to the emigrants, within my knowledge.

Eighth - When did you first hear of the attack and destruction of this Arkansas company at Mountain Meadows, in September, 1857?

Answer - I did not learn anything of the attack or destruction of the Arkansas company until some time after it occurred - then only by floating rumor.

Ninth - Did John D. Lee report to you at any time after this massacre what had been done at that massacre, and if so, what did you reply to him in reference thereto?

Answer - Within some two or three months after the massacre he called at my office and had much to say with regard to the Indians, their being stirred up to anger and threatening the settlements of the whites, and then commenced giving an account of the massacre. I told him to stop, as from what I had already heard by rumor, I did not wish my feelings harrowed up with a recital of detail.

Tenth - Did Philip Klingensmith call at your office with John D. Lee at the time Lee made his report, and did you at that time order Smith to turn over the stock to Lee, and order them not to talk about the massacre?

Answer - No. He did not call with John D. Lee, and I have no recollection of his ever speaking to me nor I to him concerning the massacre or anything pertaining to the property.

Eleventh - Did you ever give any directions concerning the property taken from the emigrants at the Mountain Meadows Massacre, or know anything as to its disposition?

Answer - No, I never gave any directions concerning the property taken from the company of emigrants at the Mountain Meadows Massacre, nor did I know anything of that property or its disposal, and I do not to this day, except from public rumor.

Twelfth - Why did you not, as Governor, institute proceedings forthwith to investigate that massacre, and bring the guilty authors thereof to justice?

Answer - Because another Governor had been appointed by the President of the United States, and was then on the way to take my place, and I did not know how soon he might arrive, and because the United States Judges were not in the Territory. Soon after Governor Cummings arrived, I asked him to take Judge Cradlebaugh, who belonged to the Southern District, with him, and I would accompany them with sufficient aid to investigate the matter and bring the offenders to justice.

Thirteenth - Did you, about the 10th of September, 1857, receive a communication from Isaac C. Haight, or any other person of Cedar City, concerning a company of emigrants called the Arkansas company?

Answer - I did receive a communication from Isaac C. Haight, or John D. Lee, who was a farmer for the Indians.

Fourteenth - Have you that communication?

Answer - I have not. I have made diligent search for it, but cannot find it.

Fifteenth - Did you answer that communication?

Answer - I did, to Isaac C. Haight, who was then acting president at Cedar City.

Sixteenth - Will you state the substance of your letter to him?

Answer - Yes. It was to let this company of emigrants, and all companies of emigrants, pass through the country unmolested, and to allay the angry feelings of the Indians as much as possible.

(Signed)   BRIGHAM YOUNG

Subscribed and sworn to before me on this 30th day of July, A.D. 1875

[L. S.]   WM. CLAYTON,

Notary Public

AFFIDAVIT OF GEORGE A. SMITH

TERRITORY OF UTAH, }
Beaver County, }

In the Second Judicial District Court of the Territory of Utah
The People, Etc., vs.
John D. Lee, Wm. H. Dame, Isaac
C. Haight, *et al.*, Salt Lake Co.

Indictment for murder, committed September 16, 1857.

George A. Smith having been first duly sworn, deposes and, says that he is aged fifty-eight years. That he is now and has been for several months suffering from a severe and dangerous illness of the head and lungs, and that to attend the court at Beaver, in the present condition of his health, would in all probability end his life.

Deponent further saith, that he had no military command during the year 1857, nor any other official position, except that of one of the Twelve Apostles of the Church of Jesus Christ of Latter-Day Saints.

Deponent further saith, that he never in the year 1857, at Parowan or elsewhere, attended a council where Wm. H. Dame, Isaac C. Haight or others were present to discuss any measures for attacking, or in any manner injuring an emigrant train from Arkansas or any other place, which is alleged to have been destroyed at Mountain Meadows in September, 1857.

Deponent further saith, that he never heard or knew anything of a train of emigrants, which he learned afterwards by rumor was from Arkansas, until he met said train at Corn Creek on his way north to Salt Lake City, on or about the 25th day of August, 1857. Deponent further saith, that he encamped with Jacob Hamblin, Philo T. Farnsworth, Silas S. Smith and Elijah Hoops, and there for the first time he learned of the existence of said emigrant train, and their intended journey to California.

Deponent further saith, that having been absent from the Territory for a year previous, he returned in the Summer of 1857, and went south to visit his family at Parowan, and to look after some property he had there, and also visit his friends, and for no other purpose, and that on leaving Salt Lake City he had no knowledge whatsoever of the existence of said emigrant train, nor did he acquire any until as before stated.

Deponent further saith, that as an Elder in the Church of Jesus Christ of Latter-Day Saints, he preached several times on his way south, and also on his return, and tried to impress upon the minds of the people the necessity of great care as to their grain crops, as all crops had been short for several years previous to 1857, and many of the people were reduced to actual want and were suffering for the necessaries of life.

Deponent further saith, that he advised the people to furnish all emigrant companies passing through the Territory with what they might actually need for breadstuff, for the support of themselves and families while passing through the Territory, and also advised the people not to feed their grains to their own stock, nor to sell to the emigrants for that purpose.

Deponent further saith, that he never heard or knew of any attack upon said emigrant train until some time after his return to Salt Lake City, and that while near Fort Bridger he heard for the first time that the Indians had massacred an emigrant company at Mountain Meadows.

Deponent further saith, that he never at any time, either before or after that massacre, was accessory thereto; that he never directly or indirectly aided, abetted or assisted in its perpetration, or had any knowledge thereof, except by hearsay; that he never knew anything of the distribution of the property taken there, except by hearsay as aforesaid.

Deponent further saith, that all charges and statements as pertaining to him contrary to the above are false and untrue.

       (Signed,)   Geo. A. Smith

Subscribed and sworn to before me this 30th day of July, A.D. 1875.

       (Signed,)   Wm. Clayton,
       [L. S.]   Notary Public

PROCLAMATION BY THE GOVERNOR

CITIZENS OF UTAH:

We are invaded by a hostile force, who are evidently assailing us to accomplish our overthrow and destruction.

For the last twenty-five years we have trusted officials of the government, from Constables and Justices to Judges, Governors and Presidents, only to be scorned, held in derision, insulted and betrayed. Our houses have been plundered and then burned, our fields laid waste, our principal men butchered while under the pledged faith of the Government for their safety, and our families driven from their homes to find that shelter in the barren wilderness, and that protection among hostile savages, which were denied them in the boasted abodes of Christianity and civilization.

The constitution of our common country guarantees unto us all that we do now or ever claimed.

If the constitutional rights, which pertain unto us as American citizens, were extended to Utah, according to the spirit and meaning thereof, and fairly and impartially administered, it is all that we could ask.

Our opponents have availed themselves of prejudices existing against us, because of our religious faith, to send out a formidable host to accomplish our destruction. We have had no privilege, no opportunity of defending ourselves from the false, foul and unjust aspersions against us before the Nation. The Government has not condescended to cause an investigating committee or other person to be sent to inquire into and ascertain the truth, as is customary in such cases. We know those aspersions to be false, but that avails us nothing. We are condemned unheard, and forced to an issue with an armed mercenary mob, which has been sent against us at the instigation of anonymous letter writers, ashamed to father the base, slanderous falsehoods which they have given to the public; of corrupt officials who have brought false accusations against us, to screen themselves in their own infamy; and of hireling priests and howling editors, who prostitute the truth for filthy lucre's sake.

The issue which has been thus forced upon us compels us to resort to the great first law of self preservation, and stand in our own defense, a right guaranteed unto us by the genius of the institutions of our country, and upon which the Government is based.

Our duty to our families requires us not to tamely submit to be driven and slain without an attempt to preserve ourselves. Our duty to our country, our holy religion, our God, to freedom and liberty, requires that we should not quietly stand still and see those fetters forging around, which are calculated to enslave and bring us into subjection to an unlawful military despotism, such as can only emanate (in a country of constitutional law) from usurpation, tyranny and oppression.

Therefore, I, Brigham Young, Governor and Superintendent of Indian Affairs for the Territory of Utah, in the name of the people or the United States in the Territory of Utah,

First - Forbid all armed forces of every description from coming into this Territory, under any pretense whatever.

Second - That all the forces in said Territory hold themselves in readiness to march at a moment's notice, to repel any and all such invasion.

Third - Martial law is hereby declared to exist in this Territory, from and after the publication of this Proclamation; and no person shall be allowed to pass or repass, into or through, or from this Territory without a permit from the proper officer.

Given under my hand and seal at Great Salt Like City, Territory of Utah, this fifteenth day of September, A.D. eighteen hundred and fifty seven, and of the Independence of the United States of America, the eighty-second.

(Signed)   BRIGHAM YOUNG

The letter and report of John D. Lee to Brigham Young, in regard to the Mountain Meadows Massacre, were here introduced as evidence. (see pages 260-2.)

REPORT OF BRIGHAM YOUNG

OFFICE SUP'T OF INDIAN AFFAIRS, G.S.L. CITY,
September 12, 1857

HON. JAMES W. DENVER, *Commissioner of Indian Affairs,*   }
    Washington, D.C.:

SIR - Enclosed please find abstract account current and vouchers from 1 to 35, inclusive, (also abstract of employee) for the current quarter up to this date, as owing to the stoppage of the mail I have deemed it best to avail myself of the opportunity of sending by private conveyance, not knowing when I may have another chance. The expenditures, as you will observe by the papers, amount to $6,411.38, for which I have drawn my drafts on the department, favor of Hon. John M. Bernhisel, Delegate to Congress from this Territory. You will also observe that a portion of those expenditures accrued, which may need a word of explanation. Santa Clara is in Washington County, the extreme southern county of this Territory, and this labor was commenced and partly performed, seeds, grain, etc., furnished prior to the time that Major Armstrong visited those parts of the Territory, hence failed to find its way into his reports, and failed being included in mine because the accounts and vouchers were not sooner brought in, and hence not settled until recently. But little has been effected in that part of the Territory at the expense of the Government, although much has been done by the citizens in aiding the Indians with tools, teams and instructions in cultivating the earth.

The bands mentioned are parts of the Piede tribe of Indians, who are very numerous, but only inhabit this Territory. These Indians are more easily induced to labor than any others in the Territory, and many of them are now engaged in the common pursuits of civilized life. Their requirements are constant for wagons, ploughs, spades, hoes, teams and harness, etc., to enable them to work to advantage.

In like manner the Indians in Cache Valley have received but little at the expense of the Government, although a sore tax upon the people. West and along the line of the California and Oregon travel they continue to make their contributions, and I am sorry to add, with considerable loss of life to the travelers. This is what I have always sought, by all means in my power, to avert, but I find it the most difficult of any portion to control. I have for many years succeeded better than this. I learn by report that many of the lives of the emigrants and considerable quantities of property have been taken.

This is principally owing to a company of some three or four hundred returning Californians, who traveled those roads last Spring to the Eastern States, shooting at every Indian they could see, a practice utterly abhorrent to all good people, yet, I regret to say, one that has been indulged in to a great extent by travelers to and from the Eastern States and California, hence the Indians regard all white men alike as their enemies, and kill and plunder whenever they can do so with impunity, and often the innocent suffer for the deeds of the guilty.

This has always been one of the greatest difficulties that I have had to contend with in the administration of Indian affairs in this Territory.

It is hard to make an Indian believe that the whites are their friends, and that the Great Father wishes to do them good, when perhaps the very next party which crosses their path shoots them down like wolves.

This trouble with the Indians only exists along the line of travel west, and beyond the influence of our settlements. The Shoshones are not hostile to travelers as far as they inhabit this Territory, except perhaps a few called "Snake Diggers," who inhabit, as before stated, along the line of travel west of the settlements.

There have, however, been more or less depredations the present season north, and more within the vicinity of the settlements, owing to the causes above mentioned, and I find it of the utmost difficulty to restrain them. The sound of war quickens the blood and nerves of an Indian. The reports that troops were wending their way to this Territory has also had its influence upon them. In one or two instances this was the reason assigned why they made the attack which they did upon some herds of cattle. They seemed to think that as it was to be war they might as well commence, and begin to lay in a supply of food while they had a chance.

If I am to have the direction of the Indian affairs of this Territory, and expected to maintain friendly relations with the Indians, there are a few things that I would most respectfully request to be done.

First - That travelers omit their infamous practice of shooting them down when they happen to see one. Whenever the citizens of this Territory travel the road they are in the habit of giving the Indians food, tobacco and a few other presents, and the Indians expect some such trifling favors, and they are emboldened by this practice to come up to the road with a view of receiving such presents. When, therefore, travelers from the States make their appearance, they throw themselves in sight with the same view, and when they are shot at and some of their numbers killed, as has frequently been the case, we cannot but expect them to wreak their vengeance upon the next train.

Secondly - That the Government should make more liberal appropriations to be expended in presents. I have proven that it is far cheaper to feed and clothe the Indians than to fight them. I find, moreover, that after all, when the fighting is over, it is always followed by extensive presents, which, if properly distributed in the first instance, might have averted the fight. In this case, then, the expenses of presents are the same, and it is true in nine-tenths of the cases that have happened.

Third - The troops must be kept away, for it is a prevalent fact that, wherever there are the most of these, we may expect to find the greatest amount of hostile Indians and the least security to persons and property.

If these items could be complied with I have no hesitation in saying that, so far as Utah is concerned, travelers could go to and from, pass and repass, and no Indian would disturb or molest them or their property.

In regard to my drafts, it appears that the department is indisposed to pay them, for what reason I am at a loss to conjecture.

I am aware that Congress separated the office of Superintendent of Indian Affairs from that of Governor; that the salary of Governor remained the same for his Gubernatorial duties, and that the Superintendent's was fifteen hundred. I do think that, inasmuch as I performed the duties of both offices, that I am entitled to the pay appropriated for it, and trust that you will so consider it.

I have drawn again for the expenditure of this present quarter as above set forth. Of course you will do as you please about paying, as you have with the drafts for the two last quarters.

The department has often manifested its approval of the management of the Indian affairs in this Superintendency, and never its disapproval.

Why, then, should I be subjected to such annoyance in regard to obtaining the funds for defraying its expenses? Why should I be denied my salary? Why should appropriations made for the benefit of the Indians of this Territory be retained in the Treasury, and individuals left unpaid?

These are questions I leave for you to answer at your leisure, and meanwhile submit to such course in relation thereto as you shall see fit to direct.

  I have the honor to be, most respectfully,

     Your obedient servant,

 (Signed)   BRIGHAM YOUNG

Governor and Ex-Officio Superintendent of Indian Affairs, U. T.

Certified to by JAMES JACK, Notary Public of Utah Territory, at Salt Lake City, August 15th, 1876.

ABSTRACT FROM REPORT OF BRIGHAM YOUNG

The following is an abstract from a letter under heading and date as follows:

       OFFICE OF SUPT. OF INDIAN AFFAIRS,

       G.S.L. City, U. T., January 6, 1858

HON. JAMES W. DENVER, *Commissioner of Indian Affairs,*

 Washington City, D.C.:   }

SIR: On or about the middle of last September a company of emigrants traveling the southern route to California, poisoned the meat of an ox that died, and gave it to the Indians to eat, causing the immediate death of four of their tribe, and poisoning several others. This company also poisoned the water where they were encamped. This occurred at Corn Creek, fifteen miles south of Fillmore City. This conduct so enraged the Indians, that they immediately took measures for revenge. I quote from a letter written to me by John D. Lee, farmer to the Indians in Iron and Washington counties. "About the 22d of September, Capt. Fancher & Co. fell victims to the Indians' wrath near Mountain Meadows. Their cattle and horses were shot down in every direction; their wagons and property mostly committed to the flames." Lamentable as this case truly is, it is only the natural consequence of that fatal policy which treats the Indians like the wolves, or other ferocious beasts. I have vainly remonstrated for years with travelers against pursuing so suicidal a policy, and repeatedly advised the Government of its fatal tendency. It in not always upon the heads of the individuals who commit such crimes that such condign punishment is visited, but more frequently the next company that follows in their fatal path become the unsuspecting victims, though peradventure perfectly innocent. Of this character was the massacre of Capt. Gunnison and party in 1853. He was friendly and unsuspecting, but the emigrant company that immediately preceded him had committed a most flagrant act of injustice and murder upon the Indians, escaped unscathed, causing the savage feeling and vengeance which they had so wantonly provoked to be poured upon the head of the lamented Gunnison. Owing to these causes, the Indians upon the main traveled roads leading from this Territory to California have become quite hostile, so that it has become quite impossible for a company of emigrants to pass in safety. The citizens of the Territory have frequently compromised their own safety and other peaceful relations, by interfering in behalf of travelers; nor can they be expected to be otherwise than hostile, so long as the traveling community persist in the practice of indiscriminately shooting and poisoning them, as above set forth. In all other parts of the Territory, except along the north and south routes to California, as above mentioned, the Indians are quiet and peaceful. It is owing to the disturbed state of our Indian affairs that the accounts of this quarter have been so considerably augmented. It has always been my policy to conciliate the native tribes by making them presents and treating them kindly, considering it much more economical to feed and clothe them than to fight them. I have the satisfaction of knowing that this policy has been most eminently successful and advantageous, not only to the settlements, but to the Government, as well as to the emigrants and travelers. But the most uniform, judicious and humane course will sometimes fail in holding ignorant, wild and revengeful Indians by the wrist, to be indiscriminately murdered. We trust, henceforward, such scenes may not be re-enacted, and the existing bad feeling among the native tribes may become extinguished by a uniform, consistent, humane and conciliatory course of superior sets, by those who profess superior attainments.

Respectfully, I have the honor to remain your obedient servant,

BRIGHAM YOUNG,
Gov. and Supt. of Indian Affairs, U. T.

Certified as correct by JAMES JACK, Notary Public of Utah Territory, at Salt Lake City, August 15, 1876.

The following circular, issued by Brigham Young and Daniel H. Wells, was then read in evidence:

GREAT SALT LAKE CITY, ⎫
Sept. 14th, 1857 ⎭

COL. WILLIAM H. DAME, Parowan, Iron County:

Herewith you will receive the Governor's proclamation declaring martial law.

You will probably not be called out this Fall, but are requested to continue to make ready for a big fight another year. The plan of operations is supposed to be about this. In case the United States Government should send out an overpowering force, we intend to desolate the Territory, and conceal our families, stock and all of our effects in the fastnesses of the mountains where they will be safe, while the men waylay our enemies, attack them from ambush, stampede their animals, take the supply trains, cut of detachments and parties sent to the canyons for wood, or on other service. To lay waste every thing that will burn - houses, fences, trees, fields and grass, so that they cannot find a particle of anything that will be of use to them, not even sticks to make a fire to cook their supplies. To waste away our enemies and lose none; that will be our mode of warfare. Thus you see the *necessity* of preparing first; secure places in the mountains where they cannot find us, or if they do, where they cannot approach in force, and then prepare for our families, building some cabins, caching flour and grain. Flour should be ground in the latter part of the Winter, or early in the Spring to keep. Sow grain in your fields as early as possible this Fall, so the harvest of another year may come off before they have time to get here. Conciliate the Indians and make them our fast friends.

In regard to letting the people pass or repass, or travel through the Territory, this applies to all strangers and suspected persons. Yourself and Brother Isaac C. Haight, in your district, are authorized to give such permits. Examine all such persons before giving to them permits to pass. Keep things perfectly quiet, and let all things be done peacefully, but with firmness, and let there be no excitement. Let the people be united in their feelings and faith, as well as works, and keep alive the spirit of the reformation. And what we said in regard to saving the grain and provisions we say again, let there be no waste. Save life always when it is possible. We do not wish to shed a drop of blood if it can be avoided.

This course will give us great influence abroad.

(Signed,)   { BRIGHAM YOUNG
                             { DANIEL H. WELLS

Certified to under seal by James Jack, Notary Public, August 16th, 1876.

CHAPTER XXII

TRIAL OF LEE CONTINUED

WHILE the documentary evidence was being read, the people had been gathering in large numbers, so much so that many were unable to obtain admission to the courtroom, to hear the statements of the witnesses.

It was by this time well understood by all parties, that the command of secrecy, which the Church had imposed on its members, had been countermanded, so far as related to John D. Lee, the defendant on trial. It was then a certainty that the witnesses would swear to as much as the prosecution was willing to hear. The result proved that these surmises were correct.

The witnesses for the prosecution were then called and sworn, after which they testified in the order and language as follows:

TESTIMONY OF WITNESSES

DANIEL H. WELLS

Sworn for the prosecution.

HOWARD - How long have you resided in this Territory? Since the fall of 1848.

Do you know John D. Lee? Yes, sir.

Did you know him in 1857? Yes, sir.

What position did he occupy at that time - official position? I don't know of any position except it was farmer to the Indians in the southern part of the Territory. He had been a Major in the military. I don't remember whether he was at that time or not. At that particular time, I think not. I think he had been suspended. I wish to ask you the question, What, from your personal knowledge, was the influence of John D. Lee over the Indians to whom he had been appointed farmer - was he interpreter also? Well, I think he understood the language imperfectly; could probably converse with the Indians.

State if he was a man of influence with the Indians, a man popular with them? He was so considered.

Cross examination waived.

LABAN MORRILL

Sworn for the prosecution.

Where do you reside? Iron County, at what is called Fort Johnson. How long have you lived in the Territory? Since 1852. Do you know the location of Mountain Meadows? No, sir. I never was there. Where did you live in 1857? I think I lived at Cedar City. How far is Cedar City from Beaver? About thirty miles. Did you, in 1857, know any thing about an emigrant train, known as the Arkansas emigrant train, passing through the Territory to Southern California, or starting to pass? By report only. Did you have any thing to do as an officer or citizen, at Cedar City, with regard to the passage of those emigrants? If you did, state what you know about their passage, in your own way. Merely by report, that there was a company come through Cedar City. I lived off at a place called Fort Johnson, six miles and a half. I was engaged at that time some little in seeing what was called the best locality, or what would do the best good for some three or four little places, Cedar City, Fort Johnson and Shirts' Creek. We had formed a kind of a custom to come together about once a week, to take into consideration what would be the best good for those three places. I happened on Sunday to come to Cedar City, as I usually came, and there seemed to be a council. We met together about four o'clock, as a general thing, on Sunday evening after service. I went into the council, and saw there was a little excitement in regard to something I did not understand. I went in at a rather late hour. I inquired of the rest what was the matter. They said a company had passed along toward Mountain Meadows. There were many threats given concerning this company.

SPICER - for Defendant - We object to these conversations, in which the witness has not shown that the defendant was present.

HOWARD - for the People - We expect to connect Mr. Lee with it in this way: We propose to show that at that council a report was made that the Indians had stopped this train of emigrants, or were about to stop them; and we propose to show further that at that time, in consequence of the condition of the country, it was claimed by some people that they should

DANIEL H. WELLS

be held until a message could be sent to Salt Lake and their passage secured; that Mr. Morrill appeared there - others being in favor of stopping the emigrants, and perhaps doing more than that. Mr. Morrill appeared there and insisted that no interference should be had with them until orders came from Brigham Young - from headquarters - and at first insisting that they should be allowed to pass unmolested. That the Indians should not be allowed to molest them if it could be avoided. That they should be prevented by all means from interfering with them. Mr. Morrill made several speeches to that council in favor of that proposition, and that finally an agreement was made that the emigrants should not be interfered with, and suspend all proceedings in regard to even stopping them until a message should come from Brigham Young. At that time Brigham Young was not only the President of the Church, but Governor of the Territory, and Indian Agent. We propose to follow it up by showing that an agreement *was* made and a messenger sent posthaste to Salt Lake. We propose to follow it up by showing that a messenger was sent to see that the Indians did not interfere with the emigrants. We propose to follow it up by showing that John D. Lee *received* that word. That that was the agreement of that council, and that he must not allow those emigrants to be interfered with. That he not only received that word, but that he made the remark that he had something to say about it. The man who carried the message was told that he had better get out of the way himself, or he would get hurt. There has been an effort made to show that others besides John D. Lee commenced this attack. We propose to show to this jury that the attack was made in defiance of the authorities. That they not only held the lives of those emigrants secure; were not only anxious that they should be allowed to pass, but that they should be protected from the Indians, in order to show their sincerity and do what was right in view of the circumstances, made a solemn agreement there among themselves that the emigrants should not be interfered with until a dispatch could be sent to Governor Young and returned. We propose to show that that dispatch was sent to Governor Young by that messenger, with instructions not to spare horseflesh, but to ride there day and night; that before this messenger returned, John D. Lee, in defiance of that council, massacred the emigrants.

SPICER - If the gentleman propose to prove that Lee did anything contrary to the orders of the Church Council, we will withdraw our objections. But we know the prosecution will fail in the effort. Lee did nothing that was contrary to Council, and the fact is, he obeyed orders.

Howard - Mr. Morrill, the court directs that you state what was done at that Council?

Ans. - As I said, there appeared to be some confusion in that Council. I inquired in a friendly way what was up. I was told that there was an emigrant train that passed along down to near Mountain Meadows, and that they had made threats in regard to us as a people - said they would destroy every d--d Mormon. There was an army coming on the south and north, and it created some little excitement. I made two or three replies in a kind of debate of measures that were taken into consideration, discussing the object, what method we thought best to take in regard to protecting the lives of the citizens.

My objections were not coincided with. At last we touched upon the topic like this: We should still keep quiet, and a dispatch should be sent to Governor Young to know what would be the best course. The vote was unanimous. I considered it so. It seemed to be the understanding that on the coming morning, or next day, there should be a messenger dispatched. I took some pains to inquire and know if it would be sent in the morning. The papers were said to be made out, and Governor Young should be informed, and no hostile course pursued till his return. I returned back to Fort Johnson, feeling that all was well. About eight and forty hours before the messenger returned - business called me to Cedar City, and I learned that the *job had been done,* that is, the destruction of the emigrants had taken place. I can't give any further evidence on the subject at present.

What was the name of the messenger sent to Salt Lake? James Haslem.

Cross examined by W.W. Bishop - You think that about forty-eight hours before the messenger returned from Salt Lake, you learned that the *job was done,* the people killed at Mountain Meadows. Do you mean by that, the killing that had been talked of at that Council? I suppose it was, sir. Who was present at that Council that you recollect? Mr. Smith. Give me the name of any there that you can call to mind? I think Isaac C. Haight was there. Was John D. Lee present? No, sir, not to my knowledge. Did you see that messenger start to Brigham Young? I did not. Did you see the message that he took to Brigham Young? I did not. Did you ever read it? I did not. Did you know, or have any knowledge that any written communication was given by the Council to any one to carry to President Young? The understanding of the Council was that one should be written out for him prior to his starting.

Do you know of your own knowledge that one was written out? I didn't see Mr. Haight, but he should have made it out in time. I didn't see the paper.

Then the understanding of the Council, as I take it, was this, that different parties presented different plans for having the people follow the emigrants; that after all this argument it was agreed by the parties there that a messenger should go to Brigham Young for instructions as to how the people should treat the emigrants in that train, and nothing should be done with those emigrants until that messenger returned? That was the agreement - I understood it so.

Who else did they agree to send a messenger to? I heard of no other but Governor Young. That was my proposition.

Then you never heard of a messenger being sent to any other place, or to any other party, from that Council? No, I did not pay any attention to any other point, or what was considered; only the one point that a messenger should go to President Young.

Redirect by HOWARD - Did you understand that a messenger was to be sent down to John D. Lee? I did, but I did not see him start. I understood that at the same time a messenger was to be sent.

What did you understand? I understood that there was to be word sent down towards Pinto Creek.

For what purpose? To have the thing stayed according to contract, to agreement made.

What do you mean by the thing being stayed? Was the massacre of that emigrant train discussed there at all? It was, sir; and some were in favor of it, and some were not.

Who were they? Bishop Smith, I considered, was the hardest man I had to contend with.

Who else spoke about it? Isaac Haight and one or two others. I recollect my companions more than any one else.

They were very anxious and rabid were they not? They seemed to think it would be best to kill the emigrants. Some of the emigrants swore that they had killed old Joseph Smith; there was quite a little excitement there.

You have given us the names of two who were in favor of killing those emigrants - who were the others? Those were my companions, Isaac C. Haight and Klingensmith. I recollect no others.

You remember that council, and the agreement that they would not do anything until word came back from President Young? Yes, sir.

Although you didn't see either of those messengers start, you understood messengers were sent each way? Yes, sir; to stay the opposition until that messenger returned.

Re-cross examination - You say you understood a messenger was to be sent to Pinto Creek. Did John D. Lee live at Pinto Creek? He lived at Harmony.

Was it mentioned in that Council that a messenger was to be sent to Pinto Creek to stay the thing until the other messenger got back? Understand me, there was nothing said in that Council in regard to Pinto, only that the thing should be stayed. They took such measures to stay it as they thought proper. After the messenger, Mr. Haslem, returned I asked Mr. Haight about it, and he said he had sent word to let them pass, of course. That was the end of my experience in regard to it.

HOWARD - Where did John D. Lee live at that time? He lived at Harmony.

How far is Harmony from Pinto Creek? I don't know.

What was his position at that time? He was a man of some influence among the Indians, and also held a position in the military.

Was he not Indian Farmer? I think he had done something towards it. One thing I passed over at that Council; I inquired by what authority they were doing it, and they said by their own authority. Says I, has Dame got a letter here; is there anything from Mr. Dame of Parowan? They said no. I demanded a written letter or order from him before I would act; they said they had none.

James Haslem testified that he went as a messenger from Haight to Brigham Young, and that Brigham Young sent back word that "those men must be protected and allowed to go in peace." He got back with the message *Sunday after the massacre,* and reported to Haight, who said, "It is too late."

JOEL WHITE

Sworn for the prosecution.

Where did you live in 1857? I lived in Cedar City, Iron County.

Do you remember the Mountain Meadows band of emigrants? Yes, sir.

Did you at that time know John D. Lee? Yes, sir.

And Klingensmith? Yes, sir.

Were you ever entrusted by anybody with a message to John D. Lee, or to any other person? No, sir, not to John D. Lee. During the delivery of which you met John D. Lee? Yes, sir. I was away from home at the time the emigrants passed through Cedar City. I came home just before night. I can't recollect the day or date, nor anything of that kind; but Mr. Haight called me as I was passing, and said he wanted a message taken to Pinto Creek, and wanted to know if I would go. I asked if it had to go tonight. He said it had, that the emigrants would pass Pinto tomorrow. He told me the nature of the dispatch. It was to the man in charge there at Pinto, to pacify the Indians if possible, and let the emigrants pass. Klingensmith was standing by and volunteered to go with me, and I accepted his company.

Did you start with that message? Yes, sir.

Tell what occurred. When I got down to the lower corner of the field, after we had started, probably a mile and a half, or such matter, I don't recollect the distance now, I met John D. Lee. It was about dark; he was coming toward Cedar. He asked us what the calculation of the people was in regard to those emigrants - in regard to letting them pass.

Did he ask you where you were going? I don't recollect. I told him - we both told him, but I told him in particular - the conclusion was to let them pass, and that I was going to Pinto with a letter to that effect, to have the Indians pacified as much as possible, to let them pass. Mr. Lee spoke up and said, "I don't know about that," or, "I have something to do about that," I don't exactly recollect the words, and drove on.

Where were the emigrants at that time? They were camped on a little stream in the mountains, between Cedar City and Pinto, just off the road. We saw them indistinctly as we passed them in the night, but as we came back next day we met them on the travel.

What place was that? Iron Springs. A very little spring, I hardly remember the locality.

The emigrants hadn't yet reached Pinto? No, sir, because we met them. The first time I had ever seen them I saw them coming up along there.

Cross examined - In which direction was Lee coming? He was coming up the road towards Cedar City.

What day was it? I don't recollect neither the day of the week nor the month.

You say it was about dark? It was about dusk then.

How long was it before the massacre? I could not say about that for certain.

About how many days? Probably four or five, may be six, may be not so long; I could not say.

You passed the emigrants then on your way that night? We passed, but didn't see them.

Who was the man that you were carrying the message to? It was the man in charge of them there in Pinto Creek at that time. I can't recollect his name.

Was not his name Richard Robinson? That is my impression, but I will not be sure, as there were several changes. There was Rufus Allen, Richard Robinson, Thornton, and different ones that had charge along about that time. I can't recollect, but I think it was Richard Robinson.

When did you move to Cedar City? I moved there in the Fall of 1853.

How long did you live there? I left there in the Summer of '58. I left there and came to Beaver, and from there went north.

Where do you reside now? I live at what is called Cedar Fort, Cedar Valley, in Utah County, five miles from Camp Floyd.

You say you passed by near the emigrants' camp, but didn't see them? Yes, sir. We saw them next day on the travel.

You afterwards saw those emigrants, I believe, at the Meadows? Yes, sir, a portion of them.

You were present at the Meadows at the time of the massacre? Yes, sir.

Redirect - You don't remember the day nor the date, but on your way back, after delivering the message, you met these same emigrants, and you know they were the Mountain Meadows emigrants? Yes, sir.

Re-cross examined - You know they were the same ones from passing them and afterwards seeing them at the Meadows after they were killed? Klingensmith was with me, and he had seen the emigrants when they had passed through Cedar City, and there were some of the principal ones that he pointed out to me as we passed by them.

Why did he point them out to you? One man that had made these threats that he had helped kill Joe Smith, and so forth.

Did you see that same party at the Meadows afterwards? I don't recollect the same party. I saw the same band of emigrants, I suppose at any rate no others had passed.

SAMUEL KNIGHT

Sworn for the prosecution.

Where do you live? I live at Santa Clara.

How long have you lived there? In the neighborhood of twenty-two years.

Where did you live in '57? 1 lived at Santa Clara; that was my house. I lived on the Mountain Meadows. I was stopping on the Mountain Meadows that Summer.

Will you state how you came up to Mountain Meadows, and how you were situated there? My family was sick at the time, and I moved my family up on account of the hot weather. I was herding stock at the Meadows and milking cows.

Who was with you? Jake Hamblin and myself were proprietors.

Describe that locality to the court and jury? The location in at the north end of what is termed Meadow Valley.

How long is the Meadow Valley? Four miles long, and about one mile wide.

Is it entirely surrounded by mountains and hills? Yes, sir, it is entirely surrounded, except a gap at this end - the gap at which Hamblin's Ranch was situated, and the gap at the other end leads you out on the desert. It has a stream that leads to the Santa Clara stream.

On the first of September, 1857, you say you were stopping there with your wife, who was out of health? A few days before she had been confined, and was lying nearly at the point of death; we were living in a wagon box by the side of Jake Hamblin's board shanty.

Did you about that time go down to your place at Santa Clara? Yes, sir, from Mountain Meadows. I went down a few days previous to this occurrence - this massacre - to see to some business down there - about watering the crop there.

What time did you return? It is not in my memory, the day of the week.

With reference to the general massacre? It was the evening after it had been done in the morning - that is, the first attack.

I mean with reference to the general massacre of the women and children? That was nearly a week, I think.

You are sure about that, are you? I don't exactly remember, but it was several days.

What do you mean by the first attack, and from whom did you get your information? What information I got was from John D. Lee.

State the particulars? As I said before, I was on my way to where I was staying at the time from my home at Santa Clara. From the ranch to Santa Clara settlement was thirty-five miles.

How far below the lower mountain of the Mountain Meadows? About ten miles to where I met John D. Lee. I think he had on a hickory shirt, a straw hat, and homespun pants.

Did you have any conversation? Yes, sir. As I was riding along he hailed me.

Who was with you? I don't know that it is proper for me to state. Had you up to that time known any thing about the attack on the emigrants? No, sir, I had not.

Did you notice any thing peculiar about John D. Lee at that time? He showed me some bullet holes in his clothing, and may be one or two in his hat.

State the conversation. All the conversation? You can tell what you recollect. I think he told me that he had made an attack with the Indians, and got repulsed.

When did he say he had made it? I think that morning at daylight, or near daylight.

Do you know whether he told you so or not? I am pretty positive he did.

Did he tell you any thing about any escape that he had had? He said he had run a narrow escape, showing me the holes in his hat and shirt, where he had narrowly escaped being shot.

State all the conversation. He rode along with us up to some eight or ten miles of where his camp was. When I saw him it was getting dusk, and we rode along together as far as the camp.

Was he alone when he met you? Yes, sir, as far as I know.

Did he tell you whether any other white man had been with him in the attack? I am not certain. I got the impression from what he told me that there was not.

Did he tell you from whom he got the bullets through his clothes, or not? I took it, of course.

Did he say he got it on that assault on the emigrants? I can't give the exact language.

What was the substance of what he told you about it? I collected from what he said that he had attacked the camp of these emigrants with the Indians, and that in making the attack he received the shots from the camp, that the bullets had come near to him, one through his shirt and another through his hat.

Did he say anything about having a narrow escape? I think he did.

What camp did he refer to? The camp of the Mountain Meadows emigrants.

You say he came back part of the way to the Mountain Meadows? I don't know but what he went clear across the Meadows, I am not positive. I know he rode back with me. He rode back to where the camp was, at least, but whether he stopped there or not I will not be positive.

Did you see him go towards the Indian camp afterwards? I didn't know where the Indian camp was. It was in the night. He came to me about dusk. It was eight or nine o'clock when we got to where the camp was located. I went right over to my home.

State whether you noticed anything peculiar about Mr. Lee's person, aside from his dress. No, nothing more than what I have stated.

State whether he had any paint on him. I didn't notice any. It was between sundown and daylight. It was nearly dusk when I first saw him. We hadn't talked but a few minutes, when it was dark.

How long a time passed until the general massacre? Some five or six days.

Did you remain there with your wife during all that time? Yes, sir, with the exception of being out after my stock once or twice.

Had you anything to do with Lee, or see him after that time? He was over at Hamblin's ranch a few times.

What was he there for? I don't know.

Did he come alone? He was there with other men, but how he came I don't know.

Did he at any time come to you to get your teams? Yes, sir.

What day was that with reference to the massacre of the men, women and children? It was the day it was done.

What time? I think it was a little before 12 o'clock, the middle of the day.

Who came with him? I think it was Klingensmith.

Where were you, and what were you doing? I was at home waiting upon my sick wife, who was there in the wagon, and doing chores necessary to be done about home.

State the conversation that took place between you and Lee, or you and Klingensmith, in the presence of Lee, about what they came for? They told me they came to get my team and wagon to go over and haul away the sick and wounded from the train, and take them back to the settlements where they could care for them, as wagons were scarce. I didn't consent st first, I told them that I didn't want to go, that my family needed my presence at home. They insisted that I should go and said that duty called me to go. I said if the team went I should go myself with it. My team was a young team and had just been broke a few days, and the horses were fractious.

From that point what was done? Well, I went over. I hitched up my team and went over. Went with a common lumber wagon and box on it.

Did you leave your wife there? Yes, sir.

Where did you go? I went right on to the Mountain Meadows, right on to the south end of the Mountain Meadows, or near there. I drove up to a camp of Indians and men camped somewhere to the left of the road, probably half a mile, may be not so far, at a little spring to the left of the road, and waited there a little while. I stopped some four or five rods from this camp and stood by my team until I was told to drive down towards the camp.

Who told you? It is not in my memory.

Did you drive down towards the camp? I did.

What camp? The emigrant camp.

Did any other conveyance go down at the same time? Yes, sir, another wagon, I went behind it.

Did you see Lee there? Yes, sir.

Tell what he did from the first time you saw him that morning on that particular piece of ground? I don't know what he did all the time. While I was waiting at the camp I don't know that I saw him while I was there.

How far was that from the emigrants? I think nearly half a mile.
Did you see anybody go to that emigrant camp? No, sir. I saw a man carrying a white flag.

Who was that man? I could not tell.

Was anybody with him? Yes, sir, I think John D. Lee was with him, or near him, and walked down to the camp.

What occurred there? They walked with this white flag near the camp, and another man met them with a white rag on a stick. He came from the emigrant camp, and they met some distance from the camp, and held a consultation for a few minutes, and then we were told to drive along, or motioned to.

Did any other man besides this man and John D. Lee go? Not any distance. I don't remember that they did.

Who held that consultation? I was not acquainted with them, and was some distance from them, but I think it was John D. Lee, the man that carried the flag, and one or two who came from the emigrant camp.

Who motioned for you to go along after the consultation? I can't tell, but the whole fraternity up there moved along with the wagons.

When you got down to the camp what occurred? My wagon was loaded with some guns, some bedding, and a few individuals.

Who superintended that loading up? John D. Lee.

What guns were loaded into your wagons? The guns from the emigrant camp.

When the emigrants came out afterwards, were they armed or not? They were not; not that I saw.

What did they load into your wagon? Guns, bedding, and some clothing of different kinds, and several persons got in. I think three or four got in.

What were those persons? As near as I can recollect, there were two men, one woman, and, I think, some children.

State whether those men were wounded then, sick men, or what? I think they were wounded, but I stood holding my team.

State whether it was quite necessary for you to give all your attention to your team? I considered it so.

Then what occurred? After they were loaded in we were told to drive on towards home.

By whom? I can't recollect.

Did you drive along? We did.

Do you know what was put into the other wagon? Mostly people.

Were both those wagons loaded from the emigrant camp? Yes, sir. I started towards my home, north across the Meadows, lengthwise of the Meadows. It led to the north.

After you started, how close did the other wagon follow? I followed it; it went ahead.

What followed you? The men, women and children; coming along after we drove out a little ways.

Did you understand, from what you saw there, that the emigrants vacated that camp and followed you? I did, sir.

As you passed along, did you go with them, or did you go faster? We traveled a little faster.

How far in advance of them did you get? I think we got, may be, a quarter of a mile. It might not have been that far, but quite a little distance.

What order did those emigrants march in, whether single file, two abreast, or how? I could not give any testimony on that. I did not look back to see.

Who accompanied you with your wagon, who came along? I remember John D. Lee being along with the wagons.

Ahead of the emigrants? Yes, sir.

Did anything occur after you had got up to the point designated as, perhaps, a quarter of a mile ahead of those emigrants? The first thing that I heard had occurred. I heard a gun fired.

Where was that gun? I don't know the locality exactly. It was behind me.

Was it near you, or down where the emigrants were? It was below.

How far behind you? I should judge nearly a quarter of a mile, the first gun I heard.

What occurred then? I looked around and saw the Indians rising up from behind the brush, and went to butchering these emigrants.

Did you see anything of them? I didn't see anything of the emigrants.

Did you see any of those emigrants in your wagon interfered with? No, sir; not after I heard the first sound of the gun. I leaped from my wagon to see to my team.

Did you see John D. Lee do anything to any of those emigrants? I saw John D. Lee raise something in the act of striking a person - I think it was a woman. I saw that person fall, but my attention was attracted at the same time to my team jumping and lunging.

What became of that woman? I could not say.

Will you state to the jury the manner of that striking? Well, as near as I can recollect it, it was done as though he had a club or gun in his hands, but which of the two I cannot tell. She was falling when I first saw her. When I turned my eyes away she was falling.

You know he struck that woman? Yes, sir.

Either with a gun or with a club? Yes, sir.

Your team, you say, became very fractious. Is that all you saw John D. Lee do? That is all I could be positive about.

What was he doing besides that? I could not be positive what he was doing all the time.

State whether all of those people were killed there and then? They were; those in the wagon were all killed.

Was it in your wagon or the one behind you that John D. Lee struck that woman? It was in the one ahead of me.

Was that woman killed? I think she was. They were all killed.

How many cattle had this emigrant train? I don't know, sir.

Should judge three or four hundred head.

Do you know who drove these cattle away from that ground? No, sir; I do not.

Do you know whose men drove them off? No, sir; only by report - by rumor.

Did you see Lee drive any of them? No, sir; I did not.

Did you hear him say anything about it? I did not.

Did Lee remain there until all in the wagons were killed? I think he did.

Where did you go then? I drove immediately home.

Which way did Lee go? I don't know - he was on the ground when I left.

Do you know the names of any of those parties who were killed there? No, sir; I do not.

Cross examined - How many people were present around the wagons when you say you saw Lee strike the woman? I don't know how many.

Were there any others there except Lee and yourself? I have an impression that there were, but I don't know who they were. I have always had an idea that there were one or two more men.

Don't you know, as a matter of fact, that there were? Yes, sir; there was another man that drove the other wagon, but how many more I don't know.

You don't know the names of the men? Not that I recollect of.

Were any Indians around there? Yes, sir.

Any around the wagons? Yes, sir.

Did you see them take any part in the killing? Yes, sir; they took some part in the killing. There were not more than one or two men there, John D. Lee and the men that drove the wagon.

How many Indians? I can't tell.

Isn't it a matter of fact that about that time you wanted to got away from there, and to see as little as possible? I paid just as little attention as I possibly could.

Didn't you make an effort to see as little of it as you could? I did, sir.

That explains why you did not see all of it? Yes, sir, I took all the pains I could to see as little as I could.

Did not the Indians raise a yell, and make a rush for the wagon before you jumped out? Yes, sir, or about that time.

Were they not surrounding the wagons at the time you saw Lee strike? Yes, sir.

There were Indians all around and close to you at the time? Yes, sir, there were Indians a round; quite a number all round there.

Did they rush toward the people in the wagons with hostile intentions? Yes, sir, with apparently hostile intentions.

You saw them kill a number of people - didn't they kill that woman? It was my impression that John D. Lee killed her.

Do you know? Yes, sir, I do.

Did you see him do anything else except strike? No, sir.

That much you did see? Yes, sir, I did.

Who was that man with you at the Meadows, the first time you saw John D. Lee, the night after the first attack? I decline to tell,

Redirect - State where those cattle of the emigrants were at the time of the massacre. They were north a little; up this way.

How soon after that were they driven away? I think next day.

Do you know whose men drove them away? I do not.

Were the emigrants' wagons destroyed there on the ground, or were they taken away? I don't know. They passed along.

Was the field cleared of the emigrant property? Yes, sir, cattle and everything.

Were any wagons burned or destroyed? No, sir, not that I know of.

How long did you stay there after that? Nearly a month.

SAMUEL McMURDY

Sworn for the prosecution.

Where do you live now? I live In Cache County, Paradise.

Did you live in any other place than Paradise in 1857? 1 lived at Cedar City. I don't recollect dates. Did you live there at the time of the Mountain Meadows Massacre? Yes, sir.

State whether you were called upon to go to Mountain Meadows? I was called upon to go and take my team and wagon.

By whom? I believe it was John M. Higbee that called me.

State from that point the circumstances? I was threshing my grain. I had my grain spread out in the yard, and was tramping it with horses at the time I was called upon. I was notified to leave in two hours' notice. It was sometime in the afternoon that I was called upon.

Of what day? I could not state.

With reference to the date of the general massacre? I think It was a day prior to it. Was it stated to you for what purpose you were to go there? No, sir.

Did you know? No, sir.

Did you go? Yes, sir.

Who went with you? There were a number that went in the wagon with me. Some I can recollect, Klingensmith for one, a man by the name of Hopkins, and two or three more besides that went during the time that I went down, I understood from the men that were in the wagon. I asked them what was the matter. They told me that the emigrants had been attacked, and we had to go down and arrest the attack, if possible. That was the purpose that I expected to go for - was to preserve the emigrants from the Indians.

What time did you get there? It was in the afternoon when we started - late. It must have been way in the night when we got there. I could not tell you the time. We traveled a good many hours in the night. Got there and turned out the horses and camped.

Did you stay until morning? Yes, sir; staid there till morning, and during the next day I got up my horses.

Anybody give you orders? Yes, sir.

Who? John D. Lee. He told me to take the wagon and follow him to camp.

What camp? The camp of the emigrants.

The emigrants that were afterwards killed? Yes, sir.

Did you go? I did.

State what you saw. I went with him to camp, and there was another wagon, if I recollect right. The man that drove the wagon was a stranger to me. I never saw him before. When we got within a short distance of the camp there was a man with a flag of truce sent out.

Who was that man? His name was Mr. Bateman.

Where is he? Dead.

Where was he sent from? Sent from where we stood with the wagons.

Who went with him? John D. Lee followed immediately afterwards.

What occurred? A man came out from the camp and had an interview with John D. Lee.

What was the substance of that conversation? I was too far off to tell. I saw Lee and this man talking.

Did you hear any of the talking? Not any that I could distinguish.

After they talked what was done? After they talked they seemed to come to an understanding, ten, fifteen or twenty minutes, then Lee ordered us to drive up the wagons. We drove up the wagons. The emigrants, assisted by Lee, loaded the wagons. My wagon was loaded with some bedding, some truck of different kinds, belonging to the people that got in. Some would have their things with them, as if they were going a journey. A number got in, men, women and children, from the emigrant camp, some of them apparently wounded. I could not say how many, it is so long ago. I never charged my memory with it. I could not state how many there were.

Go on. We were ordered to start out by John D. Lee, and we started out from that place.

State whether the other wagon was loaded also? It was.

Were there any guns put into either wagon? There were not in mine.

Did you at any time leave your team? No, sir.

When John D. Lee directed you to drive, what took place? We proceeded some distance on the Meadows. Mine was the head team.

Who accompanied you? John D. Lee was walking behind the wagon, between the two wagons.

BY THE COURT - Were there any persons in those two wagons? Yes, sir. They were loaded up with persons and things.

Were both of those wagons loaded with men, women and children from that camp of emigrants? Yes, sir, and other things besides.

How many got into your wagon? I could not say. It is impossible for me to tell. I should think half a dozen.

What were they - men and women; any children in yours? I think there were some small children.

And as you started on you saw Lee take a position between the two wagons and walk on behind you? Yes, sir.

How far behind you? I could not tell you. I had as much as I could do to attend to my team. We must have been quite a little distance ahead of the other team. My team was a very fast walking team. Lee checked me up several times. I had to hold on to the lines.

Did he give you any reasons for it? No, sir. I outwalked him. We walked very fast. How many times did he tell you not to walk so fast? Several times.

HOWARD - What occurred from that point? He called to me to halt after we got out of sight of the camp.

Who did? John D. Lee. When we got out of sight, over the hill, there is where we passed out of sight of everything. There is a rising ground there. We were this side of it, and everything back towards the emigrants was out of sight. When we got to this place Lee ordered me to halt. At that instant I heard the sound of a gun. I turned and looked over my shoulder, and Lee had his gun to his shoulder, and when the gun had exploded I saw, I think it was a woman, fall backwards. I had to tend to my team at the time.

Who discharged that gun? John D. Lee must have discharged it.

Did he hold it in his hand? Yes, sir. He must have hit her in the back of the head. She fell immediately.

Go on. I turned round. It seemed to me like I heard sounds of striking with a heavy instrument, like a gun would make, but I never saw any striking done. But I turned round to the other side a few minutes afterwards, and saw Lee draw his pistol and shoot from two to three in the head of those who were in the wagon.

Did he kill them? He must have killed them.

What were these he shot - men, women or children? Men and women.

And they fell off underneath the wagon, then and there? I could not say then and there. They must have been all killed.

Did you go back at all? No, sir.

Never wanted to go back? No, sir - never.

Who fired the first gun - which was the first gun fired? It would be impossible for me to tell. The first gun I heard was the first gun fired right at the back of me that attracted my attention.

You looked around and saw the gun in Lee's hands? Yes, sir; that was the first gun I heard.

Were there immediately volleys of firing? Yes, sir; I heard firing immediately afterwards.

Was that the signal to begin firing? Yes, sir, that was the beginning.

How long after Lee told you to halt was that firing? It was instantly done.

And you looked around and saw the gun? Yes, sir.

Cross examined - You say that you got your orders from Higbee to go down there? I believe it was from Higbee, but I am not sure. I am almost positive it was from him.

Did Higbee go with you? I don't recollect.

Where did you camp that night? On the Meadows.

How many men were there? I could not say.

About how many men were there? I could not give it, because I went in the dark, and had my team to hunt next morning. I turned them out,

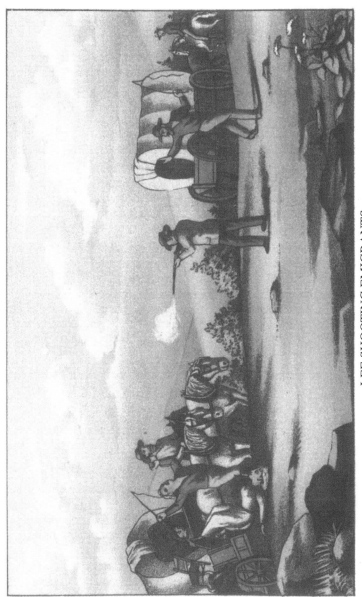

LEE SHOOTING EMIGRANTS

and it took up all my attention.

Next morning how many men did you see there? I don't recollect anything about it.

You did not see anybody there except yourself, and John D. Lee, and the man that carried the flag, did you? I saw a good many there, but they were strangers to me.

You can't tell about how many were there? I might if I had counted them, and impressed my memory with it.

Do you think there is anything you saw, during the time you were absent from home, but what is *burned* into your memory, so that it is impossible for you to forget it? Yes, sir, a number of things.

One of the principal things that you cannot recollect is the names of your friends who were there? I don't know that I had any friends there, any more than I have here.

Can you give me the names of any of the men that you saw there that day? Well, sir, I could not really recollect. I suppose not, I might if I was to sit down and think for a while. A little thing like that you would not recollect.

Will you please tell me the names of the parties that were present on the ground, at the time you started to drive down to the emigrant camp? It is impossible for me to do it.

How many men were in sight at the time you started to drive down - of your friends, parties from Cedar City or elsewhere? Well, sir, I could not say. I don't recollect seeing any of them. I was too much absorbed in my team and in my own surroundings.

What caused you to be so much absorbed? Any man that has a team to attend to under circumstances of firing of guns -

Were any guns firing then? Not then.

You did not got roused up until after they had loaded your wagon. Had anything happened to excite you previous to the loading up of your wagon at the emigrant camp? I am not aware of anything particularly.

You didn't know at that time that any one was to be killed? No, sir.

You had not even heard that any one was to be killed? No, sir.

You thought you were on an errand of mercy? Yes, sir.

You thought you had gone there in good faith to help those emigrants back to Cedar City? Yes, sir, that was my understanding.

You had driven down across the valley to the emigrant camp, and the only men you saw during that entire time were John D. Lee and this man that carried the flag? I saw a lot of emigrants around there.

I am speaking now of the people who lived in that vicinity? Outside of the men that lived at Cedar City, they were strangers to me, and I could not tell who they were.

You saw them the night before? No, sir, I did not.

Didn't you see them on the ground before you started to drive down to the emigrant camp? I could not say that I did. I don't recollect of seeing any quantity of men where I was, at all.

You didn't see any Indians that morning? No, sir.

No Indians at the time of the killing? I could not say about that. I believe there were Indians around.

Well, do you know? I don't recollect.

You do not recollect to have seen any Indians? Yes, sir, I saw Indians around there, but at the precise moment of time I could not say.

Did you see more than one or two Indians? I saw a great many Indians there after the firing commenced.

Where did those Indians come from? I don't know.

What were they doing? I could not tell.

Did you see them commit any acts of hostility? I don't recollect. I don't doubt but they did, but I can't recollect of their doing anything of the kind.

You pretend to say now that at the time the gun was fired, and from that time on, your excitement and fear were so great that you can't recollect all that did happen? Yes, sir, that's about true.

How far did you haul those people after they were killed? Left them right there.

Who took them out? John D. Lee.

Don't you think he killed a dozen? I could not tell.

Give us your best impression? My impression is that there might be half a dozen.

You did not help kill any one - did you kill any one there? I had nothing to do with it at all.

Then you did not raise your hand against any one at that time, or do any of the killing of the emigrants? I believe I am not upon trial, sir.

I ask if you refuse to answer the question? *No answer.*

Did you upon that occasion, on the day when the Mountain, Meadows Massacre took place, kill any person upon that ground or assist in the killing of any person? *I don't wish to answer.*

You say every person that was in the wagons was killed? To my best recollection and knowledge.

Don't you know, as a matter of fact, that there were some seventeen children in those wagons that were not killed? I don't recollect the number.

Don't you know there were a number of children that were not killed? Yes, sir.

Explain what you mean? I mean all of the grown persons were killed, the children were saved, sir. I believe I assisted to haul them away, to take them off.

Redirect - How many children were saved from the massacre? I have no recollection.

Where did you take them to - those that you had? They were distributed around; one went to one house, and another to another.*

NEPHI JOHNSON

Sworn for the prosecution.

Where did you live in 1857? 1 lived at a place called Fort Johnson, Iron County.

What was your business? I was living with my father - farmer.

Were you an Indian interpreter? Yes, sir; I could talk some with the Indians at that time.

Were you at the Mountain Meadows Massacre? Yes, sir.

How old were you at that time? I was in my nineteenth year.

Did you kill anybody, or help to kill anybody there? No, sir, I did not.

Tell this court and jury all you know about that? I was called on Thursday of the week they were killed. They were killed the next day.

Where were you? I was on my father's farm, finishing up my harvesting.

What occurred? There was a young man by the name of Clewes - his name has been mentioned here. I am not certain about its being Clewes, it may have been young Klingensmith, came down with a note from Isaac C. Haight, that I was wanted in Cedar City. I went to Cedar City, and he told me some men were going out to the Mountain Meadows and that I must accompany them, and I did so.

What did he tell you they were going there for? He didn't tell me. I understood they were going out to bring in the dead, slain by the

---

*See Confession where Lee describes the murderous actions and cool blooded manner with which McMurdy proceeded to butcher people for "The sake of the Kingdom." Page 248.

Indians.

Would you have gone if you had had any other understanding? No, not if I could have helped it.

Did you go there? Yes, sir.

What time did you get there? I should judge between twelve and one o'clock in the night. I got to Hamblin's ranch at that time.

Who did you see there? I saw John D. Lee and Klingensmith, and a man by the name of Western. I did not see those men until morning.

Was Hamblin at home? No, sir; he was not.

Did you learn that he had gone any where? Yes, sir.

Did you have any conversation with Lee about his having been in a fight with the emigrants? No, sir; I didn't have any conversation with him in relation to it.

Did you hear him say anything about it? Yes, sir.

What did you hear him say? In speaking to the Indians, he referred to having been in a fight with the emigrants.

What did he say? He said that the Indians and himself had made an attack on the emigrants and been repulsed.

What else did he say? Did he say anything about running any narrow risks? No, sir; he did not.

Did he show any place where his clothing was shot? There was a bullet hole which I noticed in his shirt, which the Indians told me was received down at the camp in that attack.

Anything about his hat? I didn't notice anything about his hat.

Did you notice anything about paint on him? After mature reflection, I don't think I did; I have the impression that I noticed something of that kind around his hair.

Did he say when the attack was made? He told me (those were a few Indians he was telling) there were three Indians there that had been wounded, and I was conversing with them after I got in, in the night.

Were you acquainted with the Indians - the Pah Vant Indians? Yes, sir; somewhat acquainted.

Were you acquainted with the Indians below? Yes, sir.

What was Lee's position at that time with the Indians? Well, he used to farm for them, help them to farm.

What was his influence over them? His influence was good.

Were any of the Pah Vent Indians down there? I didn't see any.

You are now at Hamblin's ranch, Friday morning. State what took place that day on the ground. I got on my horse in the morning.

Why did you do it? John D. Lee told me to, and Klingensmith told me to go with them down to the camp. The main Indian camp was down below the emigrant train, and I got on my horse and rode down with them in the morning. There were some men camped down on the meadows, down near the Indian camp. There were a few men there, and a few arrived while I was there. They were talking around. I didn't know what was said. A man went out near to the emigrant camp, and there was a white flag - a flag of truce on a stick sent down to the emigrant camp.

Who sent it down? It was John D. Lee had the management of the concern, if I understand it right - well, I will say that he did.

Follow that flag of truce, what occurred? It went down to the emigrant camp, and two men came out and met it and returned back again, and John D. Lee and another man went down to meet with the two that came out of the camp.

Did they talk? They spoke there a while, I could not hear what was said.

Did they appear to be in conversation? Yes, sir; and finally they returned, and some wagons were sent for to go down to the camp and take out some clothing and guns, and some few wounded.

Who directed those wagons to go? Well, sir, it was Klingensmith or John D. Lee, they seemed to be engineering the thing.

Did John D. Lee go down to the emigrant camp? Yes, sir.

How many people were loaded into those wagons, and who were those people? I can't tell you. Just as they went down I was where the men were. I had ridden down and tied my horse to a root on the hill; he got loose and I went for him, as the wagons went down to the emigrant camp, just as the wagons started away from the camp.

How many wagons started from the camp? *Two*.

What position did you occupy? I had not got back with my horse.

Were you on the hill - on a prominence? I was not over 800 yards from the people, where the people were passing along; the emigrants following the wagons.

How many wagons? Two.

Were these people in those wagons? Yes, sir.

Did you see Lee there? Yes, sir.

What position did he occupy when you saw him? Following between the wagons.

Which way were they going? North, towards Hamblin's ranch.

Did you see the emigrants following the wagons out of their camp?

Yes, sir.

Were they armed or unarmed? Not armed.

How far behind the wagons? The women and children along with the wagons, the men a little behind.

Do you mean along in the trail behind the wagons? Yes, sir.

And the men behind all? Yes, sir.

How many of them? I should judge about twenty-five or thirty men.

How many women? Probably there were not so many women as men.

You don't pretend to give the number? No, sir.

How far from the wagons at the head of the column were the people that were walking? The wagons got a good deal ahead.

Were the people marching in double or single file? I could not tell you. The women and children were following along promiscuously, and some of the men.

Were you where you could see the wagons plain and see Lee? Yes, sir.

Were you armed? I had a pistol.

Did you shoot it off at all? No, sir.

Did you have anything to do, in any way, shape or manner with that massacre? No, sir.

Will you tell the jury what you saw done at those wagons, and the order in which you saw it? When the wagons got up a piece ahead of the men I heard a gun fired.

Where was it? I think it was behind. I am not sure it was behind the wagons. I turned round to look, and at that the Indians and whites made a rush, and there was a general firing.

Where was that gun fired off? I think the gun fired was some distance behind the wagons.

What took place then? The people were killed.

Did you set any of them killed? Yes, sir.

Did you see John D. Lee kill any of them? I saw him fire off, and saw a woman fall as I looked down to the wagons.

What wagon was it? I am not certain. I think it was the lead wagon.

Tell what occurred? I saw his gun fired, heard the report of the gun and saw it fired, and saw a person fall, and the gun was held in his hand.

Did it kill her? I didn't go to see. The Indians rushed.

What did you see him do next? I looked down below to the men that were below, and then when I looked back again -

Was the massacre going on then down lower? Yes, sir, Indians and all along the line. I saw John D. Lee and some Indians pulling some persons out of the wagons.

What did you see him do to anybody else? I can't swear, but from the motions I should say he cut a man's throat.

Tell how he did it? I can't tell you, only I saw his arms moving around pulling men out of the wagons. They went to the left of him. I was not near enough to see, but he seemed to hold on to him.

Who pulled him out of the wagon? John D. Lee and an Indian.

Did you see John D. Lee make any motions? I did.

What were they? I thought at the time that he was cutting a man's throat, but then I was so far off.

You were in plain sight? Yes, sir.

Have you any doubt that to what he did there? No, sir.

What else did you see him do? I didn't see him do anything else at the time.

At any other time? No, sir.

Did you see him do anything else towards killing those people? No, sir.

How long a time did it occupy, that massacre? Not over five minutes - not over three minutes.

How many people were killed, do you know? No, sir, I don't.

Did you have any conversation with John D. Lee after that about it? I have had at different times, but I don't know that I can recollect the conversation that passed.

Did you ever have a conversation with him in which he told you the particulars of the first attack? He told me once something in relation to it, but it is so long ago. It was only that he attacked them; that the attack was made just as daylight was appearing in the morning. He said he went with the Indians to make the attack.

Did he give you any reasons for making the attack? No, sir.

How many cattle were there belonging to that train? That I cannot tell. There was quite a number - quite a lot of stock.

How many wagons did those emigrants have? Thirteen I counted.

Do you know what was done with the cattle? Taken to Iron Springs.

Who took them around there? I don't know who took them there - some men took them there.

Do you know of Lee having and using any of the wagons afterwards? I saw some of the wagons at Harmony several weeks afterwards.

What did you say became of the cattle? Taken to Iron Springs.

By whom? I understood by John D. Lee's orders.

Do you know what was done with the cattle? I saw some of the cattle afterwards on the Harmony range close to Lee's residence.

There under his charge? I suppose so. I am not definite about that.

Do you know whether any of them were killed by Lee? No, sir. Never saw him kill any of them; he told me once that he had given the Indians several beeves, and the Indians told me he had.

How long had you been acquainted with the Indians in Southern Utah at the time of the massacre? I had been somewhat acquainted with them for five years. I came to Iron County in the Spring of '51 and resided there until '57.

Were your relations with the Indians intimate? With some portions of them they were.

Do you know at that date, the time of this massacre, what the relations were existing between the people of Southern Utah and the Indians; whether they were hostile or whether they were friendly? They were friendly.

State whether they were in good subjection or not?

Bishop objected to the introduction of this testimony by this witness. First, because the proper foundation had not been laid to show that this witness knew how far the Indians had been placed under subjection. Second, because the prosecution had introduced written evidence, documents written by Brigham Young and John D. Lee, to show the exact condition of the Indians at that time, and before that. Third, they seek to prove that the Indians were friendly to the people of Utah; that is irrelevant and immaterial here, from this fact, that there is no question now before the court or jury as to whether the Indians of Utah were friendly with the citizens of Utah or not. It is not claimed by either the prosecution or the defense, that the Indians had made any attack at that time, or that they afterwards made any attack on the citizens of Utah. The only question on trial is as to the fate of certain people, nonresidents of Utah, and the fact as to whether this defendant was connected with their taking off or not.

After argument the question was withdrawn.

What was the influence of John D. Lee over the Indians of Southern Utah, those that were there present at, the massacre?

Objected to until it is shown that this party knows what that influence was. Question withdrawn.

Do you know the relations existing between John D. Lee and those

Indians? The relations between John D. Lee and those Indians, a small portion of Indians that roved around in there, were good; but the Indians further south, I don't know. The Indians of Santa Clara, and further on, I did not know.

Had you any information, before you went there, from John D. Lee's Indians, that he had control of, that he had promised to go there? I had information from Indians that went there.

How long was that before you went? It was on Monday evening, before the massacre on Friday.

What was that information? Objected to. Question withdrawn.

Cross examined - How old were you at the time of the massacre? I was in my twentieth year.

Where were you at the time Mr. Haight ordered you to go the Mountain Meadows? I was at Cedar City.

What time in the day was that? It was some time in the afternoon of Thursday.

The day before the massacre? Yes, sir.

How many men went with you to Cedar City? Two went with me to Cedar City.

Who were they? Klingensmith's son, and I can't recollect who the other was, came down to tell me I was wanted there. A man by the name of Charles Hopkins, and Charles Western, went with me to the Meadows. I went on horseback, and John Western went with the wagons. There were no others went at that time. There were others before, I understood.

How many did you find there when you got there, citizens of Cedar City and the surrounding country? I can't tell you the number.

How many, ten, fifteen or twenty? I should judge ten or fifteen.

Is it not a fact that there were more than twenty five or thirty men - white men - there, that you saw on the ground? There might have been.

Wasn't there that number? I could not tell you.

Why can't you tell me? Because I didn't count them. I was not there long enough to ascertain the number of men that were there.

Where did you go that night when you went on the ground? I went to Hamblin's ranch. Got there about twelve or one o'clock - not far from midnight - and lay down there till morning.

What time did you get to the Meadows next morning? It was some time in the forepart of the day.

Did you go to the camp where the citizens were located? Yes, sir.

About how many men did you find there? There were some in two places. I found some eight or ten at the place I went.

Did you go to the other place? I didn't go there.

Then how do you know men were there? I saw them.

How far off? Some were in sight.

Were they within half a mile of you? Yes, sir.

Were there any Indians on the Meadows after you got there? Yes, sir.

Where were the Indians with reference to the white men? The Indians camped some distance from the whites.

Were the Indians out of their camp and up at that of the whites? Several came up while I was there.

Then after they came up to see you they staid up there around where the white men were? Yes, sir.

What men were at the camp where you stopped? Well, sir, I didn't stop at the camp. I stayed there a few minutes and talked to Mr. Bateman.

Who did you see there? Mr. Bateman, Charles Hopkins and Klingensmith, where I was talking.

Where is Bateman? Dead.

Where is Hopkins? I understand he is dead.

Do you refer to the same Klingensmith that was a witness at the last trial? He was the man that was Bishop at Cedar City.

Where is Western? I can't tell you. I don't know whether he is dead or alive.

Did you see Isaac C. Haight? Not when I first went to the camp.

You saw him around at the Meadows? Yes, sir, I saw him at the Meadows.

Did you see a man by the name of Stewart? I don't recollect.

Did you see Higbee? Yes sir.

Wilden? I don't recollect.

Did you see old man Young? Yes, sir.

How many others did you see? I can't tell you.

You stayed there a few minutes and then went to get your horse; where was it you heard the conversation between John D. Lee and the Indians? It was at the camp at Hamblin's ranch.

Give that entire conversation that passed between John D. Lee and the Indians? I can't.

Start in and give from the first to the last of it as well as you can? I don't know as I can, sir.

What language did John D. Lee talk in to the Indians? He had an Indian boy as interpreter.

Who was that Indian interpreter? It was the Indian boy called Alma, I think, that he would talk with and then have the Indian interpret it to the Indians.

Then he talked English and the boy interpreted to the Indians? I suppose so.

You understood both languages. Do you remember whether the Indian interpreted and told the Indian what Lee said, or not? I didn't hear him tell the boy anything about the attack.

Didn't you testify that you had a talk with Lee, and that you heard him talk with the Indians, and say that he had attacked the emigrants? No, sir, I said the Indians told me so. Yes, sir; I did. Lee was talking when I went to the camp, and he did say so.

Tell me whether he talked English or Indian? He talked English to me and told me so.

Give me that conversation? He told me they attacked the camp on Monday night, and been repulsed.

What else? I can't be expected to remember all the conversation twenty years ago.

I want all that you do know. Do you know any more about it? Can you recollect anything more that he said? Nothing that I recollect.

Did he give you any reason for attacking the emigrants? No, sir.

Did you find any fault with him for attacking them? Was anything said about whether it was right or wrong? No, sir; I was a boy; I didn't consider it my business to talk to my superior officers in regard to such things.

How was that about Lee being your superior officer? I say I was a boy and didn't consider I had a right to talk to a man in his position in such matters.

Did he have any control over you? No.

What right had he to control your actions? *No answer.*

What position did he hold that gave him the right to direct your movements? I was sent there.

You have spoken of his being your superior officer. Tell me what position John D. Lee held that enabled him to control your actions? They called him Major Lee, and I was sent by Major Haight to go to the Mountain Meadows, to Major Lee.

That is the reason you considered that you had nothing to do with it?

Yes, sir.

Did Haight tell you what you were to do there? No, sir.

He simply told you to go to the Mountain Meadows? Yes, sir.

What do you mean by your evidence, when you were asked by Mr. Howard a question, and you answered that you would not have gone to the Meadows if you had known what was to be done? That is, not if I could help it.

State whether you were under any compulsion? I didn't consider it was safe for me to object.

Explain what you mean, that is what I want. Where was the danger - who was the danger to come from if you objected - from Haight or those around him - from the Indians, or from the emigrants? From the military officers.

Where? At Cedar City.

Was Haight one of those military officers? Yes, sir.

Who was the highest military officer in Cedar City at that time? I think it was Isaac C. Haight.

You thought it would not be safe for you to refuse, had you any reasons to fear danger - had any persons ever been injured for not obeying, or anything of that kind? I don't want to answer.

It is necessary to the safety of the man I am defending, and I therefore insist upon an answer. Had any person ever been injured for not obeying? *Yes, sir; they had.*

And from what you had seen before that, you thought it was your duty, under the circumstances, to obey counsel, or commands given you by Haight? Yes, sir.

Did Haight hold any office except that of Major in the military? He held the office of President of Cedar City.

An ecclesiastical office - President of that Stake of Zion, I believe you call it? Yes, sir.

Tell me how old Haight was then? I can't.

A man full grown, I presume? *Yes, sir.*

After you had caught your horse, how far were you from the wagons at the time you heard the first firing? Well, I was not over 300 yards, and perhaps not more than 250.

What was the nature of the ground? I was on higher ground; if you have ever been to the Mountain Meadows, it gradually descends down from the mountains to the meadows.

You were on the upland - above the wagons? Yes, sir.

Between you and those parties were there any trees or shrubbery, or anything of that kind? There were some to my left - kind of behind me.

You were at the left of the column? To the right of the column.

Then to your left, in between you and the wagons, there was nothing to obstruct your vision whatever? Not between me and the wagons.

At that time could you see down to the meadows to where the principal part of the emigrants were killed? I could see the head of the column of the emigrants. The lower part of the column was hid by this oak bush that is there.

Did you see any Indians there at the time you heard this first shot, or soon afterwards? Yes, sir, soon afterwards.

You stopped your horse at the time you heard the first shot and paid particular attention to what was going on? Yes, sir.

You continued there inactive until the whole thing was over? Yes, sir.

You say you saw John D. Lee there. Did you not see Samuel McMurdy, one of the drivers, there also? Yes, sir.

What did he do? He was holding his horses all the time. I did not see him let go of them.

Do you know whether he took part in the killing, or not? No, sir, I don't. I can't say.

What was Sam Knight doing? Sam Knight, when I looked around, was out on the ground holding his horses.

How long did they stand there and hold their horses? Not long. The killing did not last over five minutes.

What did they do when they let go of their horses? I saw the wagons going off. There was another white man there along with the Indians, but who he was I do not know. I can't tell. I never inquired to find out.

It was none of your business? No, sir.

And you just let the matter pass? But you did see John D. Lee killing emigrants, but you don't know who else killed any? *No, sir.*

You have not tried to find out since, have you? No, sir, I have not.

You have talked this over a great many times since, and heard it talked over, I suppose? No, sir, but very little.

You have had people ask you about the facts and circumstances frequently? Yes, sir, but it is something that I have avoided.

Is this the first time, since you arrived in Beaver City, that you have talked this thing all over, except when talking to the attorneys for prosecution? *No answer.*

From your silence I see you wish to avoid talking to me, too. You have never talked this over to any one? No, sir.

Until you came to Beaver? I might have done so. I can't recollect.

How many of the military did you see drawn up in line there on the field of the Mountain Meadows, about the time the wagons drove off? I can't tell you.

Quite a number, were there not? Yes, sir.

Who was commanding that military body drawn up in line there? I can't tell which it was, Klingensmith or John M. Higbee.

They were both there? Yes, sir, I think so.

Is it not the fact that these men were drawn up in military line - standing there with arms in their hands - within two hundred yards of the emigrant camp? I can't tell you.

Did you see them march in? I saw them marching, as I told you; when I got my horse and turned back I saw them marching.

I understood you to say that it was the emigrants that you saw marching after the wagons. Did you see the militia from Cedar City marching too, at the same time? There were men coming all along all together. I can't tell you whether they were militia or emigrants. All were marching along together.

About what time did the emigrants come out of the camp? It was some time in the afternoon, I think.

How long had you been there at the Mountain Meadows, before the massacre took place? Well, I went from Hamblin's ranch in the morning; I hadn't been there a great while.

JOHNSON - Where were you born? I was born in the State of Ohio.

How old were you when you arrived in Utah? I was some twelve years of age.

Came I suppose with your parents, to Utah Territory? Yes, sir.

Resided In Utah ever since? Yes, sir.

Reside now at Johnson's Fort, the same place you did at that time? No, sir.

Where do you live now? Shall I answer that question? Yes, sir, I live at Kanab.

How long have you lived there? About four months.

Where had you been living before that, since you lived at Fort Johnson? After the massacre how long did you live at Fort Johnson? I moved into the Rio Virgin in the fall of '58.

How long did you remain there? Well, I can count up in a minute - I lived there ten or twelve years.

Then where did you move to? I moved to the Sevier. And from there to Kanab, where you live now? Yes, sir.

You say you saw a lot of the wagons at Harmony afterward? I will not swear to but one.

Did you ever see any of the wagons at any other place - did you not see some of them at Cedar City? Yes, sir.

Where were they in Cedar City? They were at Klingensmith's.

How many did you see? Two.

What position did Klingensmith occupy at that time? He was Bishop of Cedar City Ward.

You spoke of seeing some cattle on the Harmony range. Did you ever see any of those cattle on any other range? They were running about Harmony and Kanab.

Who had possession or control of them? I can't tell you.

Do you know how they were branded after that? No, sir.

How did you recognize them? I recognized them by the brand that was on them of "S."

Did you notice that they were branded with a "B" the first time you saw them? Yes, and they were a different kind of stock; they were Texas cattle, a good many of them Texas cattle with long broad horns. There were none in the country that I ever saw until I saw those.

Go on again and tell us just exactly what you saw John D. Lee do; tell me all that you saw him do. I want you to make it just as full and bad as you can. I have told you what I saw.

Tell it to me again. I told you that I saw him fire a gun, and saw a person fall.

Go on and give it all just as you saw it; the whole thing. And then after that I saw him and the Indians pulling people out of the wagons.

What else? That is what I told you before.

I cannot help that, I am now asking you to tell what you know. That is what I did see.

Is that all you saw? Yes, sir.

You know the parties had their throats cut, I suppose? No, sir.

You went down and looked at the bodies afterwards? No, sir, I did not; I did not want to.

Then it is only a supposition, that the parties' throats were cut? That is all.

Did you ever go back to see if those persons were dead or not? No, sir, I did not; I saw them lying there after the wagons had driven away.

Do you know whether they were dead or not, of your own knowledge? No, sir, I do not. I saw persons lying on the ground dead, back below where the troops were.

How far from you? I went to them.

Then you did go back? Were they men that Lee killed, or were they men, killed by Klingensmith's men, where he and Higbee were? They were down where Klingensmith and Higbee were.

Then you did go down to that place? Yes, sir; John D. Lee sent me down to the wagons, that were down below, to keep the Indians from taking the things out of the wagons.

How did he get you there? He told me to go, and I went.

Did you ride down to him after this killing was over? I went over to where Klingensmith was and Lee came down; he sent me down there to the wagons.

What did he say when he told you to go back? He told me that he wanted me to go down to the wagons of the emigrants and keep the Indians from taking the things out.

How long did you stay there? I stayed there till John D. Lee and Isaac C. Haight came down.

Are you certain that Lee came back? Yes, sir.

Don't you know as a matter of fact that Lee went on to Hamblin's ranch? I stayed there at the wagons until after he came back from Hamblin's ranch.

How long did you stay there? I can't tell you.

Did you sleep there in the field that night with White, Klingensmith and others? I think likely I did. I stayed there until John D. Lee and Isaac C. Haight came down.

Don't you know you stayed there that night, and until the wagons were moved away? I think I did.

Don't you know that you did? Yes, sir, I do.

Who took those wagons away - who ordered the hitching up of the oxen and taking away of the wagons? I don't know.

Was it Klingensmith? No, sir; he did not.

Did John D. Lee? No, sir. I don't know.

Didn't you help drive the stock? I went with them around to the Iron Springs.

Who helped take the wagons down there - can't you give me the names of a few of them? *Witness refused to answer.*

How many whites did you see on the Mountain Meadows, at the time of the massacre? I did not count them.

About how many? There was a considerable number, as many as forty or fifty.

How far were they from where you kept watch at the wagons? About half a mile.

Half a mile from the emigrants' wagons? Yes, sir; about that far.

Who kept watch with you that night at the emigrant camp, to keep the Indians from stealing? *I don't want to bring in new names.*

I see you do not - except Lee's - how is that? I have mentioned a good many names.

You have been sworn to tell the truth, the whole truth, and nothing but the truth; and I want you to tell me the names of those men. Well, a man named Ure was with me.

What was his fall name? John Ure.

How old was he? I can't tell.

Was he a man grown? Yes, sir.

Is he living or dead? He is alive.

How long was it after you went there to keep the Indians from stealing that these other parties came to you? I don't recollect of any coming until John D. Lee and Isaac C. Haight came.

Next day? Yes, sir.

Did you succeed in keeping the Indians from stealing there? They had taken a good deal before I went there. After I went they didn't.

You had considerable control over the Indians when you got there. They knew you, and you could talk their language, and when you told them to do anything they would do it? Some of them would, and some wouldn't.

They all agreed to quit stealing, didn't they? No, sir.

How did you keep them from stealing, then? I didn't.

What did they steal after you got there? I can't tell you.

Did they steal anything - you know whether they did or not? The Indians were at the wagons when I arrived and had taken out a good deal of stuff.

What did they do after you arrived? They took off what they wanted.

Did they stop stealing when you told them to? Not altogether.

What did they take away? Bedding and blankets.

Isn't it a fact that they took just what they wanted, and that you did not stop them from stealing? I did stop some of them.

Well, didn't they carry off all they wanted? They didn't carry it all away, but they did a good part of it.

How many did you keep from stealing? Five or six.

How many Indians were there that you could not stop; how many were there around the wagons? There was quite a lot that went away with their goods.

Fifty, seventy five, or one hundred? Not that many.

How many did you see that day altogether? There was a great number - over a hundred - there was a great number of them took horses and started off.

Where did they get the horses? From around that section of country.

Emigrants' horses, I suppose? Yes, sir.

About how many horses did the emigrants have there? I can't tell you.

Didn't you see the herd? I saw the Indians with horses that they said they got there, but I did not see the herd of stock until it was started to the Iron Springs. I only came there the night before.

Did you do anything toward burying the dead after the massacre? No, sir.

Then you did not help do that? No, sir.

Were you there at the time it was being done? I saw men there working at it from where I was at the camp. They commenced burying the dead right off.

The same evening of the massacre? Well, sir, I can't tell you.

You cannot tell whether it was the same night or the next morning? I cannot.

What number of men went from there to the Iron Springs with you? There were some ten or twelve went along. I went on afterward. I had my horse. I rode my horse.

Give me the names of as many as you can that went with you from the Meadows to the Iron Springs the day afterward. I can't. I don't know as I can give the names.

If you say you cannot give the names, I will not press it. Well, I say I cannot.

You say you cannot recollect any of the names of those who helped drive the stock? No, sir, I can't.

Who had charge of property as it was driven to the springs? That I cannot tell.

What was Klingensmith doing there? I don't know. I don't recollect seeing him along.

When did you last see Higbee there on the field? Did you see him after the massacre? Yes, sir.

Did you see him the day after the massacre? I can't tell whether I did or not.

Were you present at any council that was held there on the field previous to the massacre, and hear any agreement as to the killing of the emigrants or anything of that sort? No, sir, I didn't.

You did not hear that anybody was to be killed until you heard the shooting? Yes, sir.

When? When I started after my horse I heard that the people were to be killed.

Who told you? John D. Lee told me.

I thought you said he had left you? He talked of it before he went to the camp.

Just before that, then? Yes, sir.

I wish to get at all this, because I want you to tell everything that John D. Lee did. Tell me what he said to you about it? He was talking to the men about getting the men out of their fortification.

Was this after the flag of truce had been sent? No, sir, before that.

Who was Lee talking to? Klingensmith, Higbee and others.

Who were the others? I can't tell you.

How many others? There was quite a lot of men.

Thirty or forty? I should judge there were.

Did you hear Higbee say anything? Higbee may have talked.

Did any person make any objection to the killing of the emigrants? It is a thing, sir, that I don't like to answer.

I wish you to answer my question. Did any man or men, person or persons, there on the ground, make an objection to the killing of all the emigrants? Yes, sir, *a good many objected.* But they didn't dare to say anything.

How do you know they objected? They dare not speak about it to those men.

Did they speak up at the Council and make objections? I was not at the Council.

Did any one of that thirty or forty men raise a voice against the killing of the emigrants, at the Council, on the field, or in the presence of Lee, Higbee or Klingensmith, or any one else? No, sir, they did not.

What did John D. Lee say about it in the presence of Haight and

Higbee? He said we must get them out of there.

Who was he talking to then? Higbee and the others.

Were they talking the matter over? Yes, sir.

Tell me what was said? I can't recollect.

Do you recollect what Haight said? Haight was not there.

Then how was it that Lee was talking to Haight and Higbee if Haight was not there? It was Higbee and Klingensmith he was talking to.

What was it that Klingensmith said about killing the emigrants? I can't tell.

Then you cannot recollect what any one said or did except John D. Lee? No, because John D. Lee was the most conspicuous man in the whole thing.

Klingensmith, the Bishop of the Church at Cedar City, Haight and Higbee, as Majors in the militia, all stood back and gave John D. Lee full control, did they? He had control of everything on the field. He acted like a man that had control.

Did he not have control? I can't say.

Did you not think at the time that John D. Lee had full control of everything and of every person there? He acted like it.

What do you believe about it? *No answer.*

Haight ordered you to go there? Yes, and when I got there I went to Lee; that was the instruction.

And you stayed by him and obeyed all of his orders? No, sir, he wanted me to talk to the Indians in a way I didn't want to.

Tell me how he wanted you to talk to the Indians? He wanted me to tell them that they would get the emigrants out some way, so they could get their guns and horses.

You refused to tell the Indians that, did you? Well, I talked to them some.

Did you tell them that or not? I don't wish to answer that.

COURT - You need not tell anything to incriminate yourself.

BISHOP - Can you tell me anything besides that, that you heard John D. Lee say? No, sir, I cannot. That is all I recollect.

What time of day was that, when Lee said, "We must get them out some way? It was in the fore-part of the day.

Who was in hearing distance when Lee said that? I decline to answer.

HOWARD - You don't decline because it would incriminate you, do you? No, sir.

Then you cannot decline.

BISHOP - Tell me who was present, and heard that statement of Lee's? I can't tell - there was a lot of them there.

After you arrived at Iron Springs, did you and those with you talk the matter over and agree to keep it a secret? The matter was talked over at the camp, and again at the Springs, about keeping it a secret, but I can't tell what the agreement was that was come to.

Was the subject talked over as to whether it should be talked over afterwards or not? I don't recollect.

After that did you talk it over with those who were engaged in the affair with you, in which conversation you learned it was best to keep silent concerning the whole thing? It was talked of that way - that it was best to keep still.

What reasons were given, why it was best to keep still? I can't tell you.

Do you know what the reasons were, or do you decline to answer? Is it because you forget, or why can't you tell me? It was because they didn't want it to be known - those men who were in it; the leaders in it didn't want it to get out.

I asked you whether you ever had any conversation with any one in regard to it? I can't tell you whether I had or not.

Of course such a thing as that men would talk about. That's what the matter now. It has been talked about and can't lie still.

Did you ever have a conversation with Haight about this massacre since it occurred? Not that I know of.

Did you ever have a conversation with Stewart? No, sir.

Did you ever have one with Higbee about keeping it still? Not that I know of.

Did you ever talk with Allen, Klingensmith or any other party that was there, about keeping it still? I tell you I don't recollect having a conversation about keeping it still. Such a thing was talked about, but I don't now recollect talking about it.

Did you hear either of those men talk about it, about keeping it secret? *No answer.*

Is it not a fact that after the property was all gathered up at the Meadows, and you were ready to start for Iron Springs, that speeches were made to the men present, by those in authority, in which speeches you were ordered to keep it a secret forever? There were a great many speeches made.

At the Meadows, before you left there, was it not told you in a speech then made to you, that it must be kept secret; that it would be best to keep silent? Were you not so advised by your leaders? Yes, sir.

Who gave that advice? Who ordered you to keep silent? Klingensmith and Haight gave the advice.

The cross examination was continued at great length, but the witness could not, or would not recollect anything except what be had been advised by his priestly rulers to swear to. Nephi Johnson is a fair sample of the willing tools who commit crimes for *Christ's sake*, and swear falsely for their *own sake*. I have given sufficient of his evidence to prove to the reader, that Nephi Johnson has not told the whole truth; he has only told what the Church leaders thought sufficient to convict Lee, and kept back every thing that would lead to the conviction of the other murdering wretches, who still adhere to the Mormon faith, and skulk in their hiding places, far from the haunts of law abiding citizens.

CHAPTER XXIII

TRIAL OF LEE CONCLUDED

JACOB HAMBLIN

Sworn for the prosecution.

HOWARD - Where did you live in August and September, 1867? My home was supposed to be at Clara, but I occupied the Mountain Meadows in the Summer with my stock.

What county was Mountain Meadows in at that time? It was considered in Iron County. It was before Washington County was organized.

It is in Washington County now? Yes; I believe it is.

Do you remember the time of this massacre? I was not at home; I left before it happened, and I got back seven or eight days after.

How long before it happened was it that you left home? I don't know; I met the company at Corn Creek, and camped with them there.

You were going north, to the city? Yes.

When you returned had the massacre taken place? Yes, sir; it was done before I got home - I heard of it before I got home.

When you got home, what did you find there on the ground? Well, there were the bodies of the company lying about there.

Were they dead or alive? I didn't see any live ones lying there.

How many dead ones did you see? I suppose over one hundred.

Did you count the skulls there? The next Spring, I took my man and we buried over one hundred and twenty skulls - skeletons; I don't remember exactly, something like one hundred and twenty. Two of us gathered up the bones.

Did you count the skulls? Yes, sir; we counted them.

Can you now remember how many there were? I think it was one hundred and twenty odd; I am satisfied it was over that, but I don't just remember the number.

After the massacre did you have any conversation with John D. Lee about it? I don't know as I did after I got home.

Did you see him before you got home on that trip? I did. I met him at Fillmore.

Was that after the massacre? Yes, sir; it was this side of Fillmore. I told him I heard a rumor of it among the Indians, and he told me about it.

State whether he had any boasts to make about it, or communications concerning it. If so what and how? I asked him how it came up, or something of that kind. He said that the emigrants passed through and threatened to make their outfit out of those outlying settlements, and that he could not keep the Indians back, and he had to go and lead the next attack, and he got a bullet hole through his hat and shirt, and then afterwards got more Indians and had to decoy them out.

Tell me the whole conversation? I will if you will let me. That was the conversation. I talked about it with him, and he justified himself in this way: That the Indians made him go out and go and lead the next attack; afterwards they called on the Clara Indians, and that he decoyed them out, and they massacred them.

Did he say where he decoyed them out? Decoyed them out of the emigrant camp.

Did he say why the massacre took place? Yes, I believe he gave reasons for it.

What were they? Well, that the attack had been made by the Indians, and that they could not keep them back, and it was supposed expedient. That there was an army right on our border. That they would lead to giving the people much bother and trouble, and that they would testify against them, and so on, and it was thought best to *use them up* - all that could tell tales, that is as near as I can remember.

Who did he say concluded that? I don't think he mentioned any names.

Did he tell you whether any other white men were with him or not at the time he led the attack? He said that there was no one with him.

Did he tell you how it happened that he got down there and was there alone? Yes; I told you. He went out to watch them and keep them from making their outfit from the outlying settlements, and the Indians could not be restrained.

How long did he say that attack was made before the massacre? It ran along three or four days, he told me.

Cross examined - In the conversation that you had with Lee, did he not state to you that after the attack had been made by the Indians upon the emigrants, that word had been sent to Cedar City for assistance to save the emigrants from the Indians? Yes, sir - said they sent word there. Who did he tell you sent word to Cedar City? He did - he sent word.

What did he tell you that word was that he sent to Cedar City? He sent word that the emigrants had been attacked - that the Indians were very mad, and he didn't know how to keep them down.

Give, as near as you can, the conversation that you had with Mr. Lee at the time you refer to? I believe I have.

Didn't he tell you that Haight or Higbee sent back word that the emigrants must be destroyed, because of the fact that Stewart had killed Aiden at the Springs? Didn't he mention something of that kind to you in that same conversation? I don't remember as he did. He spoke of some man being shot at Little Pinto in the course of the evening. It was after the Indians had attacked, if I remember right, that some men left the camp and undertook to go to Cedar City, and were killed on the way - one or two I think, and one or two came back.

Go on and tell all that he told you about it, about the killing of that man at Pinto - how it was done, and all about it. I don't know that I can. I remember that he said that there was one killed there that went out to see if they could get help from Cedar City. Two or three went, and one was killed and one or two came back in the night. I don't know but that they got back to camp.

Did he tell you what word was sent back to him from Cedar City after that time? Yes; he told me something about the message that came there.

Tell me what was said about it? One message came to not disturb the emigrants, and after the message went that they had been attacked, I think he said that there was one that they be all killed or used up.

Go on and tell what he said was in that last message - he was explaining it to you? I am satisfied the message was - it commenced that they should be used up, or something like that.

Did he tell you who that message was from? I don't think he did.

Did he tell you where it was from, whether from Cedar City or elsewhere? No, he used the language that he got word.

Redirect.

Do you believe what he said, that he got a message to use up those emigrants, from any authority? I don't know that I do.

Don't you know that he lied about it? No answer.

Don't you think he did? No answer.

He was telling you this in justification after the massacre? Yes, he told me that. I asked what called for such an act, and he told what the reason was.

He gave you that reply in his justification? He said he got word to use them up, that this army was on the borders.

He got word that being commenced, that on account of the army being on the borders, that he had better finish it? Yes.

Did you understand that that came from Higbee or Haight - that word? I don't think he said.

Do you know the relations existing between Higbee, Haight and Lee, so as to know from whom it came? I would expect it would come from Isaac C. Haight, if any word was sent from Cedar City; if it was north, it would be from Parowan, but I don't think he told me where it was from.

Klingensmith was in a position, I suppose, to send such word, if any was sent? Klingensmith was presiding Bishop. If it was orders in a military capacity it would be somebody else.

If it was in a military capacity, who would it have been from? The way I understand it, it would be Dame.

If he told the truth, and authority came to him from a superior military officer - and if it came from an ecclesiastical, who would it have been from? It would have been from Klingensmith.

JACOB HAMBLIN

Re-called.

HOWARD - I am not in the habit, your Honor, of recalling a witness this way, but I was not fully posted in regard to an the facts that Mr. Hamblin would testify to. I have found he knows some additional facts, and I will ask leave to examine him further

How far above this place, Beaver, was it that you had a conversation with John D. Lee? It was about some springs, this side of Fillmore, probably seven or eight miles.

How far is Fillmore from here? About sixty miles.

How far is Cedar City from here? Supposed to be fifty-five miles - fifty-three to fifty-five miles.

Is there any other place called Cedar City, except Cedar City? No, sir,' I don't know any. It is called Cedar or Cedar City.

How far is it from Cedar City to Parowan? Eighteen miles, I used to suppose it was. I have heard it called that.

How far is it from Parowan to Harmony? About thirty-five miles, it is supposed to be.

Is Harmony on the road, or is it off of the road from Cedar City to the Meadows? It is twelve miles south of the road.

Where do you leave the road going from Parowan to the Meadows, to go to Harmony? We leave it two and a half miles below Cedar City.

Then it is off to the left as you are going? Yes, sir.

Where Is Pinto? It would be within seven miles of the north end of the Meadows, where my ranch was.

What was the condition of the Meadows at that time, with regard to being a good stopping place for travelers? At that time it had a very luxuriant growth of grass all over the valley, and springs at each end. It was considered a good stopping place for companies, and was occupied by myself and two or three others at the north end. We had then formed a settlement called the Clara.

In this conversation that you had with Mr. Lee, did he say anything to you about the manner in which, or by whom, the men had been drawn into that massacre? If he did, will you state all he said, in your own way? It was a long while ago, but I recollect him telling we that there were white men there, and that they didn't know what they were going for until they got there, and some would not act and some would.

What do you know about the disposition of the property of those emigrants? There was none on the Meadows when I got there, that I saw. I saw two or three young men driving two or three hundred head of cattle, going to the Iron Springs. Afterwards I saw them on the Harmony range - that drove of Texas cattle.

Whose range was the Harmony range? It belonged to the Harmony settlement - the citizens of Harmony.

Do you know of Mr. Lee using any of those cattle, butchering or using any of them? He had charge of them.

BISHOP - To save time and trouble, we will admit the *corpus delicti*. Of course it is understood that counsel cannot admit anything against his client in a criminal case. But there will be no question raised about it. It is an undisputed fact that something like one hundred and twenty people were killed about that time and at that place. And that the number of people charged in the indictment were killed there will be no question. That they were killed at that place there will be no question. We will never argue before any court that there has not been a killing as charged in the indictment, except that we will always argue that the defendant did not do it.

Calling your attention back to that conversation, I will ask you to tell the court and jury, in your own way, what Mr. Lee told you in regard to his personal participation in that killing, if he told you anything? Well, I believe I told it here yesterday - that he spoke of white men being engaged in it, and that he made an attack at daylight; that he could not keep the Indians back. They were so mad because one of their men got killed, and another wounded, that he led the attack and got a bullet through his hat and another through his shirt. The talk was something like this: They went out there to watch the emigrants and see that they should not get their outfit from the outlying settlements; that the Indians made the attack at daylight, and one of them got killed and another wounded, and that raised their temper to such a pitch that they went for him and compelled him to lead the attack, which he did once or twice - once anyway - and got the bullet through his hat and one through his shirt. The, emigrants were so strongly entrenched they could do nothing with them. And afterwards they were under the necessity of decoying them out with a flag of trace. And they came along in the Meadows to where the Indians were lying in ambush, and they rose up and massacred them. The emigrants were unarmed.

Tell what else he told you? Well, he spoke of many little incidents.

Mention any of those incidents? There were two young ladies brought out.

Whom by? By an Indian Chief at Cedar City, and he asked him what he should do with them, and the Indian killed one and he killed the other.

Tell the story as he told you. That is about it.

Where were those young girls brought from - did he say? From a thicket of oak brush, where they were concealed. It was an Indian Chief from Cedar City.

Tell just what he said about that. The Indian killed one and he cut the other one's throat, is what he said.

Who cut the other's throat? Mr. Lee.

Tell me what Mr. Lee said; state the circumstances of that killing, what conversation passed between that Indian Chief and Lee, and the conversation between the woman and himself? I don't know that I could.

Tell all you can remember about it; you say the Chief brought him the girls. I think I have told it about all.

Go over it again; tell us all the details of the conversation of the killing. Well, he said they were all killed - all, as he supposed; that the Chief of Cedar City then brought out the young ladies.

What did he say the Chief said to him? Asked what he should do with them.

What else did the Chief say? He said they *didn't ought* to be killed.

Did the Chief say to Lee why they should not be killed? Well, he said they were pretty and he wanted to save them.

What did he tell you that he said to the Chief? According to the orders that he had that they were too old and too big to let live.

Then what did he say took place - what did he say he told the Chief to do? The Chief shot one of them.

Did he say he told the Chief to shoot her? He said he told him to.

What did he say the girl did when he told the Chief to shoot her? I don't know.

Did she cover her face? No; he didn't say she covered her face.

Did he say she pulled her bonnet down over her face? He didn't tell me so.

Who did he say were by when that shooting took place? Indians standing round - a good many.

After the Chief shot that one did he tell you what the other one said or did to him, Lee? I don't think Mr. Lee did tell me.

Did he tell you himself who killed the other one? I told you that he said it was a Cedar City Chief that killed one.

Who killed the other? He did it, he said.

How? He threw her down and cut her throat.

Did he tell you what she said to him? No.

Who did tell you that? The Indians told me a good many things.

Didn't Mr. Lee tell you that she told him to spare her life, and she would love him as long as she lived? Lee didn't tell me that.

Did you ascertain in that conversation, or subsequently, where it was that they were killed? When I got home I asked my Indian boy, and he went out to where this took place, and he saw two young ladies lying there with their throats cut.

How old was he? Sixteen or seventeen.

What was the condition of those bodies? They were rather in a putrid state; their throats were cut; I didn't look further than that.

What were their ages? Looked about fourteen or fifteen. At what point were their bodies from the others? Southeast direction, towards some thickets of oak. How far off? About fifty yards.

Were those bodies up a little ravine, a little way? Yes, on a rise of ground.

What were their ages, about? Thirteen to fifteen, I would suppose.

Did you learn from the children, or from any other source, their names? Well, I suppose I did.

What name? There was a little girl at my house, I found with my family that was in that company; she said their names were Dunlap; she claimed to be their sister.

How old was she? Eight years old, she said.

Did you go up there and find those bodies yourself, with the assistance of the Indian boy? I walked over the ground, looked at it all pretty much and saw these two bodies.

He told you where those two bodies were to be found, did he? Yes, sir. The others had been buried slightly, but those two hadn't been; there was quite a number scattering around there.

What became of the children of those emigrants? How many children were brought there? Two to my house, and several in Cedar City. I was acting subagent for Forney. I gathered the children up for him; seventeen in number, all I could learn of.

Whom did you deliver them to? Forney, Superintendent of Indian Affairs for Utah.

Were there any of the wagons or other property burned there on the ground? I never saw any sign of burning, and never heard of any being burned.

Cross examined - BISHOP: What day in September was it that you had this conversation with John D. Lee, about seven or eight miles this side of Fillmore? I don't recollect the date, I left the city about the 14th, and came directly there.

Who was present at that conversation? A man by the name of Bishop.

That was not me? No; that man had two good eyes, and you have but one.

What Bishop was that, was he a Mormon Bishop? No, he was not a Mormon Bishop; he was a merchant. He had been hauling goods from California, and dealing here some in these settlements.

Can you give me his other name? No, sir; I never heard it.

Was it Jesse Bishop? I don't know his other name.

Lee told you and this man Bishop all about it - got you two together and told you? I don't think Bishop heard the conversation, or much of it.

Did Bishop hear any of it? I don't know that he did, or that he didn't.

Then why did you say that he told you and this man Bishop? I said he was there.

You heard the conversation? Yes, I heard it; but I don't know as any other man heard it.

There was a man present by the name of Bishop? He was in the same camp.

Where were you at the time this conversation took place? I was five or six miles this side of Fillmore, at the Springs.

What time of day was it? It was afternoon sometime.

Which way was John D. Lee traveling at the time you saw him? Going north, to the city.

You were going South? Yes, sir.

Tell me what he said about the orders that he had. You have said that he told the Chief to kill the little girl, and that he killed the other, because his orders were that they were all to be used up. He said he had orders to use up all that company that could tell tales.

Where did he get these orders from? Did he tell you that? I told you no, that I don't remember that he did.

Do you recollect that he didn't? If he did I don't recollect it.

I want to get as full a statement of facts as possible. I want you to tell me everything that you think he said, or, that he did say. When did he tell you that he got those orders from Cedar City? It was my impression that he got them from Cedar City, but I could not say what the man said about it, but I had that idea.

Who else did he tell you was on the ground siding in this killing? The names I don't know as he mentioned. I think he mentioned Bishop Klingensmith being there.

Who else? He mentioned Higbee being there.

Who else did he mention? He mentioned my brother being there, bringing some Indians there. He sent him word to bring the Indians up there. Sent him word of this affair taking place, and for him to go and get the Indians, and bring up the Clara Indians.

Your brother, then, brought the Indians to the Meadows, and then left there? Yes, he told me so.

Now, how was it about the Indians making an attack about daylight? Were they repulsed? Yes.

One killed and another wounded? Yes, sir.

That enraged the Indians, and so Lee led the next attack? Yes, sir.

Who do you mean were so enraged - the Indians? Yes, the Indians. He claimed the idea that he had to do it to save his own life. They were very mad, and wanted him to help use up that company.

Did he not tell you in that same conversation that he tried to appease the Indians and keep them from attacking the train? I don't remember just the words, but he said he could not keep them from attacking them just at daylight.

Didn't he tell you that he tried to keep them off? I don't think so. I think he said he could not keep them off.

Did he say anything about the Indians calling him any names because he would not go? He went off towards the Clara and cried, and they called him crier - yah gauts.

Why did they call him this? Because he cried.

That was before he led the attack? I don't know.

Are you positive that he told you that he cut that woman's throat? Yes, I am positive of that, or I would not have told it.

How long is it since you have told anybody that John D. Lee had told you that? It has been about three seconds.

Where have you lived since the Mountain Meadows Massacre? My family has been at the Clara the most of the time; the last six years have been at Kanab.

You have lived in Utah all that time? My home has been in Utah.

That has been your home? My home has been in Utah.

Didn't Lee tell you more than you have told? Didn't he tell you about a Council that was held on the field before the massacre? He told me. We had a good deal of conversation about it.

Tell me if he did not inform you that a Council was held on the field, on Mountain Meadows, by the people from Cedar City, before the massacre, and that he opposed the killing of the emigrants until he found that he could do no good? After we had talked some time I asked the necessity of such a thing, or why it was, and he told me that he had orders to do so.

Did he not tell you that there was a Council held there at the Meadows, and that it was then decided that they should be killed? No, I never heard that there was a Council held there to make any decision, or to decide anything but the subject or counseling how to decoy them out.

Who counseled with them? There was Klingensmith, the Bishop of Cedar City.

Who else counseled with him? I think he said John M. Higbee. I am satisfied it was.

Did he tell you how long before the massacre it was that they talked this over? I don't think that he did.

You were a subagent and Indian interpreter at that time, were you not? Right away after that Forney appointed me as subagent. At that time I was no agent, nor in any particular office, unless a missionary in the south country to establish some settlements on the Clara.

What reason did Lee give you in that conversation for the killing of the emigrants? He must have given you some reason why it was necessary to commit such a deed? I asked what called for it, why they did it. He said that attack at daylight would have thrown censure upon this people.

On what people? The people that were living here.

Do you mean the whites that were living here at the time? Yes, sir.

Go on and tell all he said. I want you to make it as bad as you can - tell all that you said, all that he said? I would not undertake that.

Tell all that you can recollect? I have, the substance of it? There must have been a good deal said about the reasons for doing this thing? The cause that he always gave to me was that which I told you. That after they came through there and behaved very rough, and said that they helped kill old Joe Smith, and were going to be ready there at the Meadows when their teams got recruited, and when Johnston commenced on the north end, they would on the south end, and he was asked by authority - Haight or Dame - to go and watch those emigrants and see that they didn't molest those weak settlements. When I asked him what it was for - that in doing so, when they got there the Indians made this attack at daylight.

The Indians then made the first attack? He said they made it voluntarily - they made the first attack.

You spoke of General Johnston's army marching towards Utah. Where was it? At Fort Bridger then.

Who was it understood that Johnston was understood to be marching against them? The understanding and feeling was that he was marching against the Mormons as a people, Church or nation, and was going to try to burst up the whole concern. That was what we expected.

You expected, then, that Johnston with the army of the United States, was leading that army against this people? Yes, sir.

With the intention of exterminating them or compelling them to abandon their religion? Yes, sir, that was my belief - to do away with the Mormon religion.

How long before that had it been that this same feeling of fear or anxiety had been felt by this people, occasioned by Johnston's approach? I think it had been two or three months, it had come south at the time. I think it was the 24th of July when a celebration was held in one of the canyons, that word came that Johnston was on his way.

After that 24th of July, did that report have any effect on this people to cause them to organize as a military people? No, that was organized before that, as far as I knew and was acquainted with the counsel.

From that time on up to the time of the Mountain Meadows Massacre, tell me if the people were organized as a militia, and enrolled as such? The instructions we had from George A. Smith, who was sent as representing President Young's mind, was to save everything like breadstuff, and use it when we wanted it.

Did the people ever meet and drill, have exercises and musters, so as to make them understand the use of arms, and make them familiar with military tactics? Yes, sir, there used to be drills, sometimes, those days.

Was it not a general occurrence for them to meet and drill? Yes, they drilled at Fillmore and Cedar - I don't know about Harmony - using as much effort as possible to perfect themselves in military tactics. They were always doing that; they did that in Illinois.

Did you not understand that all the men between eighteen and sixty years of age were enrolled in the militia? Yes, I understood it so.

Who was the highest military officer in this division? William H. Dame was first in command in the southern country. He was Colonel of the Iron Militia, as I understood it. I was out a good deal.

Who was the highest military officer at Cedar City? Well, that I could not testify to, but I think it was Isaac C. Haight, but I would not testify to it, because I don't know.

State if you know whether John M. Higbee belonged to the militia or not? Well, he belonged to the militia, but whether as private or officer, I don't know.

How many men did John D. Lee tell you had gone from Cedar City to the Mountain Meadows, and that were present at the time of the Massacre? Well, if he told me I have forgotten.

Did you ever have a conversation with him, or with any other person, as to how many or about how many were there? No, I don't know that I had. I heard there was something like fifty in all from Cedar City and from below there, but that is nothing but an idea - not founded on fact - as reports.

You spoke about Lee telling you that there was a necessity for killing those young girls, because they were older than those that his orders permitted him to save. State now, if he did not tell you in that conversation some reason for the killing of the grown people. The reason was what I told you.

Did he not say that if they were permitted to go they would tell the tale in California, about what had been done there by the Mormons? His talk was and his excuses were that it would be a bad thing for the people here in Utah, if it was known, and got out in such a troublous time. It would bring much trouble on the Mormons as a people.

Was not that trouble to come from their notifying the people of California of what had been done? Well, yes. When I interrogated him about that he said - I think he said - it would have a tendency to bring trouble from California.

Did he not tell you that that was the understanding of the people, that if they were permitted to go, that it would call an army from the south, and that was the reason these instructions were sent as they were? He didn't say anything about the people.

Did he not tell you why the instructions came to him as they did? He did not tell who it came from, he said he did it by authority.

Did he not tell you that he did it by authority and the reason that authority gave was that these parties, if permitted to go, would raise a war cloud in California? I don't know as he did. He said it would lead to bringing an army down upon us; that is what he told me.

Did he tell you anything further? I think I have told you all that was important that John D. Lee said.

Did not John D. Lee tell you in that same conversation, that after the Indians made the attack the first time, that one or more men started from the emigrant camp for Cedar City, and met some men going to the emigrant camp from Cedar City; that they met at the springs, and that then Young Aiden was killed by William C. Stewart? He gave me an account of it.

Tell me what he said about it? I can't do that.

Then give the substance of it. It would be from memory, and there might be an error in it. He told me - he spoke of three men starting back to go to Cedar City to get assistance and to give information of what was going on after the first Indian attack. During that time there were three men went out in the night, and one was killed at Little Pinto, four miles this side of the Meadows. I don't know who he said killed them. I don't know as he said that he knew. I think one was killed there, and the other got back to their camp. They wounded one in the night, and the thought was this would lead to trouble if they were permitted to go, on account of this man being wounded and telling how it was done, and what had happened in the past, was about his language; what had happened would lead to bringing trouble, perhaps an army on the southern people, and especially that action at the springs, in the killing that man.

Did Lee tell you who was at the springs at that time? No, if he did, I don't remember.

Did he say this to you - that it was understood by the authorities that one man was wounded at the springs, and one man killed by Stewart, and if those people were permitted to go to California they would notify the people of California that the whites had made an attack in conjunction with the -- Indians; that they would lead an army from the south and west, and that for safety they considered it necessary as a war measure to kill those people? I think he told you that, Mr. Bishop. I told you that when I asked him, he told me that that would lead to bringing an army here. I am satisfied that is what he said. But as to the particulars of the killing at Little Pinto I could not say, only that a man was killed there and one wounded, and they had got back; that the attack at daylight was the cause of the emigrants being killed.

Mr. Hamblin, have you now detailed to the jury all of the conversation that you had with John D. Lee, at the time that you met him seven or eight miles this side of Fillmore? I think I have, that I recollect distinctly enough to mention here. I may think of something else.

You say you saw some of the cattle on the Harmony range. How many people used that range for their cattle? I think something like twenty families.

Do you know who took charge of the stock immediately after the massacre? I met two young men driving it - between two and three hundred head.

Who were they? They lived at Cedar City. I did not know them. They said they were going to drive them to the Iron Springs, and then afterwards I learned that John D. Lee took them.

Who were those young men? I do not know. I was not acquainted with them. I was not much acquainted at Cedar City. They lived there, they said.

How far did you live from Cedar City at that time? My family was then twenty-eight miles from Cedar City, at the Meadows.

Did you spend any time at Cedar City soon afterwards? When I came through I stopped about ten minutes. I was on an express.

Where were you carrying the express? I was going to overtake another company. Colonel Dame was afraid they would jump into them, and wanted me to go and see to it.

Afraid who would jump into them? The Indians.

Where did you get that express? From him.

Where at? At Wild Cat Canyon, eight or ten miles north of here.

That was when you were coming from Salt Lake? That was.

After you had left John D. Lee? Yes, sir.

Who were you carrying that express to? To the Indians - if there were any. He said he had learned they were following up this company.

What company? The company that was following up the company that was massacred. They were stopped here a while, and the Indians wounded one, or killed one, or something.

Have you ever given this conversation that you had with Lee, to any one, to the public generally? I do not ask if you have stated it to the counsel in the case, but to others? I have no recollection of it.

Have you ever given it to any court or jury, or given a statement of it? No, sir, not at all - not until now.

Have you ever given a report of it to any of your superiors in the Church, or officers over you? *Well, I did speak of it to President Young* and George A. Smith.

Did you give them the whole facts? I gave them some more than I have here, because I recollected more of it.

When did you do that? Pretty soon after it happened.

You are certain you told it fuller than you have told it here on the stand? *I told them everything I could.*

Who else did you tell it to? I have no recollection of telling it to any one else.

Why have you not told it before this time? Because I did not feel like it.

Why did you not feel like it? You felt and knew that a great crime had been committed, did you not? I felt that a great crime had been committed. *But Brigham Young told me that "as soon as we can get a court of justice, we will ferret this thing out, but till then don't say anything about it."*

There have been courts of justice in this territory ever since that time? I have never seen the effects of it yet. I have seen it tried.

Then this to the first time you have ever felt at liberty to tell it? It is the first time I ever felt that any good would come of it. I kept it to myself until it was called for in the proper place.

You feel now that the proper time has come? I do indeed.

I presume you have talked it over with friends, and they advised you that this would be a good time and place to tell it? I had an idea that if I came here that it would be a pretty good place to tell it.

And in pursuance of that idea you are going on to tell it? Yes, sir.

Are you certain that you have told all that you know about it? I am certain that I know all I tell.

Answer the other part? I think I have, all that is important.

Have you told it all? No, sir, I have not.

Then tell it? I will not undertake that now. I would not like to undertake it.

Redirect - HOWARD: How long have you known John D. Lee? Between thirty and forty years.

How long is it since Mr. Lee ceased to be so ardent in his feelings and religious zeal that he was willing to run the risk he did down there at the Mountain Meadows, to defend his religion? What I knew of him, he was always pretty zealous in what is called Mormonism - he was at that time.

How is it now?

BISHOP - We object to the question; it is not expected that a man shall be called a criminal for giving up his belief in such a Church. It is wholly foreign to the question at issue. Objection sustained.*

NEPHI JOHNSON

Re-called by Prosecution.

HOWARD - I will introduce the question I have to ask, by asking you if you know anything about this subsequent company - the Duke's company? Yes, sir.

What do you know about that? Objected to upon the ground that it

---

NOTE - To fully appreciate the evidence of this witness, Hamblin, read what Lee says about the acts of Hamblin and Nephi Johnson, in the stealing of the cattle from the Duke's train.

relates to a matter subsequent to the crime as charged in the indictment. Question withdrawn.

What conversation did you have with Mr. Lee, after the massacre? When I arrived at Harmony, John D. Lee was there.

How long was this after the massacre at the Meadows? Only a few days.

Where did you go from? I started from this city to Cedar City at my father's ranch.

Where were you going? Going with the company to see them safe through the country;

When you got to Harmony, did you see John D. Lee? Yes, sir.

Did you have any conversation with him? Yes, sir.

What conversation? He asked me to take the company into the mountains in the Santa Clara, and that he would follow with the Indians and kill them.

Did he tell you that he had authority to do that? No, sir; I said I would not do it. I said that I was sent to see the company safely through the country, and that I would do it or die. That there had been enough blood spilt at Mountain Meadows. He called me a great many names, and passed on.

Cross examined - You made up your mind, then, to die for the emigrants. Did you try to die for them at Mountain Meadows? No answer.

Nephi Johnson recalled.

HOWARD - By permission of counsel for defense I will ask one question.

BISHOP - Ask as many as you desire.

HOWARD - How long have you known John D. Lee? Since 1851.

Do you identify the prisoner at the bar as the John D. Lee spoken of by the witnesses and in your own testimony? Yes, sir.

Cross examined - Where did you live in 1851? Parowan, Iron County.

What time did you go to Iron County, Parowan? In the Spring of '51.

Where did you come from when you went there? Came from Salt Lake Valley.

Where did you come from to Salt Lake? From Illinois.

What part? Knox County, Illinois.

When did you leave Knox County, Illinois, for Salt Lake? I think it was in 1849.

Then you have lived in Utah all the time since? Yes, sir.

The defendant introduced no witnesses, but rested his case upon the evidence that had been introduced by the prosecution.

The case was then argued for the prosecution by Howard and Denney, and for the defendant by Foster and Bishop. The court instructed the jury at length.

The jury, after a few hours' deliberation, returned a verdict of "Guilty of murder in the first degree."

A motion was afterwards made and argued for a new trial. The court overruled the motion, denied the application for a new trial, and sentenced Lee to be shot.

The case was appealed to the Supreme Court of Utah Territory, and argued in that court by Hon. Frank Tilford and Sumner Howard for the people, and by Wm. W. Bishop for Lee.

The Supreme Court sustained the judgment and sentence of the District Court, and ordered the District Court to fix a day for carrying the judgment into effect. The District Court again sentenced John D. Lee to be shot to death, and fixed the day for execution on March 23d, 1877.

CHAPTER XXIV

NAMES OF ASSASSINS CLAIMED BY LEE TO HAVE BEEN PARTICIPANTS IN THE MOUNTAIN MEADOWS MASSACRE, OR PRIVY THERETO

NAMES of those who were on the ground, and aiding in or consenting to the killing of over one hundred and twenty men, women and children, at the Mountain Meadows.

1. George Adair, Jr.
2. Benjamin Arthur.
8. Ira Allen, (dead) Member of High Council of Church and City.
4. Wm. Bateman, (dead) Carrier of Flag of Truce.
5. John W. Clark, (dead) Lived at Washington, Utah.
6. Thomas Cartwright, (dead) Lived at Cedar City. Member City Council.
7. E. Curtis. Captain of "10", Cedar City.
8. Joseph Clews. Then of Cedar, now at Los Angeles, California.
9. Jabez Durfey. Cedar City.
10. -- Edwards. Cedar City.
11. Columbus Freeman. Then of Cedar, now at Corn Creek, Utah.
12. John M. Higbee. 1st Counselor to Isaac C. Haight, and Major of Iron Militia. In command at Massacre.
13. Oscar Hamblin, (dead)
14. Charles Hopkins, (dead)
15. Wm. Hawley. Now residing in Fillmore, Utah Territory.
16. John Hawley. (Died in Indian Nation)
17. Richard Harrison, of Pinto. Member of High Council of Church.
18. George Hunter, of Cedar City.
19. John Humphreys, of Cedar City.
20. Samuel Jukes, of Cedar City.
21. Nephi Johnson, of Cedar City. Indian Interpreter.
22. Swen Jacobs, of Cedar City.
23. John Jacobs, of Cedar City.

24. Philip Klingensmith. Bishop of Church at Cedar City.
25. Samuel Knight, of Cedar City.
26. -- Knight.
27. Dudley Leavitt, of Cedar City.
28. A. Loveridge, of Cedar City.
29. Daniel McFarland, of Cedar City. Son-in-law of Isaac C. Haight, and acting Adjutant at time of massacre.
30. John McFarland. Attorney at law, St. George, Utah.
31. James Matthews, (dead)
32. John Mangum, of Cedar City.
33. Samuel McMurdy, of Cedar City. 1st Counselor to Bishop Klingensmith. Assisted in killing wounded.
34. James Pearce, of Washington, Utah.
35. Harrison Pearce, of Washington, Utah.
36. Samuel Pollock, of Cedar City.
37. Dan. C. Shirts, of Harmony, now of Potato Valley, Utah. Son-in-law of John D. Lee, and Indian Interpreter.
38. William Slade, Sr., (dead) of Cedar City.
39. William Slade, Jr., of Cedar City.
40. William C. Stewart, of Cedar City.
41. Joseph Smith, of Cedar City.
42. Arthur Stratton, of Virgin City.
43. -- Tate, of Cedar City. Has since been a Captain of militia.
44. John Ure, of Cedar City.
45. Joel White, of Cedar City.
46. Elliott Wilden, of Cedar City.
47. Robert Wiley, of Cedar City.
48. Samuel White, of Cedar City.
40. Alexander Wilden,, of Cedar City.
50. John Weston (dead), of Cedar City.
51. Wm. Young (dead), of Washington, Utah.
52. John D. Lee. Executed March 23, 1877.

ACCESSORIES BEFORE THE FACT

WILLIAM H. DAME, Bishop of the Church at Parowan, Colonel of the Iron Military District, and first man in authority in Southern Utah. He gave orders to Isaac C. Haight to have the emigrants exterminated, and did not deny the same when accused of it by Haight on the field after the massacre, while examining the dead bodies.

IsAAC C. HAIGHT, President of that "Stake of Zion" at Cedar City, Utah Territory, Lieutenant Colonel of the Iron Military District - the man who directed Lee to see that the emigrants were exterminated.

GEORGE A. SMITH, one of the Twelve Apostles of the Church of Jesus Christ of Latter-Day Saints, who preached a crusade against all who were opposed to the Mormon Church, through the settlements in Southern Utah, immediately before the Mountain Meadows Massacre. (Now dead, or so reported).

ACCESSORIES AFTER THE FACT

BRIGHAM YOUNG, to whom John D. Lee made a full report of the massacre, giving names of persons engaged in the crime, and every fact within his knowledge, in less thin a month after the same was committed.

The man who said "God had shown him that the massacre was right."

The man who ordered John D. Lee to keep the whole thing secret.

The man who pretended to aid Judge Cradlebaugh to discover the guilty parties, and while pretending to do so was preaching at Cedar City and elsewhere that damnation would be the fate of all who presumed to give evidence against the brethren who had committed the crime.

The man who gave offices and concubines to John D. Lee and Isaac C. Haight, as a reward for their acts at the massacre.

The man who controls the every act of the Mormon people and makes slaves of his followers.

The man who teaches the doctrine of Blood Atonement as a religious duty to be performed by the faithful Latter-Day Saints.

The man who assumes that he does nothing except by direct authority from Heaven.

The greatest criminal of the Nineteenth Century!

DANIEL H. WELLS, the man who has done everything that he could possibly do to carry out the will of Brigham Young and defeat the United States officers in their attempts to enforce the laws of the United States. The man who directed the witnesses that it was the will of God, as made known through Brigham Young, the Prophet, Priest and Revelator under the New Dispensation, that John D. Lee must be convicted, but that no evidence should be given that would implicate any others of the brethren who aided in the butchery at Mountain Meadows.

NEXT. Every Mormon who has tried to screen the guilty perpetrators from punishment, among whom may be named -

GEORGE Q. CANNON, who disgraces the Government of the United States by holding a seat as delegate to Congress from the Territory of Utah, and who wrote many articles for publication, in the vain effort to prove that the massacre was an Indian massacre, without help or advice from the Church.

LASTLY. All who pretend that John D. Lee, and those who assisted him in the massacre, acted contrary to the orders of the Mormon Priesthood.

CHAPTER XXV

EXECUTION OF JOHN D. LEE

JOHN D. LEE was executed on Mountain Meadows, Washington County, Utah Territory, at the scene of the massacre, on the 28d day of March, 1877.

As to the reasons which prompted him to act as he did during his lifetime, we have nothing to say. Judging from his Life and Confessions, and our personal acquaintance with him, we believe him to have been an honest man, but so blinded by religious fanaticism and faith in his corrupt Church leaders, that his moral vision was perverted, and he committed crimes under the orders of his superiors, believing that he was doing right and working for the glory of God. It appears from his writings that he was used by Joe Smith, Brigham Young and other Mormon leaders, from the time that he became a member of the Church, as a tool to perform their dirty work, and when he was worn out and could no longer be of any service to them, they sacrificed him with as little compunction of conscience as a carpenter would throw away an old worn out saw or chisel.

The only wonder is that Lee, who was an intelligent man, would allow himself to be so often and so grossly deceived, and still repose confidence in his leaders. The answer to this is, that he had the utmost faith - a fanatical faith - in the truth of the Mormon religion, and believed that no other doctrine would enable him to attain immortality and future happiness. In addition to this, he had married a number of wives, who had borne him children, for all of whom he seems to have entertained a warm, fatherly affection; and if he had left the Mormon Church the law would have compelled him to give up all his wives except the first one, and his children would have been branded as bastards. His life, too, would have been in danger from his former associates, as he says himself, and they would either have *"blood atoned"* him or reported his crimes to the civil authorities and secured his conviction.

All these reasons kept him in the Church, and while there he felt that it was his duty, to himself, his family, and his God, to obey his rulers and those who were in authority over him.

The rulers of the Mormon Church teach their deluded followers that they are *inspired* men; that they act by direct authority from God, and that disobedience to their orders is rebellion against God. They also teach that those who carry out their orders in the commission of murders and other crimes, are only instruments to perform the will of God, and are not responsible for the sins which they commit in obeying the orders of their *inspired* rulers.

It is hard to believe that people. of any intelligence whatever, could be so shamefully deceived, but when men and women are thoroughly imbued with religious fanaticism, they are capable of believing or doing almost anything, provided it is sanctioned by a *"thus sayeth the Lord"* from the lips of some "holy" man or prophet, pretending to have his authority from revelation. Christianity itself furnished too many sickening examples of this kind a few centuries ago.

Thus John D. Lee was led on, step by step, from one crime to another, until his leaders had made all the use of him they could, and then they sacrificed him to a felon's death, in order to save themselves and cover up the sins of the Church.

On Wednesday preceding the day fixed upon for the execution, the guard having Lee in charge started from Beaver City, where Lee had been imprisoned, for Mountain Meadows, where it had been decided to carry the sentence into execution.

The party consisted of United States Marshal, William Nelson, a military guard, the prisoner, District Attorney Howard, a few newspaper correspondents, and about twenty private citizens.

The authorities had received information that an attempt to rescue Lee would be made by his sons and a body of his personal friends, and precautions were taken to prevent the success of any such attempt. The place of execution was kept a profound secret, except with the Marshal and a few trusted friends, and a strong guard was procured. Lee either knew nothing about the intended attempt at rescue, or else he placed no confidence in it, for he uttered no word or expression to indicate that he had any hope. He was cheerful and resigned to his fate, and seemed to have but little dread of death

The party reached Mountain Meadows about ten o'clock Friday morning, and after the camp had been arranged, Lee pointed out the various places of interest connected with the massacre, and recapitulated the horrors of that event.

A more dreary scene than the present appearance of Mountain Meadows cannot be imagined. The curse of God seems to have fallen upon it, and scorched and withered the luxuriant grass and herbage that covered the ground twenty years ago. The Meadows have been transformed from a fertile valley into an arid and barren plain, and the superstitious Mormons assert that the ghosts of the murdered emigrants meet nightly at the scene of their slaughter and re-enact in pantomime the horrors of their massacre.

The ground is cut up into deep gullies, and the surface to covered with sage brush and scrub oak. Meadows Spring, where the emigrants were encamped when they were first attacked, is situated at the lower part of the plain. At the time of the massacre this spring was on a level with the surrounding country, but it has since been washed out until it forms a terrible gulch some twenty feet in depth and eight or ten rods wide.

About thirteen years ago, Lieutenant Price and a party of soldiers collected all the bones of the murdered emigrants that could be found on the field, and erected a monument of loose stones over them, on the banks of this ravine. The monument is about three feet high, oblong in shape, and some twenty feet in length. Many of the stones of which it was composed have fallen into the ravine, and the monument is in keeping with its surroundings - dreary, desolate and decaying. The curse rests upon the whole landscape. The Marshal's party removed some of the loose stones down to the level of the earth, but no trace of bones or human remains could be found. Decay and desolation mark everything. The accompanying illustration, engraved from a photograph taken a few minutes before Lee's execution, gives a correct view of the present appearance of the Meadows.

To this dreary spot, the scene of one of the most revolting crimes that ever disgraced humanity, John D. Lee had been conveyed to bid farewell to life and be suddenly hurled into the unknown realities of eternity. His sentence, doubtless, was just, but if so, what ought to be the fate of the men who counseled and commanded him to do what he did? Among the number Brigham Young stands head and foremost, by reason of his position, and if the curse which rests upon the scene of the butchery does not follow him with the horrors of the damned fate is unjust. He proved himself a traitor to his faithful friend and slave, as well as a murderer at heart, and as sure as there is a God in Heaven just so sure will

EXECUTION OF JOHN D. LEE

be the curse of that crime come home to him. If the law should fail to reach him with its retributions. the ghost of John D. Lee will haunt his lecherous pillow and scorch his sleepless brain with visions of everlasting woe.

As the party came to a halt at the scene of the massacre, sentinels were posted on the surrounding hills, to prevent a surprise, and preparations for the execution were at once begun.

The wagons were placed in a line near the monument, and over the wheels of one of them army blankets were drawn, to serve as a screen or ambush for the firing party. The purpose of this concealment was to prevent the men composing the firing party from being seen by any one, there being a reasonable fear that some of Lee's relatives or friends might wreak vengeance upon his executioners. The rough pine boards for the coffin were next unloaded from a wagon, and the carpenters began to nail them together. Meanwhile Lee sat some distance away, with Marshal Nelson, and quietly observed the operations going on around him. The civilians, and those specially invited as witnesses, were allowed to come within the military enclosure, but all others were required to station themselves at a considerable distance to the east of the ravine.

At 10:35, all the arrangements having been completed, Marshal Nelson began to read the order of the court, and at its conclusion he turned to Lee and said:

"Mr. Lee, if you have anything to say before the order of the court is carried into effect, you can now do so."

Lee replied:

"I wish to speak to that man," pointing to the photographer (James Fennemore), who was adjusting his camera near by, preparatory to taking the group of which Lee was the central figure. "Come over here," said Lee, beckoning with his hand.

"In a second, Mr. Lee," replied Mr. Fennemore, but it was more than a minute before he could comply with the request. Lee, observing that the artist was occupied with his camera, said:

I want to ask a favor of you; I want you to furnish my three wives each a copy," meaning the photograph about to be taken. "Send them to Rachel A., Sarah C., and Emma B."

Hon. Sumner Howard, who was standing by the side of the instrument, responded for the artist, whose head at the moment was covered by the hood as he was adjusting the camera: "He says he will do it, Mr.

Lee."

Lee then repeated the names of his three wives carefully, saying to the artist, who had just approached him, "Please forward them - you will do this?"

Mr. Fennemore responded affirmatively, at the same time shaking Lee by the hand.

Lee then seemed to *pose* himself involuntarily, and the picture was taken.

He then arose from his coffin, where he had been seated, and, looking calmly around at the soldiers and spectators, said, in an even and unexcited tone of voice:

LAST WORDS OF JOHN D. LEE

"I have but little to say this morning. Of course I feel that I am upon the brink of eternity; and the solemnities of eternity should rest upon my mind at the present. I have made out - or have endeavored to do so - a manuscript, abridging the history of my life. This is to be published. In it I have given my views and feelings with regard to all these things.

"I feel resigned to my fate. I feel as calm as a summer morn, and I have done nothing intentionally wrong. My conscience is clear before God and man. I am ready to meet my Redeemer and those that have gone before me, behind the veil.

"I am not an infidel. I have not denied God and his mercies.

"I am a strong believer in these things. Most I regret is parting with my family; many of them are unprotected and will be left fatherless." (Here he rested two or three seconds.) "When I speak of these things they touch a tender chord within me." (Here his voice faltered perceptibly.) "I declare my innocence of ever doing anything designedly wrong in all this affair. I used my utmost endeavors to save these people.

"I would have given worlds, were they at my command, if I could have averted that calamity, but I could not do it. It went on.

"It seems I have to be made a victim - a victim must be had, and I am the victim. I am sacrificed to satisfy the feelings - the vindictive feelings, or in other words, am used to gratify parties.

"I am ready to die. I trust in God. I have no fear. Death has no terror.

"Not a particle of mercy have I asked of the court, the world, or officials to spare my life.

"I do not fear death, I shall never go to a worse place than I am now in.

"I have said it to my family, and I will say it today, that the Government of the United States sacrifices their best friend. That is saying a great deal, but it is true - it is so.

"I am a true believer in the gospel of Jesus Christ, I do not believe everything that is now being taught and practiced by Brigham Young. I do not care who hears it. It is my last word - it is so. I believe he is leading the people astray, downward to destruction. But I believe in the gospel that was taught in its purity by Joseph Smith, in former days. I have my reasons for it.

"I studied to make this man's [Brigham Young] will my pleasure for thirty years. See, now, what I have come to this day!

"I have been sacrificed in a cowardly, dastardly manner." (Lee enunciated this sentence with marked emphasis.) "I cannot help it. It is my last word - it is so.

"Evidence has been brought against me which is as false as the hinges of hell, and this evidence was wanted to sacrifice me. Sacrifice a man that has waited upon them, that has wandered and endured with them in the days of adversity, true from the beginning of the Church! And I am now singled out and am sacrificed in this manner! What confidence can I have in such a man! I have none, and I don't think my Father in heaven has any.

"Still, there are thousands of people in this Church that are honorable and good hearted friends, and some of whom are near to my heart. There is a kind of living, magnetic influence which has come over the people, and I cannot compare it to anything else than the reptile that enamors his prey, till it captivates it, paralyzes it, and it rushes into the jaws of death. I cannot compare it to anything else. It is so, I know it, I am satisfied of it.

"I regret leaving my family; they are near and dear to me. These are things which touch my sympathy, even when I think of those poor orphaned children.

"I declare I did nothing designedly wrong in this unfortunate affair. I did everything in my power to save that people, but I am the one that must suffer.

"Having said this I feel resigned. I ask the Lord, my God, if my labors are done, to receive my spirit."

Lee ceased speaking at 10:50, A.M. He was then informed that his hour had come and he must prepare for execution. He quietly and coolly looked at the small group of spectators. He was still very calm and resigned.

Rev. George Stokes, a Methodist minister who had accompanied Lee as his spiritual adviser, then knelt on the ground and delivered a short prayer. The minister was deeply affected by the solemnity of the occasion, and was very earnest in his supplications. The prisoner listened attentively.

At the conclusion of the prayer, Lee exchanged a few words with Mr. Howard and Marshal Nelson, saying to the latter:

"I ask one favor of the guards - spare my limbs and centre my heart." He then shook hands with those around him, removed his overcoat and comforter, presenting the latter to Mr. Howard, and giving his hat to Marshal Nelson.

The Marshal then bound a handkerchief over the prisoner's eyes, but at his request his hands were allowed to remain free.

The doomed man then straightened himself up facing the firing party, as he sat on his coffin, clasped his hands over his head and exclaimed:

"Let them shoot the balls through my heart! Don't let them mangle my body!"

The Marshal assured him that the aim would be true, and then stepped back. As he did so, he gave the orders to the guards:

"READY! AIM! FIRE!"

The five men selected as executioners promptly obeyed. They raised their rifles to their shoulders, took deliberate aim at the blindfolded man sitting upright on his coffin, about twenty feet in front of them, and as the fatal word *"fire"* rang out clear and strong on the morning air, a sharp report was heard, and Lee fell back on his coffin, dead and motionless. There was not a cry nor a moan nor a tremor of the body.

There was a convulsive twitching of the fingers of the left hand, which had fallen down by the side of the coffin, and the spirit of John D. Lee had crossed over the dark river and was standing before the judge of the quick and the dead.

His soul had solved the awful mystery, and the CURSE that hovers over Mountain Meadows had marked "ONE" upon its list of retribution.

THE END

Brigham Young

APPENDIX

LIFE OF BRIGHAM YOUNG

O N THE 29th day of August, 1877, the telegraph brought the brief announcement of the death of Brigham Young, which occurred at Salt Lake City, at four o'clock on the evening of that day. This event, of peculiar importance to the religious denomination of which he was the head and main support, was not entirely unexpected, as the infirmities of age and the effects of licentious living had been making serious inroads upon his vigorous constitution during the last few years of his life. He had anticipated the event himself, and had about completed his arrangements for the transmission of his authority to other hands.

As there is nothing to admire in the character of this gross, selfish, lustful man, except his superior natural abilities and unyielding determination, it is difficult to collect sufficient material for an extended biography, for he had no loving friends to gather up the little incidents of his life and place them on record for the use of future historians. He ruled his people as a tyrant, not as a friend, and the title of the "Old Boss," by which he was familiarly known among the Mormons, indicates the estimation in which he was held by his own people.

The only record of his early life now in existence, is a brief account written by himself, from which we learn that he was born in Whittingham, Windham County, Vermont June 1, 1801. When he was about eighteen months old his parents removed to Smyrna, Chenango County, N. Y., where they resided until 1813. Shortly after the commencement of the last war with Great Britain, they removed to Genoa, Cayuga County, N. Y., where Brigham lived until 1829. In 1830 he located in Mendon, Monroe County, where he remained but a short time, when he removed to Canandaigua, but returned to Mendon in 1832. He removed from there to Kirtland, Ohio, where he was "converted" to Mormonism, and his connection with that sect dates from that place and period.

He had four brothers, born in the following order: John, Joseph, Phineas H., and Lorenzo D., Brigham being next to the youngest. He also had five sisters.

His father's name was John Young, and his mother's maiden name was Nabby Howe.

Brigham's grandfather was a physician in the American army during the French and Indian wars, and was killed after the return of peace by a heavy rail falling upon his neck while climbing through a fence. Two of Dr. Young's sons, Joseph and John, fought in the American army during the Revolutionary War.

John Young, Brigham's father, was a farmer, and his social position seems to have been below the average. The future Prophet was reared in the humblest circumstances, and he often boasted in afterlife that he had "only been eleven and a half days at school." His natural abilities were good, but these were neglected, the boy grew up in ignorance, and as a natural consequence the grosser attributes of his character predominated.

The Young family, with the exception of Brigham, were all devout Methodists, but their religion was freely tinctured with the superstitious ideas common to ignorant minds, and which were quite prevalent at that early date; and Brigham, who possessed a naturally strong and independent character, scouted their superstitions and was considered an infidel until his conversion to Mormonism. His parents, however, had an earnest faith in his future, and believed that he would become the main pillar of the family spiritually, as he was temporally.

In early life Brigham worked on his father's farm, but he afterward learned the trade of a painter and glazier, and followed this business for eighteen years. His occupation did not afford him constant employment, and he was often forced to seek hard manual labor to earn a support for himself and family. He asserted that he "had done many a hard day's work for six bits a day," and his early privations taught him a lesson of frugality and economy that he did not forget in his more prosperous days. The spirit of industry which he infused into the entire body of people over whom he presided, was one of his few redeeming qualities. He adopted the honeybee as his motto, and permitted no idleness or extravagance to exist in his presence.

In 1824 he married his first wife, whose maiden name was Miriam

Works. She died eight years afterward, leaving two daughters, who are still living, and members of the Mormon Church. One of the daughters married Edmund Ellsworth, a relative of the famous Colonel Ellsworth who was killed during the war between the North and South. The other married Charles Dicker. The eldest is now about fifty years of age, and both are grandmothers.

About 1830 Brigham Young first heard of Joe Smith's famous "golden plates" and the doctrine of Mormon. He also obtained some advance sheets of the book of Mormon, and, with the assistance of Heber C. Kimball, who afterward became one of the most polygamous of the Mormon chiefs, began to investigate the new doctrine. He proceeded cautiously at first, and did not accept the faith until two years later. He was then baptized, and immediately afterward ordained an elder and sent on a mission to Canada. His wife having died, he placed his two children in the care of friends, and devoted himself exclusively to the ministry.

His previous poverty and habits of hard labor rendered the acceptance of Mormonism no sacrifice to him, and preaching "without purse or scrip" he felt was no lowering of his dignity. In truth he found the preaching of the new doctrine a much easier way of making a living than his former occupation, and, encouraged also by the influence and attention which his new dignity brought him, he threw his whole soul into the work, and almost immediately became one of the "bright lights." His manner of preaching was forcible and energetic, though utterly lacking in polish, and, seemingly or really in earnest himself, he conveyed the same impression to the minds of his audiences, and not only held their attention but converted hundreds of them to the new faith.

A writer of some distinction, referring to the early days of Mormonism, says:

"The preaching of the first elders was something like a resuscitation of the dispensation committed to the Apostolic fishermen of Galilee. With the acceptance of what they deemed the new revelation of Christ there was no sacrifice too great to make, and no self abnegation with which they would not strive to adorn their lives. They were earnest, fiercely enthusiastic, and believers in everything that had ever been written about 'visions,' 'dreams,' 'the ministering of angels,' 'gifts of the spirit,' 'tongues, and interpretations of tongues,' 'healings,' and 'miracles.' They wandered 'without purse or scrip' from village to village ad from city to city, preaching in the public highways, at the firesides or in the pulpits - wherever they had opportunity."

These fanatics, crazed by religious fervor and excitement, had but little difficulty in gaining the attention of the ignorant and unlettered in the communities which they visited, and the animal magnetism engendered by their excited manner and fanatical earnestness, enabled them to win converts by the thousands. The barren, speculative, carefully prepared sermons of fifty weeks in the year, chilled in the presence of the energy and demonstration of the Mormon elders, and "the number of the disciples grew and multiplied."

Ministers of other denominations, also, seeing their own flocks invaded, and prospective members won from the ranks of the outside world, began to denounce and preach against the new doctrine. Religious persecution manifested itself, several Mormon elders were tarred and feathered at different places, and the converts of the new doctrine were ostracized and driven from the society of orthodox worshippers. The result was what might have been expected, 'the blood of the martyrs became the seed of the Church," and Mormonism flourished wonderfully.

In the midst of this religious excitement Brigham Young visited Kirtland, Ohio, and for the first time met the Prophet Joseph. Heber C. Kimball and Joseph Young accompanied him on this expedition, and they had a high time of rejoicing. Brigham was so "lifted up" by the spirit upon beholding the prophet, that he "spake in tongues," which was the first time that the "gift" had been demonstrated. It was a heathenish sort of gibberish that no one understood, but Joe Smith "interpreted" the unknown sounds, and assured those present that they were "the pure Adamic language - the language in which Adam courted Eve." Brigham often resorted to this device in aftertimes, and his ignorant followers were roused to frenzy while listening to senseless ejaculations, which they believed to be the primal language of the human race.

Brigham was soon upon the most intimate terms with Joe Smith, and the latter pronounced him a "chosen vessel of the Lord." Shrewd, ready, quickwitted, enthusiastic, and practical, the new convert speedily rose among his new associates. In a community where ignorance was the rule, his ignorance passed unnoticed, while his confidence in himself, his power to read the nature of his fellowmen like the pages of an open book, and his devotion to the religion of the Latter-Day Saints soon raised him into a commanding position. He had not long been a member of the Church before he was ordained an elder, and began to preach the most stirring sermons that the infant Church had ever listened to.

In May, 1834, Joe Smith received a "revelation from the Lord," commanding him to lead an army into Jackson County, Mo., to the assistance of the Mormon colony there who had got into trouble with the neighboring "Gentiles." Accordingly an "army" was organized at Kirtland, on the 7th of May, and Smith was chosen commander-in-chief. One hundred and thirty men composed this famous "army," but it received accessions from stragglers and vagrants on the route, until when it encamped in Missouri it numbered 205 men. It was divided into companies of twelve, and each company chose its own officers.

Brigham Young accompanied the expedition as one of the leaders. The Prophet selected George A. Smith, his cousin, as his "armor bearer," and the march was conducted with great pomp and splendor.

On the 19th of June the "Lord's army" reached the vicinity of Clay County, and encamped near a company of Missourians who were waiting to attack them. During the night a dreadful storm swept over the camp of the anti-Mormons, their tents were scattered to the winds, their horses stampeded, and one of them was killed by lightning.

This relieved Smith and his followers from immediate danger, and they remained in camp until the 21st, when the cholera broke out among them with terrible fierceness. So sudden and overpowering was the attack that the strongest men fell to the ground with their guns in their hands. In four days sixty-eight were attacked and fourteen of them died. Brigham was among the stricken ones, but he overcame the disease, as be afterward stated, by the force of his will, and was soon ready for duty again.

In this crisis Joe Smith proved himself to be a true leader, for instead of becoming panic stricken, he went about laying on hands and "rebuking the destroyer," until he himself was prostrated. He ascribed this visitation to the disobedience of some of his followers, and he promised that if they would "humble themselves and obey him as the Prophet of the Lord," the plague should be staved. The Mormon historians assert that "not another was stricken with cholera from that hour."

The expedition having proved to be an ignominious failure, the Prophet very conveniently received another "revelation," and learned that "the Lord," having changed his mind, no longer desired the redemption of the Missouri "saints," who were a rebellions and stiffnecked people, and needed to be chastised by their heathen neighbors in order that they might learn obedience. The "army" was therefore disbanded, the warriors were instructed to disperse among the settlements or return to their homes, and Smith and Young, with the other leaders, returned to Kirtland.

In 1835 Brigham was ordained one of the Twelve Apostles, Smith having received a special revelation from heaven pointing him out as one of the pillars of the Church. The ordination consisted of the laying on of the hands of the three witnesses to the Book of Mormon. It may be mentioned here parenthetically that these three Saints subsequently renounced Mormonism.

When the twelve were sent to preach the gospel according to Mormon to the outer heathen, Young traveled through the Eastern States, and was the most successful preacher of them all. His presence was commanding, his speech fluent, if not polished, and his vigor and earnestness contagious. If he did not believe what he preached he certainly acted his part so well that none could discover his secret.

Soon after the return from Missouri, Joe Smith, Brigham Young, and Sidney Rigdon organized a bank at Kirtland, which they called the "Safety Society Bank," and began to issue notes in unlimited quantities, "for the relief of the Saints." The names of Joseph Smith as cashier and Sidney Rigdon as president, were signed to the beautifully engraved bank notes, and those who saw the notes with these names attached supposed the bank to be simply a savings institution in which the "saints" could deposit their earnings, which would be invested so as to pay interest, and that the notes represented actual money in the bank. The result was that the confidence of the people was gained, and the paper of the Safety Society Bank became a favorite medium of circulation with both saint and sinner.

Finally, however, other banks began to lose confidence in these notes, and the bankers of Pittsburgh deputed one of their number to visit Kirtland and learn the real condition of the Safety Society Bank. This agent was a Mr. Jones, and his account of his interview with President Rigdon was decidedly racy. He first inquired about the success of "the Lord's cause," and evinced considerable interest in the Latter-Day religion. This he claimed was a matter of courtesy, but it was unfortunate, for upon opening his satchel and producing a huge bundle of Safety Society Bank paper, which he desired to have redeemed, the whole proceeding was denounced by brother Rigdon as the "march of a wolf in sheep's clothing." He flew into a passion and asserted that the paper of the bank had been put out as a "circulating medium for the accommodation of the people, that it would be an injury to them for the notes to come home and be redeemed, as they would then have no circulating medium! His bank would redeem nothing!" Mr. Jones pleaded for a deviation from the rule in his case, and pledged himself never to return with any more of the notes for redemption if he could only get his money this time. But Rigdon was faithful to the programme of the bank, and coolly informed Mr. Jones that they had never asked him or any one else to take their paper, and referred him to that important epoch in Biblical history where the profession to which Mr. Jones belonged were scourged out of the Temple at Jerusalem.

The agent returned to his employers and reported the facts, and immediately the notes of the Safety Society Bank began to depreciate. The inspired bankers, realizing what the end would be, determined upon flight, and Brother Brigham, more sagacious than the others, set out for Missouri with his family, three weeks in advance of the president and cashier. His discretion proved his superior wisdom, for his associates narrowly escaped arrest, being compelled to seek safety in flight during the night of January 12, 1838. They were pursued by their infuriated victims for more than two hundred miles, and frequently evaded them only by the superior mettle of their horses. They finally overtook Brigham and his family, and continued their journey to Missouri, or the "promised land," arriving in Far West on the 12th of March, 1838.

Prior to this, in 1836, Thomas B. Marsh, President of the Twelve Apostles, had resigned, and Brigham Young took his place, being delegated by Smith to "preach in tongues." He did preach "in tongues" now and then, and although none of the saints understood him his oratory was vastly admired.

In 1838 there were many schisms in the church. Orson Hyde apostatized and testified against Smith; Phelps deserted the cause, the Pratts were wavering, and Dr. Arvard, one of the Danites, exposed the hidden machinery of Mormonism. Smith was arrested Sept 14, 1838, and to save his life, Brigham fled to Quincy, Ill. There he met the remainder of the twelve and some other brethren, and in the next year assisted to relay the foundation of the Mormon temple in Independence, Jackson County, Mo. The laying of the corner stone was done at midnight, and every man who participated in the ceremonies knew that his life was at the mercy of the enemies around him - the enemies who had already razed to the ground the habitations of the faithful. Still, there was no wavering, and not one jot of the ceremonial was neglected.

In 1839 Brigham, still faithful where so many had proved false, was sent by the Prophet to preach in England. He was penniless, friendless, and alone, and suffered much during the two years he spent in England. Still, supported by the charity of his audiences, he made thousands of converts, shipped 769 new Mormons to Smith, established the *Millennial Star,* a Mormon organ which lived for many years, and formed a number of churches.

Upon his return to the United States in 1841, Brigham joined his brethren at Nauvoo, being received with great enthusiasm. It was here that he first came in conflict with the Prophet; but such was his power among the people that he carried his point. At this time he preached throughout the summer and worked in the Winter.

The difficulties that environed the Saints at Nauvoo increased to such a degree that in 1842 Joe Smith prophesied that within five years they would remove to a new location in the Rocky Mountain region, and in the Spring of 1844 he sent a party to explore the unknown region, with a view to verifying his prophecy. In his private history, under date of February 20, 1844, he wrote:

"I instructed the Twelve Apostles to send out a delegation and investigate the localities, California and Oregon, and hunt up a good location where we can remove to after the Temple is completed and where we can build a city in a day and have a government of our own; get up into the mountains where the devil cannot dig us out, and live in a healthy climate where we can live as old as we have a mind to."

His idea was to found an independent State somewhere in the Rocky Mountain region, where his people could live to themselves and practice their peculiar doctrines unmolested by infidels and outside sinners. The plan was afterward successfully carried out by Brigham Young, subsequent to the death of the Prophet, so that the credit which has sometimes been bestowed upon Brigham as the originator of this fine strategic movement belongs of right to his predecessor.

On the 27th of June, 1844, Smith was shot by a mob while in the jail at Carthage, Ill. The twelve apostles were scattered far and wide, and Brigham Young was in Boston. Nauvoo was threatened by the Gentiles. Troops were in arms, and rumors of coming trouble flew thick and fast. Sidney Rigdon, who was the legal successor of Joseph Smith, assumed the mantle of the Prophet and began to peddle dispensations, confer endowments, and dictate in every way to the saints. It was the rule of a weak man, and was destined to be short lived. Suddenly Brigham appeared, and Rigdon's power crumbled into dust. He denounced Rigdon as a fraud and a hypocrite; declared that his revelations were from the devil; and finally hurled upon him anathema after anathema. The result was an election that wiped Rigdon out and made Brigham Young the Mormon ruler. Those who had voted against him, the new Prophet cursed and cut off, and by a well devised system of rewards and punishments he soon inspired love in the hearts of his friends and adherents and fear in the hearts of his enemies. John D. Lee gives an account - and doubtless the only correct one ever published - of the manner in which Brigham secured his election to the presidency of the Mormon priesthood. It is decidedly rich and worth reading twice. (see page 162)

Brigham began his administration with a reign of terror. If any person, whether Saint or Gentile, became obnoxious to him, a word or a sign to the Danites or his secret police was sufficient to seal the fate of the unfortunate offender, who would either be waylaid and murdered or enticed into some lonely place and there executed. If the offending person happened to be so prominent that his death or disappearance would cause inquiry and investigation, he would receive warning from Brigham's agent, that it was no longer healthy for him to remain in that locality, and the warning was sure to be heeded and acted upon, for the power of the new Prophet was soon understood and dreaded by all.

By this system of murdering and banishing his enemies Brigham soon had his authority firmly established, and his leading men were bound to him forever by the common fear of the penalties of the law if they should be detected or any of their number turned traitor. The Prophet felt so secure in their confidence that one day in council he openly dared them to betray him, plainly intimating that they were all in the same category and if he fell they must fall with him.

He also encouraged polygamy, both by precept and example, with the evident intention not only of gratifying his own lustful desires, but of causing his people to form peculiar social relations that could not be maintained elsewhere, and thus compelling them to remain forever a separate and distinct community. Polygamy had been taught and secretly practiced by Joseph Smith, but Brigham engrafted it upon the doctrines of the Church and caused it to become a leading feature of the new religion.

He furthermore hastened the completion of the Temple, and then administered the endowment rites to all the people. The ceremonies and obligations of these rites were of such a character as to leave a lasting impression upon the minds of those who received them, and after that but few ever had the hardihood to apostatize.

Having bound his people together by the various ties of murder, polygamy, and the endowment, more closely than any other community that ever existed, he began to make preparations to carry out the plan of his predecessor and found an independent State in the Rocky Mountain region. Their departure was hastened by the threatening attitude of the citizens of Illinois, who had endured the insolence and lawlessness of the Mormons so long that forbearance was at an end, and they had determined to drive them out by force of arms.

On the 5th of February, 1846, the first company crossed the Mississippi River on the ice, and on the following day the main body of Saints began to move. During the month of February about 1,200 wagons were transported to the Iowa shore, and started on the journey westward. Brigham Young took his departure on the 3d of March, and by the middle of May about 16,000 people were wending their way through Iowa to rendezvous on the banks of the Missouri River in the vicinity of Council Bluffs. Only about one thousand Mormons were left in Nauvoo, mostly on account of their inability, from poverty or sickness, to undertake the journey with the main body, while some were left to dispose of the property and settle the affairs of the Church. By the first of October all had taken their departure.

None knew their destination, but they faithfully followed their leader, trusting to his ability to find a resting place for them. They spent the Winter of 1846-7 in Iowa, in miserable hovels and tents, and endured great hardships on account of the lack of proper shelter to protect them against the severity of the weather.

Here the need of money began to be felt, and the U.S. Government having offered a bounty of $20,000 for a regiment to serve in the Mexican war, Brigham ordered his men to enlist, and a regiment five hundred strong was soon organized, equipped and started on the march to Santa Fe. With the money thus obtained Brigham was enabled to place his people in much more comfortable circumstances than they had previously been, and the following Spring he took 143 men and started on a prospecting tour to the West, having first organized the people into farming companies and directed them to raise a crop for their use during the coming Winter.

He and his party reached Salt Lake on the 24th of July, and there he determined to locate his colony. Leaving a portion of his company to begin farming operations, he returned with the remainder to Iowa, for the purpose of piloting his people across the plains. He found them in a sad condition, for during his absence dissensions had arisen among them, and cholera, fever and ague, and other diseases, had greatly thinned their ranks. But he went to work with his usual indomitable energy and soon restored order and good feeling, and as the Winter advanced the health of the people greatly improved.

Preparations for the journey across the plains were vigorously prosecuted, and early in the Spring of 1848 the people were ready to depart, and by the last of May they were all en route for the new "promised land."

The main body arrived in Great Salt Lake Valley in September and October, bringing with them a large amount of grain and agricultural implements, as well as the remnant of their property from Nauvoo with which to commence a new home. Great suffering was experienced during the trip, and hundreds died of disease and exposure, leaving the route dotted with graves. But the winter following their arrival at Salt Lake was mild, and the sufferings of the emigrants were greatly mitigated by that fact. During the following summer, however, their crops were damaged by drought and grasshoppers, and their sufferings during the preceding winter were almost unbearable. Indeed their condition did not materially improve until the third summer, when their harvests were abundant, and prosperity began to smile upon them.

In 1850 the Mormons became anxious for admission to the Union. They accordingly drew up a constitution of a State which they wished to call Deseret, and sent delegates to Washington. Congress granted them a territorial government under the name of Utah, and President Fillmore appointed Brigham the first Governor.

From 1850 to 1854 the growth of the Church was rapid, both as to numbers and wealth. Almost every country in Europe sent its quota to swell the number. Villages grew into towns, towns into cities. The capital, Salt Lake City, daily increased in size and importance. Brigham inculcated constant industry. In his creed to be idle was to be vicious; and so all worked

In 1854 a Governor, not a Mormon, was appointed, and Brigham began to show an inclination to resist. For three years the Territory was in an unsettled condition. The saints, acting upon the orders of Brigham, committed many crimes, the most revolting of which was the Mountain

Meadows Massacre. In 1857 President Pierce appointed Alfred Cummings Governor of Utah and sent with him a force of 2,500 soldiers. Brigham submitted with a bad grace. As he controlled the courts, the juries, and all elective offices, the power of the new Governor was of the slightest. He could plan reforms, but he could not carry them out. It was not until the Salt Lake colony had been fairly started that Brigham proclaimed the "celestial law of marriage," which sanctioned polygamy. He said that Joseph Smith had had a revelation in 1848 directing him to promulgate this doctrine; but that he had failed to do so because of the troubled times in the Church. Smith's widow and his sons pronounced this a falsehood, but the power of Brigham, chiming in with the wishes and inclinations of his people, soon made polygamy an institution. There was a schism in the Church, but the Smith faction were speedily driven to the wall.

Of Brigham's later years little need be said. Keen and farsighted he piloted his people through all their troubles into a haven of prosperity such as no people ever attained in so brief a space of time. He neither spared himself nor others. "Watch and work," not "Watch and pray," was his motto. Brigham Young was one of the most farseeing and enterprising business men in the country. He never lost an opportunity. By the establishment of the Zion cooperative stores, the working of mines, the purchase of property in places likely to grow rapidly, and by his railroad operations he accumulated one of the largest fortunes in the United States. Good authorities say that there is scarcely a city or town in the region over which he so long ruled in which he did not own property. By a system of tithe collecting, he made the people contribute directly to his coffers. The tithes were for the Church, it is true, but Brigham was the Church. In the early days of the Pacific Railroad he took a deep interest in the scheme, and was afterwards a contractor for a portion of it. That he had confidence in the stability of the national Government is shown by the fact that he was a large holder of bonds purchased in the early years of the war.

In person the "Old Boss," as his people called him, was large and portly, with a steel blue eye, a resolute month, a ruddy cheek, an imposing carriage and a very impressive manner. He was indeed a noticeable man, yet plain and simple in his dress, in his diet, and indeed all his habits. He had an excessive fondness for tobacco, and sometimes (his enemies said) took too stiff a dram of whisky; but he ate little, toast, bread and milk being his chief food. He rose early and attended to his multitudinous affairs with persevering industry, strict routine and systematic regularity. Among his intimates he was free, affable, pleasant; courteous to strangers, and full of plain, offhand, practical talk with every one. In council his power impressed every one by the cool, calm, deliberate, well considered views he was always ready to express. In the pulpit he was still more a power, fascinating his hearers by what in the lips of others would seem mere swagger and rhodomontade. His manner was unstudied, unaffected; all seemed to see that he was talking to them from his heart, and that that heart was sincere. Indeed, the secret of Brigham Young's success lay just here, that he had - or feigned irresistibly to have - an intense conviction of the truth of his mission.

Brigham's lion could roar terribly enough upon occasion. His roar was loud enough without needing to be like those of the Danites, to echo it. In 1854 the crops failed, there was a famine and the people murmured. Brigham preached a series of startling famine sermons; told them they were cursed because they were unfaithful, they had sinned and the judgment was on them, they must bow to the yoke, and ended by cursing the murmurers. There was no more complaining. None of his followers dared differ from Brigham; they were sure to be browbeaten to the very dust. His magnetism was irresistible, but this only made his anger the more terrible. He more than once showed himself implacable as granite with the Mormon offender against the Mormon law, the heretic, the traitor, the adulterer. "Gentiles" who have made trouble in the territory he has cursed from the pulpit, bustled and harried, plundered and maltreated them, until they were glad to flee naked and afraid for their lives. One of the Smiths in 1852 differed upon some point of doctrine from Brigham and attempted to set up a little Ebenezer of his own. Young bore it for awhile in silence, then suddenly, from his stand in the Tabernacle, denounced the intruder in the vernacular: "I tell Albert Smith that he had better clear right out, and that right straight, too, or I will cut his damned throat, and send him to hell across lots!" Needless to say, Smith fled at once.

On Thursday, August 23, 1877, Brigham Young was attacked with cholera morbus, said to be the result of making a hearty dinner of green corn and peaches. The attack was regarded as serious, but on Friday his physicians pronounced him convalescent. He had a relapse on Saturday afternoon, accompanied by severe pain. The symptoms yielded to the use of morphine, but on Sunday a condition of semi-stupor set in, which continued throughout the day and night. On Monday there was no change for the better. On Tuesday it became difficult to arouse him, but he retained his consciousness and recognized those about him, but experienced great difficulty in breathing, and artificial respiration was resorted to for about nine hours. His condition from this time until his death admitted of no doubt as to the result.

His last words, uttered on Tuesday night, were, "I feel better." He was able to say very little to the members of his family, as they came to bid him farewell on Sunday night. He then said, "It will make no difference whether I live or die. I am resigned." For the past few months he had enjoyed remarkable health; had preached sermons an hour in length, and been engaged actively in the reorganization of the Church in different settlements, and the appointment of new bishop's preparatory, it was hinted, to the cutting off of the lukewarm or immoral members.

At 4 o'clock on the afternoon of August 29th he passed quietly away, seemingly unconscious of all his surroundings. The members of his family were generally gathered around his bedside, and evinced deep emotion. His sons, John W. and Brigham Junior, constantly attended him during his illness.

The funeral was an impressive demonstration. On Saturday morning the body was taken from the Lion House to the new Tabernacle, where it lay in state until noon the following day. Until after midnight on Saturday there was a constant stream of people to see the body, and at daylight the next morning the rush began again, continuing until the beginning of the funeral services. Nearly eighteen thousand persons saw the corpse, which was arrayed in the sacred temple or endowment robes, consisting of the garment, shirt, apron, robe, cap, and shoes, all of fine linen. The coffin was of California redwood, varnished, and without ornament. The lining was white satin. The corpse rested on a wool mattress. The arrangements were all in accordance with written instructions given by Brigham Young in 1873, which instructions were read at the funeral, as follows:

"I, Brigham Young, wish my funeral services to be conducted in the following manner: When I breathe my last, I wish my friends to put my body in as clean and wholesome a state as can conveniently be done, and preserve the same for one, two, three, or four days, or as long as my body can be preserved in good condition.

"I want my coffin made of plain one-and-a-quarter redwood boards, not scrimped in length, but two inches longer than I would measure, and from two to three inches wider than is commonly made for a person of my breadth and size, and deep enough to place me on a little comfortable cotton bed, with a good suitable pillow in size and quality. My body dressed in my Temple clothing, and laid nicely into my coffin, and the coffin to have the appearance that if I wanted to turn a little to the right or left I should have plenty of room to do so; the lid can be made crowning.

"At my interment I wish all my family present that can be conveniently, and the male members to wear no crepe on their hats or coats; the females to buy no black bonnets or dresses nor black veils, but if they have them they are at liberty to wear them.

"And services may be permitted, as singing and a prayer offered, and if any of my friends wish to say a few words they are desired to do so.

"And when they close their services, to take my remains on a bier and repair to the little burying ground which I have reserved on my lot east of the White House on the hill. On the southeast corner of this lot I have a vault built of mason work large enough to receive my coffin, and that they may place in a box, if they choose, the same as the coffin - redwood - then place rocks over the vault sufficiently large to cover it, that the earth may be placed over it - as fine dry earth as can be had - to cover it until the walls of the little cemetery are hid, which will leave me in the southeast corner.

"This vault ought to be roofed over with some kind of temporary roof. There let my earthly tabernacle rest in peace and comfort and have a good sleep until the morning of the first resurrection - no crying world mourning with any one.

"I have done my work faithfully and in good faith. I wish this to be read at the funeral, provided that if I should die anywhere in the mountains I desire the above directions respecting my place of burial should be observed. But if I should live to get back to the church in Jackson County, Mo., I wish to be buried there.   "BRIGHAM YOUNG,

"President of the Church of Jesus Christ of Latter-Day Saints"

The tabernacle was heavily draped, and profusely decorated with flowers, the dome being festooned with roses, bouquets, and baskets of flowers, and wreaths were suspended from the pillars and the gallery. The coffin was placed in front of the elevated platform, resting on a modest catafalque. Two hours before the opening of the services the gallery and about half of the body of the building for the public were filled, and thousands of persons were unable to gain admission to the tabernacle. Ten tiers of seats in front of the stand were occupied by the family and relatives of the deceased Prophet, numbering several hundred. The arrangement was in accordance with the church rules. The stands in front of the organ were occupied by high church authorities. John W. Young and Daniel H. Wells, counselors to Brigham, and Brigham Young, Jr., and George Q. Cannon were in the upper stand. Ten of the apostles were next below, and the High Council still lower. The bishops were on the north platform, and the City Council on the south. In front, behind the family, were the quorums of seventies, high priests, elders, teachers, deacons, etc. There were not less than 12,000 persons in the building.

At 11:30 the family gathered around and gazed for the last time on the corpse. All his wives and children, with few exceptions, were present, and there were scores of grandchildren and relatives more distant. The demonstrations of grief were few, although all seemed sad and full of mourning. Previous to the services, the coffin was elevated in full view of the entire assemblage. From 9 o'clock the organ had been playing appropriate pieces, "The Dead March in Saul," Mendelssohn's funeral march, and a march composed for the occasion by a Mormon. George Q. Cannon was master of ceremonies, and promptly at noon announced the beginning with the hymn, "Hark from Afar," which was sung by the Tabernacle choir of 220 voices. The opening prayer was offered by Apostle Franklin D. Richards, who thanked God that when he took Joseph Smith he gave the saints for a leader Brigham Young, one of the noblest and purest of the royal family of heaven. Then followed a hymn, after which brief addresses were delivered by Daniel H. Wells and Apostles Wilford Woodruff, Erastus Snow, Geo. Q. Cannon, and John Taylor. Contrary to expectation, nothing was said in reference to the succession. The speakers confined themselves to laudations of Brigham and exhortations to the saints to remember and obey his counsels and advice, to proceed with the erection of temples, the foundations for four of which have been laid. All the elders expressed joy that Brigham had defeated the purposes of his enemies, and had died in his own house, surrounded by his family and friends. Mr. Cannon said that, while Brigham Young had been the brains, the Eastern star, and the tongue of the saints for more than thirty years, he was only the agent of God, who would carry on the work of Mormonism always. It was a significant fact that John W. Young and Brigham Young, Jr., both aspirants for the Presidency of the Church, occupied the seats of their father and

PRESIDENT TAYLOR, BRIGHAM YOUNG'S SUCCESSOR

his counselors. Many people thought they should have been with the family or with the apostles.

A hymn composed for the occasion and the benediction by Apostle Orson Hyde closed the services in the Tabernacle. The procession then formed and marched eight abreast to the cemetery, half a mile distant.

Four thousand persons were in the line, marching with uncovered heads. The ceremonies at the grave were brief, consisting only of a hymn sung by the Glee Club and a prayer by Apostle Woodruff, dedicating the vault, the coffin and the body. The coffin, enclosed in a rough box, was lowered into the vault, and the wives and children gathered around, but the lid was not removed. Brigham's first wife stood by the grave for some time, leaning on the arm of Amelia, the favorite. The spectators were then allowed to pass by the tomb, after which it was closed and sealed.

The vault is of cut sandstone, eight feet long, four feet wide, and three feet high, internal measurement. The stone blocks are laid in cement and pinned together with steel bars, sent through each block horizontally and vertically. The cover is of seven inch flagging, pinned to the walls with iron bars.

Brigham Young was the father of fifty-six children, forty-four of whom are now alive - sixteen sons and twenty-eight daughters. He leaves seventeen wives, not including Ann Eliza. He has left his family well provided for, apportioning property to each member. His estate is valued at from six to seven millions of dollars.

BRIGHAM'S SUCCESSORS

On the evening of September 10, 1877, the Apostles of the Mormon Church, joined by John W. Young and Daniel H. Wells, late counselors of Brigham Young, published a circular saying that on September 4 they held a meeting, and waited upon the Lord who blessed them, and who revealed to them the steps they should take. John Taylor, senior apostle, acting president of the twelve, is unanimously sustained in that position; also that a quorum of the Twelve Apostles shall be the authority of the Church. This was the plan pursued at the time of the death of Joe Smith, and was so ordered by Smith and sustained by Brigham. To facilitate the transaction of business it was ordered that President John Taylor be assisted by John W. Young, Daniel H. Wells and Geo. Q. Cannon.

A REMARKABLE LETTER

To the Inter-Ocean

MORMON WIVES TAUGHT THAT ONLY THEIR HUSBANDS CAN RES-
URRECT THEM - LECHEROUS BISHOPS WHO MARRY WHOLE FAMI-
LIES - MORMONS LIVING AS HUSBANDS TO MOTHERS AND DAUGH-
TERS, AND HAVING CHILDREN BY ALL

SALT LAKE CITY, May 21 - Among the thousands of unfortunate victims of polygamy in Utah, the case of Mrs. Brig Hampton has been
made familiar to me. The most accurate statement of the sufferings of
this "second wife," which followed the consecrated sufferings of the
Endowment house, will be found in the following complaint, drawn up
in legal form, and addressed to President John Taylor, and praying for a
divorce. When this document was drawn it was supposed that Mrs.
Hampton's only hope of divorce was in the president or Mormon
Church, as being a second wife, our courts did not recognize the legal-
ity of her marriage, and could not consider her prayer for divorce. It has
been lately discovered, however - and the discovery affords incidental-
ly another illustration of the peculiar sanctity which hedges about the
married relation in Mormon life - that Hampton's first wife was the legal
and undivorced wife of another man. Thus, Mrs. Hampton becomes,
therefore, in the regard of our law, the first and only legal wife of
Hampton. She will, therefore, make her prayer for divorce in a legal
court, and a new complaint is now being prepared. The one which I have
been at some pains to secure and inclose here, it must be remembered,
was addressed to John Taylor, the president of the church, and all reflections upon the church, or anything that could offend, are necessarily
avoided; but even in its cold and legal phraseology the story of one
woman's wrongs (in polygamy) is graphically portrayed in the following lines :

COPY

Helen Hampton vs. Brigham Y. Hampton. Application for divorce and division of property.

PRESIDENT JOHN TAYLOR: I was married to B. Y. Hampton as his second wife, in the Endowment house, November 7, 1863. After living with him a period of seven years he separated himself from me as a husband, so that I have now for nine years been virtually divorced from him, supporting myself and my children by my personal labor, aided by such uncertain and insufficient support as he has seen fit to give me.

My reasons for now requiring an actual and absolute divorce are based upon this desertion, taken together with a long continued course of neglect, cruelty and abuse, both before and since our separation. In proof of which I refer to imposition upon me for a number of years of excessive drudgery and toil, unrequired by his circumstances; his neglect of proper aid and care in times of childbirth; his neglect, indifference, and coarseness in times when my children have been dangerously sick, and even dying; his general neglect to adequately provide for our wants through a long series of years; his attempt to deprive me and my children of a home conferred upon us by repeated agreements and promises, and his attempts to accomplish his purpose by starvation and force, culminating in personal violence, the marks of which I still carry upon my person.

For the first year after my marriage with B. Y. Hampton I supported myself by dressmaking, and when he entered into the saddle and harness business I assisted him therein by making nosebags, also by boiling, extracting and spinning cattle hair to make into switches for sale, etc. For these and other labors, extra to my domestic duties, he promised to deed me a house, situated half a block west of the courthouse, as my individual property, of which house I took possession in October, 1866.

After I had occupied my new house for about three years, he demanded that I should relinquish it to a third wife, whom he had secretly married, and move into rented rooms myself. I freely offered to divide with the new wife, and give her by far the larger portion of the rooms, on condition that she would undertake the care of the first wife's family, then on my hands. If this did not suit I offered to keep the additional family myself, on condition of having the extra rooms. But this fair offer did not suit, and I was required to give up the whole of the house. Inasmuch as I refused to be turned out of my hard earned home, B. Y. Hampton stripped all the blankets from my bed - blankets which I had earned boarding teamsters; and considerable of the carpets from my floor - carpets which I had sewn myself with a baby on my lap; and in addition to a number of articles belonging to me before I was married, carried them away before my face, in spite of my entreaties, telling me at the same time, "He knew I had earned them," but that "he would have me to know that all I earned belonged to him, for my time belonged to him, and all I could make."

As a next step he demanded my two children from me, and told me to go and hire out for my support, and added, "that he would bring me to his terms or send me to keep company with Mrs. Mires," an inmate of the lunatic asylum.

The measures failing he refused all my applications for provisions for the support of my family, and for ten days we were kept without food, beyond six pounds of corn and a quart of seed beans, which happened to be in the house at the time. My children were crying with hunger and were in a state of starvation. At the end of this time I met D. Y. Hampton on the street. I had not tasted food for two days, and I begged of him to give us some bread. He gave me as much as can now be purchased for ten cents, saying he would give me no more until I complied with his demands.

He next attempted to kidnap my two children from me, but I overtook him in the act and he relinquished them on my demand, He followed behind me, however, into the house, and as I entered, kicked me in the back, causing me to fall on my face, and then struck me over twenty times on the face and arms with his brass capped walking stick. I defended myself from his murderous assault as well as I could, and he actually left me bleeding freely from the effect of his blow.

Inasmuch as I still refused to give up my home unless I was furnished with another, my demand, be it understood being only for one half the value of the one I was living in, B. Y. Hampton caused me to be summoned to appear before the High Council, presided over by George B. Wallace. The council heard my statement and decided in favor of my demand. The council decided that I should have my choice and the deeds of either of the two houses B. Y. Hampton was then negotiating for.

The repairs required by the council he has never to this day made, and he has persistently refused to give me the deeds to the property agreed upon. And here let me restate, that my rights to an independent property may be fully understood, that over and above my claims as a wife and a mother, I had done my part to earn a property of the kind, not only by furnishing for myself the support for a year, which should have been supplied by himself, and thereafter working as his assistant in the saddle and harness business, but also by manufacturing for six years all the outer clothing required by two families (including B. Y. Hampton's first wife's family and himself), washing, picking, spinning and coloring the material, and afterward manufacturing the whole into clothing; and also, by carrying the burden of an extra family of four children, in addition to my own for a series of years.

With regard to the matter of support, for a short time after the decision of the High Council, Hampton gave me $4 per week for the support of my family, which large amount it was stipulated was to include a meal a day to be provided for himself. On ceasing to dine with me soon after, he refused me any regular amount for my support, giving me only odd sums as the humor took him. In the winter time I have been compelled to go several blocks through the snow to borrow a sawbuck, and then with my own bands saw up the poles of my fence before I could procure food or warmth for my children - his other families not more than two blocks off being surrounded at the same time with every comfort. On one occasion when I sent a request by one of my children for some fuel he told my little boy to tell his mother "to go to h--l."

It will be observed that when the case of the second wife and her wrongs were appealed to the High Council of the church certain just and decent requirements were made of Brig Hampton in behalf of his injured wife. These were never carried out by the polygamous Mormon, and it will be interesting to learn that their just and inspired tribunal has punished him - by giving him an appointment on the police force of the city.

After reading this remarkable document I felt a great desire to converse with this woman who makes these statements. I found that she was living in Salt Lake City. Through the kindness of one of the ladies connected with the Ladies' Anti-Polygamy Society here I was enabled to meet her. I found her living in a little house in the outskirts of the city, where she supports her two children, born of Brig Hampton, by sewing, and is to all appearances, and I believe from assurances of this lady who accompanied me, and other Gentile ladies in Salt Lake City, she is an honest and reliable woman. She is about forty years of age, and bears upon her face marks of the great suffering she has passed through. It was only by the most earnest persuasion, however that I could get her to talk of her former troubles. She showed me the scars upon her hands from blows received from Brig Hampton, and which were spoken of in this complaint. I asked her if she would tell me how any woman of the intelligence she evidently possessed, could be induced to marry Hampton, knowing he had another wife. Her reply was: "It will be impossible for me to show you. It is something that you cannot understand, and something that you will not sympathize with."

"What was the argument they used to force you to do this?"

She replied: The argument was that I would be damned if I didn't do it. That was the argument. Brig Hampton's wife, extraordinary as it may seem to you, assisted him in inducing me to marry him. Brigham Young brought his persuasion and his authority to bear upon me. You can form no conception of the kind of persuasion, promises and threats that were used to induce me to become his wife. There were no Gentiles here then as there are now. There were no opportunities of my getting advice, nor what I needed still more, because I had my own scruples, of getting assistance to enable me to withstand this pressure. I was made to believe, a believer as I was then in the Mormon religion, that I would be damned, and that all my salvation would be destroyed if I refused to accede to the wishes of Hampton and of the leaders of the church, and this, you must know was terrible to a young girl of my age. I finally consented. After I left the Endowment house I felt, in spite of all the confidence I had in the Mormon leaders, that I had done a terrible crime; and on my way to what was to be our home I cried. Brig Hampton's first wife said, 'If any one should cry it ought to be me.' 'But I would not have married him if you had not urged me,' I said. She replied, 'I didn't want you, and I want you to understand now that I did this to please him, and that I despise polygamy, and all that I have said to you in its favor and the hopes I have held out to you of happiness and peace were false."

I asked Mrs. Hampton to describe to me her life as the polygamous wife of Brig Hampton. This she said she could not do, and even at this late date and distance from her former troubles, her distress in the recital and the recalling the instances of that horrible life were so manifest that I did not have the heart to press the inquiries. She told me, however, among other things, that in 1869 Brig Hampton and some other men came to the house where she was living and sent her into the kitchen because they wanted to talk. Brig Hampton was then what was called one of the special police, but which Mrs. Hampton said she had since found out were Danites of the Mormon Church. She went into the kitchen during this conversation, but could not resist the temptation to listen to what they were saying, and to her horror she heard all the details of a plan which they had formed for waylaying and killing some men who apostatized from the Mormons, and who are now among some of the leading men of Salt Lake City. These men were Shearman, Godbe, Armstrong and others. They were going down to Cottonwood to preach and to labor to induce other Mormons to leave the church which they had just left. The plan was stated with cold blooded accuracy to waylay them on their way down and kill them, and the horrible details were so far arranged that each man agreed upon the man which he should "get away with." "I ran around," continued Mrs. H., "to the kitchen of Armstrong, and walked through the house, not daring to stop. I stopped long enough to say, 'Don't go to Cottonwood; don't go,' and then ran back to my own house. They heeded my warning, and another terrible crime was averted."

At this time Mrs. Hampton was nearing childbirth, and the child, born soon after, has always been afflicted with terrible fits. In this conversation Mrs. Hampton told me one feature of polygamy which was new, at least to me. The endowment robe consists of several garments. One of these is a white headgear for the women, which has a flowing cape falling down from the back. During the ceremony this cape is thrown over the woman's face. At some point in the ceremony, the man she has married raises that cape from her face, and no other person is permitted to do it.. When the woman dies she is buried in her endowment robes, with this cape on her head, and when she is laid in her coffin the cape is thrown over her face. The teachings of the mormon leaders are that she cannot be resurrected until the husband raises this cape from her face; that if he pleases and is satisfied that she has been a faithful and obedient wife and true to him, he will raise this cape and she may be resurrected, but if he is not satisfied of this, then he refuses to do this, and she cannot be resurrected. One of the most common threats Mrs. Hampton said, by which Brig Hampton used to compel her to obedience, was that if she didn't obey him "she would never be resurrected," that he would not raise the cape from her head on the morning of the resurrection. This threat, Mrs. Hampton said, at any time had great terrors for her, but that she had learned now, of course, to regard it as harmless.

Polygamy in Salt Lake City is sugarcoated, so far as revealed to the public sight. The man of many wives living amid surroundings of

Christianity and civilization, and who by his wealth is able, may hide something of the deformity of this unnatural and bestial relation; but in this country, and among poor people, small means are at command and little anxiety manifested to rob it of any of its repulsiveness. When you can bring your mind to dwell for a moment upon the fact of a man being a husband to a mother and her daughters, and living all together in one house, and even in one room, you will be able to conceive the full significance and beauty of a system which "is to be perpetuated if need be, in the blood of martyrs," and which finds its sublime justification in the claim made by Mormon priests that their wives are saved in polygamy from prostitution.

The reference here made to polygamous relations between a man and a woman, and her daughters, may seem incredible to some, but can be doubted by no one who has ever investigated the system. It is a fact of as general knowledge here as that polygamy exists. I started to make a list of such cases here in Salt Lake City, given me by responsible persons, and I have already progressed so far that eight names are recorded of Mormon men who are living with sisters, with mothers and daughters, and having in some cases children by the mother and daughter both. In the case of one, a lecherous old bishop, the man was married to two sisters in the Endowment house on the same day.

J. W. R.

THE END